THE SACRED LITURGY

Source and Summit of the
Life and Mission of the Church

The Sacred Liturgy

Source and Summit of the
Life and Mission of the Church

~

The Proceedings of the International
Conference on the Sacred Liturgy
Sacra Liturgia 2013

Pontifical University of the Holy Cross, Rome
25–28 June 2013

Edited by Alcuin Reid

IGNATIUS PRESS   SAN FRANCISCO

Cover design by Milo Persic

© 2014 by Ignatius Press, San Francisco
All rights reserved
ISBN 978-1-58617-786-7
Library of Congress Control Number 2013917064
Printed in the United States of America ∞

Contents

Editor's Preface

On 4 December 1963, closing the second session of the Second Vatican Council, Ven. Paul VI spoke of the first fruit of the Council, its Constitution on the Sacred Liturgy, *Sacrosanctum Concilium*, which he had just promulgated:

> The right order of things (goods) and duties has been conserved . . . the greatest place ought to be given to God; for us our first required duty is to bring prayers to God; the Sacred Liturgy is to be the first source of that divine exchange by which the life of God is communicated to us; it is to be the first school of our spirit. . . . (Allocution, 4 December 1963)[1]

Indeed, our first duty is the worship of Almighty God. Before we act as Christians we must in fact be Christians—and it is Christ Himself at work in the Sacred Liturgy of His Church who makes us His children, who nourishes, forms, establishes and heals us in our Christian life and vocation.

The reality of the primacy of the Sacred Liturgy for Christian life led the Fathers of the Second Vatican Council to call for profound liturgical formation in order to bring about *participatio actuosa*—a conscious and life-giving connection with and immersion in the riches of the liturgical life of the Church by all of Christ's faithful. Such living participation was seen as the essential foundation for Christian life and mission in the modern world.

---

[1] Translation: M. Rafael Gonzalez. See also: Xavier Rynne, *The Second Session—The Debates and Decrees of Vatican Council II: September 29 to December 4, 1963* (London: Faber & Faber, 1964), pp. 366–74.

So too it was judged that ritual reforms would help achieve *partici-patio actuosa*. This is the *raison d'être*—the "why"—of *Sacrosanctum Concilium*.

The Second Vatican Council had primarily pastoral and not dogmatic aims.[2] Thus it is important to note that its Constitution on the Sacred Liturgy contains no dogmatic definitions—its contents are not new infallible dogmas of the Catholic Faith. Rather, it consists of liturgical theology authoritatively taught, of fundamental and general principles drawn from that theology, and of subsidiary principles and authoritative policies which seek to achieve its fundamental aims and which provide an outline of the moderate liturgical reform intended to achieve them. Taking due account of the fact that *Sacrosanctum Concilium* is an act of the Church's Magisterium, its theology, principles and policies permit of critical evaluation, particularly in the light of the need for reform and renewal in continuity in respect of the Church's theological and liturgical tradition.[3]

The Constitution's theology, read with a hermeneutic of reform in continuity and in a true spirit of *ressourcement*, rightly takes its place amidst the currents of theological renewal of the twentieth century. It is the theology taught by an Ecumenical Council and whilst it is not *de fide definita*, one would be foolish to reject it out of hand. The Constitution's fundamental principles—of seeking a true *participatio actuosa* in the Church's liturgical life for all the faithful by means of carrying out widespread and profound formation in the Sacred Liturgy (cf. n. 14)—which are in fact those of St. Pius X, Ven. Pius XII and of the twentieth-century liturgical movement, with roots deep in the previous centuries—are of perennial value. The general principles which flow from these (cf. nn. 22–34), also reflect sound liturgical tradition. Its subsidiary principles (cf. nn. 33–46) are just that: subordinate to the greater realities preceding them and may be evaluated accordingly.

---

[2] "The substance of the ancient doctrine of the Deposit of Faith is one thing, and the way it is presented is another. And it is the latter that must be taken into great consideration . . . everything being measured in the forms and proportions of a *magisterium* which is predominantly pastoral in character;" John XXIII, Allocution 11 October 1962, in: Xavier Rynne, *Letters from Vatican City—Vatican Council (First Session): Background and Debates* (London: Faber & Faber, 1963), (pp. 262–72), p. 268.

[3] Cf. Benedict XVI, "Address of His Holiness Benedict XVI to the Roman Curia Offering Them His Christmas Greetings", 22 December 2005.

The policies of the Constitution, which are found in its subsidiary principles and in the remainder of *Sacrosanctum Concilium* are and always were contingent. That the Council Fathers adopted them indicates their value in their judgment, and in the authoritative judgment of Paul VI through his promulgation of the Constitution.

Historically it is now clear that some of the liturgical reforms enacted in the name of the Council went beyond the carefully nuanced provisions *of the Council itself* as set forth in *Sacrosanctum Concilium*. It is also clear fifty years later that the widespread renewal of liturgical and indeed of Christian life for which the Fathers of the Council hoped has not been achieved: the proportion of Catholics participating regularly in the Sacred Liturgy or otherwise practicing their faith is substantially less now than it was then. Whilst this decline has many causes, the reformed liturgy as it has been implemented has not been a significant factor in arresting it.

We must have the courage, then, to admit that some of these policies, either in their conception or in their (mis-)application, have not necessarily served the Constitution's fundamental aims well. It may be that some policies, whilst judged apposite fifty years ago, in the light of radically changed circumstances in the Church and world of the twenty-first century, can be seen today to be no longer as vital as they were thought to be in 1963. It may be that the intentions behind some policies were distorted in their implementation and in fact have brought about unhelpful results. It may also be that, with the advance of scholarship, the difference, if not the distance, between *Sacrosanctum Concilium* and the liturgical tradition it sought moderately to reform, and the rites produced by the *Consilium* charged with implementing the Constitution, has become more apparent.

Yet the Council's insistence that the Sacred Liturgy is "the summit toward which the activity of the Church is directed [and] at the same time it is the font from which all her power flows" (*Sacrosanctum Concilium*, 10), remains true. In our world which so needs to hear and to live the Gospel, what are we to do if our access to the source and summit of our Christian life is not what it should be, indeed not what the Second Vatican Council intended?

The answer is that we must look again in all humility at the question of the liturgy, not with the blinkered eyes of partisans of the 'liturgy wars' that have marked recent decades, but with the vision of the fathers of the Council, who could see clearly the necessity of maintaining sound tradition whilst being open to legitimate development (cf. *Sacrosanctum Concilium*, 23). We must be prepared to make a liturgical examination of conscience, and where necessary to make amends.

In doing this we must safeguard the gains in liturgical practice since the Council. Thankfully the expectation of participating in the liturgical rites is now widespread. So too, it is beneficial that the reformed rites include a wider selection of readings from Sacred Scripture and that their reading in the vernacular has facilitated their comprehension (cf. *Sacrosanctum Concilium*, 35 § 1; 36 § 2). And the renewed use of many ancient liturgical texts, especially prefaces, is a valuable development.

We must also take into account the ecclesial experience of the past fifty years. The modern rites have been fundamental for the Christian life and formation of generations now, and that reality must not be ignored. These years have also made clear the ongoing pastoral value and rightful place in the life of the Church of the *usus antiquior*—the older form of the Roman rite.[4] Benedict XVI set the challenge of "mutual enrichment" between the two (cf. Letter, 7 July 2007), a challenge which remains. So too, he underlined the legitimate diversity possible in Western Catholic liturgy (cf. *Sacrosanctum Concilium*, 38), insisting that one such example is nothing less than a "treasure to be shared" (cf. *Anglicanorum Cœtibus*, 4 November 2009, 3).

Any reappraisal of *Sacrosanctum Concilium*'s policies, of their implementation and of subsequent liturgical practice will raise the question of a "reform of the reform." This question must be taken seriously— out of fidelity to the Council, out of fidelity to the liturgical tradition the Council received and indeed in the light of the urgent pastoral needs of our day.

Sacra Liturgia 2013 took place during the Year of Faith (2012–2013), which Benedict XVI called to mark the fiftieth anniversary of the Second Vatican Council and in order to provide renewed impetus "in the service of belief and evangelization" (*Porta Fidei*, 12). Far from be-

---

[4] The neutral and descriptive term "the *usus antiquior*" is taken from the "Letter of His Holiness Benedict XVI to the Bishops on the Occasion of the Publication of the Apostolic Letter 'Motu Proprio Data' *Summorum Pontificum* on the use of the Roman Liturgy Prior to the Reform of 1970", 7 July 2007, and is used so as to avoid language which, at least in English, has been seen to make qualitative judgments about the older and newer forms of the Roman rite.

ing motivated by an "ostentatious preoccupation" with the liturgy (cf.
Pope Francis, *Evangelii Gaudium*, 95), *Sacra Liturgia 2013* was concerned
from the outset to consider the liturgy, liturgical formation and celebration "as the point of departure for the New Evangelisation" (Bishop
Dominique Rey, Conference Announcement, 2 October 2012).

In this spirit its speakers and delegates addressed a wide range of questions from differing perspectives, with a notable absence of polemics,
united in the desire that the Sacred Liturgy should empower anew the
preaching of the Gospel of Christ in the twenty-first century. Participants prayed together—using the reformed rites and the *usus antiquior*
—and manifested their Catholic unity with and under Peter by participating in the Mass of Saints Peter and Paul celebrated by Pope Francis.

It is hoped that this volume, which makes available all the papers
from *Sacra Liturgia 2013*, will serve these ends in a similar spirit. The
unity of the contributors in seeking authentic liturgical renewal does
not necessarily imply their endorsement of all of the views of other
contributors. But it does bear witness to a widespread concern seriously to consider the questions raised herein.[5]

It is also hoped that this volume shall prove to be a useful resource
for the liturgical formation for which *Sacrosanctum Concilium* called, and
that it will assist us in looking again at the Constitution on the Sacred
Liturgy, and at what followed it, in the light of the situation and needs
of the Church and the world of the twenty-first century. Indeed, it is
hoped that this volume might contribute to that new liturgical movement for which Joseph Cardinal Ratzinger expressed the hope.[6]

Sacra Liturgia 2013 could not have taken place without the warm wel-
come given to us by the *Ufficio Eventi* of the Pontifical University of
the Holy Cross ("Santa Croce") in Rome, nor without the ready and
generous sponsorship of The Knights of Columbus, Ignatius Press,
CIEL UK, Arte Granda, The Cardinal Newman Society, Human Life
International, De Montfort Music, Arte Poli, Una Voce International,
Ars Sacra Vestments, La Nef, Libreria Leoniana, and Editions Artège.
All who draw from this volume are in their debt.

---

[5] With the exception of the Introduction and the Homilies, where authors have referred to popes due to be canonized before the publication of this volume, the title
"Saint" has been adopted.

[6] Cf. Joseph Cardinal Ratzinger, *The Spirit of the Liturgy* (San Francisco: Ignatius Press,
2000), pp. 8–9.

So too, my fellow organisers Fr. Uwe Michael Lang and Fr. M. Rafael Gonzalez as well as the team of Conference Staff—Magdalen Ross, Adrien de Germiny, Valleran Meaby, David Chadwick and Johannes Huber—each made important contributions and are to be thanked for enabling *Sacra Liturgia 2013* to achieve Bishop Rey's desire to "underline the fundamental and unique role of the Sacred Liturgy in all aspects of the life of the Church and its mission" (Conference Announcement, 2 October 2012) in the light of the example and teaching of Benedict XVI.

It is fifty years since Paul VI promulgated *Sacrosanctum Concilium*. Much has indeed happened in respect of the Sacred Liturgy since, which neither he nor the Fathers of the Council foresaw. Yet it remains true, as Paul VI said, that "the Sacred Liturgy is to be the first source of that divine exchange by which the life of God is communicated to us", and that "it is to be the first school of our spirit."

It is our task, indeed our duty, to consider this reality once again in the light of the experience of past decades, and to do what is necessary so that the Church of the twenty-first century—called anew to the imperative of evangelisation—may truly find in the Sacred Liturgy the source and summit of her life and mission.

—DOM ALCUIN REID
4 December 2013

Introduction

BISHOP DOMINIQUE REY

Bishop of Fréjus-Toulon, France

Your Eminence, Your Excellencies, dear friends:

It is my pleasure to welcome you to the Pontifical University, Santa Croce for *Sacra Liturgia 2013*. We have come together from more than 35 countries throughout the world. Welcome!

Our work has already begun with the solemn celebration of Vespers in the Basilica of St. Apollinare. This was a very deliberate act, because before we speak about the Sacred Liturgy we must be immersed in the liturgical life of the Church. The reality of the liturgy, into which we are initiated at the moment of our Baptism, precedes any study of the liturgy. To be liturgical comes first. To talk about the liturgy comes second.

But it is important to talk about and study the question of the liturgy! Here, in the aula magna, we shall listen to the contributions of many experts and leaders in this field. I am particularly grateful to Their Eminences Cardinals Ranjith and Burke, and to my brother bishops, for giving of their time to teach us. So too, I wish to thank their Eminences Cardinals Cañizares and Brandmüller who will celebrate Holy Mass and preach for us. And I thank all our speakers, especially those who have travelled far, for coming to share their expertise and insights.

Sacra Liturgia 2013 was inspired by the liturgical teaching and example of His Holiness, Pope Benedict XVI. Pope Benedict taught us the importance of the *ars celebrandi*, reminding us that "everything related to the Eucharist should be marked by beauty" (*Sacramentum Caritatis*, 41). He taught us that there needs to be no opposition between the older and newer forms of the Roman rite—that both have their rightful place in the Church of the New Evangelisation. He taught us that within the embrace of Catholic unity, other liturgical traditions can be welcomed as "precious gifts" and "treasures to be shared" (cf. *Anglicanorum Cœtibus*, § 5, III); for that reason I am particularly delighted that the Ordinary of the Ordinariate of Our Lady of Walsingham, Msgr. Keith Newton, will be present with us.

I wish this conference to be a tribute to the liturgical vision and achievements of our beloved Emeritus Bishop of Rome, Benedict XVI: may God reward him for all he has given us and grant him health and long life!

Pope Benedict initiated the Year of Faith to commemorate the fiftieth anniversary of the Second Vatican Council during which we are meeting. Our Holy Father, Pope Francis, has continued this initiative. From the outset it was my wish that we should meet here in Rome, during this Year of Faith, so as to be close to Peter, to manifest our communion with him, and to pray with him on the great feast of Saints Peter and Paul. That we have the opportunity to do this with our new Holy Father is a providential blessing.

Fifty years ago, in June 1963, the first session of the Second Vatican Council had concluded. St. John XXIII had just been succeeded by the Ven. Paul VI, who continued the work of the Council. It was Paul VI who promulgated its Constitution on the Sacred Liturgy, *Sacrosanctum Concilium*, on December 4, 1963, at the end of the Council's second session.

Fifty years later we need to look again at *Sacrosanctum Concilium*. The liturgical reform which followed the Constitution's promulgation gave us much of value, especially in its promotion of participation in the liturgy. But it also caused controversy, both in its official reforms, in its translation into the vernacular languages, and in its varied local implementations.

We need to recognise, as did St. John Paul II, that there have been both "lights" and "shadows" in the liturgical life of the Church in the past fifty years (cf. *Ecclesia de Eucharistia*, 10). We need to celebrate the legitimate progress that has been made. We need to consider the lessons that the mistakes made during these fifty years teach us. We need to look again at the liturgical Constitution and re-discover its true meaning. Perhaps we need to correct some practices or recover some things that we have lost through what Cardinal Ratzinger called a "reform of the reform". Perhaps there are areas in which that "mutual enrichment" spoken of by Benedict XVI is necessary.

Above all, we need to promote authentic liturgical renewal in all its Catholic richness and diversity. We need to promote the Sacred Liturgy celebrated as the Church gives it to us, as the Fathers and Popes of the Second Vatican Council desired.

This must not be dismissed as a marginal concern. The liturgy is not a peripheral matter for the Church. As Cardinal Ratzinger wrote in 1997: "the true celebration of the Sacred Liturgy is the centre of any renewal of the Church whatever."[1] As *Sacrosanctum Concilium* teaches us, the Sacred Liturgy is the 'culmen et fons', the source and the summit, of the life and mission of the whole Church (cf. n. 10).

The Sacred Liturgy is not a hobby for specialists. It is central to all our endeavours as disciples of Jesus Christ. This profound reality cannot be overemphasised. We must recognise the primacy of grace in our Christian life and work, and we must respect the reality that in this life *the* optimal encounter with Christ is in the Sacred Liturgy.

As a bishop it is my duty to do all I can to promote the New Evangelisation initiated by John Paul II. I wish to say very clearly that the New Evangelisation must be founded on the faithful and fruitful celebration of the Sacred Liturgy as given to us by the Church in her tradition—Western and Eastern.

Why? Because it is in the Sacred Liturgy that we encounter the saving action of Jesus Christ in His Church today in a manner in which we encounter it nowhere else. In the liturgy Christ touches us, nourishes us and heals us. He strengthens us and orders us with particular graces. When we pray liturgically we do so in communion with the whole Church, present, absent, living or dead. Yes, there are other good and valuable spiritual practices, but none enjoys the objectivity and singular efficacy of the Sacred Liturgy (cf. *Sacrosanctum Concilium*, 7).

The New Evangelisation is not an idea or a program: it is a demand

---

[1] Cf. Roberto de Mattei, "Reflections on the Liturgical Reform" in A. Reid ed., *Looking Again at the Question of the Liturgy with Cardinal Ratzinger* (Farnborough: St. Michael's Abbey Press, 2003), (pp. 130–44), p. 141.

that each of us comes to know the person of Christ more profoundly and, by doing so, become more able to lead others to Him. The only way to begin to do this is through the Sacred Liturgy, and if the liturgy is somehow not as it should be, or I am not properly prepared, this encounter with Christ will be impeded, the New Evangelisation will suffer.

That is why our celebration of the liturgy is so important. We must maximise, not limit, our connection with the action of Christ in the liturgy. If I change or re-create the Church's liturgy according to my own wishes or a subjective ideology, how can I be sure that what I am doing is truly His work? Whereas, if I faithfully celebrate that which the Church has given to us—and celebrate it as beautifully as possible —I am assured that I am a servant of Christ's action, a minister of His sacred mysteries, not an obstacle in His path (cf. Mt 16:23). Each of us, ordained ministers, religious and lay men and women, are called to this fidelity and respect for Christ, for His Church and for her liturgical rites.

And that is why liturgical formation is crucial. I must obtain 'from within' as it were, the conviction that Christ is indeed at work in the Church's sacred rites. I must immerse myself in this privileged dynamic and discover its ways. This will bring me to the person of Jesus Christ again and again. And this will enable me to bring Christ to others.

Liturgical formation, liturgical celebration and the mission of the Church: all three are intrinsically related. That is why we are here: to consider this relationship and to examine its meaning and importance for the Church at the beginning of the twenty-first century. If we do this well, we will lay very sound foundations for the New Evangelisation indeed.

It would be impossible for *Sacra Liturgia 2013* to take place without the support of many people. I am grateful to the Rector of the beautiful Basilica of St. Apollinare, Msgr. Pedro Huidobro, for welcoming us. I am profoundly grateful to our many sponsors for their material help. For the welcome we have been given here at the Pontifical University Santa Croce and for the use of their excellent facilities, we are all indebted. So too, I thank the team of organisers and volunteers who have done so much to prepare for this event.

My friends, we are here to listen, to learn and to share with others. But we are also here to pray—here in the Basilica of S. Apollinare and also with our Holy Father, Pope Francis, in St. Peter's Basilica on Saturday. If we do all of these things well we shall come closer to Christ whom we worship in the Sacred Liturgy, and we shall be empowered to become the evangelists our world so desperately needs.

May God bless our efforts!

The Sacred Liturgy, Source and Summit of the Life and Mission of the Church

Malcolm Cardinal Ranjith

Archbishop of Colombo, Sri Lanka

"Liturgy is a radiant expression of the paschal mystery, in which Christ draws us to himself and calls us to communion . . . the concrete way in which the truth of God's love in Christ encounters us, attracts us and delights us, enabling us to emerge from ourselves and drawing us towards our true vocation, which is love" stated Pope Benedict XVI in his Post-Synodal Apostolic Exhortation *Sacramentum Caritatis* (n. 35), showing us the true nature of Christian liturgical life which he calls the "veritatis splendor" or "a glimpse of heaven on earth". It is a heavenly happening, so to say.

The beauty of liturgy then, lies, not so much in what we do or how interesting and satisfying it becomes to us, as much as how deeply we are drawn into something that already happens which is profoundly divine and liberative. It is greater than us and carries with it a totally transforming effect, which we often cannot fully grasp. It is Christ's paschal victory celebrated in heaven and on earth.

Worship, the Assurance of Victory

That Liturgy is indeed the supreme priestly act of Christ in the presence of God, is clearly explained in the book of the Apocalypse. In it Christ, called the Sacrificial Lamb (cf. Apoc 5:6, 8, 12, 13; 7:9, 10, 14, 17;

12:11), sits on the throne and is adored with hymns and canticles (Apoc 5:9–10, 12, 13; 4:8, 11; 7:12; 11:17–18 etc.) and is acclaimed by the crowd of the elect who are dressed in white robes (cf. Apoc 7:12). The presentation of the celestial scenario in the Apocalypse demonstrates a strong cultic view of the eschatological events prophesied by the visionary. The setting is of the heavenly Jerusalem where God Himself and the Lamb are called the temple (cf. Apoc 21:22) "which is the new heavens and the new earth" (21:1); the altar is mentioned (cf. Apoc 6:9, 8:3) with the seven golden candles (cf. Apoc 1:12); the incense (cf. Apoc 8:4); and the sound of trumpets and songs; the ceremony of the enthronement and the worship of the Lamb is also mentioned (cf. Chapter 5:6–14). What is truly celebrated in the heavens is the realization of that final victory of God over Satan and of good over evil. Jesus, the Lamb that is offered, has become the first and the last, the Alpha and the Omega of the New Order. In the image of that new creation, the heavenly Jerusalem, everything will be made anew:

> The tabernacle of God is with men, and he will dwell with them, and they shall be his people, and God himself shall be with them and be their God. And God shall wipe away all tears from their eyes; and there shall be no more death, neither sorrow, nor crying, neither shall there be any more pain; for the former things have passed away . . . behold, I make all things new. (Apoc 21:3–5)

This message of hope for humanity is based on the assurance that the heavenly worship of God, through the Lamb that was slain, continues and would be the guarantor of the definitive and final victory of good over evil to which humanity tends. It is that which gives final direction and meaning to history. It is already happening in heaven, this celebration of the final triumph of good over evil, and so it would continue to happen on earth too. This heavenly worship of the Lamb would also be the guarantor of the coming of that new Jerusalem. The vision of the seer invites the Church to be faithful to the Lord and to be hopeful that victory will be hers, even though its faith entails great suffering at the time, for the worship of the Lamb of the sacrifice in heaven continues and it will, sort of, gradually erupt into human life, through the life of consecration and sanctification we are guided to lead on earth and in the way we ourselves worship the Lamb or associate ourselves to His eternal sacrifice. It is in this sense that Pope

Benedict spoke of how "the new Temple, not made by human hands, does exist, but it is also still under construction. The great gesture of embrace emanating from the Crucified has not yet reached its goal; it has only just begun. Christian liturgy is liturgy on the way, a liturgy of pilgrimage toward the transfiguration of the world, which will only take place when God is 'all in all'."[1]

Liturgy thus determines the whole process of true growth, transformation and sanctification of human life. Indeed salvation itself is God's own work and the Church hastens it by joining her Lord in the fullest realization of His priestly office and in the celebration of that heavenly liturgy here on earth. Liturgy in this sense forms the new people of God—the Church.

Worship and Israel's History

This formative process is clearly visible also in the very history of Israel. The text of the Pentateuch, for example, has a gravitational centre in the ancient cult of Israel. Pentateuchal history itself is woven around the Credo formulas of the community which were recited in the Sanctuary at Jerusalem (Deut 26:5):

> When you come into the land which the LORD your God gives you for an inheritance, and have taken possession of it, and live in it, you shall take some of the first of all the fruit of the ground, which you harvest from your land that the LORD your God gives you, and you shall put it in a basket, and you shall go to the place which the LORD your God will choose, to make his name to dwell there. And you shall go to the priest who is in office at that time, and say to him, "I declare this day to the LORD your God that I have come into the land which the LORD swore to our fathers to give us." Then the priest shall take the basket from your hand, and set it down before the altar of the LORD your God.
>
> And you shall make response before the LORD your God, "A wandering Arame'an was my father; and he went down into Egypt and sojourned there, few in number; and there he became a nation, great,

---

[1] Joseph Cardinal Ratzinger, *The Spirit of the Liturgy* (San Francisco: Ignatius Press, 2000), p. 50.

mighty, and populous. And the Egyptians treated us harshly, and afflicted us, and laid upon us hard bondage. Then we cried to the LORD the God of our fathers, and the LORD heard our voice, and saw our affliction, our toil, and our oppression; and the LORD brought us out of Egypt with a mighty hand and an outstretched arm, with great terror, with signs and wonders; and he brought us into this place and gave us this land, a land flowing with milk and honey. And behold, now I bring the first of the fruit of the ground, which you, O LORD, have given me." (Deut 26:1–10)

The exegete Gerhard von Rad identified other forms of this credo formula in Deuteronomy 6:20–24 and in Joshua 24:2b–13. Although this position—especially von Rad's seeking to make these formulae independent of the Sinai tradition—has since been subject to critical analysis, by and large the cultic background of the use of these formulae, their influence on the eventual coming together of the Pentateuchal history and traditions and on the very identity of Israel have been accepted as tenable. What is important for us is the fact that God's very action in the calling into existence of the people of Israel, their growth as a nation, especially through the role of the patriarchs, their liberation from slavery and eventual settling down and owning of the land have all been seen as something that God Himself had determined and which all has a liturgical orientation: Israel is called to the worship and to the adoration of the LORD in its coming into being and its very finality. In the later era, Israel gradually assumed the role of being the chosen nation to bring all the other nations on earth to the worship of the LORD in the New Jerusalem, thus becoming missionary. This latter position is markedly visible in the Prophets, especially in Isaiah who speaks of the nations streaming into the New Jerusalem (cf. Is 2:2–4; Is 66:18–21) for the worship of God. Thus the centre of gravity is truly the role of Israel in bringing all the nations on the earth to the worship of God on the Holy Mountain in Jerusalem.

Worship and the Covenant

This predominantly cultic coloring of the role of Israel in the history of salvation is very much visible in the events of Sinai too. In his book *The Spirit of the Liturgy* Joseph Cardinal Ratzinger shows how the worship of God was truly the motive behind the entire story of the exodus. The future Pope focuses attention on the key phrase used by Moses and Aaron containing the words that the Lord Himself had ordered them to pronounce before the Pharaoh "let my people go to worship me in the desert" (Ex 7:16). He observes that "these words . . . are repeated four times, with slight variations in all the meetings of Pharaoh with Moses and Aaron" (cf. Ex 8:1; 9:1, 13; 10:3)[2] He continues:

> In the course of the negotiations with Pharaoh, the goal becomes more concrete. Pharaoh shows he is willing to compromise. For him the issue is the Israelites' freedom of worship which he first of all concedes in the following form, "Go, sacrifice to your God within the land" (Ex 8:25). But Moses insists—in obedience to God's command—that they must go out in order to worship. The proper place of worship is the wilderness. . . . After the plagues that follow, Pharaoh extends his compromise. He now concedes that worship according the will of the Deity should take place in the wilderness, but he wants only the men to leave. . . . But Moses cannot negotiate about the liturgy with a foreign potentate, nor can he subject worship to any form of political compromise. . . . That is why the third and most far-reaching compromise suggested by the earthly ruler is also rejected. Pharaoh now offers women and children the permission to leave with the men: "Only let your flocks and your herds remain" (Ex 10:24). Moses objects: All the livestock must go too, for "we do not know with what we must serve the LORD until we arrive there" (Ex 10:26). In all this, the issue is not the Promised Land: the only goal of the Exodus is shown to be worship, which can only take place according to God's measure and therefore eludes the rules of the game of political compromise.[3]

The Cardinal then goes on to affirm that the true goal of the exodus was not land or statehood for the people but that of serving God in the place indicated by Him. In fact, merely attributing land to the people or even their forging themselves into a nation status would not have made them God's chosen special people. It is the special historic relationship to God as "those who serve Him" which made them what they were. That was also the basis of the covenant which God made

---

[2] *The Spirit of the Liturgy*, p. 15.

[3] Ibid., pp. 15–16.

with the people. In fact, it is ratified in a ceremony minutely regulated as an event of worship. The covenant thus embraces worship, law, and ethics as the Cardinal goes on to explain. That this covenant was cultic in orientation is made clear when Cardinal Ratzinger presents an analysis of Israelite history through the key of its faithfulness to the worship of God in his words: "[w]henever Israel falls away from the right worship of God, when she turns away from God to the false gods . . . , her freedom, too, collapses."[4]

The Cardinal then affirms the logical conclusion of all of this when he states:

> Worship—that is, the right kind of cult, of relationship with God, is essential for the right kind of human existence in the world. . . . Worship gives us a share in heaven's mode of existence, in the world of God, and allows light to fall from that divine world into ours. In this sense, worship . . . has the character of anticipation. It lays hold in advance of a more perfect life and, in so doing, gives our present life its proper measure.[5]

Creation and Worship

That the Old Testament's history of salvation is steeped in the faith and the worship forms of Israel is made clear also in the priestly account of the creation narrative found in the first chapter of the book of Genesis. Its language and style are distinctly priestly and cultic. The most important consideration in all of this is that it does not wish itself to be a scientific or cosmological study on the origins of the universe or of man, but that, underlying its affirmations, was the faith in God whom they worshipped and whose covenant with them at Sinai made them believe that He their Saviour was also their Creator. As Gerhard von Rad mentioned:

> Faith in creation is neither the basis nor the goal of the declarations in Genesis chapters 1 and 2. Rather the position of both the Yahwehist and the Priestly document is basically faith in salvation and election. They undergird this faith by the testimony that this Yahweh, who

---

[4] Ibid., pp. 19–20.

[5] Ibid., p. 21.

made a covenant with Abraham and at Sinai, is also the Creator of the world.[6]

The creation narrative is thus the natural consequence of God's election of Israel. The God of the covenant is not only Israel's redeemer but also the Creator of the setting in which that relationship is brought to fulfillment. Cardinal Ratzinger observes:

> Creation moves toward the Sabbath, to the day on which man and the whole created order participates in God's rest, in his freedom. . . . On this day slave and master are equals. . . . Now some people conclude from this that the Old Testament makes no connection between creation and worship, that it leads to a pure vision of a liberated society as the goal of human history. . . . But this is a complete misunderstanding of the Sabbath. The account of creation and the Sinai regulations about the Sabbath come from the same source. . . . The Sabbath is the sign of the covenant between God and man; it sums up the inward essence of the covenant. If this is so, then we can now define the intention of the account of creation as follows: creation exists to be a place for the covenant that God wants to make with man. The goal of creation is the covenant, the love story of God and man.[7]

This is clearly indicated also through the use of the Hebrew word "bara" which denotes God separating the elements through which the cosmos emerges from chaos and it also denotes, as the Cardinal mentions, "the fundamental process of salvation history, that is, the election and separation of pure from impure . . . the spiritual creation, the creation of the covenant, without which the created cosmos would be an empty shell. Creation and history, creation, history, and worship are in a relationship of reciprocity."[8]

The underlying affirmation in all of this is the fact that the biblical narratives and the history of Israel have as their focus the worship and praise of the one and true God and faithfulness to the covenant made with Him in Sinai. The very existence and mission of Israel is governed by this hermeneutical key. Israel could not have been, what it was called upon to achieve, in a different way. Israel is constituted as

---

[6] Gerhard von Rad, *Genesis* (London: SCM Press, 1976), p. 46.

[7] *The Spirit of the Liturgy*, pp. 25–26.

[8] Ibid., p. 27.

the community that associates itself to the heavenly worship of God (Is 6:1–4) and has as its mission that of becoming the source of salvation to all men of good will. The cultic language and the stress on the covenant which needs to be faithfully adhered to are all comparable to the thread that runs through the pages of the Bible and salvation history. Cult is found throughout the pages of biblical history giving it a truly God-centered focus. Thus it becomes not just the story of a nation but the story of a relationship, that between God and Israel.

Worship and Paschal Mystery

In the New Testament too, the role of the Lamb that is sacrificed for the salvation of the world is assumed by God Himself in the person of Christ. His sacrificial death on the Cross in obedience to God's will is that which brings about true reconciliation between God and man and the birth of the Church, the new people of the covenant. The old order has definitely been perfected. As the letter to the Hebrews mentioned: "But Christ having come now as the High Priest of the good things to come has passed through a greater and more perfect tabernacle, not made with hands, that is to say not of this order; neither by the blood of goats and calves, but by His own blood, has entered, once and for all [ephapax], into the Holy of Holies, having obtained eternal redemption for us" (Heb 9:11–12). And thus as Cardinal Ratzinger states: "Worship through types and shadows, worship with replacements, ends at the very moment when the real worship takes place: the self-offering of the Son, who has become man and 'Lamb', the 'First-born', who gathers up and into himself all worship of God, takes it from the types and shadows into the reality of man's union with the living God."[9] Hence liturgy is nothing other than the participation of the ecclesial community in the perennial and heavenly worship rendered by Christ to God along with the heavenly chorus.

The continuous offering of praise in heaven by "the Lamb that was slain" is the reality to which we as an ecclesial community associate ourselves in and through our liturgy. The paschal glory of Christ continues to be renewed and sung.

---

[9] Ibid., pp. 43–44.

Actio Christi

And so truly liturgy is primarily *Actio Christi*. It is, as articles 7 and 8 of the Constitution *Sacrosanctum Concilium* of the Second Vatican Council states:

> An exercise of the priestly office of Jesus Christ . . . performed by the Mystical Body of Jesus Christ, that is, by the Head and His members. From this follows that every liturgical celebration, because it is an action of Christ, the priest and of His Body, the Church, is a sacred action surpassing all others. No other action of the Church can match its claim to efficacy, nor equal the degree of it. In the earthly liturgy, by way of foretaste, we share in that heavenly liturgy which is celebrated in the Holy City of Jerusalem towards which we journey as pilgrims and in which Christ is sitting at the right hand of God, a minister of the sanctuary and of the true Tabernacle. (cf. Apoc 21:2; Col 3:1; Heb 8:2)

Mediator Dei, the 1947 Encyclical Letter of Pope Pius XII on the Sacred Liturgy, stated:

> In obedience, therefore, to her founder's behest, the Church prolongs the priestly mission of Jesus Christ *mainly by means of the Sacred Liturgy*. She does this in the first place at the altar where constantly the sacrifice of the Cross is re-presented and with a single difference in the manner of its offering, renewed. She does it next by means of the Sacraments, those special channels through which men are made partakers in the supernatural life. She does it finally by offering to God, all Good and Great, the daily tribute of her prayer of praise. (n. 3)

It also stated: "Along with the Church, therefore, her Divine Founder is present at every liturgical function: Christ is present at the august sacrifice of the altar both in the person of His minister and above all under the Eucharistic species. He is present in the sacraments, infusing into them the power which makes them ready instruments of sanctification. He is present, finally, in the prayer of praise and petition we direct to God" (n. 20).

Liturgy for us in the Church then is not just a series of actions or rituals but eventually a person, and that person is Christ. It is Christ who renders glory to God, invites us to unite ourselves to Him and be totally transformed in Him becoming a sacrifice pleasing to God (*logiken latreian*—cf. Rom 12:1–2), so that His mission becomes our own and we become part of His transforming, sanctifying, presence on earth. This truly is the very core of the life and mission of the Church without which she would be reduced to the level of a service of altruism only, or to an earthly association of likeminded people. It would also take away the eschatological finality of the community, for in her liturgy the Church celebrates "the now" of "the then" which leads to "the not yet" of the end times. In short, like in the case of the History of Israel, the life of the Church too becomes the story of a relationship, that between Christ and His community of disciples, whose very existence is focused on the true praise and worship of God.

It is this centrality of the role of Christ which makes liturgy sacred and places it beyond the creativity of humanity. *Sacramentum Caritatis* calls Christ "the 'subject' of the liturgy's intrinsic beauty" (n. 36). And Pope Benedict XVI then goes on to explain this: "Since the Eucharistic liturgy is essentially an *'actio Dei'* which draws us into Christ through the Holy Spirit, its basic structure is not something within our power to change, nor can it be held hostage by the latest trends" (n. 37). *Mediator Dei* called liturgy the prolonging of the priestly mission of Christ (cf. n. 3). Thus it is really not what we do that matters as much as what He does in and through us.

Ars Celebrandi

There was a time however when the popular term *ars celebrandi* was used to mean the art of celebrating as if it was all a matter of our doing it in style, with the accent placed on the role of the celebrant, and what he does, like an artist creating something *ex nihilo*. The truth is far from it. Pope Benedict XVI defines *ars celebrandi* as "the fruit of faithful adherence to the liturgical norms in all their richness" (*Sacramentum Caritatis*, 38). The *ars* thus does not connote the freedom to do as one pleases: it calls for a desire to be united to Christ the High Priest in His heavenly liturgy by means of one's faithful adherence to the norms and the inner mysticism of the celebration. He expects the *ars celebrandi* to "foster a sense of the sacred and the use of outward signs which help to cultivate this sense, such as, for example, the harmony of the rite, the liturgical vestments, the furnishings and the sacred space" (*Sacramentum Caritatis*, 40).

The *ars* is then understood, rather, as the effort we make to conform to the inner mystique of this heavenly nature of liturgy. This is because liturgy, being eventually God's action, which unfolds itself in and through human life, carries with it forms of expression and language which far surpass human understanding or means of communication: symbols, gestures, the "otherness" of the atmosphere. And the words serve to express, at least partially, the grandeur of what is happening. The Council of Trent spoke on this matter when it stated:

> And as human nature is such that it cannot easily raise itself up to the meditation of divine realities without external aids, Holy Mother Church has for that reason duly established certain rites . . . and she has provided ceremonial, such as mystical blessings, lights, incense, vestments and many other rituals of that kind from apostolic order and tradition, by which the majesty of this great sacrifice is enhanced and the minds of the faithful are aroused by those visible signs of religious devotion to contemplation of the high mysteries hidden in this sacrifice.[10]

In other words, the symbolism of the liturgy is the language through which we can read, experience, conform ourselves and be transformed in Jesus. While being deeply oriented towards man and the profoundest language of human communication, liturgy helps us to touch the divine.

This does not mean that we base ourselves on a dualistic conception of man as being merely constituted of a body and soul. Rather, we are talking of the Pauline view of man as body, soul and spirit (cf. 1 Thes 5:23), of the *soma, psuchè* and *pneuma*. It is in the sphere of the *pneuma* that faith generated in prayer becomes a profoundly transforming power—the *pneuma tēs pisteōs*—faith experienced deep down and fully (cf. 2 Cor 4:13). It is a faith that moves us to walk justly—the *dia pisteōs gar peripatoumen* of 2 Cor 5:7. Prayer leads and stimulates us to a kind of "intelligence of the heart."

---

[10] Heinrich Denzinger; Peter Hünermann, Robert Fastiggi and Anne Nash eds., *Enchiridion symbolorum definitionem et declarationem de rebus fidei et morum*, 43rd ed., Latin-English (San Francisco: Ignatius Press, 2012), n. 1746, p. 419.

Buddhism has this concept—the knowledge that stimulates the heart —"Sraddha". St. Ambrose in the hymn "Splendor Paternæ Gloriæ" calls this experience the "Sobria ebrietas", the drunken sobriety, which leads to a kind of mystical rapture and a sense of joyful enthusiasm at being touched profoundly by God. If celebrated in the proper way —according to its own proper *ars*—we would be able to be power-fully transformed by liturgy—the *"metamorphousthe"* of which St. Paul speaks in Romans 12:2.

In this manner, the whole of our Christian living would be stimulated powerfully by God's own inner action. Thus celebrating the liturgy in a way that does not reflect such nobility would deprive the Church of its profoundly divine inner dynamism. It is here that we seem to have faltered. Surely *Sacrosanctum Concilium*'s terms "noble simplicity" (n. 34), "legitimate progress" (n. 23), "unencumbered by useless rep-etition" (n. 34), and so forth did not constitute an open invitation to use the axe freely on the symbols of liturgical celebration and their inner meaning and purpose. For example, abolishing some of the gen-uflections, blessings and prayers and reducing or putting aside some of the objects that formerly constituted the requisites and furnishings prescribed for the celebration of the Eucharist, did give the wrong sig-nal to many. We sort of emptied the liturgy of its "heart" or its inner dynamism, making it a matter rather of the head.

Neither were the quasi or total reduction of the use of Latin, Gre-gorian chant and some of the symbols and gestures that gave expression to the sacredness of what happens at the altar, as well as the denuding of the sacred precincts of symbols that spoke of the celestial aspects of the most Holy Sacrament, anywhere near what the Conciliar Constitution itself advocated. A careful reading of *Sacrosanctum Concilium* would be sufficient to be convinced of this. It did not call for such radicalism.

Liturgical Consistency

And so liturgy should not be easily tampered with, for it is at the very core of the Church's life and mission. Indeed it is Jesus Himself who posited this when He told the Samaritan woman: "The hour comes and now it has, when true worshippers shall worship the Father in Spirit and in truth, for, the Father wants that kind of worship, God is

Spirit and those who worship must worship in Spirit and truth" (Jn 4:23). "Worship in Spirit and truth" here, according to the exegete Raymond Brown, refers to the role of Jesus Himself as the worshipper par excellence of the eschatological times. Jesus becomes the temple and "worship in Spirit" is only possible by "those who possess the Spirit by which God begets them, the Spirit by which God begets them from above (Jn 3:5)."[11] Worship in Truth is seen also as "coherence" which is what Jesus demanded of us, for He is the Truth (cf. Jn 14:6). It is here that in the liturgy, faith is turned into its coherent living out, what St. Paul called the *logiken latreian* (cf. Rom 12:1). That this meant a pleasing sacrifice of life-transformation is how St. Paul explains "*latreian*": "Do not be conformed to this age but be transformed [*metamorphousthe*] by the renewing of your mind that you may discover that which is good and well pleasing and perfect to God's will" (Rom 12:2). Liturgy is thus linked not only to its celebrational aspect but very much more to its parenetic coherence. The *lex orandi* becomes the *lex credendi* and the *lex vivendi* of the community of Christ's disciples, the Church. Pope Benedict XVI called this "*Eucharistic consistency*" (*Sacramentum Caritatis*, 83).

Latin and Liturgy

With regard to the use of Latin in the liturgy it must be stressed that what the Council decreed was that "the use of the Latin language is to be preserved in the Latin rites" (*Sacrosanctum Concilium*, 36). It allowed the use of the vernacular in the following areas: the readings and directives and some of the prayers and chants. Of course, it allowed for the competent territorial ecclesiastical authority to decide whether and to what extent the vernacular is to be used in the liturgy, subject however to the approval of the Holy See. With regard to Gregorian chant too the Council was circumspect in that while opening up to "other kinds of sacred music, especially polyphony" it stated that the Church "acknowledged" Gregorian chant as being proper to the Roman liturgy and "should be given pride of place in liturgical services"

---

[11] Raymond E. Brown, *The Gospel According to John* (New York: Doubleday, 1966), p. 180.

(n. 116). This limited concession of the Council allowing the use of the vernacular in the liturgy was rather adventurously extended by the reformers in that Latin almost totally vanished from the scene and became the best-loved orphan in the Church.

This I state not because I am a fanatic of the Latin language. I come from a mission land where Latin is hardly understood by most of my community. But it is a fallacy to believe that a language needs to be always understood by all. Language as we know is a means of communication of an experience which most of the time is greater than the word itself. Language and words are thus secondary and follow the experience and the person sharing it in importance. Language always carries with it a *kenosis*—an impoverishment in its expression. The more this experience undergoes trans-communication into other languages it tends to be increasingly less expressive of the originality of what happened. The word "OM" in the Hindu liturgy, for example, is untranslatable. Besides, the oriental religions use a language which is strictly limited to their prayer and worship forms. Hinduism uses Sanskrit, Buddhism uses Pali, and Islam, Koranic Arabic. None of these languages are spoken today. But they are used for worship. Each of these languages has been respected and reserved from the very beginning for the expression of "something beyond the level of sounds and letters." Judaism, for example, uses the Tetragrammaton to indicate the unpronounceable name of God. In itself the four letters of the Tetragrammaton may have no linguistic nuance but it stands for the most sacred name of God in the written tradition of the Masora.

The liturgical use of Latin in the Church, even though it starts somewhere in the fourth century A.D., gives rise to a series of expressions which are unique and which constitute the very faith of the Church. The vocabulary of the *Credo* is quite clearly filled with expressions in Latin which are untranslatable. The role of the *lex orandi* in determining the *lex credendi* of the Church is very much valid in the case of its use of Latin in the liturgy. For doctrine often evolves in the faith experience of prayer. For this reason a healthy balance between the use of Latin and that of the vernacular languages should, I believe, be maintained.

The re-introduction of the *usus antiquior*—the older form of the Roman liturgy—by Pope Benedict XVI was thus not a retrograde step as some called it, but a move to bring back to Sacred Liturgy a deeper sense of awe and mysticism and a way in which the Pope sought to prevent a blatant banalization of something so pivotal to the life of the Church. This initiative should be given due value and support. It may also lead to the evolution of a new liturgical movement which could be a step in the direction of the "reform of the reform" which has been an ardent desire of Pope Benedict XVI.

Erroneous Ideas

Another aspect of the process of ushering in a truly profound renewal of the Church, given the decisive role that worship plays in its life and mission is the need to purify the liturgy of some of the erroneous ideas that have entered its portals in and through the euphoria of reform ushered in by some liturgists after the Council. These, I must state, were never in the minds of the Council Fathers when they voted on the historic Constitution on the Sacred Liturgy, *Sacrosanctum Concilium*.

Archeologism

First among these is a kind of false archeologism which echoed the slogan: "let us go back to the liturgy of the early Church." In this was an implicit assumption that only what happened in liturgy in the first millennium of the Church was valid. This was supposed to be part of the process of *aggiornamento*.

Mediator Dei indicates that this view is in error when it states: "The liturgy of the early ages is most certainly worthy of all veneration. But ancient usage must not be esteemed more suitable and proper, either in its own right or in its significance for later times and new situations, on the simple ground that it carries the savor and aroma of antiquity" (n. 61). Moreover, since information on the liturgical practice of the early centuries is not so clearly attested to in the written sources available to us from that era, the danger of a simplistic arbitrariness in defining these practices is greater and runs the risk of being pure conjecture. Also, it is not respectful of the natural process of growth of the traditions of the Church over the subsequent centuries. Neither is it consonant with the belief in the action of the Holy Spirit in the Church down the centuries. It is also highly pedantic and unrealistic.

The Ministerial Priesthood

Another such reformist misconception in the matter of liturgy has been the tendency to confuse the altar and the nave. It is often noted that the essential distinction in liturgy between the role of the clergy and that of the laity had been mixed up due to a misunderstanding of the difference between the priestly office of all the faithful (the common priesthood) and that of the clergy (the ministerial priesthood), a difference clearly highlighted in the Second Vatican Council's Dogmatic Constitution *Lumen Gentium*. This explained that, although the common priesthood of all the baptized which the Church has always upheld (cf. Apoc 1:6; 1 Pet 2:9–10; *Mediator Dei* 39–41, *Lumen Gentium*, 10) and the ministerial priesthood are in their own way "a participation in the one priesthood of Christ", "they differ from one another in essence and not only in degree" (n. 10). The Liturgical Constitution of the same Council, in fact, asserted that "the liturgy makes distinctions between persons according to their liturgical function and Sacred Orders" (*Sacrosanctum Concilium*, 32). *Mediator Dei*, of course, was even more categorical when it stated that "only to the Apostles and thenceforth to those on whom their successors have imposed hands, is granted the power of the priesthood" (n. 40).

The result of this confusion of roles in the modern era has been the tendency to clericalize the laity and to laicize the clergy. Indicative of this confusion has been the increasing removal of the altar rails from our sanctuaries and the sitting or squatting of everyone around an *ad hoc* altar. Far too many people have started to walk about or get into the sanctuary, so much so, that there is much distraction and disturbance at many of our liturgical services. The Holy Eucharist in such a situation becomes a show and the priest the showman. The priest, as in the past, is no more, as K. G. Rey wrote in an article entitled "Coming of Age: Manifestations in the Catholic Church":

> The anonymous go between, the first among the faithful, facing God and not the people, representative of all and together with them offering the sacrifice, while reciting prayers that have been prescribed for him. Today he is a distinct person, with personal characteristics, his personal life style, his face turned towards the people. For many priests this change is a temptation they cannot handle . . . to them,

the level of success of their personal power and thus the indicator of their feeling of personal security and self assurance.[12]

The priest here becomes the main actor playing out a drama with other actors on the altar and the more dramatic and sensational they all become, the more they feel that they are performing well. The central role of Christ fades away in such a scenario. Even though at first it may sound nice, later on it becomes a big bore.

Actuosa Participatio

Yet another and quite often largely misinterpreted liturgical concept is that of *actuosa participatio*. *Sacrosanctum Concilium* coined this term when it stated that "mother Church earnestly desires that all the faithful be led to that full, conscious and active participation in liturgical celebrations which is demanded by the very nature of liturgy" (n. 14). It further stated that "in the restoration and promotion of the Sacred Liturgy, this full and active participation by all the people is the aim to be considered before all else" (n. 14). Unfortunately though, this has led more often to distractions and showmanship than to a true service of devotion and prayerfulness in the liturgy. In *The Spirit of the Liturgy* the future Pope Benedict described *actuosa participatio* as a spirit of total and devout assimilation in the very action of Christ, the High Priest.[13] He asks: "What does it mean . . . ? Unfortunately the word was very quickly misunderstood to mean something external, entailing a need for general activity, as if as many people as possible and as often as possible, should be visibly engaged in action."[14]

Already in *Mediator Dei* Pope Pius XII explained what that participation should be. He wanted the faithful to participate in the Eucharistic Sacrifice "not in an inert and negligent fashion, giving way to distractions and day dreaming, but with earnestness and concentration" (n. 80). The Pope wanted the faithful "to be as closely united as possible with the High Priest (Christ)" (n. 80). They, in imitation

---

[12] K. G. Rey, *Pubertätserscheinungen in der Katholischen Kirche*, Kritische Texte 4 (Einsiedeln: Benziger, 1970), p. 25.

[13] *The Spirit of the Liturgy*, p. 172.

[14] Ibid., p. 171.

of Christ, should "in a humble attitude of mind, pay adoration, honour, praise and thanksgiving to the supreme majesty of God" (n. 80).
There should be a sort of synergy, of a spirit of profound communion
between us and the Lamb whose divine sacrifice of praise continues
in time in the heavenly liturgy. In *The Spirit of the Liturgy*, Cardinal
Ratzinger states: "The point is that, ultimately, the difference between
the *actio Christi* and our own action is done away with. There is only
one action, which is at the same time his and ours—ours because we
have become 'one body and one spirit' with him."[15] In *Sacramentum
Caritatis* Pope Benedict XVI names some of the personal dispositions
needed in order to achieve such a sense of participation with Christ
among which the "Spirit of constant conversion", "Sacramental confession and fasting", "Greater awareness of the mystery being celebrated and its relationship to life", "Holy Communion" where we are
totally assimilated to Him, and even "recollection and silence" (cf. nn.
53-55). In short "participatio" is eventually a matter of "being" rather
than "doing"—without that, as Cardinal Ratzinger wrote we would
radically misunderstand the "theo-drama" of the liturgy, lapsing into
mere parody.[16]

The Church's Mission and the Sacred Liturgy

And so it is necessary that liturgy be taken seriously by all concerned.
It is not something about which we, even as communities, or still more
as individuals can decide. While it is profoundly Christ that celebrates
in our liturgy, it is a matter entrusted to the Church. It is that which
enhances and brings to fulfillment the mission of the Church. The Second Vatican Council is clear in this when it states that "as often as the
Sacrifice of the Cross by which Christ our Pasch is sacrificed (1 Cor
5:7), is celebrated on the altar, the work of our redemption is carried
out. At the same time in the Sacrament of the Eucharistic bread, the
unity of the faithful, who form one body in Christ (cf. 1 Cor 10:17)
is both expressed and brought about" (*Lumen Gentium*, 3).

The Eucharist thus redeems humanity and builds the Church. And
so the Church becomes as St. Pope John Paul II stated: "a sacrament

---

[15] Ibid., p. 174.
[16] Cf. ibid., p. 175.

for humanity, a sign and instrument of the salvation achieved by Christ
. . . for the redemption of all" (*Ecclesia De Eucharistia*, 22). The Pope
adds: "from the perpetuation of the sacrifice of the Cross and her
communion with the Body and Blood of Christ in the Eucharist, the
Church draws the spiritual power needed to carry out her mission.
The Eucharist thus appears as both the source and the summit of all
evangelization" (n. 22). And so the Eucharist is that through which
the community of the faithful and every single disciple of Christ is absorbed unto Christ in that He assumes us and becomes one with us. We
are made to partake in His redeeming mission and while being purified
ourselves, we become part of the community of those redeemed. The
Church thus is formed in her liturgy and draws from it the strength
to carry out her mission on earth.

What really happens is that due to this intimate link to Christ, the
High Priest, in her very existence and mission, the Church moves
into the realm of God's own salvific action. God takes over. Thus the
Church does not engage in her mission as a human community or an
association of altruists but becomes the channel through which God's
own salvific action realizes itself. The absolute indispensability of the
Church for the redemption of humanity stems from that unique relationship.

In fact Jesus and the Church, His mystical continuance in history,
are interlocked in a most absorbing union that it is truly His power
that animates and bears fruit in the mission. He did confirm thus when
He assured the Apostles that He would make them fishers of men, not
they (cf. Mk 1:17). He did affirm that missionary fruitfulness would
very much depend on the Apostles' communion with Him as in the
case of the vine and the branches (cf. Jn 15:5). It is in and through
her liturgy and specifically the celebration of the Eucharist that such
communion is brought about most efficaciously. And the more united
the Church is to Christ, which happens in a most powerful way in the
Eucharist and in the celebration of its liturgical life, the more fruitful
its mission would become because it is finally Christ and His eternal
sacrifice which would redeem the world. Not just what we do.

The Liturgy and the Church

That itself places a grave responsibility on the Church—that is to give due weight to its liturgical life. The seriousness of this matter has been made clear to all, down the centuries, by the Church. Speaking of the rites, Cardinal Ratzinger stated: "They elude control by any individual, local community, or regional Church. Unspontaneity is of their essence. In these rites I discover that something is approaching me here that I did not produce myself,—that I am entering into something greater than myself, which ultimately derives from divine revelation."[17] And so the clear demand of the Conciliar Constitution is normative: "Therefore, no other person whatsoever, not even a priest may add, remove or change anything in the liturgy on their own authority" (*Sacrosanctum Concilium*, 22 §3).

Since Christ is the main subject of liturgical action it is not up to us to arbitrarily change or tamper with the essential orientations or norms of liturgy. Otherwise we would be not so different from those who, impatient at waiting for Moses to descend from the mountain, constructed a golden calf and worshipped what was made by their own choosing. They made their own ritual, eating, drinking and merry making—"playing god" in the process—and the Holy Scriptures mention what then happened to them.

In our own times too we get such people who wish to make the liturgy more "interesting" or palatable to what they call "our times". They make their own rules. And so, they run the risk of emptying liturgy of its essential inner dynamism and the end result would be that the so-called worship forms eventually become tasteless and boring. If such improvisation is that which makes liturgy most effective and interesting, why then is it that, with such experimenting and creativity, the number of those attending Sunday Mass has fallen rapidly in some areas today? This is a question we need to face with courage and a spirit of humility. It is one thing to consider the anthropological requirements of a healthy liturgy, especially with regard to the symbols, rubrics and participation; yet it is another thing to ignore the fact that

---

[17] Ibid., p. 165.

these have no meaning unless they are co-related to that essential call of Christ to join Him in His timeless Sacerdotal Action.

Conclusion

There are many more points which we can and need to consider on the matter of liturgy and its centrality for the life of the Church. I would like to conclude with a beautiful reflection from the Holy Curé of Ars. This humble servant of the Eucharist wrote on the Holy Mass in his *Little Catechism*:

> All good works together are not of equal value with the sacrifice of the Mass, because they are the works of men and the Holy Mass the work of God. Martyrdom is nothing in comparison; it is the sacrifice that man makes of his life to God; the Mass is the sacrifice that God makes to man of His Body and His Blood. Oh how great is the priest! If he understood himself he would die. . . . God obeys him; he speaks two words and our Lord comes down from heaven at this voice and shuts Himself up in a little host. God looks upon the altar. "That is my beloved Son," He says, "in whom I am well pleased." He can refuse nothing to the merits of the offering of this Victim. If we had faith, we should see God hidden in the priest like a light behind a glass, like wine mingled with water.[18]

---

[18] *The Little Catechism of the Curé of Ars* (Rockford, Ill.: TAN, 1951), p. 37.

2

Liturgical Music and the New Evangelization

GABRIEL M. STEINSCHULTE

It gives me particular pleasure to speak for the first time at the beginning of a major international liturgical conference on the theme of *musica sacra*, which otherwise will not be discussed in detail during these days, and yet which is related to and spiritually present in almost all the other topics.

"Fides ex auditu", goes the wise old axiom: "Faith comes from hearing." Or as Sacred Scripture puts it: "Blessed are those who have not seen and yet believe" (Jn 20:29). Perhaps we should reflect on these connections in greater depth, especially in the Year of Faith; after all, hearing is, as everyone knows, the first and the last sense by which a human being perceives, both before birth and also as a person is dying, even when brain function is no longer measurable.

Music as non-verbal communication with meaningful, ordered sound is present at the cradle of humanity, as shown by the term "jubilation", which is derived from the name "Jubal" in the account of creation.[1] Music always serves to communicate, either between human beings or between humanity and divinity. Therefore it goes without saying that all rituals of any culture and religion whatsoever, including the secularized societal and political derivatives of a deliberately godless society,

---

Translated from the German original by Michael J. Miller.

[1] According to Gen 4:21 Jubal is the ancestor of all who play the lyre and pipe, that is, wind instruments as well as string instruments, thus symbolic of instrumental music in general. In this connection see also the valuable publication by Rudolf Pohl, *Enchiridion Musicæ Sacræ: Musica Sacra in den Zeugnissen des Glaubens und der Kirche* (Aachen: Einhard, 2010).

and even sports, have their musical forms of communication and continually develop them. Celebrating and mourning without music is simply unthinkable.

It is the most spiritual form of all human activity and it happens only in the now, intangibly, never again to be repeated identically, unique at every moment, because it is inseparably connected with the living human being, whose mind supports it and whose heart modulates it. It is similar to love and comparable to fire, in that when divided it is not necessarily diminished, and it makes one forget pain, hunger and thirst. Sacred Scripture therefore has good reason to tell us about the angels singing on Christmas night and the eternal praises of the heavenly hosts before the throne of the apocalyptic Lamb; we are privileged to join our voices with theirs in the *Trisagion* or to listen to them when the choir allows us to have a presentiment of the heavenly praises in a more dignified form.

At no time in history was as much music ever consumed as nowadays —and "consumed" is the right word, because people do not produce it themselves. On the contrary: one might observe instead that perhaps never before has so little music, whether vocal or instrumental, been performed by individuals as today. Indeed, who personally still sings at all? If you do not go to church or to the stadium, the only remaining possibility is usually the shower. On the other hand our everyday routine is inundated with piped-in music selected to stimulate the desired behavior: in the supermarket, in the restaurant, in the hotel room, in the discotheque, in the elevator, in the parking lot, and so forth. Even radio or internet news broadcasts require an audio treatment, in keeping with the concept of so-called "infotainment". And is not the great expense on the musical score an essential part of the recipe for success of the film industry in the United States?

In this world of rampant relativism we speak about the music *of* the Sacred Liturgy, please note, and not about music *in* the liturgy, for the latter designation, in deliberately functional terms, obviously intends to leave open the essential question as to the kind of music, consciously avoiding the concept of *musica sacra*—a familiar strategy since the struggle over the 1967 Instruction *Musicam Sacram*.[2] Actually, however, the

---

[2] Thus Johannes Overath, president of the *Consociatio Internationalis Musicæ Sacræ* (CIMS), whom Paul VI allowed to read the manuscript before it was signed, was still

liturgy possesses its own suitable music, which through the action of the Holy Spirit becomes *musica sacra*,[3] and thus something more than is implied literally by the term "sacer, sacra", which means "offered up" or "set aside".

Remarkably, every sort of music has its communicative meaning. Even apparently meaning-free music is deployed in order to distract from reflecting or listening. Thus the background music in restaurants serves precisely this purpose, namely to prevent indiscreet eavesdropping, especially when there are few patrons. For low volumes are enough to alter or greatly to impair our ability to concentrate. How much greater a disturbance, then, must be a kind of music that is felt to be completely out of place! It is obvious, therefore, that every community seeks the type of music suitable for their purpose. For the Church, which since the days of the primitive Church has prayed by singing, this means: *lex orandi*—*lex credendi*, which is, in my opinion, the central point on which this conference turns.

A Look at History and the Present

Whereas "orandi" implies many other aspects, such as language, posture, orientation of prayer, and so forth, here we intend to focus our attention on the sonic garment of prayer, a garment that was woven in the first centuries of the martyrs and of the young, enthusiastically believing Church, in faithful adherence to Scripture and to sound Tradition. At the same time, musical-motivic gems from the past were just as carefully preserved as the new treasures of the young Christian peoples were gratefully welcomed. This music of the liturgy, which grew up organically in the first millennium of the Church under the inspiration of the Holy Spirit, with its more than four thousand vocal pieces in so-called Gregorian chant alone, born out of the texts of

---

able to correct important things, among them the absurd prohibition of all polyphonic settings of the *Sanctus*, as well as the proposed misleading Arrenga-terminology "musicam in liturgia" which was typical of the authors of the draft.

[3] Cf. Gabriel Maria Steinschulte, ed., *Musica Spiritus Sancti numine sacra: Contributi alla teologia della Musica Sacra dalle pubblicazioni della Consociatio Internationalis Musicæ Sacræ*, Italian-German edition (Rome: Consociatio Internationalis Musicæ Sacræ and Libreria Editrice Vaticana, 2001).

Sacred Scripture, correlated for every hour and every day of the whole year in a great, organic and meaningful whole—this music (almost the sung Bible) can without hesitation be regarded as the greatest musical artwork of all ages, which moreover is by no means concluded, as long as the liturgy is alive.[4]

The theme of the New Evangelization is not new. Rather it has appeared again and again in history. Before we turn our attention to the present, therefore, it seems to me that a brief glance at the history of the Church's music will be useful, because—just as in the field of dogma —many liturgical wrong turns and corrections logically run parallel and periodically recur.

The development of the early Church took place within the external legal framework of the Roman Empire, yet from the very start encountered altogether different cultures, from Judaism via the various peoples of Asia Minor and North Africa, then Greece, to Rome itself and its Gallic provinces in particular. It was an initial evangelization of peoples with various musical cultures, who were united among themselves in only one thing, namely their mania for the most frenzied entertainment possible, the pre-eminent luxury instrument of which was the *hydraulis*, the so-called "water organ".

Now when the Christian communities flatly rejected all these sorts of music, both liturgically and extra-liturgically, this was not a sign of antipathy toward music, but on the contrary only the consequence of clear discernment. Unlike their pagan fellow citizens, they would already be singing the divine praises at an early morning hour; a new concept arises, *psallein*, the "singing" of those formally quite variegated songs from the Old Covenant as though they were Christ's own hymnal—songs that from the new perspective of redeemed mankind were rediscovered as precious texts of revelation that already include all the central statements of the Gospel.[5] From its earliest hour, Christianity has lived by its joy in the Resurrection. Easter is the central point of the liturgy and of the Church year. And precisely this great Easter season is

---

[4] Cf. Bonifacio G. Baroffio, "Le chant grégorien, forme musicale la plus achevée, pour toute l'année, pour chaque jour, et pour chaque heure", in: Symposium *La Bible Chantée*, Chartres 1994, *Musicæ Sacræ Ministerium*, Anno XXIX–XXX, nn. 1 & 2 (Rome: Consociatio Internationalis Musicæ Sacræ, 1995), pp. 50–57.

[5] *Psallein* was sooner part of the Apollonian tradition of spiritualized singing—in stark contrast to the predominant Dionysian practice of carnal, sensual music.

drenched with the happy imperatives, "Sing, exult, rejoice", citations unerringly selected from the psalms.

Services of divine worship were sung as a matter of principle, even the readings, as was already the case at the time of the Jews,[6] and not just for technical reasons to overcome considerable distances when communicating. Rather, a human being who sings finds himself comparatively speaking in an exceptional condition, he is almost beside himself, he is exalted. At the same time he becomes vulnerable and is aware of the need for humility, since in the tightrope walk between the enchanting and the ridiculous there is a very small margin of error.

Hopeless melancholy, anger and wickedness, nevertheless, cannot or will not sing.

Therefore the Church by no means adapted to existing musical customs; when in doubt, as a matter of principle she renounced the use of musical instruments so as to avoid syncretistic misunderstandings. This liturgical memory has remained alive to this day in Orthodoxy. The purely *a cappella* tradition of the Sistine Chapel (as the papal "private choir") has its roots here too, whereas in countries with less of the musical tradition of antiquity, an increasing impartiality in the use of musical instruments then became widespread over the course of the second Christian millennium;[7] precisely because there was no longer any clear and present danger of psychological confusion with pagan thinking.

This early Christian singing of psalms and hymns was not restricted to liturgical gatherings, but lived on in the so-called house music. Christians already knew, therefore, that extra-liturgical spiritual music must have a certain relation to worship, and so to speak must lead to it. The liturgical event should therefore radiate into the everyday routine, and not vice-versa.

Since today's New Evangelization in many places is again *de facto* an initial evangelization and is taking place in an era that in many respects

---

[6] Giacomo Baroffio, "Continuità e rottura con il mondo antico nella liturgia romana", in: *Atti di un convegno del 2011*, in: Rosa Bianca Finazzi and Paola Pontani, eds., *Dal mondo antico all'universo medievale: nuove modulazioni di lingue e di culture* (Milan: EDUCatt, 2013), pp. 7–11.

[7] The secular pipe organ was even ennobled and declared a liturgical instrument *expressis verbis* in the directions of the Second Vatican Council, for the first time in history with such lofty authority.

is pagan or else hedonistic and nihilistic, in posing our question we are especially close to the problems and experiences of the early Church.[8]

Over the centuries of the early Church we also observe the constant effort to establish generally binding liturgical ordinances under the control of the local bishop and in the broadest possible conformity with the developing ecclesiastical provinces. In this process the Latin Church looks steadfastly to the East and learns from the prototypes among Egypt, Jerusalem and Constantinople, while the provinces of a Gallic character often are more concerned about old liturgical treasures and Tradition than Rome itself is. This care about a binding form of the liturgy and of the manner of singing it originates in turn from the care about the content of the Faith and about deepening it. For the early Church already knew that *non*-binding form leads to *non*-binding content. This holds true today as it did then.

The first great wave of hymn composition in Constantinople was contagious: soon, in the Latin Middle Ages, Latin poetry blossomed with all its flowerings and false starts. The Carolingian spring even brushed aside older, precious traditions of sacred song for the sake of union with Rome. Here already it becomes clear that in reality it is not a matter of purely musical questions when judgments are to be made about liturgical music.

In the following centuries, eras of religious decline alternate in an undulating motion with periods of reform, which as a rule are supported by the religious orders: to the apogee of Cluny—the Latin answer to liturgical Constantinople—the response was the Cistercians with their principle: "back to the roots", whereby in their well-intentioned mutilation of Gregorian chant they were of the opinion that they were now singing the "older", "more authentic" chant, although to this day

---

[8] At any rate our brethren and "colleagues" from the first half of the first Christian millennium would probably recoil in horror if we tried to inform them that it is good policy in pastoral work with youth to sing the liturgy in Gregorian chant first and then to invite them to an evening dance with rock and pop music. Actually this hypothetical case is hardly realistic, because in what youth Mass nowadays do they hear even one selection from the authentic sung music of the liturgy? Not only in this setting did the sound of pagan music conquer the sanctuary years ago. Therefore either today's Church has gone terribly astray, or else the early Church made life unnecessarily difficult for itself.

no one has been able to see any increased spiritual attractiveness in it. One is tempted to liken it to today's semiological zeal.

Just like the Cistercians, the Franciscans too were convinced above all by their personal experience of the monastic ideal of poverty, which had sunk into oblivion elsewhere, while they—at the time of their founder and in the first centuries of their history—still took very seriously the sung monastic Liturgy of the Hours and, in their satchels, spread the *Missale Romanum* throughout Europe and overseas. With their fondness for popular piety they opened a door in music history, not only in Italy: the importance of this seems to be underestimated frequently. Thus, for example, the so-called Franciscan *Laudes* are a valuable compendium of high-quality spiritual folk songs in the Italian language, which is yet to be discovered by contemporary pastoral ministry. Likewise the Latin rhymed little offices could clear a new path to the Church's Liturgy of the Hours.[9]

Not liturgical-musical poverty, but rather the opposite was historically the hallmark of a Franciscan Order, which did live in the world but was not of the world and which intensified the pastoral significance of *musica sacra*.[10]

All initial steps to renew religious life with the help of the liturgy are essentially supported by a sort of restoration of liturgical music.[11]

---

[9] The first priests on the ships of the explorers and pioneers of the New World were Franciscans, who in South America—as opposed to North America—built up in the following centuries a distinctive church music culture that was largely driven out by incorrectly understood reforms after the Second Vatican Council. On this subject see both the comprehensive studies by Antonio A. Bispo on the history of church music in São Paulo as well as the publications written or edited by him on the historical heritage of sacred music in Latin America in the annual series *Musices Aptatio* of the CIMS Institute for Hymnological and Ethnomusicological Studies (Cologne) in the 1980s and 1990s.

[10] One might understand in this sense also the warning by Benedict XVI that the Church should detach itself from "worldliness", as he put it in his address during the meeting with catholics engaged in the life of the Church and society at the Concert Hall, Freiburg im Breisgau, on Sunday, 25 September 2011.

[11] We can trace further the stages of the new religious orders with their respective beginnings and also look at the famous Bull by John XXII, *Docta Patrum*, in the early fourteenth century, with which he put a stop to the affectations of the so-called *ars nova* in the liturgy at that time and reminded the Church again of the essentials. Cf. Max Lütolf, "Die Constitutio *Docta Sanctorum Patrum* (1324) von Papst Johannes XXII", in:

Drastic measures to alter the musical structure only serve the sole purpose of making the substance of the event more evident again.

This outline could also describe the whole reform effort of the Council of Trent, which, faced with Protestant idiosyncrasies and forms of subjectivism, removed tens of thousands of Latin hymns and hundreds of sequences from liturgical use and placed tighter restrictions on the polyphony.

This had been preceded by Martin Luther's Reformation, which fetched German hymns that had existed since the Middle Ages and numbered around 800 even before the Reformation (!) out of the realm of folklore and para-liturgy and brought them into the Lutheran worship service, preferably in place of the Latin propers. Besides the favor of the princes, it was not theological argumentation, but rather this chessboard move of "looking at what comes out of the people's mouths" that obtained for the Reformation its great initial successes. But what had happened? The reliable proper texts, which had grown up over the course of more than a thousand years from the readings, the psalms and other passages of Scripture, had been replaced by interchangeable, individual, subjective songs, the texts of which only in the rarest cases correspond halfway adequately to the readings and the specific liturgical day and theme; musically they are at best good folk songs, yet far removed from the melodic masterpieces of the Latin liturgy, which stands within the liturgical context of the entire Church year, is obligatory regardless of language barriers, and therefore unites peoples.

Recognizing this weakness, gifted authors then tried, for example in the form of the so-called *Psalmenlied*, to pour the contents of a psalm textually and musically into the form of a hymn, and sometimes they were even halfway successful. At any rate, during the Reformation period we can observe the problematic nature of the folkloric hymn and ultimately its unsuitability for the Sacred Liturgy. For centuries, with good reason, the Church had kept these genuinely valuable folk songs, which after all are not an invention of the Reformation, in the para-liturgical sphere of devotions, processions and house

Musicæ Sacræ Ministerium, Anno XXXVIII (Rome: Consociatio Internationalis Musicæ Sacræ, 2000/2001), pp. 32–43.

music.[12] In competition with its Protestant counterpart, a considerable repertoire developed, especially in confessionally mixed countries: hymns of widely varying quality on all themes, which mirror the history of piety.

The likewise inflationary and usually ill-qualified production of a flood of vernacular songs in countries that hitherto had been largely Catholic, and their almost exclusive use *in* the liturgy as a matter of principle after the Second Vatican Council—contrary to its instructions—is a major reason for the loss of liturgical identity and single-minded faith.

What the vernacular hymn was for the Reformation, the splendor of the Baroque orchestral Mass was for the Counter-Reformation. Everybody was invited to hear the most beautiful music possible at the time; in the high caliber of its ceremonies, vestments, architecture and above all in its music, this sort of Mass took its standard from the princely court. Even today this tradition lives on in many regions, because it is loved by people with some degree of higher education who are otherwise so modern.[13]

In the nineteenth century, ecclesiastical life arose again from the ruins of liturgical music resulting from the French Revolution only through Dom Prosper Guéranger and his monks of Solesmes, on the one hand, and through the Cecilian Movement of Regensburg, on the other. Once again it was the way of sung prayer, of the liturgy, which fanned a new fire in recovering the life of faith in the second half of the century, with its young religious communities, whereas the episcopate *en masse* clung to the status quo of the music style of the operetta. Despite St. Pius X and Vatican II, this attitude has essentially —and naturally with a few happy exceptions—not changed to this day,

---

[12] Through the collaboration of the CIMS-Institut für Hymnologische und Musikethnologische Studien in Cologne [see note 9], in a few years the eight-volume critical edition of the German-language hymns from the time before the invention of printing will be completed and available; to date six volumes have been published in Kassel.

[13] In places where the clergy forcibly prevent it, those who attend move on to the nearest concert halls, which very often have meanwhile befriended these new patrons and offer a program with this great church music on Sunday morning, usually at 11:00.

except that the operetta has meanwhile turned into a sort of "variety show".[14]

In young Churches and non-Christian cultures, nevertheless, missionaries behaved until the mid-twentieth century much as the early Church had done in pagan antiquity: to avoid running the risk of substantial dogmatic misunderstandings, they preferred to make use of relatively simple European hymns and simple Gregorian chants. Then, instead of a conscientious and cautious openness to the liturgical integration of precious elements of the native musical cultures, as foreseen by the Second Vatican Council,[15] the dam burst and what followed was unscrupulous arbitrariness unparalleled in history.

Artistic demands and groundbreaking musical-anthropological research aimed at avoiding syncretistic misunderstandings were to a great extent ignored by those with pastoral responsibility. "Just do it" became the watchword of the hour. Every musical dilettante is welcome. It comes as no surprise that the results are up to neither the minimum artistic standards of European musical culture nor those of the respective native musical cultures outside of Europe.[16]

Unless new "quality offensives" are mounted in the near future against the rampant liturgical-musical Bollywood kitsch, the missionary force of the Church will weaken, precisely with regard to the elites.

The situation in the countries of Western musical culture is different and yet similar: instead of preserving with the utmost care ("summa cura"), as the Council puts it, the "treasure" of the native *musica sacra*, which has grown up for two thousand years in the liturgy, with the liturgy and around the liturgy, it has to a great extent been thrown overboard and replaced with cheap, short-lived products. Whereas Gradual and Alleluia chants inspired by the Holy Spirit had resounded between

---

[14] Thus the music *in* the cathedral liturgy today—too often it is not music *of* the liturgy!—resembles a mixed bag of individual songs, short-lived mini-antiphons, nice choral compositions and now and then isolated bits of Gregorian chant and Latin polyphony, framed by a relatively loud organ, which in the best case is played by a virtuoso, to whom the liturgy is often nothing more than a programmed sequence of not only musical numbers.

[15] See Article 119 of the Conciliar Constitution *Sacrosanctum Concilium*.

[16] More on this topic in: Gabriel M. Steinschulte, "Zur grundsätzlichen Bedeutung der Musik für die Evangelisation nach dem II. Vatikanischen Konzil", in: Emilio Casares and Carlos Villanueva, eds, *De Musica Hispana et aliis: Miscelánea en honor al Prof. Dr. José López-Calo S.J., en su 65° cumpleaños*, vol. II (Universidade de Santiago de Compostela, 1990), pp. 419–32.

the readings since the days of the early Church, what is heard now are compositions on a par with ringtones and radio jingles. Even for the musical requirements of papal Masses these days, makeshift music and the services of dilettantes are thought to be adequate.

After the sickeningly sweet kitsch of the nineteenth century and the coy kitsch of the theologically shallow 'SacroPop' and so-called "new spiritual songs" of the twentieth century (which have long since lost their novelty), musical helplessness is becoming increasingly widespread, and Catholics wonder where to go from here. This can be observed in the music of World Youth Days as well, for a form suited to the content is lacking.

Superficial externals and highly subjective sentimentality do not spring from what is substantial, nor do they lead to anything substantial. Spiritual and artistic quality does not take its bearings from popular demand, but rather from the central meaning and depth of the truths of the Faith. Something can be beautiful and good only if it is unambiguously aligned with the truth and with artistic ability.

Taking the Directives of the Second Vatican Council at Their Word—Finally

Experience has shown that councils produce their intended effect only one hundred years later; if so, then fifty years after Vatican II it is high time to reexamine the course that has been charted, for the Council's directives on *musica sacra* were not meant as material for discussion or as a snapshot of a given moment. If the changes in the liturgy in the post-conciliar period had not been made while disregarding the music that is organically connected with it—despite all the warnings of the experts who had been consulted[17]—many aberrations and mistakes could have been avoided.[18]

---

[17] On the eve of the Council the Fourth International Congress for Church Music in Cologne had not only demonstrated the wealth of high-caliber liturgical-musical possibilities, but had also pointed out lurking dangers and misunderstandings, as could be gathered especially from its moderate *vota* (recommendations). See: Johannes Overath ed., *Ipsi canamus gloriam: IV. Internationaler Kongress für Kirchenmusik: Dokumente und Berichte*, Schriftenreihe des Allgemeinen Cäcilienverbandes für die Länder der deutschen Sprache. Privately printed at Bachem's in Cologne, 1962, vol. IV, pp. 356–58.

[18] The disastrous nosedive is well known and is acclaimed only by those who were

Anyone who wants a fresh start has to start here first, since today especially, in the audio-visual world of signs and "music colors", the liturgy supports evangelization in the long run more than any intellectual appeals, publicity and other pastoral efforts. Every media professional knows today that the musical tag of a broadcast is decisive for its identity and thus ultimately for its long-term acceptance by the public, whereby music and content absolutely must correspond to each other.

"The New Evangelization in formerly Christian regions of the secularized West requires [of course] first a change of consciousness in those who still belong to the Church", as Nicolaus Buhlmann correctly writes,[19] and therefore also a change in the consciousness of those who bear the responsibility for conditions today.

Since the hoped-for New Evangelization in many regions and population sectors is actually a re-evangelization, one can *still* often make a connection with the old Christian roots, insofar as they are still engaged psychologically in the people's memory in a positive way. In contrast to many other ecclesiastical departments, one can nevertheless generally observe precisely among those who are rather distant from the Church—for whatever reason—a nostalgic longing for the lost forms of liturgical solemnity, while younger generations listen in unbelieving astonishment and perplexity. There is still a glow in the liturgical ashes. Given good will or at least basic fairness, therefore, it should be a missionary imperative and a commandment of love to give back to the people in the old formerly Christian regions this sacred music which is their own, the sound of the liturgical home of their childhood,[20] and to stop withholding it from the younger folks.[21]

In general, in all the initiatives and activities of the New Evangeliza-

---

responsible for it. The world of culture has meanwhile recoiled from it in horror; the lay faithful with liturgical education (a vanishing breed) have retreated in resignation. For young people who are relatively distant from the Church, what worship ought to be is often enough as interesting as an evening with their stodgy parents or else an exaggerated kindergarten ceremony.

[19] Nicolaus Buhlmann, "Wir wollen wieder wachsen", in: *Vatican-magazin* 11/2011 (Journal) (Kisslegg: Fe-Medienverlags GmbH), (pp. 34–42), p. 35.

[20] In the growing retirement homes of aging Western societies a mighty pastoral task awaits, whereby the traditional *musica sacra* could aid felicitously in bringing joy and consolation; with the technological resources of our time, musically trained pastoral assistants could be of great help.

[21] Who as a rule have never yet experienced, for example, a Latin High Mass with chant schola and choir.

tion we will have to ask ourselves: Who needs to be re-evangelized? Someone who in today's world, with its atheistic, hedonistic and heterodox groups of all sorts, professes the Roman Catholic Faith not out of habit or because of group dynamics but because he is seeking, is a demanding person. There is no good reason to prevent him from making the challenging climb into the fascinating mountains of the musical beauties of the liturgy and beyond that to the worship and experience of God.

In his booklet on the New Evangelization in the Year of Faith, Bishop Dominique Rey has marked out all the essential position lights that can serve as points of reference from a wide variety of perspectives. Unmistakably he declares concerning the concept of the New Evangelization: "New" means "reevaluating" our pastoral practices.[22] Faced with the external challenges of secularism, relativism and the loss of the Christian memory, Bishop Rey considers it necessary for the Church ceaselessly to rediscover her own identity and her missionary structure.[23]

Applied to the music of the liturgy, and in complete agreement with the wisdom of the missionary Church since the beginning, this means: no uncritical adoption of secular musical forms and sound patterns, but rather a distinctive identity with unmistakably special music.

And sacred music is not the *ancilla liturgiæ*, the Cinderella of the liturgy, as an old misunderstanding supposed. The Council very deliberately avoids that expression.[24] The Archbishop of Rio de Janeiro, indeed, had made it clear that *musica sacra* has an "ancillary" or subordinate function only with respect to its action ("quoad actionem"), but not with respect to its nature ("quoad naturam"). "By its nature it is and remains a necessary and integral component of the solemn liturgy."[25] By its nature, therefore, it belongs not to the so-called liturgical Martha-services, but rather with its loving intuition to the Mary-services (to stay with the same figure of speech).[26]

---

[22] Dominique Rey, *Paroisses, Réveillez-Vous! Au défi de la nouvelle évangélisation* (Paris: Éditions de l'Emmanuel, 2012), p. 18.

[23] Ibid., p. 21.

[24] Johannes Overath, "Die liturgisch-musikalischen Neuerungen des II. Vatikanischen Konzils", in: *Geschichte der Katholischen Kirchenmusik* (Kassel: Karl Gustav Fellerer, 1976), (pp. 370–80), p. 378.

[25] Johannes Overath, "Bestimmungen der Konzilskonstitution", in: ibid., (pp. 381–94), p. 388.

[26] See Joseph Cardinal Ratzinger, Les figures de Marie et de Marthe, in: Autour de

Noteworthy too nowadays is Christ's reaction to the apostles' criticism of the extravagant outpouring of the costliest nard on Jesus' head. They say that it would have been better to sell the perfume and to give the money to the poor, but Christ answers this rebuke: "You always have the poor with you" (Mt 26:11). Do we not have here the textbook case of a classical dispute in the Church, whenever *musica sacra* costs money that might also be given to the poor?

Like Mary Magdalene on Easter morning, sacred music too sets out in search of the Christ-encounter, if necessary even without encouragement from the hierarchy. The Sacred Liturgy however is for us the most perfect place to meet Christ, as Bishop Rey remarks.[27]

St. Ambrose goes a step further when he says, "Christus in Ecclesia cantat." (Christ sings in the Church). From the Trinitarian perspective, the Holy Spirit himself—as Bishop Wilhelm Kempf said in the Council hall as *relator* of the German bishops for the liturgy—is called in the language of the Church *jubilus Patris et Filii* (the joyful melody of the Father and of the Son).[28] He went on to say (and we quote him verbatim):

> A liturgy that tried to dispense with pneumatic song, the *jubilus* of the well-tuned heart, and singing and playing in the Lord, would be not only a stunted liturgy but a downright denial of its own nature. This is not just about some categories of aesthetics, but about genuine categories of theology. It is about restoring to *musica sacra* the theological status that belongs to it, which for many reasons it has regrettably lost.[29]

In contrast to the free-form devotional exercises or worship service gatherings of Protestant congregations, the objective Eucharistic Presence of the Lord gives rise to a different situation, in which instead of arbitrary subjective elements only an objective order and form is appropriate. For this reason the Council particularly recommends, as

---

la question liturgique, Actes des Journées liturgiques de Fontgombault 22–24 Juillet 2001, Fontgombault, (pp. 6–9), p. 9; ET: Joseph Cardinal Ratzinger, Homily, "Mary and Martha", in: Alcuin Reid, ed., *Looking Again at the Question of the Liturgy, Proceedings of the July 2001 Fontgombault Liturgical Conference* (Farnborough: St. Michael's Abbey Press, 2003), (pp. 13–15), p. 14.

[27] Interview with the Journal *La Nef*, April 2013, p. 247.

[28] Overath, "Bestimmungen der Konzilskonstitution", p. 387.

[29] Ibid., cited from *Musica Sacra* (Journal of the General Saint Cecilia's Federation for the German speaking countries), vol. 83 (1963): p. 155.

St. Pius X already had done, in addition to Gregorian chant the works of so-called classical polyphony, because in them the requisite balance between objectivity of form and lively subjective expression is achieved, probably in a way not found in other genre of music whatsoever.

The specific musical directives of the Council are therefore by no means to be understood merely as illustrative examples; rather, hidden within these directives is a clearly outlined repertoire and job description for the professional musician in the service of the sacred. Again and again they make the demand for true art, which (as everyone knows) presupposes first of all talent, and then of course training, praxis, experience and furthermore—surprise!—even a suitable living wage and respect for author's rights. If *musica sacra* constitutes a "treasure of inestimable value" ("thesaurum . . . pretii inæstimabilis") which "is to be preserved and cultivated with greatest care" ("summa cura servetur et foveatur"), as Vatican II prescribes,[30] it requires first-class artistic personnel in the liturgical service, for the Council issued no instructions for the concert business. And liturgical masterpieces cannot be performed adequately by amateur musical hobbyists. All this does not happen by itself in the long run; it demands the applied pastoral attention of the bishop. Likewise this status in liturgical law is worth something only insofar as it is taken seriously by the bishops and by the pope.

If music always participates in the cultural dynamic of every era, then we can understand also the by now familiar fashion of so-called historical performance practice, which influences the praxis of liturgical music in ways that are both beneficial and harmful. Proven historical facts can enlighten and enrich the present; nevertheless in the liturgy they must not become an end in themselves or art for art's sake.

Philological fanaticism, however, turns out to be just as misleading as the unwritten "dogma" of *sola Scriptura*. Only those styles of Gregorian chant that have proved effective every day, day and night, in the sung prayer of non-professional singers can be taken seriously in the liturgy.[31]

---

[30] *Sacrosanctum Concilium*, articles 112 and 114.

[31] It is well known that all the potential data contained in the manuscripts can no longer be performed with artistic authenticity; attempts to do so belong instead in workshops, and many of them perhaps in the cabaret. Moreover, for liturgical performance today the question as to the sound pattern at a particular time in history is extremely relative, at any rate not decisive and at best valuable for orientation. Scientifically, it is simply false and misleading to view Gregorian chant merely as a repertoire of ancient music. What

There are not many alternatives, but certainly many aberrations. These aberrations are especially dangerous in convents and cloisters, where the celebration of the liturgy is central to the monastic vocation. The beauty of community prayer in choir is the vital elixir of contemplative life. Anyone who disrupts it by an extravagant style of singing or— worse yet—by vernacular substitutes that are as artificial as they are bloodless, endangers the future of the community.[32]

In contrast, hidden in the "melodic miracles" of Gregorian chant —as Paul Hindemith put it—is an inexhaustible mine of inspiration, which precisely in connection with very specific texts from Sacred Scripture can accompany the singer and the listener meditatively for hours as an audio-perfume or a so-called musical hook, quite in keeping with the words of the Psalmist: "O Lord, I meditate on your law day and night" (Ps 1:2).

Actually, the fact that great liturgical music and especially Gregorian chant can be taught to ordinary non-musicians and to the average faithful should be generally known, since for more than sixty years in many countries of the world the Ward Method, developed by Justine Bayard Ward in the United States, has made it possible for thousands

---

is still lacking in regard to Gregorian chant is a scientific theory that not only examines the meaning, possibilities and limitations of notation and ethnomusicological evaluation from a historical perspective, but also includes and understands the theological understanding of the Church and of her liturgy on her journey through the ages.

[32] No less a personage than Dom Prosper Guéranger even described awful ways of singing Gregorian chant, which turn it into a "sluggish, dreadful series of choppy notes . . . that evoke no feeling and cannot speak to the soul", as "the work of the devil." In the foreword to the book *La Méthode raisonnée* by Canon Gontier of Le Mans he wrote: "The melodic rendition of Gregorian chant is so important for this chant that even ownership of the Antiphonary used by St. Gregory would hypothetically be no advantage whatsoever, if you also had to listen to how its marvelous pieces were sung without any sense of rhythm and expression. It would be a hundred times better to take the most faulty and incorrect of the editions that we have today and to perform the pieces contained therein—however distorted they may be—according to the rules known and practiced in antiquity." Cf. Guy-Marie Oury, *Dom Prosper Guéranger*, (Solesmes, 2001) [citation translated into English from the authorized German edition (Heiligenkreuz, no date), p. 549.]

What is needed today, therefore, is not so much a dubious restoration of melodies (as though there were an "original version", which is an anachronistic short-circuiting of musical archaeology!), as instead the "restoration" of chant in general that would be experienced as halfway musical by people who pray today. Moreover: no high-class opera company in the world today would dare to allow a work to be sung in a more or less poor translation.

upon thousands of average children to learn Gregorian chant and complex polyphony as a game. All that is needed is collaboration between school and pastoral ministry.[33]

What Can We Improve?

Bishop Rey mentioned a threefold deficit: communication, attractiveness and credibility.[34] In all three of these legitimate points the real music of the liturgy can be helpful.

Firstly, it *is* communication, which can be used on the social media, without language problems, ecumenically, discreetly or strikingly, meaningfully and in a way that is accessible to everyone; most importantly, though, beyond all words it is the messenger of the ineffable mystery of God.

Secondly, since listening to or even producing music is a favorite occupation of youth, an inspiring and competent director (a few continuing education courses are not enough!) can manage economically or at almost no cost to convey to them an attractive repertoire out of the immense wealth of the "treasure of sacred music",[35] so as to make choirs places of real encounter and lasting association, which incidentally in a de-Christianized world are often enough sought out as ideal marriage markets for like-minded people.

Thirdly, if the singers and musicians live out their faith, music performed even by untrained musicians can have a convincing and moving effect. When the boys' choirs at the cathedrals were still conducted by faithful priest-musicians, those choirs were reliable sources of priestly vocations. Liturgical choirs and especially boys' choirs therefore need special pastoral attention.

Today, most importantly, there is an opportunity to win over again to the Gospel members of the educated classes. This same opportunity, however, is frequently ruined by the use of trivial or even painful music in the liturgy.

---

[33] See Gabriel M. Steinschulte, *Die Ward-Bewegung: Studien zur Realisierung der Kirchenmusikreform Papst Pius X. in der ersten Hälfte des 20. Jahrhunderts*, Kölner Beiträge zur Musikforschung 100 (Regensburg: Bosse-Verlag, 1979).

[34] Rey, *Paroisses, Réveillez-Vous!*, p. 19.

[35] See *Sacrosanctum Concilium*, articles 112 and 114.

It is entirely in keeping with the image of the "salt of the earth", to see the future Church in a network encompassing the territorial spiritual centers that are increasingly developing around monasteries and convents, pilgrimage churches and special parishes. What could be more important than to make these centers unforgettably and enduringly attractive as a home for the soul through dignified music of the sung liturgy?

To do that requires a new educational initiative and consciousness-raising with regard to *musica sacra*, especially for all who are responsible for the liturgy, therefore especially for priests and religious—and not just the so-called lower clergy! The indispensable foundation, at any rate, is the teaching and legislation of the Church, as found in the documents of the Council and of the Holy See. It is not enough to concentrate this educational initiative merely on the musical material and the training of personnel. Instead musical horizons must be broadened theologically, historically, acoustically, ethnologically, psychologically and sociologically, with an entitlement that is just as scientifically well-grounded as the subjects in the study of theology.

However, since today we are practically back to square one again with this entitlement, it will be necessary initially to train the teachers of such liturgical music in the first place. Before general structural recommendations can be made in this field, conscientious bishops at the diocesan level should set up coordinated, specific courses in the subject at their major seminaries, whereby at the same time two indispensable principles should be heeded: (1) the instructors must in every case have an academic formation in their field and; (2) at the same time be rooted in liturgical praxis and have a share in pastoral responsibility.

It would already be a success if, after this conference, one or two dioceses started to put this new plan into practice, so that, with the help of the experiences gained there, very soon imitations could be offered generally in a permanently improved form, in a way that transcends boundaries.

Since the qualifications demanded of the instructors will to a considerable extent be interdisciplinary, a lively exchange or an organic collaboration should of course exist and be fostered among these instructors.

As for the contents of this curriculum, the *Consociatio Internationalis*

Musicæ Sacræ already designed a draft plan six years ago, which is included as an appendix to this paper.[36]

Even though the religious orders, especially the new liturgical communities, do not need a general education in all aspects of *musica sacra* to the same extent as the diocesan clergy do, educational opportunities should be offered to these communities too, so as to avoid abuses that are as deplorable as they are unnecessary.[37]

Another area of fatal musical mistakes is provided by architecture and interior decoration: who ever consults musical specialists in this regard? And then later everyone wonders why the singing and the organ sound bad. Then all the parish needs is an expensive and inappropriate installation of microphones in order to go completely astray musically. Is there a major seminary anywhere in which one can learn how to deal with microphones and in what spaces, and that there are, for example, very different sorts of microphones?

The indirect demands of the Council, in particular on priests, in matters of musical competence are much higher than is generally assumed; they are an indispensable prerequisite for any *ars celebrandi*. Apart from the fact that the celebrant really should be able to sing the solemn Latin liturgy according to the rules and must not leave the tones of the collects, for example, to chance or an arbitrary whim, he has to make sure, as a music teacher among other things, that the congregation can sing all the parts belonging to it, including the appropriate Ordinary prayers and *Credo*, and so forth in Latin as well.[38] But with regard also

---

[36] CIMS paper, "Formazione del Clero e dei Religiosi alla Musica Sacra", Rome, 2007; see appendix, "Formation of Clergy and Religious in Sacred Music."

[37] Thus we often come across altogether refined or even exemplary liturgical chant side by side with inappropriate organ music, either from an electronic synthesizer that is expensive, when pro-rated over its lifetime (despite the unambiguous conciliar demand for a pipe organ—because every imitation is a lie and thus liturgically just as unusable as electric candles) or in the form of a courtly Baroque organ, on which one might play the repertoire of an aristocratic salon, but nevertheless to a great extent is liturgically unusable and superfluous.

With regard to the celebration of the *usus antiquior*—the older form of the Roman rite—moreover, most organists need additional training which at the moment is offered at no music academy, namely in Gregorian liturgical improvisation, intonation and accompaniment.

[38] Here we deliberately speak only about the Latin form, because the sometimes hastily produced vernacular versions often enough are artistically demanding and therefore cannot be sung "correctly" at all in the strict sense.

to the selection of repertoire, he should have his own academically well-founded opinion about all songs for liturgical use, if he does not want to be clueless and thus caught unawares by the fantastic wishes of particular groups, wedding parties and funeral planners. Likewise, on the occasion of outdoor Masses and processions one should keep in mind the acoustical possibilities and limitations when selecting repertoire.

Above all every priest should be aware of the widespread error that Latin sacred music belongs to the so-called "old rite", whereas the Council requires vernacular songs only. On the contrary, *musica sacra* can, like no other expression, bridge ritual variations and even interdenominational differences. The noble expressive forms of Gregorian chant and polyphony are highly esteemed in all Christian communities [in Europe], a royal road of ecumenism. Moreover, in its soul-stirring power and doctrinal depth, *musica sacra* and particularly Gregorian chant quite often in the past was what prompted artists and musicians to repent or convert. If we want to bring the Gospel again to today's world, and not just to the ecclesiastical periphery of the real artists and intellectuals, we must return to the great liturgical music!

While liturgical education as a sort of catechesis addresses the reason and the body, *musica sacra* reaches the heart and the soul too. Generally participation in the apostolate of church music has the effect of a catechetical experience for all who are directly and indirectly involved.[39] Liturgical music becomes a factor of identification and association that extends to relatives and friends. The most convincing argument for all these sacrifices is disarming beauty in the service of the holy, which can be grasped only by St. Augustine's remark, *"Cantare amantis est"* (To sing belongs to one who loves).

It should come as no surprise, therefore, that out of this societal milieu of singers of liturgical music very frequently other commitments for the message of the Church develop, including even the defense of human life.

---

[39] If the boys in a cathedral choir need to be brought to several rehearsals each week, and then on Sunday both in the morning to the Solemn Mass and also in the afternoon to Vespers, the relation between Church and family remains an issue; indeed, the family is compelled to grapple with the contents of the Faith, because vacation times, daily routines, eating habits and efforts of all sorts have to be attuned to the commitment to *musica sacra*.

Liturgical singing is almost always a missionary activity, as an expression of the Faith, of an understanding of the Faith, or even of disbelief. Therefore we should not leave the music in the liturgy to the devil. Indeed, he is all too capable of correctly assessing its priceless value for those respective purposes, as can easily be observed. If the Sacred Liturgy is the *fons et culmen vitæ et missionis ecclesiæ* (source and summit of the life and mission of the Church), it can be inferred that one cannot overestimate the importance of her *musica sacra*.

As we have seen, *musica sacra* runs through all the liturgical themes like a *basso continuo*. The complexity and expressiveness with which the harmonies and agogics of this *basso continuo* are executed, however, are left to the particular interpretation.

Appendix

FORMATION OF CLERGY AND RELIGIOUS IN SACRED MUSIC

Consociatio Internationalis Musicæ Sacræ, 2007

I. Introduction

Liturgy: An Experience of Beauty

Everyone knows that the Second Vatican Council paid particular attention to the way in which the liturgy is celebrated. In the Introduction to the *Constitution on the Sacred Liturgy* it says:

> For it is the liturgy through which, especially in the divine sacrifice of the Eucharist, "the work of our redemption is accomplished," and it is through the liturgy, especially, that the faithful are enabled to express in their lives and manifest to others the mystery of Christ and the real nature of the true Church. The Church is essentially both human and divine, visible but endowed with invisible realities, zealous in action and dedicated to contemplation, present in the world, but as a pilgrim, so constituted that in her the human is directed toward and subordinated to the divine, the visible to the invisible, action to

contemplation, and this present world to that city yet to come, the object of our quest. (n. 2)

Let us call to mind also the basic statements formulated in the first chapter of the Constitution on the Liturgy of the Second Vatican Council:

> In the earthly liturgy we take part in a foretaste of that heavenly liturgy which is celebrated in the Holy City of Jerusalem toward which we journey as pilgrims, where Christ is sitting at the right hand of God, Minister of the holies and of the true tabernacle. With all the warriors of the heavenly army we sing a hymn of glory to the Lord. . . . (n. 8)

Therefore it seems fair to conclude that the expressive scope of the liturgy, in its human and visible aspect, being by its very nature ordained to the divine, requires *the noblest expression of the realities that can be perceived by means of the senses*: in this context the word "noble" does not always have to be equated with material things that are precious and costly. When we speak about the principles that refer to what is in a certain sense the "external" form of the liturgy, perceptible to the senses, we mean something that goes further and deeper.

When we speak about the living experience of beauty in the liturgy, we are not focusing on the object-related and accidental elements. The experience of the liturgy concerns its own full accomplishment and hence in particular what can be heard: *"Fides ex auditu."* ("Faith comes from hearing.") In this regard we mean especially the sung liturgy with its specific "pneumatic" character (originating from the Holy Spirit), by which we partake in a "foretaste" of the heavenly liturgy.

Of all things, music, which begins where words leave off, allows us to advance a little further in presenting the mystery of God without speaking.

Liturgical song and accordingly liturgical *music*—bound up in truth and beauty with the persons who together celebrate the liturgy—is extolled by the Second Vatican Council in an altogether special way *above all the other arts*.

The musical tradition of the universal Church is a treasure of inestimable value, greater even than that of any other art. The main reason for this pre-eminence is that sacred singing united with the words forms a necessary and integral part of the solemn liturgy (cf. *Sacrosanctum Concilium*, 112).

Liturgical song is therefore in and of itself liturgy. We do not sing *in the liturgy*, but rather *the liturgy* is sung.

II. The Theological Foundation

We reprint part of the academic inaugural lecture given by then-Cardinal Joseph Ratzinger at the opening of the proceedings of the Eighth International Church Music Congress in Rome in 1985, organized by the CIMS on the occasion of the European Year of Music:

> Liturgical music is a result of the demands and of the dynamism of the Incarnation of the Word, for music means that even among us, the word cannot be mere speech. The principal ways in which the Incarnation continues to operate are of course the sacramental signs themselves. But they are quite misplaced if they are not immersed in a liturgy which as a whole follows this expansion of the Word into the corporeal and into the sphere of all our senses. It is this fact which justifies and indeed renders necessary images, in complete contrast to Jewish and Islamic types of worship. This is also the reason why it is necessary to appeal to those deeper levels of comprehension and response which become accessible through music. Faith becoming music is part of the process of the Word becoming flesh. But at the same time, this "becoming music" is also subordinated in a completely unique way to that inner evolution of the Incarnation event which I tried to hint at earlier: the Word become flesh comes to be, in the Cross and Resurrection, flesh become Word. Both are permeated with each other. The Incarnation is not revoked, but becomes definitive at that instant in which the movement turns around, so to speak: flesh itself becomes Word, is "logocized", but precisely this transformation brings about a new unity of all reality which was obviously so important to God that He paid for it at the price of the Son's Cross.
>
> When the Word becomes music, there is involved on the one hand perceptible illustration, incarnation or taking on flesh, attraction of pre-rational and suprarational powers, a drawing upon the hidden resonance of creation, a discovery of the song which lies at the basis of all things. And so this becoming music is itself the very turning point in the movement: it involves not only the Word becoming flesh,

but simultaneously the flesh becoming spirit. Brass and wood become
sound; what is unconscious and unsettled becomes orderly and meaningful resonance. What takes place is an embodiment or incarnation
which is spiritualisation, and a spiritualisation which is incarnation
or em-"body"-ment. Christian "incarnation" or "embodiment" is always simultaneously spiritualisation, and Christian spiritualisation is
em-"body"-ment into the body of the *Logos* become man.[1]

III. The Specific Demands of Vatican Council II

Unfortunately we must note that in many places of the Catholic Church
the state of sacred music at the present moment exhibits remarkable
inconsistencies and many difficulties. They can make equally difficult
any formational activity in the field of music. For this reason the following proposals are to be understood as a long-term objective.

The *sine qua non* condition for any formation is an in-depth knowledge of the conciliar texts concerning sacred music (*Sacrosanctum Concilium*, chapter VI). In this document we find in detail almost a catalogue
of the fundamental requirements for formation, not only of musicians
in the service of the liturgy, but indirectly also of the one responsible
for the liturgy, namely the priest. Thus the Council itself composed
the curriculum:

Article 116

Gregorian chant as part of pastoral responsibility: this does not mean
having extensive paleographical training, but rather a basic, comprehensive view of its historical, artistic and especially sociological importance
in the overall present-day situation: in the different social strata, in different cultures, in light of current aesthetics and musical styles.

Unfortunately it does not seem superfluous to emphasize the indispensable necessity and duty to be able to sing correctly all the liturgical

---

[1] Joseph Cardinal Ratzinger, Robert Skeris trans., "Liturgy and Sacred Music", in:
Christus in Ecclesia Cantat (Rome: Consociatio Internationalis Musicæ Sacræ, 1986), (pp.
74–88), p. 83.

formulas, readings, prayers, prefaces, intonations, acclamations, and so forth, that belong to the celebrant as the one repertoire of Gregorian chant. Familiarity with the Gregorian (melodic) formulas in Latin will also make it possible for the celebrant to attempt an eventual adaptation into the vernacular languages.

It is of course a requirement of good education and pastoral competence to be able to sing also all the Gregorian chants that are supposed to be sung by the faithful, for example the chants of the *Ordinarium Missæ* (Ordinary of the Mass).

Given that article 116 is also concerned with all the other musical forms suited to the liturgy, the priest needs to have at least an elementary knowledge of the *Thesaurus Musicæ Sacræ* (treasury of sacred music) of all the centuries down to modern times (art. 114). Moreover he needs to have the criteria to distinguish suitable repertoire from what is not suitable for the liturgy, liturgical sacred music from music that does not have the qualifications.

Article 118

The historical and often precious repertoire of popular sacred songs can be very different from one country to another, or even from one region to the next. Therefore in his pastoral ministry the priest needs to have a deep knowledge of the musical heritage of his flock, and must have good judgment so as to distinguish between what is good and what is less good, between songs that are deeply felt and those that are superficially tolerated, between genuine folk art and artificial imitations, and so on.

It should be noted especially in evaluating new contemporary songs that these criteria are necessary in order to make a serious judgment.

Article 119

In a culture without its own Christian tradition the priest needs to have a special preparation so as to be ethnologically competent in musical matters, in order to avoid serious dogmatic misunderstandings: a particular sort of music may be closely connected to another religion and faith according to a possible psychological identification in the non-Christian culture.

Article 120

In order to understand the clear instruction of the Council when it speaks explicitly about the pipe organ, the priest must be acquainted with the artistic value of this musical instrument, which is different from any electronic imitation. To generalize, he must learn to distinguish between the truth of an original instrument and the falsehood of an imitation that sounds like it; this is another criterion for the admission of an instrument in the liturgy. Moreover the pastor is normally the person who makes decisions about the maintenance and/or acquisition of a pipe organ. Therefore he needs basic good judgment specifically concerning the value of an historical organ, so as not to be totally dependent on the judgment of some outside consultant.

Although this is not an everyday topic of discussion, the same is true also for church bells, with the special difference that a profound symbolic significance is attributed to the church bell throughout the world of sound.

What was already said in reference to articles 118 and 119 applies to the admission of other musical instruments into the liturgy.

Article 121

Anyone interested in the creation and performance of new compositions must be aware of the circumstances, the conditions and the rights that proceed from them. Thus a basic orientation in the administrative aspects within sacred music seems to be more than advisable.

General Formation for Pastoral Needs

The Diffusion of Sound

Every space has its own acoustic. Consequently one must study and practice the proper use of the microphone. One should also be generally acquainted with the effect of ornaments and carpeting, for example, on the diffusion of sound.

A new demand: designing sound systems for open-air ceremonies, which involves the technological creation *ex novo* of a virtual acoustical space.

Sacred Music and Architecture

Not even the most sophisticated microphones are capable of resolving possible problems of an acoustical nature; on the contrary, they often aggravate them. The architecture in the first place already implies a choice of the suitable musical repertoire. Not every sort of music can be performed well in every setting.

Particularly important is the position of the source of sound in the setting, especially of the celebrant, but also of the organ and the choir.

Musical Pedagogy

Where the schools and public education do not offer elementary musical training, the pastor himself ought to have at least a basic plan, or else entrust the program to qualified members of the faithful, who can produce adequate results, especially by working with the youth and the children.

Psychology of Choirs

In order to maintain or create choirs of musical groups in the parish the one with pastoral responsibility needs in addition a certain "feeling". He must be acquainted with the particular psychology of choirs made up of amateurs, suspended in a delicate balance between a deeply-felt faith and a joyous, musical response.

These suggestions should be experienced and not just read. It takes the implementation of each one, and not just occasionally or selectively, but rather during the whole liturgical year: how else could a worshipping community understand in their entirety the architectonic details of that ideal cathedral of sound that is established by the complete liturgical arch? Only experience develops esthetic taste and deep understanding, by creating indelible liturgical memories.

3

Ars Celebrandi in the Sacred Liturgy

Bishop Peter J. Elliott

Auxiliary Bishop, Melbourne, Australia

Responding to the Synod on the Eucharist in the Apostolic Exhortation *Sacramentum Caritatis*, Pope Benedict XVI continued the Eucharistic project that characterised the last years of St. John Paul II. I believe that *Sacramentum Caritatis* may be summarized in a guiding principle: *the Eucharist as Sacrifice and Sacrament takes absolute priority over the liturgy.* This provides a timely corrective to a defective understanding of "liturgy" in the Western Christian traditions, that is, through a rather Cartesian distinction between the visible "externals" (rites, rituals, ceremonies, music, symbols, and so forth) and the inner spirit of worship.

Having reflected on the Eucharistic Mystery in the opening chapters of *Sacramentum Caritatis*, Pope Benedict developed the liturgical dimension of the Eucharist around action, hence the expression *ars celebrandi*, meaning the "art of celebrating" or, as he qualified it, "the art of proper celebration" (cf. nn. 38–42). As an auditor at the 2005 Synod, I heard bishops welcoming these words.

Under the heading of the *ars celebrandi* he presented the bishop as liturgist: "The bishop, celebrant *par excellence*", the one whose example, particularly in his cathedral, sets the tone and standard for the liturgies of a particular Church (cf. n. 39). He repeated this message in an allocution to French bishops.[1]

In *Sacramentum Caritatis* Pope Benedict called for *respect for the rites*

---

[1] Cf. Benedict XVI, Allocution to the Bishops of France, November 19, 2012.

handed to us by the Church, so "The *ars celebrandi* is the fruit of faithful adherence to the liturgical norms in all their richness . . ." (n. 38, responding to *Propositio* 25 of the Synod). That theme was already evident in his writings as cardinal. The liturgy is "given" to us, a gift of God, a gift of the Church. Moreover God gathers us for worship; we do not gather ourselves for some activity we control or even manipulate. While the liturgy is deeply influenced by human cultures it is not subject to culture.[2]

Interiority and the *Ars Celebrandi*

The *Eucharistic spirituality of the priest* was a major theme in the post-synodal Exhortation. The daily celebration of the Eucharist was strongly commended (cf. n. 80, echoing *Propositio* 38 of the Synod). Mass is to be celebrated in "a faith filled and attentive way" (cf. n. 80). Preparation and thanksgiving may need to be adapted in busy pastoral situations, but the *Liturgy of the Hours* is useful here. In the sacristy a more recollected atmosphere is essential, and to this end I would propose the official provision of vesting prayers for the ordinary form. This will help the priest to keep the Eucharist ever before him in all his liturgical actions and words.

However, on the sanctuary and at the altar, the priest celebrant needs to overcome what I described earlier as a Cartesian distinction, even a separation, between outer form and spiritual interiority. The good celebrant integrates the "externals" and his own spiritual interiority. Word, gesture, prayer come together like the union of body and soul. The Cartesian temptation should fade away. It undermines the "art of proper celebration" by suggesting that our actions do not matter as long as inner faith is present. But prayer and action are integrated in the *ars celebrandi*, which evokes two happy personal memories.

I think of a young monk celebrating the *usus antiquior*—the older form of the Roman rite—in the Abbey of Fontgombault and of concelebrating according to the reformed rites with the monks of the Abbey of Solesmes. Actions flowed into prayer. Each movement and gesture

---

[2] On inculturation, see: Joseph Cardinal Ratzinger, *The Spirit of the Liturgy* (San Francisco: Ignatius Press, 2000), pp. 143–48, 198–99.

was gracious, unhurried, but never theatrical or contrived. The *ars cele-brandi* seemed effortless, because the Eucharist maintained priority and liturgical action rested on sound foundations.

Foundations: Understanding and Knowledge

The foundation of the "art of proper celebration" is *understanding what you are doing*. We are guided by the words of the bishop to the newly-ordained priest at the *porrectio instrumentorum*: "Receive the oblation of the holy people, to be offered to God. Understand what you do, imitate what you celebrate, and conform your life to the mystery of the Lord's Cross." In this context "understanding" is a sacred gift of the Holy Spirit, resting in turn on another sacred gift, knowledge. To welcome understanding and knowledge, we all need the *sine qua non* of the *ars celebrandi*, humility—in the form of a willingness to learn.

Understanding and knowledge first come together in a priest's forma-tion in the doctrine, sacramental theology and spirituality of the Mys-tery of Faith. This formation should maintain the principle in *Sacramen-tum Caritatis*: *the Eucharist as Sacrifice and Sacrament takes absolute priority over the liturgy*. Eucharistic formation is thus cultivated by praxis in the seminary, by daily Mass and Communion and regular Eucharistic Ado-ration. But as priesthood approaches, and after ordination, knowledge comes to the fore in a practical sense.

In the perspective of the post-conciliar rites we cannot expect an *ars celebrandi* from clergy who do not know, or have never read, the *General Instruction of the Roman Missal*. Yet this is a widespread problem today. The publication of a more accurate and richer English translation of the Mass is having salutary effects in the Anglophone world. The new edition of the *Missale Romanum* of Ven. Paul VI is an opportunity to call priests to study and understand the revised *General Instruction* as a source of essential knowledge. I hope that this will also happen in other language groups as they move towards better vernacular texts.

When we come to the *usus antiquior*, I wonder how many priests are familiar with what appears at the front of the *Missale Romanum* of St. John XXIII (1962), the *Ritus servandus in celebratione Missæ* and the accompanying *De defectibus in celebratione Missæ occurentibus*?

A friend of mine was ordained during the Council so, for some years, he celebrated according to the *usus antiquior*. I once asked this devout celebrant how he learnt the classical rite. He replied that he did not go to the usual authorities on rubrics, such as Fortescue-O'Connell,[3] but directly to the *Missale Romanum* itself, to the *Ritus servandus*. His knowledge began with the primary sources and so he developed a gracious *ars celebrandi*.

Practice and Experience

From understanding and knowledge comes practice. Celebrating Mass and the Sacraments is an "art" which requires what all artists need: experience, discipline and practice, but always open to a willingness to develop and refine skills. For the *ars celebrandi* this requires respectful attention to the rubrics and related details, but also an intelligent grasp of the *whole action of the Mass*, particularly the solemn forms. This holistic approach also applies to the rites for the Sacraments and complex ceremonies such as the Holy Week rites, ordinations, and so on.

To "know what comes next" is a skill in itself, which some people find difficult. I have heard some priests say, "I never know what comes next!" But when the whole rite is prepared and studied carefully, it can be understood as unfolding in stages, a series of moments in one great action. To develop such a holistic understanding, I would hope our seminaries provide a systematic theological and historical formation in the "shape" of the liturgy, free from outdated polemics and irrelevant theories—and not easily derailed by a youthful obsession with liturgical trivia.

Here I touch on the role of the Master of Ceremonies, not only as he supports and guides the clergy, but as he puts into practice his own distinct *ars celebrandi*. He needs to bring together qualities which I would sum up as: being unobtrusive, never dominating or pushing people around, showing confidence without signs of hesitation, being calm and never panicking—even if he knows that the whole enterprise is falling apart! I speak from past experience. However, a good example of an *ars celebrandi* is given by the Papal Master of Ceremonies,

---

[3] Cf. Adrian Fortescue, J. B. O'Connell and Alcuin Reid, *The Ceremonies of the Roman Rite Described*, 15th ed. (London: Burns & Oates, 2009).

Msgr. Guido Marini. He provides a humble and efficient model that should be followed by all who seek to work in this demanding technical field.

Continuity and the *Ars Celebrandi*

If celebrating the liturgy is meant to be a well-founded art, the "art of proper celebration" should never become too specialized, that is, an elite exercise for only a few people, which is the case with so much "art" in Western societies. Therefore I prefer to understand the art of celebrating in terms of a "craft", something accessible to all of us, whether we think we are "liturgically minded" or not.

In the *centro storico* of Rome, in streets around the University of the Holy Cross, skilled artisans work every day in their little shops. When I lived nearby in the Domus Paulus VI, these artisans fascinated me. The *ars celebrandi* is very much like their creative skills. So my ideal is that *the priest should be a good liturgical craftsman, an artisan of the worship of God.*

A craft is passed on from the master to his apprentice, often from father to son. In a healthy family this maintains continuity. How wisely Pope Francis has presented the Church first and foremost as the family of God.[4] In a family environment much is passed on by example or in subtle ways similar to the transmission of Sacred Tradition in the Church. Tradition is supported by many traditions, often embodied in various customs. I think, for example, of a gracious Northern Italian way of incensing the Blessed Sacrament, similar to the reverent style customary in some monastic houses.

This is why, in my own ceremonial manuals, I use the expression "the continuity of our tradition",[5] which is obviously related to the greater "hermeneutic of continuity". But how do we describe our liturgical tradition? Roman liturgical tradition is best understood in light of the somewhat misunderstood ideal, "noble simplicity". Long before that expression was favored, great liturgists commented on the

---

[4] Cf. Allocution at the General Audience, 29 May 2013.

[5] See Peter J. Elliott, *Ceremonies of the Modern Roman Rite*, revised edition (San Francisco: Ignatius Press, 2004), Introduction, nn. 16–24, and *Ceremonies of the Liturgical Year* (San Francisco: Ignatius Press, 2002), Introduction, nn. 12–13.

sobriety, restraint and simple forms of the Roman rite. "Noble simplicity", rightly understood, characterizes the continuous ethos or style of the Roman rite across the ages and in both the rites promulgated after the Second Vatican Council and the *usus antiquior.*

Suggestions for Both Forms of the Roman Rite

Permit me to offer some practical suggestions that may demonstrate the "art of proper celebration" as this applies to both forms of the Roman Rite.

The precise rubrics of the *usus antiquior* require a discipline of the body, the hands, the eyes, levels of the voice, and these have been further refined by the rubricists. That precision is not evident in the *General Instruction* of the modern rites, although the revised edition of 2002 is clearer. But even if discipline is observed precisely, according to the rubrics of the *usus antiquior,* this does not automatically ensure an *ars celebrandi.*

Take for example the different ways a celebrant can make that gracious gesture of raising and joining his hands. For some priests it is a prayerful act, for others just a rapid disjointed movement. The same applies to the multiple signs of the cross made over the *oblata.* Low Mass can be celebrated in great haste, the Latin uttered in a rapid unintelligible way—so the *usus antiquior* can be misused.

To underline the need for a deeper interpretation of rubrics, permit me to share one of my unhappy liturgical memories. As a layman, I assisted at a Solemn Mass celebrated at the high altar of the cathedral of Seville, in October 1968, that is, a year before the *Novus Ordo Missæ* was introduced.

The priest, deacon and subdeacon acted like robots, correct in every detail but so mechanical, functional and cold. They completely ignored a team of disorderly altar boys who competed in races, running up the many altar steps, trying to get to the predella first. The altar boys were "supervised" by an elderly Master of Ceremonies, who seemed to enjoy childish chaos. There was a total disconnection between the sacred ministers and the servers, and that is instructive. Team work is essential in both forms of the Roman rite. The *ars celebrandi* is inclusive, for it is not restricted to the celebrant.

In the wider world of the modern rite of the Mass we encounter other problems, one in particular. Words become dominant. Actions, gestures, symbols are overshadowed by words and more words. Behind the altar the celebrant becomes a talking torso; his homily is long and he always chooses the short Eucharistic prayer. The Eucharist as Sacrifice and Sacrament cannot take absolute priority over such an unbalanced liturgy.

Some Problems

In the ordinary form a tendency to concentrate on words takes the form of *didacticism*, which reduces the liturgy to a method of teaching people. As cardinal, Pope Benedict criticized an emphasis on making worship "edifying". "Only when the sacrament retains its unconditional character and its absolute priority over all communal purposes and all spiritually edifying intentions does it build community and edify humans."[6]

The Mass is primarily worship. Maintaining this principle reduces the didactic tendency and helps maintain or restore the continuity of our tradition, for every liturgical abuse is a moment of rupture.[7] A *sense of worship* is at the heart of a good *ars celebrandi*. The skilled celebrant with a recollected demeanor never gives the patronizing impression that he is giving lessons to his people. He has humbly absorbed that wider guiding principle *the Eucharist as Sacrifice and Sacrament takes absolute priority over the liturgy*. He expresses something that the people sense, that he is involved in an action much greater than himself, an action which does not need his words of explanation.

However, when we come to actions at the altar and comportment on the sanctuary, some celebrants have as much style as an unskilled butcher, and let me add that butchering done well is a fine craft. These priests may have great inner faith, but who can tell this from their clumsy or casual behavior? Again we see a Cartesian disconnection between what is seen and what is unseen. In that perspective, and drawing on the need to integrate internal faith and external actions, it is

---

[6] Joseph Cardinal Ratzinger, *A New Song for the Lord* (New York: Crossroad, 1996), p. 75.

[7] See *Sacramentum Caritatis*, 3, note 6, Pope Benedict's explicit reference to the hermeneutic of continuity.

important to maintain consistent behaviour and to attend to matters of detail, as any good craftsman knows. But here I touch on a delicate nerve. There are times when a painful lack of the *ars celebrandi* calls for *prudent* fraternal correction among priests, or some *kindly* intervention by the bishop or his appropriate episcopal vicar.

However, while "style" is important, I add a word of caution for I am uncomfortable with a popular liturgical expression "presidential style". The good celebrant avoids an artificial style. He is not trying to play a role as if he were in a theatre. In this regard I turn to ancient China.

Confucius quoted another Chinese philosopher Yu, who said: "in practicing the rules of ceremonial ('li'), a certain naturalness is desirable."[8] Apparently *li* is close to our concept of "liturgy". This is interesting, coming as it does from the ancient cultures of China and Japan where ceremonial is so precise and, to Western eyes, often rather lifeless, stiff or mechanical, but that was not their ancient ideal.

Ceremonial Details

As cardinal, Pope Benedict wrote wisely about the body and liturgy with a strong doctrinal basis, the Incarnation. For him, liturgy is not some "other worldly" activity. *liturgy is always incarnational*, grounded in our concrete material world where the Logos became flesh.[9] He said: "The body has a place within the divine worship of the Word made flesh, and it is expressed liturgically in a certain discipline of the body, in gestures that have developed out of the liturgy's inner demands and that make the essence of the liturgy, as it were bodily visible."[10]

In good ceremonial the body moves with dignity, first in walking and posture, even sitting, then through gestures, movements and ritual actions such as genuflecting and bowing, making clear and reverent signs of the cross, carrying out the customary kisses of altar and book without haste, and using a thurible with skill and restraint. Above all, at the heart of the Mass, the Host and Chalice should be elevated *rev-*

---

[8] Confucius, *Analects* I, 12.

[9] Cf. *The Spirit of the Liturgy*, part 4, ch. 2, "The Body and the Liturgy".

[10] Ibid., pp. 176, 177.

erently and slowly. As the rubric of both forms require,[11] the celebrant "shows" the Body and Blood of the Lord to the people gathered by God for the divine Sacrifice.[12] Quickly waving the Host or Chalice in the air is not showing the Eucharistic Lord to His people.

By evoking a sense of mystery, of wonder and awe in the divine presence, the *ars celebrandi* is at the service of God's People. And again I return that perennial enemy of the *ars celebrandi*—haste, wanting to hurry through the rite, as if there were something more important waiting to be done. But liturgical humility before the Mystery of Faith whispers in our priestly hearts: "There is nothing more important than this. . . ."

The Voice

The *ars celebrandi* obviously calls for the competent use of the voice, particularly in vernacular celebrations of Mass and the Sacraments. Clergy need to be intelligible, clear, measured in phrases, striking a balance between moments that call for the language of symbolic drama or a more direct expression of the meaning of the Gospel and the teaching of the Church in a homily.

This leads to the place of preaching within the "art of proper celebration". The *ars celebrandi* needs to be complemented by the *ars prædicandi*. In an age of instant communication and social media the art of homiletics is in transition, which may partly explain why there is so much poor preaching. Clergy feel inadequate because they must compete with the world's skilled communicators. Bishops can develop a better *ars prædicandi* among clergy and seminarians through providing practical workshops, animated by the grace of encouragement.

Liturgical preaching expounds the Word of God, but in a particular way in a specific context. The voice of the priest or deacon in his sermon or homily is different from the levels and style of his other liturgical voices, but "how" it is different needs to be explored by practice.

---

[11] *Missale Romanum* 2002: "Hostiam consecratam ostendit populo, reponit super patenam"; *Missale Romanum* 1962: "hostiam consecratam . . . ostendit populo, reponit super corporale". A slow pace is also desirable when giving Eucharistic benediction.

[12] Through a reverent and unhurried consecration and elevations, Pope Francis provides an ideal model for all clergy.

The words of consecration said aloud in the vernacular surely call for a lowering of the voice and a slower pace, to underline the great Mystery of Faith. Combine this control of the voice with what I have already called for, gracious elevations of the Host and the Chalice, and "something" immediately happens. In the church there will be silence, the same silence evoked during the silent consecration and elevations in the *usus antiquior*. This is one central area where we perceive one of the hopes behind the 2007 Motu Proprio of Benedict XVI, *Summorum Pontificum*, that there should be an interaction between the two forms of the one rite.

Nevertheless, each form of the Roman rite has its own genius, its own integrity. So the well understood *ars celebrandi* accepts different nuances in each form. To celebrate the modern rite *versus populum* with the same style as the *usus antiquior* is regrettable. To attempt the vernacular style of communication of the post-conciliar rites when celebrating the *usus antiquior* in Latin can be rather foolish. Each form has its own "voice" and style.

Many of us can sing, if we try. Those who cannot sing well may compensate by cultivating good proclamation, which is in itself an art.

Celebrants of the modern rites should also rediscover silence, an essential component in the *ars celebrandi*. Let them never imagine that sound must always surround the assembly or otherwise the people will become bored. This is when the devil of "entertainment" takes control. Moreover, must the offertory prayers, "Blessed are you . . .", always be said aloud? In the Missal and *General Instruction* that is not the first option. Will it really delay my breakfast or dinner if I pause after Communion in silence?

We should also recover silence in our churches before and after worship.[13] When I am about to celebrate Confirmation in some parishes I think I am in a cinema, such is the noisy effect of secularization among our people in my country.

The Inclusive *Ars Celebrandi*

The priest skilled in the "art of proper celebration" encourages others —choir, organist, altar servers, readers and especially the sacristans. He

---

[13] Francis has rightly ended the practice of applauding as the Pope enters for Mass.

does not usurp or eliminate their ministries, saying, for example, "We don't need servers here", which really means "We don't follow the Roman rite here." He encourages the choir to provide peaceful and reflective song, not always leading the people, nor, on the other hand, just performing a concert.

He draws his collaborators into his own *ars celebrandi* by requiring high standards based on training to develop skills and to correct errors. He should expect dedication and never settle for less. Nevertheless he does not play the "sacristy priest", because he delegates liturgical training and formation to those he has already formed in the wider *ars celebrandi*.

A good liturgical craftsman is a pastor who nourishes his people with variety within the parameters of the missal and lectionary. Should we ignore those optional memorials? What about a votive Mass now and again? Surely the Saturday Mass of Our Lady should be chosen above other options. Can we not find days when a Requiem Mass may be pastorally welcome, never forgetting the inestimable help the Lord's Sacrifice brings to our dear departed?[14]

Learning from the East

As we seek to understand the *ars celebrandi*, another question inevitably arises: what can we learn from the Christian East? St. John Paul II spoke of the "two lungs" of the Church, East and West. This applies to our understanding and practice of worship.

Some years ago I concelebrated the Divine Liturgy at the funeral of Bishop Ivan Prasko, the retired Ukrainian Eparch in Australia. This was an opportunity to experience the Byzantine Rite in its most solemn form, but as a priest at the altar, that is, within the iconostasis.

These were my impressions. Byzantine liturgical action moves along, without any self-consciousness about "Now we're doing this" "Now we will do that". It moves in such a way as to carry clergy, servers, choir and people within it. We know we are involved in something much greater than a human action, something that goes on and will go on whether we like it or not—for we have entered the eternal worship of heaven. The Divine Liturgy also seems to flow with continuity as

---

[14] Cf. *Institutio Generalis Missalis Romani* 2002, n. 379.

one action. It is not a series of disparate or separate items, which can be a weakness in the post-conciliar form of the Roman Rite.

However there is also an *anthropological* dimension to Eastern Christian worship. At first sight, the Byzantine Rite seems to be all about the glory of God, yet at the same time there is a constant affirmation of the innate dignity of the human person. Christians at worship are all the sons and daughters of the Father, redeemed by Christ's Sacrifice, divinized by the Holy Spirit. There seems to be a natural integration between the priesthood of Christ's faithful and the priestly ministry of the ordained; all are made one in the hierarchic ordering of the eternal oblation of Christ the High Priest. Yet this is achieved without lecturing, instructing or admonishing people.

Moreover, in Eastern liturgies the community is never turned in on itself, in dialogue with itself, which is a problem in celebrating Mass *versus populum*.[15] The sense of all being turned towards the Lord is facilitated by celebrating the Eucharist *ad orientem*, which is normal in the liturgies of the Eastern Catholic Churches.[16] Nonetheless I believe that Mass celebrated *versus populum* in the ordinary form of the Roman rite can evoke this Eastern sense of the sacred, but only if the celebrant has a developed *ars celebrandi*.

However, we should not over idealize Eastern liturgy. Problems are also apparent in the demeanor of some clergy celebrating Eastern liturgies: formalism, a certain nonchalance or a matter-of-fact approach, even apparent boredom. However, this is the human factor when a strong liturgy backed by centuries of tradition carries the clergy along with its action. They can be tempted to take their liturgical ministry for granted and just "float along with the tide". That problem may also manifest itself in our *usus antiquior*, as I have already indicated.

The Effects of the Enlightenment

The Christian East invites us to rediscover a pre-Enlightenment approach to Christian worship, because, in historical terms, that is pre-

---

[15] On self-centric worship see: Joseph Cardinal Ratzinger, *Feast of Faith* (San Francisco: Ignatius Press, 1990), pp. 142–43 and: *A New Song for the Lord*, loc. cit.

[16] Why have Maronite Catholics and certain other Eastern Churches succumbed to post-conciliar "Romanization" and abandoned their classical tradition of celebrating "ad orientem"?

cisely what it offers. In a post-Enlightenment world, in a post-modern society, the attraction of Eastern Christianity is the way it bypasses rationalism or intellectualism and opens "doors to the sacred". But that also raises the current question of why we have to promote the *ars celebrandi*, why we need to correct a desacralized style of worship that has become dominant in not a few places since the Second Vatican Council. The Council Fathers who issued *Sacrosanctum Concilium* did not envisage a secularized or banal liturgy and it is not supported by the text of the *General Instruction of the Roman Missal*.

This is my interpretation of the causes of problems with the rites promulgated after the Council today, at least in the area of the *ars celebrandi*. Those who drafted the first edition of the *General Instruction of the Roman Missal* seemed to work with two naïvely idealistic misconceptions.

First they assumed that the old ceremonial skills and customs would naturally pass on from older to younger clergy, so there was no need to spell them out precisely in rubrics or directives. This naïveté ran parallel to the collapse of catechesis and the systematic religious education of children and young people. That disaster rested, not only on a false theology of Revelation, but on the assumption that the basics of doctrine would pass on naturally from generation to generation, and we know that this did not happen.

Secondly, in the idealistic spirit of zeal for the reform, those who drafted the *General Instruction* imagined that all priests are eager liturgists, able to bring understanding and knowledge to worship. One can understand such idealism in the mood of the post-conciliar Church, but it implies that over-optimistic interpretation of the capacities of the human person that flowed from the Enlightenment.

Loss of basic skills, such as using the thurible properly, explains why the *General Instruction* had to be revised and redrafted, why some of us have had to write ceremonial manuals and, now, why the Congregation for Divine Worship and the Discipline of the Sacraments is preparing a guide for the *ars celebrandi*.

Those who framed the rubrics of the *usus antiquior* in the sixteenth century were much more realistic about clergy. In the atmosphere of Tridentine reform, they did not expect priests to be skilled or eager liturgists. They provided precise and binding rubrics to control abuses and rein in the widespread problem of the poor celebration of Mass and the Sacraments. The priest in the village, the chaplain at court, the monk in the abbey, the friar in the city, they all knew exactly what was expected of them: *"Read the black and do the red"*. The rubrics carried these priests in their weakness and, at the same time, invited them to welcome the grace of God through the prayerful and reverent celebration of the Mass.

Out of the Enlightenment also emerged what I would call modernist problems undermining the *ars celebrandi*. I have already outlined didacticism, the liturgy reduced to teaching or edification. But that led to the liturgy being used to improve people, to free them from the superstition and ignorance of the past. The ill-fated Synod of Pistoia expressed the contempt of Enlightenment intellectuals for simple folk and their "old fashioned" popular piety. That snobbish mentality has returned in our post-conciliar era. To counteract it, the priest craftsman with an *ars celebrandi* needs to have a pastoral heart, humbly open to the popular piety and devotions of his people, tolerant of aspects he personally may find distasteful. He maintains the priority of the Eucharist and liturgical celebrations, but he never restricts his community to these acts of worship.

Theatricality was another modernist tendency, first evident in the liturgical decadence of the eighteenth and nineteenth centuries when sung Mass became the vehicle for a concert. This decadence returned after the Council, but in a twentieth-century form focused around the individual. Some celebrants imagined that they were entertainers, imitating a television personality with off-the-cuff comments and jokes, even amidst the prayers of the Mass. I have no problems with some humor in the homily, for pastoral warmth is useful there, but the priest skilled in the "art of proper celebration" knows where to draw lines and he keeps within those limits. Moreover, there is no such thing as a "spontaneous liturgy", as any priest working hard to achieve an *ars celebrandi* knows well.

Beauty

It is significant that Pope Benedict introduced the chapter in *Sacramentum Caritatis* that includes the *ars celebrandi* with a theme envisaged in *Sacrosanctum Concilium* chapter VII, *the beauty of the liturgy*. In divine worship we see the glory that the apostles beheld in Jesus Christ. "Beauty, then is not mere decoration, but rather an essential element of the liturgical action, since it is an attribute of God himself and his revelation" (*Sacramentum Caritatis*, 35).

Art is meant to be at the service of worship, summed up in a small sentence: "Everything related to the Eucharist should be marked by beauty" (n. 41). He also offered some guidance on that dimension dear to his heart, good sacred music, especially song (cf. n. 42).

The Liturgical Setting

In the perspective of beauty a noble liturgical setting sustains the *ars celebrandi*. In shaping the environment for worship, good art and architecture serve the liturgy (cf. n. 41, responding to *Propositio* 27 of the Synod). The celebrant consciously dedicated to "the art of proper celebration" knows that he cannot isolate himself from sacred space. Mass can be celebrated well in an ugly church, but the church remains ugly, and the people deserve a better place for their Eucharist.

Catholic worship calls for a spacious and beautiful sanctuary, not cluttered up with useless furnishings, irrelevant decorations or banners or, worse still, posters adorned with distracting slogans. In this sacred space the feasts and seasons of the liturgical year should be visible every day through variations of color and design in the lectern fall, the altar antependium, the veil on the tabernacle (and it should be veiled). In some churches it could be Good Friday all the year round, so bare is the sacred space. In other churches the good ladies raise mountains of flowers, even during Lent. It is not only a question of rules here, but of the wisdom they contain. Liturgical time and color support a good *ars celebrandi*. They contribute to a deepening, even a recovery, of a *sense of the sacred*, or what is called "resacralization".

The altar is the focus of the liturgy. I would invite every priest to take a long look at the altar in his church. This is not just a matter of technical conformity to rules requiring a solid altar that is accessible on all sides,[17] but of going back to the vision of divine beauty that informs the *ars celebrandi*. Is this altar beautiful? Does it speak to us of God, his sacrifice and banquet? Is it made of noble materials, dressed with dignity, adorned with fine candlesticks? Might we also follow the

---

[17] Cf. *Institutio Generalis Missalis Romani*, nn. 298–301.

word and example of Pope Benedict and place a crucifix, of suitable proportions, at its centre?[18] During Mass *versus populum*, Jesus Christ is meant to be central, not the celebrant, certainly not his personality. People do not come to Mass to see the priest, bishop or Pope. Christ calls the celebrant to be humble, for as he acts *in persona Christi* so he serves and leads, and as he prays so his people pray.

The Eucharistic vessels also call for the critical eye of the liturgical craftsman. Are they truly noble, fashioned by other craftspeople? Or are they mass-produced, even secular? This is not only a question of following clearer rules about metal vessels,[19] rather it is a question of whether *hæc præclarum calicem* evokes a sense of the sacred, speaking to us of its sacred finality, for God and for His People. Money may need to be spent, but many old vessels can be restored without much cost and most parishes have someone wanting to offer something beautiful for God. And if there are too many chalices in a sacristy surely they can be given to poor parishes.

The vestments in his sacristy cupboard reveal how seriously a priest takes his liturgical craft. As they travel from parish to parish, bishops come across all sorts of vestments, even in various stages of dirt and decay. While cleanliness and neatness are essential, can we not go a step further and seek beautiful vestments? In their noble simplicity let them speak of the sacred action that passes through a priest's hands, for that is symbolized in what clothes his body, what modifies or even conceals his personality, what reduces his ego. The vestments call us to an *ars celebrandi* that should always be marked by humility.

The Pastoral Ideal

The *ars celebrandi* extends to all who offer worship in the liturgy, as Pope Benedict said in *Sacramentum Caritatis*:

> In the course of the Synod, there was frequent insistence on the need to avoid any antithesis between the *ars celebrandi*, the art of proper celebration, and the full, active and fruitful participation of all the faithful. The primary way to foster the participation of the People of

---

[18] Cf. Ratzinger, *Feast of Faith*, pp. 143–45; *The Spirit of the Liturgy*, pp. 82–84.
[19] Cf. *Institutio Generalis Missalis Romani*, nn. 328–30.

God in the sacred rite is the proper celebration of the rite itself. The *ars celebrandi* is the best way to ensure their *actuosa participatio*. (n. 38)

In this paper I have emphasized the celebrant and those who assist him, but the pastoral, indeed evangelizing, effects of a developed "art of proper celebration" animate the faithful for their mission in this world. Have people been inspired to deeper commitment to Christ Jesus by assisting at the Mass of a devout priest? Have people been converted to the Catholic Faith through experiencing a liturgy celebrated well? I return to the words of Pope Benedict: ". . . indeed, for two thousand years this way of celebrating has sustained the faith life of all believers, called to take part in the celebration as the People of God, a royal priesthood, a holy nation (cf. 1 Pet 2, 4–5, 9)" (*Sacramentum Caritatis*, 38).

Conclusion

Speaking to priests at the Mass of the Chrism on Holy Thursday 2013, Pope Francis reflected on the meaning of the chasuble. He related the vestment of the Catholic priest to the vestments of the High Priest in tabernacle and temple and the ministerial anointing of Aaron. He said:

> The priest celebrates by carrying on his shoulders the people entrusted to his care and bearing their names written in his heart. When we put on our simple chasuble, it might well make us feel, upon our shoulders and in our hearts, the burdens and the faces of our faithful people, our saints and martyrs of whom there are many in these times. From the beauty of all these liturgical things, which is not so much about trappings and fine fabrics than about the glory of our God resplendent in his people, alive and strengthened, we turn to a consideration of activity, action. (*Homily, Mass of the Chrism*, 2013)

The Holy Father's words integrate priestly ministry, pastoral spirituality and the mission of the Church with the proper celebration of the liturgy, that is, when *the Eucharist as Sacrifice and Sacrament takes absolute priority over the liturgy*. In celebrating the divine mysteries well, any priest who is committed to the *ars celebrandi* is called to be a loving pastor. He gives glory to God as he seeks to nourish Christ's faithful day by day.

4

The Early Christian Altar—Lessons for Today

STEFAN HEID

1. Periodic Transformations of the Worship Space[1]

In every age there have been transformations of worship spaces. In this development the space surrounding the altar has proved to be the most precarious zone. In the Middle Ages, when the liturgical arrangement of St. Peter's was imitated outside of Rome also, sanctuaries were destroyed everywhere so as to install a crypt.[2] The construction of gothic choirs in the Middle Ages and the new architecture of the Baroque period resulted in thoroughgoing changes. Even the present era has

---

Translated from the German original by Michael J. Miller.

Abbreviations: CCL = *Corpus Christianorum Series Latina*; CSEL = *Corpus Scriptorum Ecclesiasticorum Latinorum*; FC = *Fontes Christiani*; GCS = *Die griechischen christlichen Schriftsteller*; PG = *Patrologia Græca*; PL = *Patrologia Latina*.

[1] Basic literature: E. Reisch, "Altar", in: *Paulys Real-Encyclopädie der classischen Altertumswissenschaft*, vol. 1, J. B. Metzlersche Verlagsbuchhandlung, Stuttgart 1894, pp. 1640–91; *"Altaria"*, in: *Thesaurus Linguæ Latinæ*, vol. 1 (Leipzig: Teubner, 1900), pp. 1725–29; J. Braun, *Der christliche Altar in seiner geschichtlichen Entwicklung*, vol. 1, (Munich: Alte Meister Guenther Koch & Co.); B. Kruse, "Mensa", in: *Paulys Real-Encyclopädie der classischen Altertumswissenschaft*, vol. 15, (Stuttgart: J. B. Metzlersche Verlagsbuchhandlung, 1932), pp. 937–48; J. P. Kirsch and Th. Klauser, "Altar", in: *Reallexikon für Antike und Christentum*, vol. 1, (Stuttgart: Hiersemann, 1950), pp. 310–54; K. Wessel, "Altar", in: *Reallexikon zur Byzantinischen Kunst*, vol. 1 (Stuttgart: Hiersemann, 1966), pp. 111–20; "Altarbekleidung", in: *Reallexikon zur Byzantinischen Kunst*, vol. 1 (1966), pp. 120–24; *"Mensa"*, in: *Thesaurus Linguæ Latinæ*, vol. 8 (Leipzig: Teubner, 1966), pp. 738–45; *"trápeza"*, in: G. W. H. Lampe, *A Patristic Greek Lexicon* (Oxford University Press, 1976), pp. 1399–1400; *Thesaurus cultus et rituum antiquorum*, vol. 4 (Los Angeles: The J. Paul Getty Museum, 2005).

[2] A. Klein, *Funktion und Nutzung der Krypta im Mittelalter: Heiligsprechung und Heiligenverehrung am Beispiel Italien* (Wiesbaden: Reichert, 2011).

not been spared. Since the Second Vatican Council thousands of new altars have been set up, and in the process venerable old altars were not infrequently destroyed,[3] displaced or mutilated.[4]

All told, such epoch-making changes have left their mark on church art and culture, for better or for worse. In the process tempers have flared and much ink has been spilled. At each point, the current theology and contemporary taste imposed changes by force, which then continued for a time until they were rejected or further developed by later generations.[5] If you take up Joseph Braun's monumental study, *Der christliche Altar*, you will understand what an immense variety of forms altars have assumed over the course of Church history.

So there is no reason to think that the post-conciliar changes are now over or that they are the final, definitive word on the subject of altars. Much will of course remain as it is, following the law of inertia, but much will disappear again too, including both beautiful and shabby artistic creations. At best, excesses will be removed and mistakes corrected.

2. The Problem of the *Norma Patrum*

One particularly influential formula of the Second Vatican Council was the expression *norma patrum* (*Sacrosanctum Concilium*, 50), that is, the standard of the Church Fathers, which was supposed to guide the reform of the *Ordo Missæ*. Subsequently not only the liturgy but also the worship space and the sanctuary were transformed. Overall we can observe a megatrend toward the early Christian ideal, which started with the liturgical movement in the late nineteenth century and through the Council acquired a universal dimension.

The attempt to push back from one's own era to the liturgy of the Early Church is nothing new. As early as the eighth century, Charlemagne petitioned Pope Adrian for a "pure" Sacramentary that would

---

[3] One sad example is the church of the *Campo Santo Teutonico*, Vatican City, whose historic Baroque altar was destroyed in the 1970s.

[4] One example of an outright mutilation of altars is the Cathedral of Pesaro, in which the *mensæ* of all the side altars were sawn off or the steps were removed.

[5] A discussion, which is also quite critical, of the altar after the Second Vatican Council can be found in: F. Debuyst *et al.*, *L'altare: Mistero di presenza, opera dell'arte* (Bose: Edizioni Qiqajon, 2005).

contain the original Roman and thus the apostolic liturgy. The Council of Trent inaugurated its reform of the Mass under the motto of the *norma patrum*.[6] Of course the reception of the Church Fathers was limited at the time to a few established authors.[7] The scholarly study of historical monuments did not yet exist, so that the Baroque era lacked reliable knowledge about early Christian church structures and their liturgical appointments. Even though the churches of Rome were considered ancient and venerable, that was a far cry from preserving an early Christian worship space for its own sake.[8] Instead a Baroque "permanent" [hairstyle] was given to these churches too, which covered over the early Christian impression and the medieval arrangement. Then came the new Baroque constructions, which were entirely freed from the traditional basilica style.

No doubt the Baroque period brought about one of the most thoroughgoing and brilliant transformations of the worship space. But the *norma patrum* played no supporting role in it; the more important elements were catechesis, the cult of the saints and sacramental piety. Meanwhile and most importantly, what remained constant was the traditional liturgy, which was essentially left untouched. The Baroque church served as a cosmic-Catholic stage for the divine mysteries. Theologians liked to speak, with Augustine, about the "sacrament of the altar". The enormous buildings and the impressive number of altars were supposed to set the infinite value of every Sacrifice of the Mass before the eyes of the faithful.

With the same slogan of the *norma patrum*, the Second Vatican Council had much greater repercussions, as we will show. Of course the theological disciplines of exegesis, Church history and patristics had been established meanwhile. Increasingly the hitherto uniform image of the Early Church began to dissolve and to fall apart into various ecclesiastical provinces. Most importantly, research now contrasted classical

---

[6] Pius V, Apostolic Constitution *Quo Primum* (14 July 1570): *"ad pristinam Missale ipsum sanctorum Patrum normam ac ritum restituerunt"* ("restored the Missal itself and the rite according to the original standard of the holy Fathers").

[7] Ibid. *"necnon veterum consultis ac probatorum auctorum scriptis"* ("and having consulted the writings of the ancient, approved authors"). A study of the Council of Trent's reception of the Church Fathers is currently being written by Mathias Mütel.

[8] Of course many Baroque measures can be understood as restorative interventions or else as an aesthetic upgrading of early Christian and medieval churches.

patristics with the pre-Constantinian Church and even early Christianity. In this ambivalence lay a danger for the conciliar reception of the *norma patrum* from the outset: Which Christianity corresponded to the *norma patrum*? Was it the classical patristics of the fourth and fifth centuries or should early Christianity be taken as the standard?

3. The Influence of Christian Archaeology

Besides patrology, the nineteenth and twentieth centuries saw advances in Christian archaeology, which provided, so to speak, the material side of the *norma patrum*. For the first time, through expeditions and excavations, scholars had a firsthand impression of what an early Christian church actually looked like.[9] Italian conservation of historical monuments adopted the new findings. Already in the early twentieth century early Christian basilicas were being restored by the removal of Baroque encrustations, for example San Vitale in Ravenna (since 1898) and Santa Sabina in Rome (1914–1919). Ultimately the result was artificial worship spaces robbed of their historical texture. Nevertheless these prominent monuments became model churches of a modern trend, which demoted the Middle Ages and the Baroque era to the status of old-fashioned liturgical epochs.

Christian archaeology also had an influence on the liturgy. It inspired those liturgists who before and after the Council drafted a new liturgy in the spirit of the Early Church. The central figure of this group, Annibale Bugnini, had studied from 1942 to 1945 at the Pontifical Institute for Christian Archaeology. The new liturgy was supposed to take its bearings from the churches of the early period in their "noble simplicity" (*Sacrosanctum Concilium*, 34):[10] at the same time they were supposed to follow the example of the Augustinian-African liturgy, which

---

[9] The Pontifical Institute for Christian Archaeology, founded in 1925, immediately began under its founding director Johann Peter Kirsch to research the Roman titular churches systematically, with regard to both their architecture and their interior liturgical appointments. Kirsch was familiar with the article "Altar" of the *Reallexikon für Antike und Christentum*, which was planned by Theodor Klauser even before World War II (see note 1 above).

[10] Cf. A. Da Rocha Carneiro, "Realizzazioni di altari in Francia e in Belgio", in: F. Debuyst *et al.*, *L'altare* (Bose: Edizioni Qiqajon, 2005), (pp. 99–111), pp. 102–4.

had as little to do with the Roman Tridentine Rite as Baroque church architecture did with the restored churches of Rome and Ravenna.

The altar was directly affected by all these efforts. The greatest influence in this development was exercised by a priest from Augsburg, Franz Wieland (1872–1957), who between 1906 and 1912 published three studies about altars.[11] Wieland, who had studied Christian archaeological evidence in Rome, vehemently defended the opinion that originally there was no Eucharistic Sacrifice and no Christian altar. When first- and second-century writings spoke about sacrifice and altar, these were to be understood spiritually. According to this theory, only during the third century did the development of sacral and priestly elements in divine worship set fundamentally new coordinates. Although Wieland's books were placed on the *Index of Forbidden Books*, they became widely accepted right down the line. They found their most influential disciple in another German priest Theodor Klauser (1894–1984).[12]

4. The Thesis of the Eucharistic Meal Table

The Wieland-Klauser thesis of the Eucharistic meal table starts with the assertion that the Christian altar is derived from the table at the Last Supper. Today this view is shared unanimously by all who speak about the origin of the Christian altar.[13] According to this opinion, the first generations of Christians had held the community meal [*agape*] and the Eucharist on the same table. Later, when the Eucharist was separated from the community meal, the table form was deliberately retained in memory of the Last Supper. Hence in the first two centuries there were only arbitrary dining tables (made of wood) for the Eucharist. To this day, therefore, scholars derive the early Christian altar from the dining

---

[11] F. Wieland, *Mensa* und *Confessio* I (Munich: Lentner, 1906); *idem*, "Die Schrift *Mensa* und *Confessio* und P. Emil Dorsch S.J.: Eine Antwort", (Munich: Lentner, 1908); *idem, Altar und Altargrab der christlichen Kirchen im 4. Jahrhundert* (Leipzig: J. C. Hinrichs, 1912). About Wieland personally, see Stefan Heid and M. Dennert, eds., *Personenlexikon zur Christlichen Archäologie*, vol. 2 (Regensburg: Schnell & Steiner, 2012), p. 1321.

[12] Concerning him personally, see *ibid.*, pp. 738–40.

[13] E. Mazza, "Tavola e altare: Due modi non alternativi per designare un oggetto liturgico", in: F. Debuyst *et al.*, *L'altare* (Bose: Edizioni Qiqajon, 2005), (pp. 55–79), p. 57.

table of antiquity.[14] Not until the beginning of church construction in the late third century were permanent tables set up, and only then did these acquire the sacral significance of real altars.[15]

Around the year 100, of course, the ecclesiastical authors already speak alternatively about the "table" (*mensa, trápeza*) and the "altar" (*altare, thysiastérion*). It was claimed now that the first mentions of an "altar", for instance in the Letter to the Hebrews and in the writings of Ignatius of Antioch, were to be understood metaphorically. Moreover, as compared to "table", "altar" was supposedly a later linguistic usage. To shore up this thesis, it was said that the first Christian gatherings had taken place in normal family homes, where there were no rooms reserved for worship, and people occasionally used an arbitrary dining table as an altar.[16] Another thesis claimed that in the house churches the dining room (*triclinium*) was used for the Eucharist; couches were set up in a semicircle around a sigma-shaped table. From this arrangement, supposedly, was later derived the apse of the basilicas with benches for the priests running along the back wall.[17]

The only textual support for this was a fabulous third-century document from East Syria. In it, a bench is prepared as a table on one occasion, and another time the table of a *triclinium* is used in celebrating the Eucharist.[18] Furthermore Christian archaeology seemed to help the

---

[14] Kirsch and Klauser, "Altar", pp. 334–35; Wessel, "Altar", pp. 111–12; N. Duval, "Church Buildings", in: A. di Berardino and W. H. C. Frend, eds., *Encyclopedia of the Early Church*, vol. 1 (Oxford University Press, 1992), (pp. 168–75), p. 171: "It is quite clear that the Christian altar is directly derived from the Roman dining-table (*mensa*)." Similarly R. Riesner, "What does archaeology teach us about early house churches?", in: *Tidsskrift for Teologi og Kirke* 78 (2007): (pp. 159–85), p. 169; F. W. Deichmann, "Vom Tempel zur Kirche", in: *Mullus* (Münster: Aschendorff, 1964), (pp. 52–59), p. 56; J. A. Iñiguez, *El altar cristiano* 1 (Pamplona: Ediciones Universidad de Navarra, 1978), p. 17; N. Duval, "L'autel paléochrétien: Les progrès depuis le livre de Braun (1924) et les questions à résoudre", in: *Hortus Artium Medievalium* 11 (2005): (pp. 7–17), pp. 11–13.

[15] V. Saxer, *"Altare"* in: *Augustinus-Lexikon*, vol. 1 (1994), (pp. 241–45), pp. 241–42.

[16] Kirsch and Klauser, "Altar", pp. 334–35.

[17] K. Gamber, *Domus Ecclesiæ* (Regensburg: Friedrich Pustet, 1968), pp. 33–62, pp. 86–94. Cf. Riesner, "What does archaeology teach us about early house churches?", p. 169.

[18] *Acta Thomæ* 49, pp. 131–33 (*Acta Apostolorum Apocrypha* 2, 2, 165. 238–40). The bench was covered with a cloth. Thus the cloth seems to safeguard the sacredness; cf. Wessel, "Altarbekleidung", pp. 123–24. Mazza too, in "Tavola e altare", relies on this peculiar passage to uphold his claim about movable profane dining tables.

thesis. For in the search for the earliest representations of the Eucharist, it was claimed that it was celebrated in the first centuries as at the Last Supper (Mt 26:20), as a meal eaten while reclining, and was depicted as such in the catacombs,[19] for example the fresco in the *Capella Græca* of the Catacombs of St. Priscilla from the third century. The low meal table (round or semicircular), around which the meal companions lay on couches, was viewed as the Eucharistic table.[20]

Such theses are popular to this day.[21] However they are neither demonstrable nor probable, because scholars have learned meanwhile that the sepulchral depictions of meals eaten while reclining are meals for the deceased.[22] Moreover the early Christian depictions of the Last Supper as a reclining-meal (on mosaics in Ravenna or on ivories) show historical scenes without any liturgical-eucharistic connotation. Therefore we can find no Eucharistic tables either.[23] Moreover to date no

---

[19] J. Wilpert, *Fractio Panis* (Freiburg im Breisgau: Herder, 1895), p. 81.

[20] J. Braun "Die Entwicklung des christlichen Altars bis zum Beginn des Mittelalters", in: *Stimmen der Zeit* 110 (1926): (pp. 161–72), pp. 164, 167; V. Saxer, "Mensa", in: A. de Berardino and W. H. C. Frend, eds., *Encyclopedia of the Early Church*, vol. 1 (Oxford University Press, 1992), p. 554.

[21] R. Messner, "La direzione della preghiera, l'altare e il centro eccentrico dell'assemblea", in: Debuyst, *L'altare*, p. 208 (original German text, "Gebetsrichtung, Altar und die exzentrische Mitte der Gemeinde", in: A. Gerhards *et al.*, eds., *Communio-Räume* [Regensburg: Schnell & Steiner, 2003], pp. 27–36). "Tale concezione poggia sull'errata ipotesi di una continuità che andrebbe dalle tavole cultuali del cristianesimo primitivo (raffigurate come simposi ellenistici, in cui i commensali giacevano intorno a basse tavole), alla figura a noi famigliare, della messa in cui chi presiede sta a un unico altare, dove né si mangia né si beve." ["This concept is based on the erroneous hypothesis of a continuous development from the cultic tables of primitive Christianity (depicted as Hellenistic symposia, in which the table companions reclined around low tables), to the picture familiar to us, of the Mass in which the presider stands at a single altar, where the others neither eat nor drink."]

[22] Kirsch and Klauser, "Altar", p. 335; J. Engemann, "Der Ehrenplatz beim antiken Sigmamahl", in: *Jenseitsvorstellungen in Antike und Christentum* (Münster: Aschendorff, 1982), (pp. 239–50), p. 248; R. M. Jensen, "Dining with the Dead: From the Mensa to the Altar in Christian Late Antiquity", in: L. Brink and D. Green, eds., *Commemorating the Dead* (Berlin and New York: De Gruyter, 2008), (pp. 107–43), pp. 123–24; N. Zimmermann, "Zur Deutung spätantiker Mahlszenen: Totenmahl im Bild", in: G. Danek and I. Hellerschmid, eds., *Rituale, identitätsstiftende Handlungskomplexe* (Vienna: Verlag der Österreichischen Akademie der Wissenschaften, 2012), pp. 171–86.

[23] Nor is the table in the Catacombs of St. Callistus (sacrament chapel), at which two people stand, by any means proved to have been an altar; contrary to Mazza, "Tavola e altare", p. 59.

house church has ever been found in which the *triclinium* was used as the place for the Eucharist.[24]

The real weakness of the Wieland-Klauser thesis lies in the fact that it uncritically assumes that the Eucharistic "table" was a dining table on account of the Last Supper. It is well known that in antiquity a meal table, at meals that were eaten reclining, was a round or semi-circular low table.[25] But obviously there were no low altars, and high altars with a semicircular *mensa* are the exception and extremely rare. The almost exclusive form of an altar is instead a high "table" with a rectangular top.

Archaeologically, since the fourth century essentially three equally privileged types of altars have been authenticated: table altars, *stipes* altars (with a tabletop resting on a stand) and chest-shaped altars.[26] Not one of these types is reminiscent of an ancient meal table. Nevertheless the Church Fathers from the earliest times speak alternatively about the "table" or the "altar". They therefore do not associate the Eucharistic "table" with a meal table at all, but rather with an altar. "Table" and "altar" do not mean different things for them, but rather are names for one and the same object,[27] even though "altar" can be ascribed more to the sacrifice and "table" more to the meal.[28] "Table" was simply a synonym for the Christian altar. In this connection it may also have been a block of stone.[29] The oldest preserved altar, from the period around 300, which was recently discovered in Megiddo near Jerusalem, was made up of such blocks[30] and is nevertheless referred to as a "table" in the inscription found on it.[31]

---

[24] L. Bouyer, *Liturgy and Architecture* (South Bend, Ind.: University of Notre Dame Press, 1967), p. 41.

[25] Kruse, "Mensa", p. 941.

[26] Kirsch and Klauser, "Altar", pp. 337–41.

[27] Braun, *Der christliche Altar*, vol. 1, p. 26.

[28] For example Peter Chrysologus, *Sermo* 67, 7 (CCL 24A:404–5); 95, 3 (587).

[29] Gregory of Nyssa, *In diem luminum* (PG 46:581C).

[30] This sort of construction does not indicate the foundation of a pillar but rather an altar; cf. Reisch, "Altar", p. 1672. Contrary to Riesner, "What does archaeology teach us about early house churches?", pp. 168–69.

[31] Y. Tepper and L. di Segni, *A Christian Prayer Hall of the Third Century CE at Kefar 'Othnay (Legio): Excavations at the Megiddo Prison 2005*, Israel Antiquities Authority, Jerusalem, 2006. See Ezekiel 40:42.

5. The Early Christian Sacral Table

Doubts as to whether by Eucharistic "table" the ecclesiastical writers meant an ordinary meal table arise also when we look at the origin of the celebration of the Eucharist itself. For Christians by no means celebrated the Eucharist as a constantly repeated Last Supper, but rather as a cultic act instituted by Christ within a supper. At first this cultic act was performed during a meal eaten to satisfy hunger, but later it was separated from it. Therefore they probably used special tables for the Eucharistic rite of bread and wine.

The possibility that the Eucharistic "table" was such a sacral table[32] has hardly even been considered seriously by scholars.[33] Philo of Alexandria reports that during the cultic meals of the Therapeutæ a cultic table was brought in during a meal eaten to satisfy hunger. Some of them carried the "most clean table" (Lev 24:6, Douay-Rheims) into the meeting room for the "most holy food", namely leavened bread with salt, in memory of the "holy table" in the porch (or vestibule: *prónaos*) of the Temple in Jerusalem.[34] Remarkable here is the practice of bringing in a table in imitation of the showbread table, for the latter was a sacral table (cf. Heb 9:2).

It is very plausible that the first Christians in their community meals used a special cultic table for the Eucharistic ceremony. Surely the Christian altar cannot be derived, in either its form or its function, from the altar of holocaust or the altar of sacrifice. There is a general scholarly consensus about this. Early Christian iconography can be adduced as evidence of this also. The altars of sacrifice depicted in it in no way resemble the later established forms of the Christian altar.

---

[32] A student of Klauser, Otto Nussbaum thoroughly discusses sacral tables in: "Zum Problem der runden und sigmaförmigen Altarplatten", in: *Jahrbuch für Antike und Christentum* 4 (1961): p. 20 (pp. 18–43), but then becomes completely fixated on meal tables. At the end (p. 36) he returns to the sacrificial table, without drawing the appropriate conclusions from it. Similarly Braun, *Der christliche Altar*, vol. 1, p. 23.

[33] H. G. Thümmel, "Versammlungsraum, Kirche, Tempel", in: B. Ego *et al.*, eds., *Gemeinde ohne Tempel* (Tübingen: Mohr Siebeck, 1999), (pp. 489–504), pp. 490–91, tries to derive the altar not from sacral tables but rather from *Prunktischen* [grandiose tables displaying wealth]. But the latter could also have served as sacral tables.

[34] Philo, *De Vita contemplativa*, 73, 81. However see also *De Congressu eruditionis gratia*, 168: golden table in the holy of holies.

This does not mean, however, that the Christian altar has nothing to do with sacrificial worship in late Antiquity. The fact that the "table of the Lord" (1 Cor 10:21) means for Paul a table of sacrifice is clear from the context.[35] For he is speaking about the altar and the sacrifice of the Jews and also about the table and the sacrifice of the pagans (1 Cor 10:18–21). By analogy with them there is the "table of the Lord", which is reserved for the sacral act of the Eucharist. In this passage Paul is by no means playing off the sacrifice of the others against the meal of the Christians, because the Israelites and the pagans have sacrificial meals too, inasmuch they eat of the sacrifices that they offer. Sacrifice and meal form one complex cultic act among the Israelites, pagans and Christians.

Of the utmost importance in this connection is the fact that in the ancient sacrificial meal the food was not sacrificed and eaten at one and the same table. The sacrificial food was not eaten *at* the altar, but rather *from* the altar.[36] The same can be said of the sacral table. That is why Paul speaks about "partaking" of the "table of demons" or else of the "table of the Lord" (1 Cor 10:21; cf. Heb 13:10). Whereas in the Corinthian meal eaten to satisfy hunger everyone consumed his own food and in doing so obviously ate from his own table (1 Cor 11:21), at the "Lord's supper" (1 Cor 11:20) there was only one "table of the Lord" on which stood the one "cup of the Lord" (1 Cor 10:21; 11:27).[37]

The expression "table of the Lord" already allows us to conclude that there was a sacral table reserved for the Lord.[38] This sacral table was not a symposium table, not a meal table in the usual sense, since one did not eat at this table. Therefore Enrico Mazza is wrong in concluding from the fact that Paul speaks about the "Lord's supper" and about

---

[35] Mazza "Tavola e altare", pp. 57–58. Cf. Ambrosiaster, *Commentary on 1 Cor 10:21* (CSEL 81, 2, 115): *mensæ domini id est altario Domini* ["to the master's table, *i.e.* to the Lord's altar"].

[36] See above, note 21.

[37] A hypothetical and not very helpful discussion of the table question is K. Vössing, "Das 'Herrenmahl' und 1 Cor 11 im Kontext antiker Gemeinschaftsmähler", in: *Jahrbuch für Antike und Christentum* 54 (2011): pp. 41–72.

[38] On the exclusive character of altars see Reisch, "Altar", p. 1642.

spiritual food, that this was a profane meal table.[39] The sacral table is precisely what explains why the Eucharistic furniture was designated as "table" and "altar" from the beginning, because the ancient sacral table had already been called both "table" and "altar".[40]

Ancient sacral tables (*hierá trápeza, mensa sacra*) were not derived from community meals and dining tables, but rather were part of sacrificial worship. One stood at such tables, just as one approached the altar standing (Heb 10:11); only rarely did one sit at the altar or at the sacral table. Sacral tables were as a rule four-legged tables with a rectangular top; they were lighter and more movable than altars.[41] They were used to set down the sacrificial gifts or the instruments of sacrifice and stood beside altars,[42] in temples and in front of images of the gods. They were just as sacral, taboo and exclusive (in their use) as altars. Whether they were movable, large or small, wooden or stone, was a secondary matter.[43] In their religious context, the altar and the sacral table were so closely related that the terms were interchangeable: the altars were also called tables, and vice-versa, the tables were called

---

[39] Mazza, "Tavola e altare", pp. 57–58.

[40] Wrong in every respect is the argument of A. Chavarría Arnau, *Archeologia delle Chiese* (Rome: Carocci, 2010), p. 95: *"La sua origine è quindi duplice: da un lato deriva dalle are sacrificali romane, dall'altro dal tavolo dell'Ultima cena, il che spiega la terminologia (ara e mensa) usata per nominarlo."* ["Its origin is therefore twofold: on the one hand it is derived from the Roman sacrificial altars, on the other from the Last Supper, which explains the terminology (altar and table) used to designate it."] This statement probably relies on Duval, "L'autel paléochrétien", p. 11.

[41] Chr. Goudineau, "ΙΕΡΑΙ ΤΡΑΠΕΖΑΙ" in: *Mélanges d'Archéologie et d'Histoire* 79 (1967): 77–134; *Thesaurus cultus et rituum antiquorum*, vol. 5 (Los Angeles: The J. Paul Getty Museum, 2005), pp. 230–40.

[42] The frescos of the synagogue in Dura Europos depict the showbread table beside two altars in the Temple of Jerusalem. Concerning altar and table see also N. Zimmermann and S. Ladstätter, *Wandmalerei in Ephesos von hellenistischer bis in byzantinische Zeit* (Vienna: Phoibos, 2010), p. 126, fig. 226. Concerning sacral tables, in which as in this case the *mensa* rests on two marble slabs set up edgewise, see Nussbaum, "Zum Problem der runden und sigmaförmigen Altarplatten", p. 20, n. 31; E. Pernice, *Hellenistische Tische, Zisternenmündungen, Beckenuntersätze, Altäre und Truhen* (Berlin and Leipzig: De Gruyter, 1932), plate 2.3 and 2.6.

[43] Reisch, "Altar", pp. 1663–64. Movable sacral tables and portable altars were as holy as they were sturdy; Reisch, pp. 1648–50, 1685. Sacral tables with legs and *mensa* existed also as permanently installed stone tables (*Thesaurus cultus et rituum antiquorum*, vol. 5, pp. 231–32).

altars. In the same cult, the "holy table"[44] at one moment served the same needs as an altar did at the next.[45]

All this is true of the culture in which early Christianity developed its own sacred furnishings. In fact and with regard to its function, the Christian sacral table was indistinguishable from an altar. Christians had to reject altars of bloody sacrifice, because they had no use for them, but they used sacral tables, because they understood bread and wine to be sacrificial gifts. Usually an epithet was added—"table of the Lord", "holy table", and so forth—to distinguish the Christian "table" from other tables.[46]

The Letter to the Hebrews (Heb 13:10) and Ignatius of Antioch speak around the year 100 about the Eucharistic "sacrificial altar" (*thysiastérion*) in the sense of a real cultic furnishing. This term alludes not to the pagan altar but rather to the Jewish altar (as 1 Cor 10:18 did already), and it certainly could have meant the sacral showbread table also. This language about the Christian sacrificial altar does not contradict the statement by the Roman author Minucius Felix. Around the year 200 he said that Christians possessed neither temples nor altars. Minucius Felix is speaking however only about pagan temples, images of the gods and altars of bloody sacrifice[47] and allows for Jewish worship, which had its temple and altars,[48] as a legitimate institution.

6. The Form of the Earliest Altars

There is much evidence therefore that sacral tables were at the beginning of the history of the Christian altar. Since the ancient sacral table could vary in its concrete form, just like the altar,[49] there was leeway to

---

[44] Kruse, "Mensa", p. 946.

[45] Reisch, "Altar", p. 1676; Kirsch and Klauser, "Altar", pp. 312–13, 319; A. V. Siebert, *Instrumenta Sacra: Untersuchungen zu römischen Opfer- Kult- und Priestergeräten* (Berlin and New York: De Gruyter, 1999), pp. 98–102.

[46] Cf. Reisch, "Altar", pp. 1656–59; Braun, *Der christliche Altar*, vol. 1, pp. 26, 29.

[47] Minucius Felix, 32, 1 (CSEL 2, 45). Similarly Origen, *Contra Celsum* 8, 17 (FC 50, 5, 1352) and Arnobius, *Adversus gentes*, 6, 1 (CSEL 4, 214) with a clear reference to pagan altars.

[48] Minucius Felix, 33, 2 (CSEL 2, 46).

[49] Reisch, "Altar", pp. 1669–77. The many depictions of pagan and Jewish altars for holocausts and sacrifices in early Christian art furnish evidence of their diversity.

choose forms that were suited for Christian sacrificial worship. In this sense the early Christian altar, whether of the *mensa* [tabletop], *stipes* [on a stand] or chest-shaped variety, is best understood as a genuinely Christian invention. Christians wanted to set themselves apart clearly from the pagan altar, but not by choosing a meal table. Rather, the form of the Christian altar developed from the sacral table and practical considerations. It was important for there to be room on it for the Eucharistic gifts, and possibly for other sacrificial and votive gifts of the faithful.[50] Finally, the priest and the sacrificial ministers, namely the deacons, had to stand at this table or altar.[51] This required a high, large, fixed altar top. The aforementioned oldest preserved altar in Megiddo was probably a *stipes* altar made of stone. Therefore what we read again and again in scholarly literature can no longer be true, that the oldest authenticated altars had the form of a table on slender legs.[52] Cyprian and Augustine speak sometimes about the *mensa*. Hence scholars like to say that in North Africa movable wooden tables were normally used, which retained the form of the original meal table. By now we know on the basis of more accurate archaeological observations, that even in North Africa the altars were much more commonly made out of stone than was previously thought.[53] Even wooden tables, though, had nothing to do with profane meal tables, since despite the term *mensa* it was definitely a matter of offering bread and wine on the altar, as both Cyprian and Augustine emphasize.[54]

---

[50] Cf. Reisch, "Altar", p. 1661. A different explanation is given by Kirsch and Klauser, "Altar", p. 350.

[51] Origen, *In Libro Iudicum homeliæ*, 3, 2 (GCS 7, 481, 23–25).

[52] Cf. P. Volti, "L'altare cristiano dalle origini alla riforma carolingia", in: Debuyst, *L'altare*, (pp. 81–95), p. 83.

[53] Duval, "L'autel paléochrétien", p. 7.

[54] Cyprian, Ep. 63, 5 (CSEL 3, 2, 704): *"Sed et per Salomonem spiritus sanctus typum dominici sacrificii ante præmonstrat, immolatæ hostiæ et panis et vini sed et altaris et apostolorum faciens mentionem . . . mactavit suas hostias, miscuit in cratera vinum suum et paravit suam mensam."* ["But through Solomon too the Holy Spirit prefigured the type of the Lord's sacrifice, mentioning the immolated victim and bread and wine and also the altar and the apostles . . . he slaughtered his victims, mixed his wine in bowls and prepared his table."] Augustine, *Sermo* 310, 2 (PL 38:1413): *"in eodem loco mensa Deo constructa est, et tamen mensa dicitur Cypriani, non quia ibi est unquam Cyprianus epulatus . . . sed in qua sacrificium Deo . . . offeratur."* ["In that same place a table was built for God, and nevertheless the table is said to be Cyprian's, not because Cyprian ever dined there . . . but on that table sacrifice is offered to God."]

The mosaic of Abraham's three mysterious visitors in San Vitale in Ravenna (sixth century) shows a domestic meal table at which the men sit on a bench.[55] But the altar table depicted in the same church, at which Abel and Melchizedek offer sacrifice standing, is not to be identified as a meal table, precisely because it is covered with a cloth.[56] Cloths for meal tables are only found infrequently in Antiquity.[57] Table coverings were used however for the official tables of the magistrates, decorated with the Emperor's image, like the ones in the *Notitia Dignitatum* (fifth century) and in the *Codex Purpureus* of Rossano (sixth century).[58] The altar cloth therefore signaled sacrality and authority rather than a meal situation.[59]

Theodor Klauser speculated as to whether the table at the Last Supper was semicircular. He concluded that the original form of the altar was a profane semicircular or round table. As the congregation became larger, this meal table was then raised, so that the priest now distributed the Eucharistic food while standing at such a table. What supposedly still remained of the old seating arrangement in early Christian churches was the semicircular bench for the priests. According to this theory, not until the altar table was moved away from this bench was the round altar replaced by the rectangular altar.

His student Otto Nussbaum tried to prove this thesis archaeologi-

---

[55] A table without a tablecloth, at which one ate seated; see Th. B. Stevenson, *Miniature Decoration in the Vatican Virgil* (Tübingen: Ernst Wasmuth, 1983), fig. 83 (mosaic from the Bardo Museum, Tunis).

[56] Altar cloths are documented from the third century on; Kirsch and Klauser, "Altar", p. 349; Wessel, "Altarbekleidung", pp. 120–24. The altar cloth covers also the reliquary; Peschlow, 198. Admittedly, one finds artistic representations of *mensa*/altars without tablecloths, but only outside of the celebration of the Eucharist (e.g. in the baptistery of the Cathedral of Ravenna).

[57] Kruse, "Mensa", pp. 942, 944. For examples of semicircular tables with a tablecloth, see Engemann, "Der Ehrenplatz beim antiken Sigmamahl", plates 14a and 19b; J. G. Deckers et al., *Die Katakombe "Santi Marcellino e Pietro"* (Vatican City and Münster: Aschendorff, 1987), plate 64a.

[58] Cf. F. J. Dölger, *Antike und Christentum*, vol. 2 (Münster: Aschendorff, 1930), pp. 174–75. For another example see W. de Grueneisen, *Sainte Marie Antique* (Rome: Max Bretschneider, 1911), fig. 255.

[59] Contrary to Mazza "Tavola e altare", p. 57: *"Anche in quegli altari cristiani che non sono a forma di tavola, il richiamo alla tavola è garantito dall'esistenza della tovaglia."* ["Even on those Christian altars that are not in the form of a table, the presence of a tablecloth guarantees that it will be reminiscent of a table."]

cally.[60] He did not succeed, however. There is nearly no evidence for an early Christian semicircular altar table.[61] It is interesting in this connection that in the fifth century on the island of Samos a main altar with a semi-circular top does in fact turn up.[62] To all appearances, the round side of the *mensa* faced the apse; the priest stood at the straight side and consequently looked East toward the apse.[63]

This unique case proves that the Christian altar has nothing to do with a dining table.[64] For precisely in the fifth and sixth centuries there are many depictions of the Last Supper, in which Christ reclines with his disciples at a semicircular table,[65] for example the mosaic of the Last Supper in Sant'Apollinare Nuovo from the sixth century. It would have been obvious to design the altar in a church in a semicircular form so as to recall the Last Supper or to emphasize the Eucharist as a community meal. But this idea occurred to no one; on the contrary, in depictions

---

[60] Nussbaum, "Zum Problem der runden und sigmaförmigen Altarplatten", pp. 18–43. Nussbaum tries to approach the original Christian altar via the *mensa* of the meal for the dead. Similarly Jensen, "Dining with the Dead", pp. 134ff., sees the *mensa* of the meal for the dead as the origin of the Christian altar. All this is still purely hypothetical. There are no literary references to round or semicircular altars. Basil of Seleucia, *Vita s. Theclæ*, 1 (PG 85:560A) speaks not about a round altar but rather about an altar that is surrounded on all sides by ciboria (contrary to Lampe, *A Patristic Greek Lexicon*, p. 1399).

[61] The claim by Volti in "L'altare cristiano dalle origini alla riforma carolingia", p. 85, about the semicircular altar is absolutely wrong: *"era largamente diffuso in tutto il mondo cristiano della tarda antichità"*. ["It was widespread throughout the Christian world in late Antiquity."]

[62] E. Chalkia, *Le mense paleocristiane* (Vatican City: Pontificio Istituto di Archeologia Cristiana, 1991), pp. 113–14. The supposed semicircular altar on two ivory pyxes is actually a throne; W. F. Volbach, *Elfenbeinarbeiten der Spätantike und des frühen Mittelalters* (Mainz: Von Zabern, 1976), n. 177, 184.

[63] A. M. Schneider, "Samos in frühchristlicher und byzantinischer Zeit", in: *Mitteilungen des Deutschen Archäologischen Instituts*, Athenische Abteilung, 54 (1929): (pp. 29–141), pp. 108–109. The great majority of the tabletops are of unknown origin (from churches?); they could have been used for symposia or meals for the dead. The Egyptian semicircular altars are medieval; I. Sastre de Diego, "Una nuova espressione del potere: Altari, martiri e religiosità: Il ruolo del Nord Africa nella Hispania tardoantica", in: M. Bastiana Cocco *et al.*, eds., *L'Africa romana*, vol. 2 (Rome: Carocci, 2012), (pp. 1280–90), pp. 1283–85; Kirsch and Klauser, "Altar", p. 343.

[64] Concerning another possible semicircular altar, see Duval, "L'autel paléochrétien", p. 12.

[65] Last Supper in Sant'Apollinare Nuovo in Ravenna, in the Codex Rossanensis (W. de Grueneisen, *Sainte Marie Antique* [Rome: Max Bretschneider, 1933], p. 375, fig. 302) and in the Chapel of John VII in St. Peter's Basilica (ibid., PL. IC. LXVI and LXVII).

of the Apostles receiving communion, in which Christ stands at the altar and administers the Eucharist to the disciples, the semicircular table is omitted. Instead Christ now stands at a rectangular altar.[66] See, for example, the Byzantine silver bowl depicting Apostles receiving communion from the sixth century from the Dumbarton Oaks collection. We cannot speak about any Last Supper symbolism of semicircular altars, furthermore, because semicircular tabletops were found in private homes, in connection with burials, and in baptisteries and sacristies.[67]

7. The Sacrality of the Early Christian Altar

A basic trend in modern theology in the wake of the Enlightenment is the minimization of the cultic character of Christianity.[68] Supposedly Christianity was originally a religious movement without worship. Accordingly the Eucharistic table had as little sacral character as the table at the Last Supper had had. In this view, not until a particular table was used permanently for the Eucharist did it become a sacred object.[69] Nevertheless Paul already speaks about the "table of the Lord" and contrasts it with Israel's altar and the tables of the idols. The "table of the Lord" is therefore a table that belongs to the Lord, which implies a lasting sacral character.

Ancient sacral tables, like altars, were reserved exclusively for the sacrifice or the sacrificial gifts of a particular deity and were withdrawn from any profane use (*res religiosæ*).[70] It was probably no different in Christianity. As early as the third century there is proof of the special holiness of the altar or table, and in the fourth century it is regularly described as holy, awesome, royal, divine or mystical.[71] A

---

[66] E. Gagetti, " *'Sanctum altare tuum domine subnixus honoro.'* Preziosi vasi eucaristici tra IV e VI secolo d.C.", in: *Costantino 313 d.C.: L'editto di Milano e il tempo della tolleranza* (Milan: Electa, 2012), (pp. 129–35), p. 131.

[67] Wessel, "Altar", p. 117; Chalkia, pp. 111–31.

[68] K. Backhaus, "Kult und Kreuz: Zur frühchristlichen Dynamik ihrer theologischen Beziehung", in: *Theologie und Glaube* 86 (1996): pp. 512–33; *idem, Der Hebräerbrief* (Regensburg: Friedrich Pustet, 2009).

[69] Braun, "Die Entwicklung des christlichen Altars bis zum Beginn des Mittelalters", pp. 162–63.

[70] Siebert, *Instrumenta Sacra*, pp. 93–96, pp. 255–56.

[71] F. J. Dölger, "Die Heiligkeit des Altars und ihre Begründung im christlichen Al-

quasi-consecration of an altar, resulting in its use exclusively for the Christian sacrifice, took place through the Eucharist itself: once a table was used for the Eucharist, it was holy, and from then on it could be used only for this worship. Then in the late fourth century a special consecration ceremony developed, but this does not mean that Christian altars were previously not regarded as holy.

It should be assumed that wherever there was a specially designated worship space, the altar was permanently installed as well, even if the altar in question was movable in principle. In the house church of Dura Europos from the year 256 there is against the eastern wall a podium on which the altar could have stood.[72] In the house church of Megiddo from the end of the third century the lower part of the altar has been preserved.[73] Spectacularly, in this case there is an inscription of the benefactress, saying that this "table" was dedicated to the "God Christ".[74] Therefore the altar belonged exclusively to the "God Christ". Consequently this "table" was not a dining table for a symposium, but rather a sacral table or altar.[75]

In the early fourth century Christians began to cordon off the altar and thus to delimit a sacred area,[76] which as a rule only clerics entered. In the Baroque era the early Christian enclosures, insofar as they extended into the nave, were taken down, because the so-called *schola cantorum* was no longer needed (see for example Santa Prassede and Santa Maria in Cosmedin in Rome). Only in San Clemente in Rome and some other churches did it remain standing. In individual cases, such enclosures were set up again in the twentieth century as part of the restoration of early Christian churches (for example, Santa Sabina

---

tertum", in: *Antike und Christentum*, vol. 2 (Münster: Aschendorff, 1930), pp. 161–83; Kirsch and Klauser, "Altar", p. 352.

[72] U. M. Lang, *Turning Towards the Lord: Orientation in Liturgical Prayer* (San Francisco: Ignatius Press, 2009), p. 72. Riesner, "What does archaeology teach us about early house churches?", p. 160, argues unconvincingly that a large pedestal measuring 1 × 1.5 meters could not have supported an altar but was rather the pedestal for a seat.

[73] Tepper and di Segni, *A Christian Prayer Hall of the Third Century CE.*

[74] "The God-loving Akeptous offered the table to God Jesus Christ as a memorial."

[75] Contrary to Sastre de Diego, "Una nuova espressione del potere", p. 1281. It can hardly have been the basis for a low semicircular table, because with a masonry table one would expect masonry couches as well.

[76] Kirsch and Klauser, "Altar", pp. 351–52. Concerning the ancient *témenos*, see Reisch, "Altar", pp. 1641, 1654, 1685.

in Rome, Sant'Apollinare Nuovo in Ravenna). The Baroque era left the barriers of the actual *presbyterium* standing, where they served as communion rails.

Of the utmost importance for the sacral character of altars from the fourth century on was also the association with a martyr's grave or else with relics; this was the case both in the West and in the East.[77] Already in the New Testament there is an important basis for the connection between altar and entombed relics (Rev 6:9). Through the remains of those who had borne witness to God, the altar itself became a witness (*martýrion*) to the fact that God is the Lord (Josh 22:34). It became the source of special, miraculous power, which was poured out on the faithful through the martyrs' remains. The relics recalled that the sacrifice offered on the Christian altar was not of objects alone, but of the living Body of Christ, the First Martyr, whom the martyrs imitated in laying down their lives.[78]

8. The Fantasy of an Early Christian "People's Altar"

Until the Second Vatican Council, practically all altars stood against the wall. After Christian archaeology discovered more and more free-standing altars, the notion became widespread that for the Eucharist the Early Church had deliberately used tables around which the congregation gathered as though at a meal.[79] Already in the course of the liturgical movement, but also through the restoration of historical churches in the early Christian style, free-standing altars began to be set up. Finally, during the Council the instruction was issued that an altar may be free-standing so that Mass can be celebrated at it *versus*

---

[77] Kirsch and Klauser, "Altar", pp. 343–47; F. W. Deichmann, "Märtyrerbasilika, Martyrion, Memoria und Altargrab", in: *Mitteilungen des Deutschen Archäologischen Instituts*, Römische Abteilung 77 (1970): pp. 144–69; U. Peschlow, "Altar und Reliquie: Form und Nutzung des frühbyzantinischen Reliquienaltars in Konstantinopel", in: M. Altripp and C. Nauerth, eds., *Architektur und Liturgie*, Akten des Kolloquiums vom 25. bis 27. Juli 2003 in Greifswald (Wiesbaden: Reichert, 2006), pp. 175–202; A. Kalinowski, *Frühchristliche Reliquiare im Kontext von Kultstrategien, Heilserwartung und sozialer Selbstdarstellung* (Wiesbaden: Reichert, 2011), pp. 28–36.

[78] Kirsch and Klauser, "Altar", p. 344. See also Augustine, *Sermo* 310, 2 (PL 38:1413).

[79] Gamber, *Domus Ecclesiæ*, p. 94: "Die ursprüngliche Mahlgemeinschaft um den gemeinsamen Tisch". So too J. Jungmann, in: *Lexikon für Theologie und Kirche*, Das Zweite Vatikanische Konzil, vol. 1 (Freiburg im Breisgau: Herder, 1966), p. 105, note 5.

populum [facing the people].[80] The "people's altar" became the symbol of the new liturgy. At the Eucharistic meals, so they claimed, people reclined in a half circle around a table. The presider took the place at one end and turned toward the others.[81] From this it was concluded that priest and people celebrated face to face. For this reason Giulio Belvederi, the first Secretary of the Pontifical Institute for Christian Archaeology, had the depiction of a meal in the *Capella Græca* of the Catacombs of St. Priscilla installed as a mosaic on the wall behind the altar in the chapel of the Benedictine convent of Priscilla, and he himself celebrated facing the people.

The influence of Theodor Klauser was more momentous. He thought that in the Early Church the priest stood behind the altar as a matter of principle; only in the Middle Ages did the observance of orientation cause the priest to step in front of the altar.[82] His student Otto Nussbaum tried to prove this archaeologically.[83] Most early churches exhibit a priest's chair in the apse and the altar standing in front of it. So Nussbaum assumed from the outset that the bishop walked from the *cathedra* to the altar and celebrated facing across the altar.

Then there was the suggestive force of images, for instance Melchizedek on the altar in Sant'Apollinare in Classe (seventh century) or the ivory in the Liebieghaus (Frankfurt) with a depiction of the *Sanctus* (tenth century). Such depictions, which for purely artistic reasons give a frontal view of the priest at the altar, gave the impression that the priest was celebrating while facing the viewer.[84] All this did not fail to have its effect, so that today celebration facing the people is thought

---

[80] Instruction, *Inter Œcumenici*, 26 September 1964, n. 91.

[81] Engemann, "Der Ehrenplatz beim antiken Sigmamahl", pp. 239–50, shows that in late Antiquity too images of meals recognize the place of honor in the middle.

[82] Kirsch and Klauser, "Altar", p. 348; a similar view however is found already in: J. Braun, "Altar", in: *Lexikon für Theologie und Kirche* (Freiburg im Breisgau: Herder, 1930), vol. 1 (pp. 294–97), pp. 294–95. See also M. Righetti, *Manuale di storia liturgica*, 3rd ed., vol. 3 (Milan: Ancora, 1966), p. 374. Even today this thesis is extremely widespread thanks to Wikipedia https://de.wikipedia.org/wiki/Volksaltar.

[83] O. Nussbaum, *Der Standort des Liturgen am christlichen Altar vor dem Jahre 1000: Eine archäologische und liturgiegeschichtliche Untersuchung*, 2 vols. (Bonn: Peter Hanstein, 1965).

[84] On the ivory only the sanctuary is depicted. The singers in front of the celebrant are the subdeacons who recite the responses (*Ordo Romanus* I, 87). Given the orientation of a church, as a rule, the celebrant therefore looks East toward the apse or the cathedra; the nave should be imagined behind his back. See *Kunst und Kultur der Karolingerzeit*, vol. 2 (Mainz: Von Zabern, 1999), pp. 830–31.

to be the authentically correct form of celebration corresponding to the *norma patrum*.

Even early Christian church buildings were then remodeled accordingly, and today they give the impression that there were people's altars there. A particularly blatant example is the pilgrimage church Tabgha on the Sea of Galilee, which was excavated by the Görres Society starting in 1932. The church is oriented with its apse to the East. The original altar displays steps on the western side. Therefore the priest doubtless stood with his back to the faithful.[85] In doing so he looked at the famous floor mosaic with the breadbasket that was located behind the altar and was supposed to associate the miracle of the multiplication of the loaves with the priest's Eucharistic action.[86] The restoration in the 1980s however followed Nussbaum, who contrary to all the evidence maintained that the priest had always stood behind the altar in this church. Accordingly the bread mosaic was shifted to the front of the new table altar, so that now the only possible way to celebrate is facing the people. Pilgrims marvel at today's arrangement of the mosaic and the altar, but it is definitely a modern invention and not an early Christian design; the original condition could easily have been established based on the archaeological findings, but that was not desired, because it did not fit in with the preconceived idea of a people's altar.

Today no serious scholar in the fields of Christian archaeology and liturgical studies still subscribes to the theories of Klauser and Nussbaum.[87] The people's altar is an historical fiction similar to the catacomb church, the *disciplina arcani* or other faddish notions. In the Early Church there was great variety in the disposition of the altar in the worship space, and no one theory fits them all. Celebration facing the people, however, was the less common practice, and it was certainly

---

[85] Nussbaum, *Der Standort des Liturgen am christlichen Altar vor dem Jahre 1000*, vol. 1, pp. 71–72, asserts the opposite. But both the inscription and the bread mosaic are visible from the West. Altar steps for pilgrims make no sense, because they did not approach the altar, but rather crept under the altar to honor the holy stone.

[86] A. E. Mader, "Die Ausgrabung der Basilika der Brotvermehrung und ihrer Mosaiken bei Et-Tabga am See Genesareth", in: *Atti del III Congresso internazionale di Archeologia Cristiana* (Rome: Pontificio Istituto di Archeologia Cristiana, 1934), (pp. 507–21), p. 513, fig. 4.

[87] Duval, "L'autel paléochrétien", p. 8. Ideological preconceptions may have played a role in Nussbaum's arguments, as is correctly noted by A. Gerhards, "Vom jüdischen zum christlichen Gotteshaus?" in: R. Voderholzer, ed., *Der logosgemässe Gottesdienst* (Regensburg: Friedrich Pustet, 2009), (pp. 111–38), pp. 124–25.

not justified by the meal character of the Eucharist. It resulted instead from the specific local situation. The most important case was when the church entrance faced East, so that the priest had to stand behind the altar.

A look at the history of religion helps us to view correctly the free-standing altar in Early Christianity. Altars that were usually free-standing were known even in Antiquity. In the Old Testament (Ps 26[25]:6), as well as in pagan religions, there was circumambulation of the altar.[88] Synagogues too may have had altars (at which to offer incense) standing in the middle of the room.[89] In none of these cases can we speak about a gathering for a meal. Even in the Christian liturgy no meal-related significance was attributed to the circumambulation of the altar. For the Roman Canon speaks about the *circumstantes* as people offering sacrifice, not as partakers of a meal: "*pro quibus tibi offerimus vel qui tibi offerunt hoc sacrificium laudis*" ("on whose behalf we offer to You, or who themselves offer to You, this sacrifice of praise").

Although ancient altars were free-standing and usually had no superstructure, they were oriented. The people played no role in this. Instead, while offering sacrifice the priest looked at the image of the deity to whom the altar was dedicated, which stood on one side of the altar or on the *mensa* of the altar itself.[90] The designs of steps in monumental temple altars also indicate that the priest looked toward the

---

[88] Reisch, "Altar", p. 1689; Kirsch and Klauser, "Altar", p. 326. The clergy stood around the altar; Pseudo-Cyril, *Catech. mystag.* 5, 2 (FC 7:146).

[89] E. R. Goodenough, *Jewish Symbols in the Greco-Roman Period* (New York: Pantheon, 1964), pp. 26–27; *Aufstieg und Niedergang der römischen Welt*, series II, vol. 16, 1 (Berlin: Walter de Gruyter, 1978), p. 601. Some suspect that older references to such altars in the rabbinical literature fell victim to censorship. Mention is made of Jewish altars (in synagogues) in: Irenaeus, *Adversus hæreses* 4, 18, 2 (SC 100:598) and Minucius Felix 33, 2 (CSEL 2:46). Cf. F. W. Deichmann, "Vom Tempel zur Kirche", in: *Mullus* (Münster: Aschendorff, 1964): (pp. 52–59), p. 54, fig. 11: In the eschatological Temple the only remaining sacrifice is of incense.

[90] Siebert, *Instrumenta Sacra*, pp. 100, 102. For sacrificial ceremonies directed toward the image of an idol, see *Thesaurus cultus et rituum antiquorum*, vol. 4 (Los Angeles: The J. Paul Getty Museum, 2006), plates 54–55; *Thesaurus cultus et rituum antiquorum*, vol. 2 (Los Angeles: The J. Paul Getty Museum, 2004), plates 104–105; F. Matz, *Die dionysischen Sarkophage*, vol. 3 (Berlin: G. Mann, 1969), plates 200, 230; H. P. L'Orange and A. von Gerkan, *Der spätantike Bildschmuck des Konstantinsbogens* (Berlin: De Gruyter, 1939), plate 39b; G. Kaschnitz-Weinberg, *Sculture del magazzino del Museo Vaticano* (Vatican City: Max Bretschneider, 1936), plate LXXVII, 417; Grueneisen, p. 221.

image of the deity. When no image of a deity was present, the priest chose the western side of the altar so as to face East. Ideally the image of the deity stood on the eastern side too.[91] These rules, established by Vitruv (to which there are of course exceptions),[92] made sense inasmuch as the sacrifice was offered to the deity. The spectators were not the ones to whom the sacrifice was addressed and hence the priest did not look at them.

It was no different among the Christians. We have to assume, based on the written sources, that in the third century fixed altars were widespread and that even movable tables were not needlessly moved away from their place.[93] These altars were oriented, but the direction was determined neither by free placement nor by the faithful who were present. Cyprian says in a remarkable passage that the clergy left their benches and cleared away the altar of the Lord so that in its place a pagan altar could be set up, along with an image of the deity on the priest's bench.[94] Cyprian therefore takes it for granted that the priest at the altar offers the Sacrifice toward the apse, that is, toward the image of the deity. The decisive factor in evaluating the free-standing altar in early Christianity is of course the orient-ation of prayer (the custom of praying while facing East).[95] This is not a medieval innovation. Rather it is documented from the second century on that Christians prayed toward the East, and this influenced church architecture both in the East and the West, despite all regional differences. Most churches were situated with the apse toward the East, or at least on the East-West axis. This was true in Rome also.[96] The sole meaning of such an alignment

---

[91] In Jerusalem the priest stood between the Temple, in which there was no cultic image, and the altar and thus while offering sacrifice looked East, toward the Mount of Olives; Cyprian, *Fort.* II (CCL 3, 1, 204).

[92] Reisch, "Altar", pp. 1643, 1654–55; Kirsch and Klauser, "Altar", pp. 320–21. In exceptions to the rule this orientation becomes even clearer: The two altars of the Sacred Area near Sant'Omobono in Rome, the two altars are oriented (to the East) instead of the temples they belong to, which are on the North-South axis; F. Coarelli, *Rom: Ein archäologischer Führer* (Freiburg im Breisgau: Herder, 1975), pp. 282–83.

[93] F. J. Dölger, *Antike und Christentum*, vol. 2 (Münster: Aschendorff, 1930), pp. 164–65.

[94] Ibid., 161–62.

[95] Stefan Heid, "Gebetshaltung und Ostung in frühchristlicher Zeit", in: *Rivista di Archeologia Cristiana* 82 (2006): 347–404.

[96] S. de Blaauw, "In vista della luce: Un principio dimenticato nell'orientamento

of buildings was to determine the direction in which the faithful faced while praying. The fact that the orientation of prayer applied to the celebrant at the altar too is clear from the mere fact that the altar was the place of prayer par excellence. In most cases the priest therefore looked toward the apse when he stood at the altar.[97] The fact that the *cathedra* stood there bothered no one. In Syria, where the *cathedra* did not stand in the apse, the altar was often moved right up to the East wall,[98] but such cases occur even in the area of Byzantine influence.[99]

For this reason too, the free-standing altar of the Early Church is not a people's altar in the contemporary sense, because while praying all the faithful lifted their hands and their eyes to heaven. While praying, therefore, they did not look at each other, even when they stood facing one another. In an oriented church, the priest and the faithful prayed while looking together toward the apse. In doing so, their glance often fell on a mosaic that depicted the cross in heaven or Christ on the clouds. Images in the apse had a strictly liturgical function, in that they determined the place to which one looked while praying.[100] In the sixth century there were individual cases of crosses on the altar.[101] All these things had the liturgical function of replacing the old images of the deities by determining the direction of prayer.[102] This can be demonstrated by a mosaic in San Vitale in Ravenna (sixth century), on which Abel and Melchizedek lift up their sacrificial gifts to God's hand in heaven and to the cross.

---

dell'edificio di culto paleocristiano", in: P. Piva, ed., *Arte medievale: Le vie dello spazio liturgico* (Milan: Jaca Book, 2010), pp. 15–45. This article is of fundamental importance for the question of architectonic and liturgical orientation.

[97] Instructive material can be found in: M.-C. Comte, *Les reliquaires du Proche-Orient et de Chypre à la période proto-byzantine (IVe–VIIIe siècle)* (Turnhout: Brepols Publishers, 2012).

[98] Wessel, "Altar", p. 118; Comte, ibid., pp. 263ff.

[99] For example the *sacellum* under San Vitale in Ravenna.

[100] Heid, "Gebetshaltung und Ostung in frühchristlicher Zeit", pp. 366–77.

[101] Evagrius Scholasticus, *Historia ecclesiastica* 6, 21 (PG 86/2:2876C). See also Nussbaum, *Der Standort des Liturgen am christlichen Altar vor dem Jahre 1000*, vol. 1, pp. 429–32.

[102] Already in Antiquity images of the gods could be placed in niches in the wall, before which the altar stood; Reisch, "Altar", pp. 1648, 1655.

9. Conclusions and Lessons for Today

1. The liturgical developments of the twentieth century took their inspiration mainly from the Early Church, or at least from an imaginary picture of early Christianity. A certain confidence in scholarship had led people to regard many half-baked theories that were being discussed by patrologists and Christian archaeologists as definitive findings. On occasion they should have listened to sound Tradition (*Sacrosanctum Concilium*, 4) instead of the latest rage among the experts. For not all the practical implementation that resulted in the last fifty years can meet the standard of the *norma patrum*. The exaggerations of the past do not mean, however, that we would do better now to adopt a hands-off policy with regard to the Church Fathers. On the contrary: the present era must also allow itself to be informed and re-formed according to the *norma patrum*. Of course, if the *norma patrum* is not to become an empty phrase that only serves to promote one's own ideas, historical scholarship must critique itself and revise its erroneous judgments. It must clearly indicate the provisional character of its findings and guard against anachronistic manipulations.

2. At the same time recourse to the *norma patrum* must be relativized. The Early Church offers no easy-to-follow practical directions. And of all things, the liturgical arrangements of the early period were quite diverse in the various regions.[103] Are all possible early Christian church buildings supposed to serve now as the *norma patrum*? Should the Egyptian and Syrian arrangements of the worship space be applied to Catholic church architecture too? Such archaeologism, which Pius XII already warned against[104] (referring even to modern altar designs!), runs the risk of making the Early Church increasingly a mere quarry for all sorts of ideas, which may be beautiful citations but are devoid of religious and cultural plausibility. The worst derailment of this sort in

---

[103] Chavarría Arnau, *Archeologia delle Chiese*, pp. 96–97.

[104] Pius XII, *Mediator Dei* (1947), in: *Acta Apostolicæ Sedis* 39 (1947): p. 545: *"non sapiens tamen, non laudabile est omnia ad antiquitatem quovis modo reducere. Itaque, ut exemplis utamur, is ex recto aberret itinere, qui priscam altari velit mensæ formam restituere."* "But it is neither wise nor laudable to reduce everything to antiquity by every possible device. Thus, to cite some instances, one would be straying from the straight path were he to wish the altar restored to its primitive table form."

recent times is the red semicircular table in a Baroque church in Graz, Austria (the "*Welsche Kirche*"). Such theories should be countered by the argument that there is no such thing as "decline" from a pure liturgy, nor are there allegedly inferior phases in the development of liturgy.

This has two consequences for the Early Church. First, the downright ideological separation of early Christianity and the classical patristic era, which is associated with the slogan "the Hellenization of Christianity", must stop.[105] Only in this way can today's liturgy be situated in continuity with its authentic origin. Secondly, the Middle Ages and the Baroque period should be regarded as a legitimate continuation of the liturgical praxis of the Early Church. Medieval and Baroque altars must not become museum pieces or be destroyed in favor of allegedly "early Christian" altars. Otherwise we will fall into the same error as the classical archaeologists who wiped out all traces of the Middle Ages just to bring to light a few remnants of walls from classical antiquity.

3. The chorus of voices claiming that the Eucharistic table was originally a profane meal table lays the axe to the root of the Christian altar. Because the implication is that now we would actually have to design new altars as meal tables. The path marked out by Enrico Mazza— defining the original Christian altar as a meal table formally and as an altar functionally[106]—ultimately leads in the same direction as a continual desacralization. Yet the fact that after the reform of the liturgy new altars were set up everywhere accelerated this process. For they necessarily convinced people that the altars previously used for centuries were outmoded, indeed even wrong. The divine sacrifice was now replaced by the community meal, at eye level, so to speak. This was understood less and less as a cultic meal and more and more as a meal of a community, of sinners. Admittedly, one cannot dispute the legitimacy of the people's altar for the new liturgy, especially since its introduction was based on an astonishingly unanimous reception

---

[105] Christoph Markschies, *Hellenisierung des Christentums: Geschichte und Bedeutung eines umstrittenen Konzepts* (Leipzig: Evangelische Verlagsanstalt, 2012).

[106] Mazza, "Tavola e altare", p. 75: "*dal punto di vista teologico che la tavola dell'eucaristia va chiamata altare, mentre dal punto di vista della forma essa è, e resta, una tavola.*" ["from the theological perspective that the table of the Eucharist should be called an altar, whereas from the formal perspective it is and remains a table."]

process throughout the Universal Church. But the fact remains that the altar is not a meal table.[107] Hence every effort must be made to make such tables still recognizable at all as places for the ministry of the Eucharistic Sacrifice. At the very least we should make sure that the altar is clearly distinguished from a mere table. Already in the Early Church this was effectively achieved by the visible addition of relics. Even today reliquaries can help to guarantee the specifically Christian form and sacral character of the altar.

4. The reintroduction of the free-standing altar after the Second Vatican Council restored the *norma patrum* in a merely external way. In making the free-standing altar a people's altar by celebrating Mass facing the congregation, however, this recourse to the Church Fathers, while meaningful in itself, was debased. By celebrating *versus populum*, the last remnant of the early Christian orientation of prayer was relinquished. Prayer facing East was the ritual expression of the reference to God or, as Augustine put it, of the *conversio ad Dominum* (turning toward the Lord). Such a *conversio*, however, was maintained from the Middle Ages down to recent times by having the priest at the altar pray with the people in the same direction, regardless of what geographical direction the altar faced. This ritual visibility of the eschatological, vertical dimension of Christian prayer was abandoned in celebration facing the people.[108] Reinhard Messner has strikingly pointed out this problem.[109] If we take the *norma patrum* seriously, we will be skeptical of celebration *versus populum*, which is universal today, and the manner in which it is practiced.

From an ecumenical perspective too, it is still possible to restore

---

[107] Messner, "La direzione della preghiera", p. 208: *"La presunta funzione dell'altare come tavola è un costrutto—non scevro da ideologia—del XX secolo: da quando, infatti, c'è un altare nella celebrazione eucaristica, questo non è mai stato una tavola."* ["The presumed function of the altar as a table is a twentieth-century construct and not free from ideology: since, in fact, it is an altar in the Eucharistic celebration, it never was a table."] Cf. A. Gerhards, "Der christliche Altar: Opferstätte oder Mahltisch?" in: A. Gerhards and K. Richter, eds., *Das Opfer* (Freiburg im Breisgau: Herder, 2000), pp. 272–85.

[108] Cf. Peter Chrysologus, *Sermo* 26, 3 (CCL 24:149): *"qui ante deum stat iugiter, versatur in altaria semper, neque a dei oculis recedit unquam . . . non potest nisi in ipsa dei facie inter sanctorum sancta peccare."* ["A man who continually stands before God, and always remains at His altars, nor ever withdraws from God's sight . . . cannot help but sin in the very presence of God within the Holy of Holies."]

[109] Messner, "La direzione della preghiera", pp. 201–12.

the custom of celebrating at free-standing altars with one's back to the people, according to the Orthodox practice. At least an easily visible cross should stand on the altar, to which the priest can look up.[110] For no doubt the general introduction of the cross in the Middle Ages served the purpose of giving a visual reference point to the *conversio ad Dominum*.

5. From the sixth century on there was a marked increase in the number of side altars, whereas since the Council we can observe the addition of main altars. In principle the multiplication of main altars, which comes about through the additional erection of people's altars, is unfortunate. The preservation of monuments and the modern liturgy are of course in conflict here and force us to make compromises. To sacrifice an historical high altar for a people's altar is dubious from the perspective of art history and liturgically superfluous. The 1996 guidelines of the Italian Bishops Conference for adapting existing churches to the liturgical reform (n. 17) assign only a subordinate significance to the preservation of monuments. They leave open the question of whether an historical high altar should be kept or destroyed. If it is kept, it should be rendered nonfunctional, so to speak, by removing the altar cloth and relics.

Such guidelines are not only disgraceful in themselves, but must also be revised on the basis of the 2007 Motu Proprio *Summorum Pontificum*. For now there is a reason for two main altars. It is obvious to use the high altar for the *usus antiquior*, the older form of the Roman rite, and the people's altar for the post-conciliar form. In any case it would make no sense to celebrate at the people's altar with one's back to the congregation if there is a high altar. If there is only a people's altar, it should be set up as a joint altar so that it can be used from either side. As a matter of principle, of course, it is true that the rubrics allow for the celebration of the modern as well as the older forms of the Roman rite at either the high altar or the people's altar.

6. In weighing whether or not to tear down an historical altar, one must consider, besides the mere preservation of monuments, religious and moral aspects of the question much more emphatically than has been customary to date: for instance, whether the altar in question is

---

[110] Stefan Heid, "Haltung und Richtung: Grundformen frühchristlichen Betens", in: *Internationale katholische Zeitschrift Communio* 38 (2009): pp. 611–19.

a privileged altar or a legacy altar. Often altars were left as bequests by the faithful for the salvation of their souls, and occasionally they were bequeathed together with burial monuments. As such they must have a generous guarantee of continued existence. Legacy altars are in keeping with the *norma patrum*, for there is ample evidence for this practice already in the Early Church.[111] The very first altar anywhere that has been uncovered archaeologically, namely the one in the house church of Megiddo from the period around 300, was donated by a woman. The inscription to this effect had precisely the purpose of declaring the altar to be a sacrosanct bequest.

---

[111] Many supporting references can be found in the Roman *Liber Pontificalis*.

5

The *Usus Antiquior* and the New Evangelisation

Tracey Rowland

The title of this paper suggests that the *usus antiquior*—the older form of the Roman rite—is something more than an emergency pastoral measure for elderly Catholics who woke up one morning in 1969 to find that the only Mass that they had ever known was now in most parts of the world suppressed. Rather, the title invites the question: what can the *usus antiquior* contribute to the new evangelisation? Since the expression "New Evangelisation" refers in a special way to the people who live in countries which were once Christian but have now become secularised, one can rephrase the question by asking, what role can the *usus antiquior* play as an antidote to secularism?

I wish to approach this question, not as an academic liturgist but as someone interested in the question of how meaning is conveyed through cultural practices, and also as someone interested in the theological critiques of the cultures of modernity and post-modernity.

In his two-volume magnum opus, *La Tradition et les traditions*, published during the era of the Second Vatican Council (1960–1963), Yves Congar argued that if 'tradition in its dogmatic foundation is an interpretation of scripture continuing that of Christ and His Apostles, the liturgy is truly the holy ark containing sacred tradition at its most intense'.[1] He then rhetorically asked how the Catholic Tradition could possibly be transmitted to new generations after successive centuries of 'demolition work' (a reference to the theological misadventures of

---

[1] Yves Congar, *The Meaning of Tradition* (San Francisco: Ignatius Press, 2004), p. 142.

at least four centuries) and in a passage which now reads as poignant, he concluded:

> But we need only step into an old church, taking holy water, as Pascal and Serapion did before us, in order to follow a Mass which has scarcely changed, even in externals, since St. Gregory the Great. . . . Everything has been preserved for us, and we can enter into a heritage which we may easily transmit in our turn, to those coming after us. Ritual, as a means of communication and of victory over devouring time, is also seen to be a powerful means for communion in the same reality between men separated by centuries of change and affected by very different influences.[2]

Congar was not what today we would call a 'traditionalist'. He was one of the many members of his generation who were frustrated with the pre-Conciliar theological establishment and believed that the intellectual presentation of the Faith was in rather poor condition. Nonetheless for him the *usus antiquior* was nothing less than 'the holy ark' preserving the Catholic Tradition at its most intense, a victory over devouring time and a means of communication between Catholics separated by centuries of change.

Implicit in Congar's judgement is the idea that the Deposit of the Faith is not handed on solely through the teaching of doctrine, but rather that participation in the liturgy is itself an education in the Tradition of the Faith. This is not the same as claiming that the liturgy exists for educational reasons. Joseph Ratzinger/Benedict XVI, Aidan Nichols and other lesser names have argued that the liturgy exists to worship God and that if we promote it for any other reason we are promoting sub-theological ideologies.[3] The most common of these are

---

[2] Yves Congar, *Tradition and Traditions* (London: Burns & Oates, 1966), p. 429.

[3] Joseph Cardinal Ratzinger, *A New Song for the Lord* (New York: Herder, 1996), especially chapter 4; Aidan Nichols, *Beyond the Blue Glass: Catholic Essays on Faith and Culture*, vol. 1 (London: Saint Austin Press, 2002), pp. 171–91, and "Re-enchanting the Liturgy" in: *Christendom Awake* (Edinburgh: T. & T. Clark, 1999), pp. 21–41. At 31 Nichols remarked: "The de-railing of the essentially theocentric act of worship onto sidelines of social edification and group-psychological therapy was not an intended result of the liturgical reform carried out by the papacy of Paul VI Montini in the name of the Second Vatican Council, during the twenty years or so that followed that Council's close. It is hardly necessary to add that neither was that 'entertainment ethos' in church which—for sometimes excusable though ill-judged motives of 'attracting youth'—in many parishes and chaplaincies has come to reign."

liturgy as group therapy and liturgy as community building. Nonetheless, it is possible to hold that while the sole purpose of liturgy is worship, there are obvious spiritual and educational side effects and it is in this context that the *usus antiquior* can play an important role in the New Evangelisation.

Specifically the *usus antiquior* may be an antidote to the ruthless attacks on memory and tradition and high culture, typical of the culture of modernity, and it may also satisfy the desire of the post-modern generations to be embedded within a coherent, non-fragmented tradition that is open to the transcendent. In arguing this one need not take the view that the *usus antiquior* should be the only form of the Roman rite. Again, as Pope Benedict XVI and Fr. Aidan Nichols have argued, the older and the newer forms of the Roman rite should be *mutually* enriching. So, more precisely the question becomes: what is it about the *usus antiquior* that might enrich the modern form of the Roman rite and operate as an antidote to secularism?

At least one place to begin any such analysis is the study of the mediation of meaning in the culture of modernity.

The sociological phenomenon of the mediation of meaning through liturgical and other cultural practices rather than through mere words is a central theme of the scholarship of the Catholic philosopher Alasdair MacIntyre.

MacIntyre grew up on a Scottish island where he was immersed in four different cultures—a Gaelic culture, an English culture, the culture of Wee-Frees Protestantism (which is a particular sub-species of Calvinism) and the Catholic culture of the Scottish crofters. This immersion in four different cultures gave him an insight into how meaning is transferred through practices as well as through words, and how different words and concepts are difficult to transpose from one linguistic register to another.

MacIntyre is a proponent of what linguistic philosophers call 'the expressivist theory of language' according to which words cannot be understood apart from their cultural context. This differs from the instrumentalist theory of language, according to which words can be transposed from one language into another, without reference to the cultural context.

One way to understand the expressivist theory is to consider the Australian folk-song "Waltzing Matilda". This song is the unofficial national anthem of Australia. It's a song every Australian knows but it cannot be the official national anthem because it is about a sheep thief who commits suicide. The first verse of the song is: "Once a jolly swagman, camped by a billabong, under the shade of a coolabah tree, and he sang as he watched and waited while his billy boiled, you'll come a Waltzing Matilda with me." Although all of these words are English words one needs to be an Australian to know that they are about a homeless person singing a love song to his sleeping bag which he had affectionately named Matilda. The words swagman, billabong and billy are all Australian English nouns. Tramp, pond and tin can are the closest equivalent in British and American English but they do not carry the same resonance. They lack the capacity to make homesick Australians cry. They engage the intellect only, not the heart as well.

In contrast to the expressivist theory of language which holds that the meaning of words is intrinsically linked to their place within a culture, the instrumental theory of language requires no particular cultural formation. A classic example of the instrumental theory of language may be found in the opening address of St. John XXIII to the Second Vatican Council. In a now famous paragraph, John XXIII remarked:

> What is needed is that this certain and immutable doctrine, to which the faithful owe obedience, be studied afresh and reformulated in contemporary terms. For this deposit of faith, or truths which are contained in our time-honored teaching is one thing; the manner in which these truths are set forth (with their meaning preserved intact) is something else.[4]

Although this statement referred only to doctrines, it was quickly appropriated to other areas of the Church's life, especially the liturgical. Four years after this opening address, on 22 October, 1966, the Jesuit publication *America* carried an article by someone called Gareth Edwards who claimed that the Second Vatican Council's *Constitution on the Liturgy* implied that "the nearer the language of the Eucharist can be brought to a modern vernacular, the greater the resulting benefit" and further "that our democratic society and informal habits make it necessary for us to think of God as a friend, not as a king". It would be a great pity, wrote Edwards, "if, at the moment when it bursts out

---

[4] John XXIII, "Opening Address to the Second Vatican Council," 11 October 1962.

of the strait jacket of Latin, it allowed itself to be enclosed in that of Anglican English. . . . If the Church wants to sweep the world like the Beatles, it must use language as contemporary as theirs".[5]

Three years later in 1969 Ven. Paul VI said something very similar in an address which may be described as his eulogy for the *usus antiquior*. He described Latin as the language of the angels and he acknowledged that in adopting the new Missal Catholics were parting with the speech of Christian centuries and becoming like "profane intruders in the literary precincts of sacred utterance".[6] Nonetheless he concluded that: 'Participation by the people is worth more—particularly by modern people, so fond of plain language which is easily understood and converted into everyday speech'.[7]

Whatever may have been the truth of the sociological judgment that modern people are fond of plain language, linguistic philosophers now agree that there is no such thing as easy transpositions from one language to another. Today the instrumental theory of language is regarded as naïve. Francis Cardinal George raised this issue in his doctoral thesis on the treatment of culture in the thought of St. John Paul II. As a matter of principle Cardinal George stated:

> Cultural forms and linguistic expressions are, in fact, not distinguished from the thoughts and message they carry as accidents are distinguished from substance in classical philosophy. A change in form inevitably entails also some change in content. A change in words changes in some fashion the way we think.[8]

Referring to John XXIII's Opening Address, Cardinal George concluded:

> Implicitly, Pope John's statement seems to support an instrumental view of language, regarding language as the means whereby a speaker gives expression to thoughts which exist independently of language, through employment of words whose meanings are the object of explicit agreement between prospective speakers. By contrast,

---

[5] Gareth Edwards, "Modern English in the Mass", in: *America*, 22 October 1966, (pp. 483–86), pp. 483, 484.

[6] Paul VI, General Audience Address, 26 November 1969.

[7] Ibid.

[8] Francis Cardinal George, *Inculturation and Ecclesial Communion: Culture and Church in the Teaching of Pope John Paul II* (Rome: Urbaniana University Press, 1990), p. 47.

an expressivist view of language holds that thought has no determinate content until it is expressed in a shared language.[9]

Today an example of the majority academic opinion can be found in the following statement of Susanna Rizzo of Campion College, Sydney. In an endorsement of the judgment of the German literary critic and philosopher, Walter Benjamin, Rizzo argues that:

> Translation is not just the *transference* of meaning from one language into another, but a more complex process, one in which the translator is never in control as it is language itself with its structures and genealogies of sense which inescapably orients meaning. . . . This is because words in a sentence are not just *tesserae* of a mosaic but parts of a living organism: words are in a structural relation with other words within a lexicon and each word has a history, a genealogy and a generative force (*vis verbi*).[10]

In summary, one might argue that the relationship between words and cultures is symbiotic and that the project of transposing the language of Christian centuries into plain language vernacular, however well intended, had baleful effects for the transmission of the Tradition.

One needs to be immersed within a culture to understand the meaning of words, their genealogy and generative force, and conversely, the use of words also helps to build a culture. One example of this is the way that Shakespearian English and the English translation of the King James Bible helped to build an educated English culture. The project of the 1960s generation was one of transposing a high sacral language into the vernacular of a low mundane culture, with the result that something sacred became more mundane, and when the sacred becomes mundane, it becomes boring. No one speaks of the plain language vernacular translations contributing anything to the cultures into which they were received, the way that the translations of the King James Bible contributed to the development of the English language and the English imagination. No one says of these translations that "they live on the ear, like music that can never be forgotten" a statement made of

---

[9] Ibid., 88.

[10] Susanna Rizzo, "Born in Translation: the Discursive Origins of the West", Lecture delivered at Campion College, Centre for the Study of the Western Tradition, Friday, 7 December 2012.

the King James Bible by the nineteenth-century English convert Frederick William Faber, author of the hymn *Faith of our Fathers*. The pastoral leaders who decided that modern men needed a liturgy in plain language, indeed according to some, in language as contemporary as the Beatles, were making decisions without any reference to linguistic philosophy or the philosophy of culture. They were not *au fait* with the science of the transmission of meaning through cultural practices.

A more sociologically acute judgement may be found in the following paragraph penned by Henri de Lubac S.J. in 1969:

> The message of Christ, contained in the gospel and formulated by the Church in the first centuries, split wide open certain categories, both profane and religious, of pagan antiquity (and in certain cases, even Jewish antiquity). It will always be thus, and so it must be today as well, with reference to any other language—despite any tendency to some sort of pure "contemporaneity". Eternally new, this message remains eternally "scandalous" and "wonderful". For this reason it is an illusion that makes people demand, for instance, a Eucharistic prayer expressed solely in the language of "current" or "everyday life" using only "familiar concepts".[11]

The alternative to the correlation to modernity of pastoral strategies is the idea that it is the liturgical language of Christian centuries that should be penetrating contemporary cultures, not the idioms and practices of contemporary cultures penetrating the Church's liturgy. As Matthias Joseph Scheeben expressed the principle more broadly: "Christianity bears within itself an essential determination to bring to particular cultures its religious ideas and principles in order, through its divine energy, to change them, to penetrate, transform, ennoble and raise them from the natural sphere".[12]

Similarly, Jean Borella has argued that a sense of the supernatural is a sense of a higher nature or a sense that the possibilities of existence do not limit themselves to what we ordinarily experience. Accordingly, in

---

[11] Henri de Lubac, *The Christian Faith: An Essay on the Structure of the Apostles' Creed* (San Francisco: Ignatius Press, 1986), p. 289, n. 88.

[12] Matthias Joseph Scheeben, "*Das allgemeine Concilium und die Wissenschaft*" in: *Das ökumenische Konzil*, vol. 1, 1870: pp. 100ff., cited in Thomas F. O'Meara, *Church and Culture: German Catholic Theology 1860–1914* (South Bend, Ind.: University of Notre Dame Press, 1991), p. 58.

order for this sense to be awakened in people, they need to have an experience of forms which by themselves refer to *nothing of the mundane*: "While elements of the physical world are always involved—otherwise no experience of it would be possible—they are set aside from the natural order to which they originally belonged and consecrated in order to render present realities of another order".[13] As Louis Dupré argues "the purpose of a ritual act is not to repeat the ordinary action which it symbolizes, but to bestow meaning upon it in a higher perspective".[14]

In wrapping the Faith in the forms of speech of the contemporary culture and generally correlating the liturgy to the norms of the mass culture, the 1960s generation of pastoral strategists unwittingly fostered a crisis in liturgical theology and practice. They de-railed the transmission of the Tradition as the precise meaning of the sacral language was occluded in lowest common denominator translations, they dismantled a high Catholic culture by removing its cornerstone and they left subsequent generations of Catholics in a state of cultural poverty, confusion and boredom.

In a recent blog, a student who was struggling to understand James Joyce's *Ulysses* wrote:

> There's Latin on the first page. It was one of those times I wish I had had a classical education, and I could translate any Latin I encountered without even thinking about it and read on. Instead I came screeching to a halt. Fortunately, Google came to the rescue, *Introibo ad altare Dei* means "I go to the altar of God".[15]

When a Catholic student reading James Joyce has to use Google to find that the phrase *Introibo ad altare Dei* means "I will go to the Altar of God", this is, as the French say of Eurodisney, evidence of a cultural Chernobyl.

A Catholic who is ignorant of a form of the Mass which was the carrier of a high Catholic culture throughout the "Christian centuries" is like a student who majors in English literature but is unfamiliar with Shakespeare or a student who majors in German and has never heard of

---

[13] Jean Borella, *The Sense of the Supernatural* (Edinburgh: T. & T. Clark, 1998), p. 59.

[14] Louis Dupré, *Symbols of the Sacred* (Grand Rapids, Mich.: Eerdmans, 2000), p. 13.

[15] http://greatulyssestalesof.blogspot.com.au/2006/08/introibo-ad-altare-dei-3-of-783.html

Goethe. There is absolutely nothing about the Catholic Faith that says that philistinism is a virtue. The dark ages were dark because hordes of barbarians remained unbaptised, uncatechised and largely illiterate. But the great achievement of Christian civilisation was that the barbarian hordes were eventually baptised, catechised, taught to read and write and to participate in a liturgical high culture. As the philosopher Roger Scruton expressed the idea:

> The high culture of Europe acquired the universality of the Church which had engendered it. At the same time the core experience of membership survived, to be constantly represented in the Mass—the "communion" with God which is also an enactment of community. It is in this experience that our common culture renewed itself, and the art of our culture bears witness to it, either by honouring or defiling the thought of God's Incarnation. The high culture of Europe has therefore begun to assume a vast importance. It is our last glimpse of the sacred, the last memorial to an experience without which our free and easy manners will bring us face to face with Nothing. It stands as a bulwark between us and the uninterpreted world.[16]

At the height of the enthusiasm for liturgical change in the 1960s there was a general anti-European spirit animating the international intellectual elite. An ostensibly Christian civilisation had been responsible for two world wars, genocide and a sometimes rapacious colonialism. Given these historical facts the so-called third world looked morally superior. However these wars and the genocide and the economic exploitation of colonised peoples were driven by ideological forces which were alien to Christianity. Nationalism is linked to an idolatry of the state which is something that Christian civilisation sought to overcome and the genocide of the Nazis was justified by reference to neo-pagan myths which were explicitly hostile to Christianity. That such forces could take root in Christian cultural soil is however an indictment on European Christian civilisation. Something had to have been terribly wrong for this to happen.

An analysis of these pathologies is beyond the scope of this paper, but it may be argued that in the midst of so much Christian decadence and neo-pagan violence, the *usus antiquior* was the one thing that could

---

[16] Roger Scruton, *The Philosopher on Dover Beach* (Manchester: Carcanet, 1990), p. 123.

bring the warring European tribes together. A very poignant theatrical presentation of this fact can be seen in the movie *Joyeux Noel*, based on the true story of soldiers from hostile armies abandoning their trenches on Christmas Eve and gathering together to participate in the Mass. In 1914 the one thing that could actually triumph over Bismarckian nationalism was the Mass said in a language which was the common heritage of all the nations involved, thereby transcending the national and linguistic divisions.

It is noteworthy that one of the leading princes of the Church who has emphasised the value of a specifically liturgical language that has the capacity to transcend national divisions is Cardinal Arinze. He could probably do so without the fear of being accused of Eurocentrism, since he is a Nigerian who converted to Catholicism from a tribal religion.

It is not surprising therefore that in her seminal work, *After Writing: On the Liturgical Consummation of Philosophy*, the Anglican scholar Catherine Pickstock defended the superiority of the *usus antiquior* over the Missal of 1970 by placing the issue within the context of a general critique of the culture of modernity.

Specifically Pickstock argued that those who presided over the 1960s liturgical changes were correct to acknowledge a link between the form of the Mass and the cultural matrix from which the form and gestures of the liturgy are derived. However she suggested that they erred to the extent that they concluded that because there was a close nexus between culture and liturgy in the medieval period this meant that 'modern man' should have a Mass which incorporates elements from *his* contemporary culture. For liturgical action to be authentic, Pickstock argued that it must share Christ's own time-transcending and time-transforming character. Unlike the culture of Christendom however, the culture of modernity lacks time-transcendent properties. Indeed it is now an academic cliché to say that its most striking hallmark is its neurotic obsession with the present moment. It is also disenchanted and hostile to tradition. In 1970 the Belgian literary critic, Paul de Man, observed that "Modernity exists in the form of a desire to wipe out whatever came earlier in the hope of reaching at last a point that could be called a pure present, a point of origin that marks a new departure." He argued that the "combined interplay of a deliberate forgetting with an action that is also a new origin, reaches its most powerful expression in the idea of modernity."[17]

Pickstock concurs with de Man's judgment but adds her own assessment that modernity "has produced a parody of the liturgical, a sort of anti-liturgical liturgy that confirms the dominance of politics and art without liturgy."[18] In reaching this conclusion she drew on material in Paul Connerton's *How Societies Remember.* Connerton argued that:

> The temporality of the market and of the commodities that circulate through it generates an experience of time as quantitative and as flowing in a single direction, an experience in which each moment is different from the other by virtue of coming next, situated in a chronological succession of old and new, earlier and later. The temporality of the market thus denies the possibility that there might exist qualitatively different times, a profane time and a sacred time, neither of which is reducible to the other.[19]

Similarly in his *Worship as Revelation* Laurence Paul Hemming drew a link between the mechanical character of our contemporary commodity-driven culture and contemporary attitudes towards worship:

> Our current age sees everything as an object of manufacture, as something which can be got hold of and improved, or altered, to produce *better* or *more effective* outcomes. This is our present fate, especially in the West, to understand all things in this way—and it is inevitable that we should transfer even to our sacred worship the same outlook.[20]

In an interview with Jeffrey Tucker from the journal *Sacred Music* Pickstock also argued that the post-Conciliar liturgists "misinterpreted the many oral features of the text [of the Rite of Antique Usage] (such as repetitions) as grandiose rhetorical additions, or even as messy nuisances" and "failed to see them as part of an overall apophatic theology

---

[17] Paul de Man, "Literary History and Literary Modernity", in: *Daedalus*, vol. 99 (1970) (pp. 384–404), p. 388.

[18] Catherine Pickstock, "Liturgy and Modernity", in: *Telos*, vol. 113 (Fall, 1998), (pp. 19–40), p. 19.

[19] Paul Connerton, *How Societies Remember* (Cambridge University Press, 1989), p. 64.

[20] Laurence Paul Hemming, *Worship as a Revelation* (London: Continuum, 2008), p. 10.

thoroughly medieval in character."[21] They replaced the poetic repetitions with asyndetic or list-like syntax which "encourages the sense that the reality they describe comprises atemporal changeless units of simplified matter."[22] She added that "such forms of language are useful to politicians and bureaucracies, and it is no accident that political speeches and other jargon make frequent use of these characteristically 'modern' parts of speech", "though the hidden assumptions of these language-forms are wholly hostile to liturgical purpose."[23]

In contrast she noted that the pre-1970 Roman rite deployed a polyphonic texture of voices and poetic positions:

> Its constant play of differences modulate through narrative, dialogue, antiphon, monologue, apostrophe, doxology, oration, invocation, citation, supplementation, and entreaty. This manifold genre disarms in advance any assumption of an authoritarian or strategic voice of command, for as we have seen, even God Himself, whose Word is the optimum fiat which gives rise to our very being, speaks in many guises.[24]

Pickstock concluded that the form of the Missal of 1970 was modern in the sense of rationalistic and mechanical: "They ironed-out the liturgical stammer and constant re-beginning; they simplified the narrative and generic structure of the liturgy in conformity with recognisably secular structures and rendered simple, constant and self-present the identity of the worshipper."[25]

The summary indictment of the Pickstock critique is that to the degree that the forms of speech and structure of the Missal of 1970 affirmed certain secularising moves within the culture of modernity, they undermined the human person's quest for self-transcendence through worship.[26] One might say that the harder the liturgists tried to be relevant to the culture of modernity, the less relevant they were to the

---

[21] Catherine Pickstock, "More than Immanent" in: *Sacred Music*, vol. 134 (4), (Winter, 2007) (pp. 63–72), p. 64.

[22] Ibid., p. 63.

[23] Ibid., p. 63.

[24] Pickstock, *After Writing*, p. 213.

[25] Ibid., p. 176.

[26] I also make use of Pickstock's critique in: Tracey Rowland, "Liturgical Hermeneutics in the Thought of Joseph Ratzinger" in: Craig Hovey and Cyrus P. Olsen, eds., *The Hermeneutics of Tradition* (Eugene, Ore.: Cascade Books, 2014).

promotion of a specifically Catholic culture and the transmission of the Catholic Tradition. As Aidan Nichols remarked:

> To hand down authentic Tradition while manifesting insouciance towards the forms in which Tradition is embodied (the immemorial rites and customs that compose Catholic Christianity's received culture) has been, in recent decades, the somewhat contradictory policy of numerous representatives, some highly placed, of the Latin Church.[27]

In his many publications on liturgical subjects, Joseph Ratzinger/ Benedict XVI made it clear that he understood this problem. He compared the pastoral strategy of bringing God down to the level of the people with the Hebrew's worship of the golden calf and he described this practice as nothing less than a form of apostasy.[28] He also observed that people who prefer the *usus antiquior* had been treated like lepers and he sought to address their grief in his Motu Proprio *Summorum Pontificum* of July 7, 2007.[29] During his pontificate a new English translation of the post-conciliar missal was also promulgated with reference to principles set out in the Congregation for Divine Worship's 2001 instruction *Liturgiam Authenticam* on the right implementation of *Sacrosanctum Concilium*. Paragraphs 20 and 27 of that document pick up on some of the criticisms which have been made by Pickstock and others.

More recently, in an address delivered to the Plenary Assembly of the Pontifical Council for Culture of February 7, 2013, Pope Benedict remarked that "we cannot . . . content ourselves with reading the cultural youth phenomena according to the established paradigms, which by now have become commonplaces, or analyse them with methods that are no longer useful, starting from out-dated and inadequate cultural categories". He did not offer any specific examples of these outdated and inadequate cultural categories but in the territory of liturgical theology one often finds that Catholic leaders are embarrassingly behind the times in the sense of being stuck in the 1960s and 1970s mind-set and even distressingly ignorant of contemporary scholarship in the fields of the philosophy and sociology of culture. Often this is

---

[27] Nichols, *Christendom Awake*, p. 59.

[28] Cf. Joseph Ratzinger, *The Spirit of the Liturgy* (San Francisco: Ignatius Press, 2000), p. 22.

[29] See also: Joseph Ratzinger, *God and the World: A Conversation with Peter Seewald* (San Francisco: Ignatius Press, 2002), p. 416.

because these subjects do not form part of the seminary curriculum and thus priests are only familiar with them if they happen to have had a strong humanities education before undertaking their studies for the priesthood. It would be a major advance if those responsible for liturgical decisions could at least get the message that modernity has not been fashionable since the 1960s. 1968 is usually taken as the watershed year when the culture of the Western world began a serious post-modern turn.[30] In 1990 the American writer Walker Percy had this to say about modernity:

> The old modern age has ended. We live in a post-modern as well as a post-Christian age. . . . It is post-Christian in the sense that people no longer understand themselves, as they understood themselves for some fifteen hundred years, as ensouled creatures under God, born to trouble, and whose salvation depends upon the entrance of God into history as Jesus Christ.
>
> It is post-modern because the Age of Enlightenment with its vision of man as a rational creature, naturally good and part of the cosmos, which itself is understandable by natural science—this age has also ended. It ended with the catastrophes of the twentieth century.
>
> The present age is demented. It is possessed by a sense of dislocation, a loss of personal identity, an alternating sentimentality and rage which, in an individual patient, could be characterized as dementia.[31]

This is merely one of the scores of descriptions of the end of modernity and pathologies of post-modernity which can be found in literature. In so many contemporary novels a common theme is the loss of self-identity. People are always trying to find themselves. And yet, notwithstanding the volumes that have been written on this subject, liturgists still talk about how young people like things to be modern and informal, when they are actually crying out for something that is eternal, transcendent and beautiful.

An excellent analysis of the role of solemn, transcendent liturgy in the recovery of the lost ego may be found in Peter A. Kwasniewski's

---

[30] See, for example, the seminal work of Jean-François Lyotard, *The Postmodern Condition* (Manchester University Press, 1984).

[31] Walker Percy, *Signposts in a Strange Land* (London: Picador, 2000), p. 309. The author is indebted to Edward Short for this reference.

essay, "Aquinas on Eucharistic Ecstasy: From Self-Alienation to Gift of Self".[32] Kwasniewski concluded:

> The avoidance of merely "common" modes of speaking and acting in the liturgy is *by design*, to help us break free from a profane mindset, to awaken us to the Presence that surrounds and penetrates the entire world. Hence, making the liturgy more common, more everyday, casual, horizontal, is self-defeating; it obliterates the liturgical as such, exactly where it cultivates the holy, the divine, the Other who is more myself than I. Ironically, too, a liturgy stripped of its mysterious *alteritas* would be reduced to the place of last among worldly equals, for it cannot compete against the secular on the latter's terms. And so, it would be effectively sterilized in its power to fecundate outlying culture, prevented from casting an otherworldly light on the potential sacredness of the ordinary elements of this-worldly life.[33]

If modernity is a culture of forced forgetting, post-modernity is more of a fragmented culture of retrieval, the mood is less self-assured and more melancholy and nostalgic. Post-modernity, unlike modernity, is not hostile to tradition. In reacting against the rationalism of the eighteenth century, post-modernity is open to tradition and memory but hostile to the idea that the human intellect can be used to discern that one tradition is to be preferred over another.

Most post-moderns tend to think that one's preference of tradition is likely to stem from one's aesthetic sensibility rather than from intellectual judgement. Leaving aside the obvious Catholic criticism that this is anti-intellectual and fosters a culture of relativism, it is nonetheless true that post-moderns are fascinated by traditions, and Catholics, who have grown up in a post-modern culture, like other members of their generation, are keenly interested in the roots of their tradition, especially the cultural practices. Elements of Catholic culture which were suppressed by the 1960s generation of pastoral leaders are being rediscovered by younger Catholics who treat them like treasures found in their grandmother's attic. The popularity of the Camino pilgrimage is just one of the many examples of this social phenomenon, but so too is the interest in Latin hymns and solemn ceremonies. Catholics of

---

[32] Peter A. Kwasniewski, "Aquinas on Eucharistic Ecstasy: From Self-Alienation to Gift of Self" in: *Nova et Vetera*, vol. 6 (1) 2008, pp. 157–204.

[33] Ibid., pp. 196–97.

the post-modern generations want to know how the Church looked,
how the Faith was practiced, when there was a coherent Catholic culture.

It is also commonplace for younger priests and lay Catholics to say
that they obtained a deeper understanding of the Mass through having to learn to say or follow the *usus antiquior*.[34] Participation in this
form of the Rite does require a deeper intellectual engagement if one
is not to get completely lost, but this form is also more contemplative,
allowing lay people to get lost in a good sense, in the sense of lost in
the contemplation of the divine mysteries, especially during the silent
Canon. There is a paradox in the fact that the language of the Missal of
1970 has been described as rationalistic—in the sense of paring down
the poetry of the *usus antiquior* to the barest doctrinal propositions expressed in the plainest vernacular—and yet it is the far less rationalistic and more poetic language of the *usus antiquior* which more readily
engages the intellect by first stimulating the imagination.

A further significant factor about the *usus antiquior* as a vehicle for
evangelisation is that it gives great emphasis to the moment of consecration and the sacrificial nature of that moment. The whole structure
of the *usus antiquior* engenders a deeper sense that there is a sacrifice,
not a mere meal. This is partly due to the fact that the language of sac-

---

[34] In *Christendom Awake*, published in 1999 and thus some eight years before Pope
Benedict's Apostolic Letter *Summorum Pontificum*, Aidan Nichols wrote: "the survival of
the old Roman rite, whose continuing legitimacy as an expression of the worship and
spirituality of Western Catholics was acknowledged by Pope John Paul II in his Letter
Ecclesia Dei Adflicta of 2 July 1988, should be welcomed as providing a valuable reference
point, a norm of Tradition, which can guide priests and people in their own use of the
reformed Missal of Paul VI. The continuance of this rite, if it is sufficiently visible and
widespread, will impede liturgical revisionism that would push the Mass of Paul VI, as
further 'adapted' or in its de facto celebration, towards a deepening discontinuity with
the historic Roman liturgy. For this purpose, the Pope, as Western patriarch, and in that
capacity the responsible guardian of the treasures of the Western liturgy, should require
bishops to allow the faithful ready access to this ritual embodiment of the Mass—on the
prior condition, however, that the rite itself be (soberly!) modified to take account of
the *manifest* (not conjectural) wishes of the Conciliar Fathers of Vatican II—expansion
of Lectionary resources, some use of the vernacular (and hence, logically, much use of
Latin!), a litanic prayer of intercession, priestly concelebration and lay reception of the
chalice where appropriate. The result should be to draw the historic Roman rite closer
to the rites of the East rather than, has too often been the case in recent years, toward
Geneva'', p. 34.

rifice is most pronounced in the Roman Canon, or what is called Eucharistic Prayer I, which is not commonly used in the modern form of Mass because of its length. The so-called Second Eucharistic Prayer is used much more often and it contains much less sacrificial language.[35] Also absent from the second, third and fourth Eucharistic Prayers are the long lists of saints recounted in the Roman Canon, all bar one of whom were martyrs. As one scrolls down the honour board—Ignatius, Alexander, Marcellinus, Peter, Felicity, Perpetua, Agatha, Lucy, Agnes, Cecilia and Anastasia—one's mind tends to be transported to the Rome of the anti-Christian emperors and is brought to reflect on the blood of the martyrs, the cost of discipleship and the centrality of self-sacrificial love in the Christian narrative. There is really no greater antidote to secularism and what Pope Francis calls a "self-referential Christianity" than a reflection on martyrdom and the sacrifice of Calvary and the Roman Canon sustains a person's reflection on this reality.

One of the most beautiful descriptions of what happens at the moment of consecration can be found in paragraph 11 of Benedict XVI's Apostolic Exhortation, *Sacramentum Caritatis*, in which the Pope was keen to make the point that while the Last Supper occurred during the Passover, the institution of the Eucharist was something radically new. It was not simply a meal that Jesus shared with His friends. As St. Thomas Aquinas poetically expressed the idea: *Et antiquum documentum / Novo cedat ritui*. Pope Benedict wrote:

> Jesus thus brings his own radical *novum* to the ancient Hebrew sacrificial meal. For us Christians, that meal no longer need be repeated. As the Church Fathers rightly say, *figura transit in veritatem*: the

---

[35] For an excellent analysis of the provenance of the Second Eucharistic Prayer see: Matthieu Smyth, "The Anaphora of the So-called *Apostolic Tradition* and the Roman Eucharistic Prayer" in: *Usus Antiquior*, vol. 1, n. 1 (January, 2010), pp. 5–25. The author is indebted to Owen Vyner, a graduate of the Liturgical Institute of Mundelein Seminary, for this reference. Smyth concluded that "the Eucharistic Prayer II of the Roman Missal of 1970 was destined to be adapted to the taste of the day." As a consequence, "the great Christological praise was relieved of all concepts that the experts of the *Consilium* judged unsuitable for the contemporary mentality: *exeunt* 'the last times', the 'inseparable Word', the manifestation of the Son, the victory over Hell, the deliverance from suffering, the institution of the 'rule' of the sacrifice . . . the enlightenment of the just." Smyth described the Eucharistic Prayer II as "an original composition, painted in bright colours" which faithfully reflects "the concerns of a small group of liturgists in the middle of the twentieth century."

foreshadowing has given way to the truth itself. The ancient rite has been brought to fulfilment and definitively surpassed by the loving gift of the incarnate Son of God. . . . "More than just statically receiving the incarnate *Logos*, we enter into the very dynamic of his self-giving." Jesus "draws us into himself." The substantial conversion of bread and wine into his body and blood introduces within creation the principle of a radical change, a sort of "nuclear fission," . . . which penetrates to the heart of all being, a change meant to set off a process which transforms reality, a process leading ultimately to the transfiguration of the entire world, to the point where God will be all in all. (*Sacramentum Caritatis*, 11)

A neo-pagan sociologist observing the recitation of the Second Eucharistic Prayer out of intellectual curiosity might just miss the point of the whole exercise, but the same person following the Roman Canon could be left in no doubt that the moment of consecration is really the centre point or fulcrum of the whole ritual.

In an era when globalisation is regarded as a good thing and governments spend millions of dollars of tax-payers' money to keep alive the memory of minority languages and pre-modern cultural practices, the Church should not be ashamed of her own cultural treasures. It is good that Roman rite Catholics around the globe can attend a Latin Mass and feel at home regardless of where they are on the planet. It is also good that at world youth day events, a million Catholic youth can stand together and chant the *Credo* in their most common liturgical language. Latin transcends national boundaries. If one opposes its use on the political ground that it is derived from the culture of ancient Rome and Rome is in Europe and the adoption of elements of European culture is now a politically incorrect practice, then one might as well become a Congregationalist since so many of the cultural dimensions of the Faith can be traced back to Europe.

In summary, the *usus antiquior* is something much more valuable than a bone to be thrown to disgruntled Catholics as a pacifier. It has a part to play in the work of the new evangelisation since it so effectively resists secularism and satisfies the post-modern hunger for coherent order, beauty and an experience of self-transcendence.

Nonetheless, this conclusion comes with are a few caveats which have nothing to do with the Rite as such but with the culture of some of the communities who worship according to it. Some proponents

of the *usus antiquior* can be their own worst enemies and foster practices and attitudes which deter so-called 'mainstream' Catholics from
attending Masses according to this form.

First, there is the problem of aestheticism or the attitude of beauty
for the sake of beauty. The term aestheticism was used by then-Cardinal
Ratzinger in his book *A New Song for the Lord: Faith in Christ and Liturgy
Today*. In this work he included a whole section on the problems of
"aestheticism as an end in itself." He saw this mentality as a pathology
operating at one polar end of a spectrum with the pathology of "pastoral pragmatism as an end in itself" operating at the other extreme
end.[36] The pastoral pragmatists are those who do not care about beauty
at all but only about what is popular.

In some communities the problem of aestheticism manifests itself
in the habit of holding a post-mortem on the liturgy the moment it is
over, taking it apart like a performance at the opera. While one should
certainly aim to make every Mass as beautiful and perfect as possible
the 'after Mass post-mortem report' should not be released beyond the
sacristy, at least not to the families with young children who want this
time of the week to be a peaceful time, not a time when their children
over-hear adults being uncharitable about one another's performance
and bickering over the relative merits of different styles of vestments
and music. Spikey aesthetes for whom no "performance" is ever good
enough, are something of a deterrent to parents with children who
want their children's experience of parish life to be an experience of
embodied charity.

Second, some Catholics who attend the *usus antiquior* are not only opposed to the post-conciliar form of the Mass but they are also opposed
to contemporary modes of dress. While there is no doubt that some
contemporary fashion styles are highly problematic from the point of
view of feminine dignity, one can dress modestly without turning out
like an escapee from an Amish farm. If mainstream Catholics who attend *usus antiquior* Masses feel as though they have landed on the set
of a movie based in a nineteenth-century American mid-west or Penn-
sylvanian town, populated by Protestants who have a problem with

---

[36] Cardinal Ratzinger appears to have adopted this terminology from the work of
Calvin M. Johansson, especially Johansson's *Music and Ministry: A Biblical Counterpoint*
(Peabody, Mass.: Hendrickson Publishers, 1984).

modern forms of transport, they are not likely to come back. People like to feel as though they are mixing in a milieu where people are socially well-adjusted. They don't want to join a community which feels like a ghetto.[37]

Theologically the problem here seems to be that members of traditionalist movements often lack a hermeneutical framework for cultural analysis. In the absence of any framework for judging what elements of contemporary culture to accept and which to reject, they often end up adopting practices from a past 'golden' era. This is sometimes connected to the problem of an understanding of tradition which is static rather than organic.[38] Those who operate by a static notion of tradition sometimes end up in a similar position to the non-conformist Protestant groups, especially those with a Brethren-style background. While both Catholics and Brethren-style Protestants have good reasons to be critical of elements of the culture of modernity, the theological explanations and remedies *are different*. This is especially so in the territory of attitudes towards women and the human body. While there have been Puritan-style movements within the Catholic Tradition (one thinks

---

[37] This issue is not a problem in every community which worships according to the *usus antiquior*. It appears to arise in social contexts where those who take a stance of outright opposition to all things modern are either tacitly or consciously influenced by the anti-modern movements within Protestantism. When this paper was first delivered at *Sacra Liturgia 2013*, which took place on the premises of the Opus Dei University in Rome the author was accused by 'rad trad' bloggers and Twitterers of being a member of Opus Dei, whose secret purpose was to undermine support for the *usus antiquior*. The author is not, and never has been, a member of Opus Dei or any other new ecclesial movement. The author is a member of the Sovereign Military Order of St. John of Jerusalem, Rhodes, and Malta, a very old ecclesial movement, formally founded in 1113 to serve the sick and the poor and to defend the Faith from all forms of aggression. The author is also a member of the Equestrian Order of the Holy Sepulchre devoted to the support of Christians and Sacred Sites in the Holy Land. The author's objective was to defend the legacy of Pope Benedict XVI which calls for the mutual enrichment of the newer and older forms of the Roman rite and which interprets the documents of the Second Vatican Council through a hermeneutic of reform.

[38] For an overview of different interpretations of the concept of 'Tradition' from the Council of Trent through to the contemporary period, see the author's chapter on "Tradition" in the *Oxford Handbook of Theology and Modern European Thought*, edited by Nicholas Adams, George Pattison and Graham Ward (Oxford University Press, 2013): 277–301. Joseph Ratzinger/Benedict XVI's view of Tradition is clearly influenced by the theology of Bl. John Henry Newman and the nineteenth-century Tübingen school. It is not a static account of Tradition.

of medieval Albigensians and more contemporary Jansenists), these movements have never been part of mainstream orthodox Catholicism, however problematic they may have become.[39]

John Paul II offered an intellectual antidote to Jansenism with his *Catechesis on Human Love*, and in works such as his Apostolic Letter *Mulieris Dignitatem* he rejected the idea of the ontological inferiority or second-class status of women. The magisterially endorsed Catholic theology holds that men and women share a common humanity. John Paul II taught that both ways of being human belong to the image of God—and that within this shared humanity, there are differences which reflect unique 'missions' or callings in the imaging of God's inner life and His work in the economy of salvation. These differences take place 'inside' the absolute equality of a common humanity—a humanity which John Paul II thought of in Trinitarian terms—and cannot for this reason be thought of according to categories of rank or value.[40] The 'difference', then, between masculinity and femininity does not translate to ontological superiority or inferiority.

Thirdly, and most importantly, so called ordinary Catholics do not want to feel as though in attending the *usus antiquior* they are making a political stand against the Second Vatican Council. They are clearly taking a stand against the *zeitgeist* of the 1960s. They may or may not be survivors of Beatlemania. However they probably are people who can distinguish between the genuine Conciliar reforms and what Cardinal Ratzinger called the "rationalistic relativism, confusing claptrap and pastoral infantilism"[41] which was marketed as the fruit of the Council in the 1960s and 70s. Some members of traditionalist communities however continue to believe that the 'claptrap' *was the Council* and they hold onto that belief with great tenacity. Their world-view

---

[39] Anna Krohn, the Convenor of the Australian Catholic women's network called *Anima*, has suggested that a distinction can be drawn between a 'smart retro look' which can even be avant-garde, and the Amish puritan style based on Protestant critiques of the culture of modernity and Protestant scriptural exegesis and its corresponding anthropology.

[40] The author is indebted to Dr. Conor Sweeney for insights into this issue. Sweeney's STL thesis, defended at the Pontifical Lateran University in 2010, was on the subject of headship in the theology of John Paul II and Hans Urs von Balthasar.

[41] Joseph Cardinal Ratzinger with Vittorio Messori, *The Ratzinger Report: An Exclusive Interview on the State of the Church* (San Francisco: Ignatius Press, 1985), p. 121. See also: Joseph Cardinal Ratzinger, *A New Song for the Lord: Faith in Christ and Liturgy Today* (New York: Crossroad, 1997), pp. 32, 112ff.

would be shattered if they suddenly realised that for twenty-seven years John Paul II and Joseph Ratzinger laboured to present Catholics with a wholly different understanding of the Council and that their interpretation was carried over into the eight-year pontificate of Ratzinger/Benedict and now the pontificate of Francis. Ironically, it sometimes looks as though there are two groups in the Church for whom it is forever 1968—supporters of Hans Küng and disciples of Marcel Lefebvre. The rest of the Church, however, has moved on.

To make a sociological observation, the more attendance at *usus antiquior* Masses is de-politicised within the Church, the more popular such Masses are likely to be with mainstream people who long for an escape from the mundane and ordinary and for a foretaste of eternity and some moments of silent contemplation. Conversely, the more such mainstream people feel as though a whole raft of theo-political baggage comes with attendance at the *usus antiquior* Masses (primarily opposition to the Council and the genuine theological renewal it has engendered), the less likely they are to avail themselves of the opportunity to attend them.[42] In short, liturgical issues need to be disentangled from the interpretation of Vatican II issues.

While there is an overlap between the two in so far as some theologians did indeed interpret the Council as a call to accommodate or correlate the Church's culture, especially her liturgical culture, to the

---

[42] An excellent exposition of this problem may be found in the essay by Thaddeus Kozinski entitled "The Gnostic Traditionalist" in: *New Oxford Review*, vol. 74 (June, 2007), pp. 24–33. Kozinski draws a distinction between an ideological and neurotic consciousness of being a "traditionalist" as distinct from being just an ordinary Catholic who loves the Tridentine Mass and the Tradition of the Catholic Church. A subsidiary issue is what John Paul II identified in paragraph 4 of his Apostolic Letter *Ecclesia Dei Adflicta* (2 July 1988), as "an incomplete and contradictory notion of Tradition." Referring to the unlawful episcopal consecrations by Archbishop Marcel Lefebvre, John Paul II wrote: "The *root* of this schismatic act can be discerned in an incomplete and contradictory notion of Tradition. Incomplete, because it does not take sufficiently into account the *living* character of Tradition, which, as the Second Vatican Council clearly taught, 'comes from the apostles and progresses in the Church with the help of the Holy Spirit.' There is a growth in insight into the realities and words that are being passed on. This comes about in various ways. It comes through the contemplation and study of believers who ponder these things in their hearts. It comes from the intimate sense of spiritual realities which they experience. And it comes from the preaching of those who have received, along with their right of succession in the episcopate, the sure charism of truth."

culture of modernity, there is an alternative reading of the Council, what might be called the Trinitarian Christocentric reading. This gave rise to a great renewal of the Church's theological anthropology and moral and sacramental theology which can be tracked through the encyclicals of John Paul II and Benedict XVI. If one reads the documents of the Council with a Christocentric accent as both of our immediately previous Popes have recommended, instead of a Kantian accent or a Lockean accent or even worse, a Schillebeeckxian accent, the Traditionalist communities might find that their spirituality is enriched and that it is now safe to come out of the ghetto.

In 1997 the British Anglican theologian, John Milbank, wrote a book called *The Word made Strange*. A central message of the work is that in order to evangelise post-modern people one has to make the Christian narrative, so to speak, strange. It has to appear to be something starkly different from the secular culture post-modern people imbibe which is a culture parasitic upon the Christian tradition but completely decadent. To put this proposition another way, secularism is another name for decadent Christianity, or Christianity gone to seed.

Secularism holds itself out as being able to produce the fruits of a Christian culture without any actual belief in Christ, the Trinity, grace, sacraments or the Church. The more ecclesial leaders try to accommodate ecclesial practices to this culture the more boring and irrelevant the Church appears. Milbank argues that while the Incarnate Word is always mediated by human discourses, He registers His presence by transfiguring these discourses down to their very roots.

In the midst of the decadence and fragmentation and philistinism, the *usus antiquior* can continue to be, in the words of Congar, a holy ark, a victory over devouring time, and a means of communication between Catholics separated by centuries of change. It can help to 'make the Word strange'—to present Christian revelation as something radically different, fresh and liberating. For this to happen it does however need to be disentangled from a ghetto culture either ignorant or suspicious of the genuine reforms of the Council.

6

Liturgy: the Foundation of
Monastic and Religious Life

Dom Jean-Charles Nault O.S.B.

Abbot of Saint-Wandrille, France

Monastic Life, Liturgical Life
and the New Evangelization

It might well seem presumptuous, even rash, for me to talk about liturgy and religious life in the context of the New Evangelization. As a monk and the abbot of a Benedictine monastery in the tradition of Solesmes, I seek, along with my brethren, to lead the monastic life according to the Rule of St. Benedict, within our monastic enclosure, and without any direct apostolic activities in the outside world. The liturgy founds and structures our life. However, the way we celebrate the liturgy reflects our life's specific character. We spend about four hours a day in liturgical prayer, with full ceremonial, sober solemnity, mainly in Latin and in Gregorian chant. Nonetheless, the monastic character of our prayer may turn out to address the issues that are at the heart of this conference.

I was asked to discuss "liturgy and religious life", not "liturgy and monastic life". Even so, I have decided to examine "liturgy and monastic life", and for two reasons. First, it is always best to speak about something you know! Second, I am certain that this decision will not take us off topic. This is because monastic life constitutes the "stem cells" as it were of religious life as it was led during the first millennium of the Church's history, before the differentiations it underwent in the course of the second. What is true of monastic life must be true of other forms of religious life, with the adjustments needed to take into account the charisms of different religious families. Furthermore, monastic life, like religious life, is rooted in baptismal life; that is to say it is rooted in and is an unfolding of the Paschal Mystery. As a result, although monastic life may seem to be far removed from, even opposed to, Christian life as it is lived in the world, I hope to show that it can be a source of inspiration for all the baptised, whatever their state of life in the Church.

The specific character of monastic life can also help us to see an important truth. Its sole purpose is to seek God in the solitude of the desert. It does not attempt to influence the outside world, to convert unbelievers, or to teach the ignorant. In point of fact, it has done and it continues to do all this, but almost as if by accident. Monastic life exercises an influence on the world inasmuch as it remains faithful to its Rule: seeking God in prayer and in silence, away from the world. Our monastic *ars celebrandi* reflects what we might call a contemplative and theocentric orientation, for it is when liturgy seeks nothing but the greater glory of God that it is able to sanctify mankind.[1]

Should not this characteristic of monastic liturgy belong to the whole Church? This approach would help defend against the constantly recurring temptation to instrumentalize the Sacred Liturgy, the temptation to make it serve a cause external to the liturgy itself. Contemporary culture is constantly concerned with practical efficiency. This concern has its place, of course, but efficiency should never be the benchmark for discernment in the life of the Church, whether in matters of pastoral care or of liturgy. Christ leads us in the way of the cross, but for the world, the cross is a way of inefficiency! The "use" of the liturgy is the service of Almighty God, and not, at least not directly, mission, evangelization, or catechesis. This does not mean that these matters are totally foreign to the liturgy, but that they need to be put in perspective.

I would like to consider this in three parts. In the first, I will explain what I mean by "instrumentalization" of the liturgy. The starting point will be an article written by Fr. Louis Bouyer over half a century ago, but that has lost none of its relevance. In the second part, I will show

---

[1] See *Sacrosanctum Concilium*, 33, which shows how the liturgy's capacity to teach is dependent on its principal characteristic of "the worship of the divine majesty".

how the Paschal Mystery is at the heart of the New Evangelization, because it is at the heart of the liturgy. In the third, somewhat longer, part, I will compare the current Rite of Christian Initiation of Adults with the rites and stages of the reception of a newcomer into monastic life, which I hope will permit a better understanding of Christian initiation. Along the way, this study will uncover a number of challenges for evangelization in the contemporary world. I hope to show that the Church's liturgy possesses the resources needed to confront them.

Liturgy: a "Means" of Reconquest in a Dechristianized World?

The temptation to instrumentalize liturgy is not new. The *Centre de pastorale liturgique* of Paris was founded seventy years ago, in May 1943, and held its first Congress in a monastery of Benedictine nuns in the Paris suburb of Vanves in January 1944. *La France, pays de mission?*, [France, A Mission Territory?],[2] a book by Frs. Godin and Daniel calling for a "reconquest" of the dechristianized "working-class masses", had just been published. Among those present at the Vanves meeting were figures like Fr. Georges Michonneau, of the Congregation of the *Fils de la Charité*, whose parish in Colombes was already an important centre for apostolate among the working classes.[3] It was in this context that the Oratorian Fr. Louis Bouyer, who was also at the Congress, put pen to paper to lay out "Some Remarks about the Meaning and the Rôle of the Liturgy".[4] In his paper, Fr. Bouyer warns against the temptation to use liturgy as a means to an end:

> We do not pretend that the liturgy is a panacea. There are vital tasks in the life of the Church that it cannot undertake. In particular, let us consider the problem of *apostolate among the working classes and liturgy.* We are convinced that these two realities are deeply related, and it is

---

[2] Henri Godin and Yvan Daniel, *La France, pays de mission?* (Lyon: Éditions de l'Abeille, 1943).

[3] Cf. Georges Michonneau, *Paroisses, communautés missionnaires* (Paris: Cerf, 1945).

[4] Louis Bouyer, "Après les journées de Vanves. Quelques mises au point sur le sens et le rôle de la liturgie", in *Études de pastorale liturgique*, "Lex Orandi" 1 (Paris: Cerf, 1944), pp. 379–89 and in Gaston Morin, *Pour un mouvement liturgique pastoral*, "La Clarté-Dieu", 13 (Lyon: Éditions de l'Abeille, 1944), pp. 59–75.

our burning desire that by shedding light upon this relationship it may be fully exploited. But we are just as much if not more persuaded that it makes no sense to identify one with the other. This is the question: is the liturgy a *direct* means (and I underline direct) of working-class apostolate? Certainly not.[5]

He goes on to affirm that this kind of instrumentalization would be the ruin of liturgy, and also of the apostolate, what we now usually call evangelization:

It would be a total delusion to see in this [the apostolate of the working classes] the usefulness of the liturgy and the interest of a liturgical movement, even of the most pastoral of liturgical movements. Contact with reality would bring us rapidly to this conclusion: liturgy is not made for winning over crowds.[6]

What is the "usefulness of the liturgy"? Liturgy is certainly "useful", but this "usefulness" does not consist of being part of some sort of "apostolic tool-kit." It is the very nature of liturgy that is at stake here:

Liturgy is not and cannot be a direct means of mass apostolate, because the apostolate, *by its nature*, is for those who are outside the Church, whereas liturgy, *by its nature*, is for those who are within the Church. I hasten to repeat that liturgy can and should have an effect on the apostolate (and the apostolate should have an effect on liturgy); but liturgy is no more a direct means of apostolate than are dogma, asceticism, or mysticism. Liturgy is a thing of the Sanctuary, in the most literal sense. It is not at all made for the non-Christian to be converted. It is not directly made for (and in its principal elements is no more made for) the catechumen. It is made for the faithful.[7]

Fr. Bouyer shows that the liturgy is above all a means of living the Christian life; it is "the source of the collective interior life of the Church", and, at the same time, it is "the active realization of this life."[8] Vatican II says exactly the same thing when it affirms that the liturgy is the "source and summit" of the life of the Church.[9] This is

---

[5] Bouyer, "Après les journées de Vanves", p. 380.
[6] Ibid.
[7] Ibid., pp. 380–81.
[8] Ibid., p. 389.
[9] *Sacrosanctum Concilium*, 10.

why it cannot be reduced to being an instrument for something else, which would end up being a *bricolage* of catechesis, formation for Christian living and ritual. This does not mean that Fr. Bouyer thinks liturgy and evangelization should be separated. Rather, he aims at fostering a correct "use" of the liturgy, a "use" which can be a source of great pastoral and evangelical fruitfulness. For it is only when we let liturgy be "useless" that it reveals the extent of its "usefulness" in the life of the Church and the New Evangelization![10]

Liturgy and the Paschal Mystery

Liturgy can be the "source" and "active realization" of "the collective interior life of the Church" because it is the actualization of the Paschal Mystery, a mystery that Vatican II presents thus:

> For His [Christ's] humanity, united with the person of the Word, was the instrument of our salvation. . . . The wonderful works of God among the people of the Old Testament were but a prelude to the work of Christ the Lord in redeeming mankind and giving perfect glory to God. He achieved His task principally by the paschal mystery of His blessed passion, resurrection from the dead, and the glorious ascension, whereby "dying, he destroyed our death and, rising, he restored our life."[11] For it was from the side of Christ as He slept the sleep of death upon the cross that there came forth "the wondrous sacrament of the whole Church." (*Sacrosanctum Concilium*, 5)[12]

The Paschal Mystery is also a cultic mystery, a *sacramentum*, because it is through worship that the baptised participate in this mystery as a life-giving reality. Hence according to the first oration *ad libitum* for the Vigil of Pentecost,[13] God willed that the *paschale sacramentum* be contained in the "mystery of fifty days": *Deus, qui paschale sacramentum*

---

[10] For this paragraph, see: Patrick Prétot, "L'initiation chrétienne comme célébration de la foi", in: *La Maison-Dieu*, 273, 2013/1, pp. 48–52.

[11] *Missale Romanum* 1970, Easter preface I.

[12] Ibid., first oration *ad libitum* after the seventh lesson of the Easter Vigil; this oration followed the second prophecy before Pius XII's reform of Holy Week, and was restored in 1970. Hence it is not in the 1962 *Missal*.

[13] *Missale Romanum* 1970. This oration is not in the 1570/1962 *Missale Romanum*; it is drawn from the *Gelasian Sacramentary*, where it is the first oration of the Mass of

quinquaginta dierum voluisti mysterio contineri. It was Dom Odo Casel of Maria Laach who re-injected the concept of "Paschal Mystery" into sacramental and liturgical theology. In a Pauline perspective, he defined "mystery" as ". . . a deed of God's, the execution of an everlasting plan of his through an act which proceeds from his eternity, realized in time and the world, and returning once more to him its goal in eternity."[14]

It is the historical mystery of Christ in His Incarnation, culminating in His death and resurrection, and encompassing His ascension, His glorification, the sending of the Holy Spirit and His coming again in glory.[15]

Christianity is thus a "mystery", and worship is the ritual expression of this "mystery". Dom Casel's fundamental intuition was received in the French-speaking world largely thanks to one of Fr. Bouyer's most important books, "The Paschal Mystery".[16] This is how Fr. Bouyer defines his title:

> All Christian worship is but a continuous celebration of Easter. . . . The Christian religion is not simply a doctrine: it is a fact, an action, and an action, not of the past, but of the present, where the past is recovered and the future draws near. Thus it embodies a mystery of faith, for it declares to us that each day makes our own the action that Another accomplished long ago, the fruits of which we shall see only later in ourselves. . . . Here is the meaning of the pasch: it points out to us that the Christian in the Church must die with Christ in order to rise with Him. And not only does it point out . . . but it accomplishes the very thing it points out.[17]

For Fr. Bouyer, the "Paschal Mystery" means that Christians imitate Christ by becoming sacramentally conformed to Him;[18] we receive the

---

Pentecost Sunday: *Liber sacramentorum romanæ æclesiæ ordinis anni circuli (Sacramentarium gelasianum)*, ed. Leo Cunibert Mohlberg, "Rerum ecclesiasticarum documenta, Series maior, Fontes" 4 (Rome: Herder, 1960), 637, p. 100.

[14] Odo Casel, *The Mystery of Christian Worship and Other Writings* (Westminster, Md.: Newman Press, 1962), p. 9; the author makes reference to Eph 1:9ff. and 3:2ff., Col 1:25–27 and 2:2, 1 Cor 2:7, Rom 16:25ff.

[15] Cf. *Sacrosanctum Concilium*, 5, quoted above, n. 10.

[16] Louis Bouyer, *The Paschal Mystery. Meditations on the Last Three Days of Holy Week* (Chicago: Henry Regnery Company, 1950).

[17] Ibid., pp. xiii–xiv.

[18] Ibid., p. xvi.

gift of participation in the Paschal Mystery though the Church's liturgical and sacramental celebration.

Fr. Bouyer's book may well have struck a chord because the expression "Paschal Mystery" was already present in the Roman liturgy according to the 1570 Missal as it was universally celebrated at the time. These ancient examples of the expression, which date at least from the historic sacramentaries of the early Middle Ages, can be divided into three categories:[19]

A first category consists of the expressions *sacramentum paschale* and *sacramenta paschalia*, in reference to the sacraments that are celebrated at Easter and that confer paschal grace. This meaning is found in the oration that followed the reading of the sacrifice of Abraham (third prophecy, Gen 22:1–19) at the Easter Vigil before Pius XII's reform:

> *Deus, fidelium Pater summe, qui in toto orbe terrarum, promissionis tuæ filios diffusa adoptionis gratia multiplicas: et per paschale sacramentum, Abraham puerum tuum universarum, sicut iurasti, gentium efficis patrem; da populis tuis digne ad gratiam tuæ vocationis introire.*[20]

Here, *paschale sacramentum* principally indicates baptism, in which God's promise to Abraham that he would become the father of all nations is fulfilled.

In the postcommunion of the Easter Vigil, Easter Sunday, and Easter Monday, the Church asks God to make *concordes* those whom he has filled with the *sacramenta paschalia*:

> *Spiritum nobis, Domine, tuæ caritatis infunde: ut, quos sacramentis paschalibus satiasti, tua facias pietate concordes.*[21]

These *sacramenta* are both Baptism—the *Exsultet* evokes the baptisms conferred during this night with the expression *concordiam parat*—and the Eucharist, the sacrament of unity.

On Easter Tuesday, the postcommunion asks that the *paschalis perceptio sacramenti* continue their work in our souls:

---

[19] We here follow the analysis of Aimon-Marie Roguet, "Qu'est-ce que le mystère pascal?", in: *La Maison-Dieu* 67, 1961/3, pp. 6–8.

[20] In the *Missale Romanum* 1970 this oration, slightly recast, once again follows the same pericope, the second reading in this edition of the *Missal*.

[21] In the *Missale Romanum* 1970 this postcommunion is only used at the Easter Vigil.

Concede, quæsumus, omnipotens Deus: ut paschalis perceptio sacramenti, *continua in nostris mentibus perseveret.*[22]

These *sacramenta* are doubtless the three sacraments of Christian initiation together; the prayer asks God to cause them to bear fruit throughout the Christian lives of those who have received them.

A second category of texts seems to have a broader meaning; while retaining a link with Christian initiation, these texts refer to a context of liturgical celebration, bringing them closer to the meaning of the title of Fr. Bouyer's book. The oration that followed the vision of the valley of bones (seventh prophecy, Ezek 37:1–14) before Pius XII's reform seems to consider the celebration of the Easter Vigil, and in particular its Liturgy of the Word, as a ritual unity:

Deus, qui nos ad celebrandum paschale sacramentum, utriusque testamenti paginis instruis: da nobis intelligere misericordiam tuam; ut ex perceptione præsentium munerum, firma sit expectatio futurorum.[23]

The prayer affirms that through the pages of both Testaments, God teaches us to celebrate the *paschale sacramentum.*

It is rather more difficult to understand the secret of Saturday *in albis*:

Concede, quæsumus, Domine, semper nos per hæc mysteria paschalia gratulari: ut continua nostræ reparationis operatio, perpetuæ nobis fiat causa lætitiæ.[24]

It contains a request that by the *mysteria paschalia*, we may always give thanks (*gratulari*), in order that "the continual work of our restoration may be for us a cause of perpetual joy". This text seems to present the Paschal Mystery as a sacramental reality; from an objective point of view it ceaselessly continues the work of salvation, and from a subjective point of view it allows us to give never-ending thanks for this

---

[22] In the *Missale Romanum* 1970 it is the postcommunion for the Octave of Easter.

[23] In the *Missale Romanum* 1970 this oration follows (*ad libitum*) the seventh and last reading from the Old Testament, Ezek 36:16–28 (a new heart and a new spirit); it thus acts as a transition towards the epistle and gospel.

[24] This oration remains the *super oblata* of Saturday in the Octave of Easter in the *Missale Romanum* 1970; it is also the *super oblata* of the Tuesdays following the second, fourth, and sixth Sundays of Easter, and of the Wednesdays after the third and fifth Sundays of Easter.

work. The current French liturgical translation certainly understands it thus:

> [the] mysteries of Easter . . . continue your work of redemption in us, may they be for us an unfailing wellspring of joy.[25]

The oration for Easter Friday affirms with even greater force the relationship between Christ's work in history, the sacraments, and Christian living:

> *Omnipotens sempiterne Deus, qui* paschale sacramentum *in reconciliationis humanæ fœdere contulisti: da mentibus nostris; ut quod professione celebramus, imitemur effectu.*[26]

"God . . . who instituted the *paschale sacramentum* as the covenant for the reconciliation of humanity, grant to our souls that we may imitate by our acts what we celebrate by our profession." The *paschale sacramentum* places us in communion with the mystery of the cross, because it coincides with the new covenant that Christians celebrate in the sacraments, and that they are called to imitate in their daily lives.

The final text in this category is not to be found in the 1570 *Missale*; it was introduced by the 1956 *Ordo Hebdomadæ Sanctæ* as third oration after communion on Good Friday:

> *Reminiscere miserationum tuarum, Domine, et famulos tuos æterna protectione sanctifica, pro quibus Christus, Filius tuus, per suum cruorem instituit* paschale mysterium.[27]

This prayer asks God to sanctify by His protection His servants "for whom Christ [His] Son instituted the *mysterium paschale* through His Blood." Here, the Paschal Mystery is presented as the means that Christ instituted to allow those who seek to serve Him to enter into communion with the mystery of the cross.

---

[25] "[Les] mystères de Pâques . . . continuent en nous ton œuvre de rédemption, qu'ils nous soient une source intarissable de joie."

[26] This oration is to be found at the same place in the *Missale Romanum* 1970.

[27] This oration is from the Gelasian Sacramentary: *Liber sacramentorum romanæ æclesiæ ordinis anni circuli,* 334, p. 54, where it is the first oration of Monday in Holy Week. It is included in this study because it is in both the 1962 and the 1970 editions of the *Missale Romanum,* and so forms part of the *lex orandi* of the Roman Church by this double title. In the *Missale Romanum* 1970 it is the first of two orations *ad libitum* of the Celebration of the Passion on Good Friday.

The third category consists of just one oration, occurring three times in the 1570 *Missale*, as secret of the Masses of the Easter Vigil, Easter Sunday, and Easter Monday:

> *Suscipe, quæsumus, Domine, preces populi tui, cum oblationibus hostiarum:*
> *ut* paschalibus initiata mysteriis, *ad æternitatis nobis medelam, te operante,*
> *proficiant.*[28]

This text was long misunderstood; in Latin-French hand missals, it was often translated as commending to God "the sacrificial offerings consecrated by the paschal mystery."[29] But in a precise scholarly study published in 1947, Dom Botte showed that the neuter *initiata* could not possibly modify *oblationes hostiarum*, and that the verb *initiare* had never meant "consecrate".[30] Moreover, in liturgical Latin, the neuter plural usually has an indeterminate meaning. This prayer should thus be understood as a request to God to let us benefit from what we celebrate, "inaugurated by the paschal mysteries". Here, the expression "paschal mysteries" refers to these same mysteries in their very origin: the passion and glorification of Christ in their historical and theological unity.

Clearly, the expression "Paschal Mystery" was not completely unknown in the mid-twentieth century. However, it went virtually unperceived, and this apparent novelty gave its rediscovery a greater impact. As we have just seen, "Paschal Mystery" covers a range of meaning reflecting the riches of the reality that the expression seeks to convey. These riches, and this apparent novelty, also attracted incomprehension and resistance. The theology of the Paschal Mystery is emphatically not some sort of covert attempt to abandon the cross so as to focus on the resurrection alone.

On the contrary, this approach seeks to articulate these two poles of Christ's saving action within its unity. The resurrection is not the happy ending tacked onto a fairy tale. Unlike the tendency to separate passion and resurrection, the Paschal Mystery underlines that Christ's death and His risen life form a dynamic unity. Nonetheless, the Paschal

---

[28] In the *Missale Romanum* 1970 it is the *super oblata* of the Easter Vigil.

[29] "Offrandes sacrificielles consacrées par le mystère pascal."

[30] Bernard Botte, "Paschalibus initiata mysteriis", in: *Ephemerides Liturgicæ*, 61/1, 1947, pp. 77–87.

Mystery changes the emphasis in soteriological discourse.[31] When we speak of "redemption", and there is nothing wrong with doing so, we run the risk of focusing almost exclusively on the passion, and treating the resurrection as an afterthought. But when we talk about Easter, we think immediately of the risen Christ, risen, of course, *from the dead.* The resurrection no longer looks like an epilogue, but is revealed as the goal that sums up the whole mystery of salvation. The cross is not abandoned, for the risen Christ continues to bear His glorious wounds; the Lamb once slain of the Apocalypse proclaims to all eternity that He has emerged victorious from the fight. Far from being the end of the tale, the resurrection is the beginning of the story, because it is the beginning of the new creation. This new creation is not an inaccessible golden age projected into the future; no, it has already begun, and we have become part of it through baptism. Here and now, our task is to participate in this new creation, as we ask in the collect of Easter Friday to express "by our whole life this mystery that we have celebrated in faith."

Christian Initiation and Monastic Life

This brief presentation of liturgical texts that refer to the Paschal Mystery has brought us to Christian initiation. It could seem far-fetched to compare the Rite of Christian Initiation of Adults as restored after Vatican II and monastic life, but in fact the two are intimately related. We will consider this relationship in three stages: the baptismal character of monastic profession; the analogy between the stages by which a novice becomes part of a monastic community and the structure of the Rite of Christian Initiation of Adults; and finally, the importance of perseverance and dependence in the living out of baptism.

---

[31] For a Thomist perspective on the causality of Christ's resurrection in the work of our salvation, see: Jean-Pierre Torrell, *Saint Thomas d'Aquin, maître spirituel,* "Vestigia— Pensée antique et médiévale" 19, 3rd ed. (Paris: Cerf, and Fribourg: Academic Press— Éditions Saint-Paul, 2008), pp. 176–77, with reference to *Summa Theologiæ,* III, q. 56, a. 1.

The Baptismal Character of Monastic Life

In the Constitution on the Church *Lumen Gentium*, the Fathers of Vatican II chose to deal with religious life in chapter 6, hence after the chapters on the laity (ch. 4) and on the universal call to holiness (ch. 5), but before the chapter on the eschatological character of the Church (ch. 7). In chapter 6, *Lumen Gentium* explains that religious life, "though it is not the hierarchical structure of the Church, nevertheless, undeniably belongs to its life and holiness" (n. 44). In the decree on religious life *Perfectæ Caritatis*, the Council points out that it "constitutes a special consecration, which is deeply rooted in that of baptism and expresses it more fully" (n. 5). The Fathers thus wished to present religious life as a call addressed to all Christians to live out their baptism. This baptismal understanding of religious life is founded on an ancient tradition that considers monastic profession to be a "second baptism." This expression, "second baptism", is inadequate, because there is only one baptism; however, it leads us to the relationship between baptism and monastic profession.

An important example of this tradition is a book written in the early twentieth century by a monk of Maredsous, Dom Germain Morin: *L'idéal monastique et la vie chrétienne des premiers siècles*,[32] (The Monastic Ideal and the Christian Life in the Earliest Centuries), a book that is still read in the novitiates of our Congregation. At the end of the chapter entitled "Baptism and Profession", Dom Morin, writing for a primarily monastic readership, declares:

> Let us thank God for having placed at the disposition of those whom he loves this second baptism, that restores and grants to so many of the faithful the sublime prerogatives of the first. Both of them are our joy and our glory; they both merit our eternal gratitude, just as the Church reminds us each year in the introit of Whit Tuesday: *Accipite iucunditatem gloriæ vestræ, gratias agentes Deo, qui vos ad cælestia regna vocavit.*[33]

---

[32] Germain Morin, *L'idéal monastique et la vie chrétienne des premiers siècles*, "Pax" 3 (Paris: Lethielleux-Desclée de Brouwer, 1921).

[33] Ibid., p. 65.

But what does this expression, "second baptism", really mean? It should first be noted that when monastic life first appears in the history of the Church, it was considered to be equivalent to martyrdom. Without attempting to reply to the question "Did monasticism appear as a reaction against an alleged watering-down of Christian living following the end of persecution, or on the contrary did it emerge because of an increase in fervour brought about by the example and the grace of the martyrs' sufferings?", we can still affirm:

> Monastic life thus bears the aspect of a substitute for martyrdom, in a *passio* renewed every day, in the same way that the early Church considered martyrdom to be a substitute for baptism. For the Christians of the first centuries spoke of martyrdom as a "baptism of blood", and it was accepted that it could remit sins and open the gates of the Kingdom.[34]

As well, the oldest forms of monastic profession consisted of a simple change of clothing, sometimes accompanied by tonsure. But fairly soon, these rites took on two correlative additions: a *renunciation*: of the world, of parents, and of self;[35] followed by an *engagement* to follow Christ, through a promise to embrace the community's way of life.[36] There is a clear parallel with the rites of baptism: a triple renunciation, followed by an engagement to follow Christ within the community.[37]

We can take the analogy further. The monk who makes profession, like the catechumen who receives baptism, enters a process of death and resurrection with Christ, as shown by a study carried out by Edward Malone, who compared the commentaries by Cyril of Jerusalem in the *Mystagogical Catecheses* and the profession rite in the *Armenian Ritual* of Jerusalem.[38] This comparison shows clearly that the ritual of monastic

---

[34] Christophe Vuillaume, "La profession monastique, un second baptême?" in: *Collectanea Cisterciensia* 53, 1991 (pp. 275–92), p. 277; cf. Justin, *Dialogue with Trypho* 46,7 and Origen, *Exhortation to Martyrdom* 30 & 39.

[35] *Vita Pachomii* 24 and Cassian, *Conferences* 3:5, where the renunciations are of the world, passions and earthly things.

[36] Basil, *Great Rule* 14 and *Letter* 99; *Vita Pachomii* 24, *First Greek Life*, in: A.-J. Festugière, *Moines d'Orient*, t. 4/2 (Paris: Cerf, 1965), p. 170.

[37] For this paragraph, see: Pierre Raffin, *Les rituels orientaux de la profession monastique*, "Spiritualité orientale" 4 (Bellefontaine, 1968), pp. 11–15.

[38] Edward E. Malone; Anton Mayer, Johannes Quasten, Burkhard Neunheuser, eds., "Martyrdom and Monastic Profession as a Second Baptism" in: *Vom christlichen*

profession derives from the ritual of baptism: the symbolism of place, the rites and the texts—in particular the renunciation of Satan and the clothing with a new garment—as well as the *Ritual*'s affirmation:

> And then he shall raise up the novice that is prostrate before him, whose raiment is to be sealed, and that as it were with a second sealing over again. For the grace of the Holy Spirit manifestly descends upon the new offering, as on the day of illumination.[39]

The rites that derive from the description that St. Benedict gives in his *Rule*,[40] consist of a renunciation, an engagement, a rite that expresses mystical death, and the giving of the insignia of new life. After the renunciation, in reply to the questions posed by the abbot, the novice "makes profession", just as catechumens profess their faith in the rite of baptism. The novice adheres to Christ by a threefold engagement, whose elements correspond to the triple renunciation: *stabilitas*, which joins him to the community over and above any other family tie or worldly affection; *conversatio morum*, which obliges him to renounce the spirit of the world in ever greater depth; and *obœdientia*, by which he submits in everything to another's judgement and renounces his self-will. He makes this engagement by writing and signing a *petitio*, which he then lays on the altar where Mass will be celebrated. This triple engagement then receives a ritual expression by means of a twofold action that corresponds to baptismal immersion: the new brother sings the triple *Suscipe*, whilst prostrating himself three times, thus evoking the idea of death and burial, followed by resurrection.

By participating in the Paschal Mystery, we die in order to receive a renewed and transformed life. This divine life, received in the waters of baptism, must then continue to bear fruit throughout earthly life. This is why the neophytes, who have become "other Christs", receive a white garment, confirmation with holy Chrism, the peace

---

Mysterium. Gesammelte Arbeiten zum Gedächtnis von Odo Casel (Dusseldorf: Patmos, 1951), (pp. 115–34), pp. 125–26.

[39] *Rituale Armenorum. Being the Administration of the Sacraments and the Breviary Rites of the Armenian Church Together with the Greek Rites of Baptism and Epiphany Edited from the Oldest Manuscripts*, ed. Frederick C. Conybeare and Arthur John Maclean (Oxford: Clarendon Press, 1905), 24, "Initiation of Monks", p. 148. Here "illumination" clearly means baptism. Cf. Auguste Piédagnel, ed., Pierre Paris, trans., Cyrille de Jérusalem, *Catéchèses mystagogiques*, "Sources chrétiennes" 126 (Paris: Cerf, 1966), ch. 1–2, pp. 82–119.

[40] Cf. *The Rule of St. Benedict*, ch. 58.

of Christ, and a lighted candle, before participating in the Eucharist for the first time. If all the preceding rites are only carried out once, this last rite, the Eucharist, must be repeated, repeated every Sunday (and even more often, but the fundamental rhythm of the Eucharist is weekly). For it is the Eucharist that is the sacrament of Christian perseverance, and it is every Sunday that the baptised have the right, which is also a duty, to come to the assembly, to the *ekklesia*, as well as the duty so to live each day that they may receive the Body and Blood of Christ in Holy Communion every Sunday and thus bear the fruits of holiness in the Church. Regular participation in Sunday Mass is the first and fundamental testimony of our Faith.[41]

The same elements can be found in the rite of monastic profession, albeit in a more austere guise. The brother receives a new garment, the cowl. The anointing with the oil of gladness is symbolized by the fraternal kiss that the new monk receives from his brethren as they sing Psalms 47 and 132, the second of which evokes the precious oil running down Aaron's beard and robes. Monastic profession, like baptism, is oriented toward the Eucharist. The renunciations of monastic life receive their meaning and their efficacy only inasmuch as they are rooted in Christ's paschal sacrifice. Like all the baptised, monks need to receive their weekly, indeed daily, food from this unfailing source of indestructible life. Each reception of Holy Communion is a stage of our divinisation, that transformation of our entire being into Him who is received sacramentally by the power and the action of the Holy Spirit.

The text of the *Armenian Ritual* of Jerusalem quoted above also refers to this eucharistic transformation that the Christian undergoes in receiving communion, a transformation which is the reason for the

---

[41] "One who has received baptism is already a member of God's family by this baptism, but he is not qualified to take part in the Church's public worship as long as he has not been confirmed by the Spirit and thus given the capacity to give an ecclesial testimony to the faith received . . . one who has been confirmed receives a gift of the Holy Spirit that strengthens him in the action of manifesting his identity as a child of God, called to testify to the divine life of his baptism by his conscious and active participation as a member of the Church, God's family. This approach makes the *ecclesial* dimension of the grace of confirmation stand out . . . participation in the Eucharist is a confirmed Christian's first and greatest act of testimony." Marc Cardinal Ouellet, "La confirmation, sacrement de l'initiation chrétienne" in: *Communio* (French edition) 38/2, 2013 (pp. 116–25), p. 121.

substantial transformation of the bread and wine into the Body and Blood of Christ: "the grace of the Holy Spirit descends manifestly upon this new offering."[42] This is certainly an allusion to the anaphoral epiclesis; it is important to remember that Cyril of Jerusalem, a contemporary of the rite described in the *Armenian Ritual,* is the first author to present a consecratory epiclesis:

> We beseech God, the lover of humanity, to send the Holy Spirit upon the gifts placed here, to make the bread the body of Christ, and the wine the blood of Christ, because everything that the Holy Spirit touches is sanctified and transformed.[43]

This ritual parallelism is based on a theological truth. Like baptism, monastic profession is an expression of the double movement that St. Paul presents (Rom 6:4–11) as a renunciation of the world and of self (death and burial) that renews our being by the gift of a new creation (resurrection with Christ). Thus, if the expression "second baptism" is to be retained, it must be understood analogically:

> Profession is not made to complete something that would be lacking in the truth or the efficacy of baptism, but simply to accomplish it in one of the states of life to which Christ calls his disciples. By making his engagement in and for the Church, the religious does nothing else but realize in a particular way of life . . . the meaning of his baptism.[44]

The Stages of Incorporation into a Monastic Community

The rite of profession is part of a longer series of rites by which the novice is progressively made part of the community that receives him. Dom Germain Morin presents these rites as a sort of catechumenate, and attempts to establish a correspondence between the stages of the

---

[42] Quoted in Malone, "Martyrdom and Monastic Profession as a Second Baptism", p. 126.

[43] "Nous supplions le Dieu philanthrope d'envoyer l'Esprit Saint sur les dons ici déposés, pour faire le pain corps du Christ, et le vin sang du Christ; car, tout ce que touche l'Esprit Saint, cela devient sanctifié et transformé." Cyril, *Catéchèses mystagogiques,* ch. 5, 7, p. 155; cf. Kent J. Burreson, "The Anaphora of the Mystagogical Catecheses of Cyril of Jerusalem", in: *Essays on Early Eastern Eucharistic Prayers,* ed. Paul F. Bradshaw (Collegeville: Pueblo, 1997), (pp. 131–51), p. 144.

[44] Vuillaume, "La profession monastique, un second baptême?", p. 288.

novitiate and those of the catechumenate.[45] Here again, there is analogy, but not identity, between the two processes. This analogy resides in a common dynamic of conversion, in a journey structured by a number of stages which function in the same manner.

The *Prænotanda* of the Rite of Christian Initiation of Adults describe the catechumenate as a "journey [that] includes not only the periods for making inquiry and for maturing . . . , but also the steps marking the catechumen's progress, as they pass, so to speak, through another doorway or ascent to the next level."[46] Thus a "period of evangelization and precatechumenate" can lead to becoming a catechumen, and the catechumenate leads to election or the enrollment of names by the bishop. This call leads in turn into the time of purification and illumination during Lent, in preparation for the celebration of the paschal sacraments of initiation. This sacramental celebration opens the time of mystagogy, the beginning of the Christian life of the newly baptised, which is itself a time of preparation for the face-to-face meeting with Christ beyond bodily death, in the expectation of the final resurrection. The rites that structure this period are not "certificates" proving that the candidate has succeeded in following the prescribed course. They are something quite different: celebrations by means of which God grants the grace necessary to go forward, a grace that will continue to unfold over time. Not all of these rites are sacraments, but they all participate in one way or another in a certain sacramentality. The image of going up a flight of stairs can illustrate what is going on: as you go up, the support of each step permits you to continue to the next.

The *Prænotanda* give the bishop and those who assist him a number of criteria for discernment concerning the admission of catechumens to the sacraments. These criteria show that this is a journey of conversion: the catechumens should demonstrate evidence of inner conversion and of the practice of charity, possess an appropriate knowledge of the Christian mystery and an enlightened faith, participate in the life of the Christian community whose heart is the liturgical assembly, and manifest an explicit desire to receive the sacraments.[47] These are

---

[45] Morin, *L'idéal monastique et la vie chrétienne des premiers siècles*, pp. 52–54.

[46] *Rite of Christian Initiation of Adults. Study Edition* (Collegeville: Liturgical Press, 1988), n. 6, p. 4; *Ordo Initiationis Christianæ Adultorum* (Rome: Typis Polyglottis Vaticanis, 1972), n. 6, p. 8.

[47] *Ordo Initiationis Christianæ Adultorum*, nn. 23, 134.

exactly the same sorts of criteria that St. Benedict gives the novice master for the discernment of a monastic vocation: "Et sollicitudo sit, si revera Deum quærit, si sollicitus sit ad opus Dei, ad obœdientiam, ad opprobria."[48]

The primary concern here is not to know things—even though, in both cases, there are certainly things to know!—but to show the outward signs that an interior conversion is taking place.

Baptismal Life: Perseverance and Dependence

Conversion takes time. This need for time has a theological foundation which can be summed up in Tertullian's saying: "*fiunt, non nascuntur, christiani.*"[49] The fact that we are not born Christian but that we become Christian has important consequences in the day to day life of the baptised. We need to acquire a Christian way of living, one that is more and more at odds with the way the world lives. This way of living sets us free from the sin of Adam, who wanted to be "like God", to decide for himself what was good and evil: *like* God but *without* God. Adam's sin disfigures humanity in its very being:

> [The] root of human sin is located in the act of knowing good or evil by oneself rather than in dependence on God. . . . The effects of this introduction of disorder attain the "being" of the human creature. Within a biblical perspective, being means situating the self and living in a just relationship with God the Creator.[50]

This is to say Adam sinned by attempting to define good and evil for himself, instead of submitting to God's judgement upon sin, and thus "placing himself in a state of independence from the gift of God."[51] Christ, by accepting to drink of the cup of the passion in filial obedience to the Father's will, destroyed this sin at its root. In the waters of

---

[48] "Let him examine whether the novice truly seeks God, and whether he is zealous for the Work of God, for obedience, and for humiliations." *The Rule of St. Benedict*, ch. 58.

[49] Tertullien, *Apologétique*, 18, 4 (Paris: Les Belles Lettres, 1998), p. 92.

[50] Frédérique Poulet, "Baptism: Renouncing the Knowledge of Evil" in: *Studia Liturgica* 42, 2012/1–2 (pp. 217–30), p. 220.

[51] Ibid., p. 221.

baptism, the baptismal renunciation of sin is endowed with ontological reality, for baptism restores humanity in its being. It does not merely restore us to our original state as created beings, it also raises us to the dignity of sons and daughters in the Son. The oration of Thursday of the fourth week of Easter begins by affirming: "Deus, qui humanam naturam supra primæ originis reparas dignitatem . . .",[52] and that of the fifth Sunday of Easter says that God accords redemption (*redemptio venit*) and adoption (*præstatur adoptio*) to his beloved children (*filios dilectionis tuæ*):[53] by grace, the obedience of the baptised is the obedience of a child of God.

The renunciation of evil that restores and renews the baptised takes place once for all, and in a fundamental renewal of their very being. But this transformation must take flesh in concrete actions, every day, ceaselessly. This can help us to see how the celebration of the sacraments of Christian initiation, like the various stages of the catechumenate, and indeed the rite of monastic profession, far from being a point of arrival, is in fact a point of departure. Unlike the preceding stages, the celebration of the sacraments of initiation is fully sacramental; their celebration contains and grants the grace it signifies, a grace destined to unfold over time. If they are celebrated only once, they are in fact never finished in this life. We become Christians, not just by baptism, but by being inserted into the Paschal Mystery, that is to say the death and resurrection of Christ, through the gift of the Holy Spirit. As long as we remain in this life, we will always need to come together to be fed on God's Word and on the bread and wine transformed by the Holy Spirit into the Body and Blood of Christ, in that communion of the body of Christ that seals our insertion into His Body and founds the Church's unity. Baptism and confirmation are administered once in order to graft us into the Paschal Mystery in the depths of our being, but it remains for this transformation to become a living reality as it bears fruit throughout our Christian life. It is the Eucharist, celebrated from Sunday to Sunday, that allows this transformation to take flesh day by day.

The baptised Christian has renounced evil, yet he remains in conflict with sin. When the monk withdraws to the desert, is not to live a quiet

---

[52] *Missale Romanum* 1970, oration of Thursday after the fourth Sunday of Easter.
[53] *Missale Romanum* 1970, oration of the fifth Sunday of Easter.

life away from the concerns of his fellows in humanity, but rather to confront the devil who shows himself more openly in the wilderness. But all Christians must enter this spiritual combat; as St. Ambrose explained to his neophytes in Milan: *Ubi certamen, ibi corona.*[54] This is why newly professed monks do not leave the novitiate right away, but remain there a while in order to learn how to fight on their own. One of the roles of mystagogy should be formation for spiritual combat. More than a simple explanation of rituals, mystagogy should teach neophytes to live what they have received, how to take up the weapons of spiritual combat. This combat takes place under God's command. We depend on God, not as slaves, but as sons and daughters. The warfare will probably be long, because it only ends with death. Hence one of its principal arms is perseverance.

Formation for perseverance and dependence is certainly a major challenge for the Church today, because perseverance and dependence are seen in a largely negative light by a contemporary society that exalts autonomy and looks for instant satisfaction of its desires. So many of us demand what we want, demand to have it now, and refuse to tolerate delay. But the liturgy teaches us *dependence*, precisely because we receive the liturgy from the Church as a gift. The liturgy also introduces us to *perseverance over time*, because the liturgy takes its time, and opens us to God's own time: eternity.

Conclusion: Receiving the Gift of God

Is not learning dependence through perseverance over time a way of learning to receive grace as a pure gift? Formation with a view to openness to the gift of God is doubtless a third challenge for the Church. Today's world is structured to reason in terms of "rights." Indeed, in French, people often say, "Do I have the right to do such and such?" when in fact what they really mean is, "Am I allowed to do such and such?" But if something is a right, it is also a due, and so it is not a gift.

---

[54] "Where there is contest, there is a crown." Bernard Botte, ed. and trans., Ambrose, *De mysteriis*, 1, 4, "Sources chrétiennes" 25bis (Paris: Cerf, 1980), (cf. 1 Cor 9:24–25), pp. 62–63. The direct object of Ambrose's commentary is the baptismal renunciation, but it is clear that this renunciation opens a struggle that will last throughout life, and will only receive its crown in heaven.

If we forget how to receive a gift, we will no longer know how to say "Thank you", we will no longer be able to give thanks. It seems to me that the inability to ask forgiveness for sin has more to do with an inability to receive a gift as a gift than with a lack of the sense of sin; if the world owes me everything, how can I possibly understand forgiveness? Our society knows perfectly well what sin is, for it promotes transgression in so many domains. In this perspective, we can see how liturgy teaches the real sense of sin, not by instilling unhealthy feelings of guilt, but by opening us to receiving the gift of God, to receiving God's forgiveness with thanksgiving.

Since its beginning, the first Christian Pentecost, the Church has evangelized, following St. Peter: "God has made Him both Lord and Christ, this Jesus whom you crucified" (Acts 2:36).

Ever since, moved by the Holy Spirit, the Church has gone out of the Upper Room to bring the Good News to the ends of the earth. As Pope Francis said while still a cardinal during the General Congregations before the conclave that elected him Pope:

> Evangelizing presupposes a desire in the Church to come out of herself. The Church is called to come out of herself and to go to the peripheries, not only geographically, but also the existential peripheries: the mystery of sin, of pain, of injustice, of ignorance and indifference to religion, of intellectual currents, and of all misery.[55]

The liturgy also invites us to take part in this exodus, but it also teaches us that its movement is twofold. Going out to meet others is one aspect, but there is also the movement that takes us into ourselves, *habitare secum*,[56] as St. Gregory the Great puts it in his *Life* of St. Benedict. For it is the heart of man that has the greatest need of evangelization, for it is there that the "mystery of sin" dwells. The heart awaits freedom from enslavement to the "mystery of sin" through the gift of participation in the Paschal Mystery. This interior evangelization is the foundation of all evangelization.

This brings us to another double movement. The dynamic of the liturgy goes from the exterior to the interior, and leads us to "internalize

---

[55] http://www.news.va/en/news/bergoglios-intervention-a-diagnosis-of-the-problem
[56] Gregory the Great, *Dialogues II*, 3, 5, "Sources chrétiennes" 260 (Paris: Cerf, 1979), p. 142.

the *exteriora*".[57] We do not produce the liturgy's texts, readings, chants, and orations ourselves, and neither do they necessarily relate to our inner state at the moment we pray them. Nonetheless, the Church our mother asks us to make them our own. St. Benedict tells his monks: *sic stemus ad psallendum, ut mens nostra concordet voci nostræ.*[58] This receptive attitude goes beyond the texts. In the liturgy, we have everything to receive; not only the texts, but what the texts signify: grace. This comes to its fullness in the Eucharist, when we receive the Body and Blood of Christ in all their reality under the appearances of bread and wine. As we receive them and seem to make them ours, they in fact transform us into what they themselves are. Once we have become what we have received,[59] we can enter into the second movement, going from the interior to the exterior, "journeying, building, confessing", to borrow an expression from the first homily of Pope Francis.[60]

All this leads to the conclusion that the liturgy is most certainly not a tool, an object to be manipulated in a search for evangelical effectiveness. But although liturgy, as Fr. Bouyer said, is a "thing of the sanctuary", it is not for all that foreign to evangelization. On the contrary, the liturgy is its source and summit. However, it can only fulfil its proper role if we respect its true character and steer clear of the temptation to instrumentalize it. If evangelization is the proclamation of the Paschal Mystery of Christ who died and rose again for the glory of God and the salvation of the world, it is in and through the liturgy, where we participate by grace in the Paschal Mystery, that this historical truth becomes a fountain of life. The Paschal Mystery is always a confrontation with death—whether it be death that awaits the Hebrews on the shore of the Red Sea, the death of Christ on the cross, or the many

---

[57] "This is close to the perspective of the spiritual figures of the seventeenth-century *École française* (Bérulle, Condren, Olier), so different from the law of 'letting it all hang out'. . . . Celebrating 'with sensibility', as St. Vincent de Paul put it, means above all receiving the Signs in the very act of their attentive confection and interiorizing them as such." Jean Yves Hameline, "Observations sur nos manières de célébrer" in: *La Maison-Dieu* 192, 4, 1992, (pp. 7–24), p. 21.

[58] "And so sing the psalms that mind and voice may be in harmony." *The Rule of St. Benedict*, ch. 19.

[59] *Missale Romanum* 1970, Postcommunion for the Memorial of St. Augustine: "Sanctificet nos, quæsumus Domine, mensæ Christi participatio, ut, eius membra effecti, simus quod accepimus."

[60] Homily, 14 March 2013.

forms of death that confront us daily, and that can be summed up in our inevitable bodily death—but beyond this confrontation, death is transformed into an irruption of life, by a direct and sovereign act of God.[61]

This life is anything but an abstraction. It implies renunciations, because participation in the Paschal Mystery means passing with Christ through death, a passage whose starting point is the fundamental renunciation of deciding for oneself what is good and what is evil. The beginning of the journey is difficult. St. Benedict warns the postulant who knocks at the monastery door of this difficulty. But participation in the Paschal Mystery is also the gift of life: "as we progress in conversion and in faith, our hearts shall be enlarged, and we shall run on the path of God's commandments with the inexpressible delight of love."[62] This path is the path of the liturgy. It teaches us to be ready to wait on God, to depend on Him, to receive everything from Him as a free gift and in thanksgiving. Liturgy is the first and the best school of the Lord's service.

---

[61] Roguet, "Qu'est-ce que le mystère pascal?", pp. 14–15.
[62] *The Rule of St. Benedict*, Prologue.

7

The Sacred Liturgy and the New Communities

BISHOP MARC AILLET

Bishop of Bayonne, Lescar and Oloron, France

I would like firstly to examine the kinds of spiritual riches to be found in the new communities and then address the liturgical question, pointing out several ways to make the life of these new communities and their apostolate increasingly fruitful. I will conclude with a few considerations about the need for interior renewal, not only for these communities, but also for us.

The Riches of the New Communities

As Pope Benedict XVI said in his last address to the clergy of Rome, concerning what he called the Council of the media:

> This was the dominant one, the more effective one, and it created so many disasters, so many problems, so much suffering: seminaries closed, convents closed, banal liturgy . . . and the real Council had difficulty establishing itself and taking shape; the virtual Council was stronger than the real Council. But the real force of the Council was present and, slowly but surely, established itself more and more and became the true force which is also the true reform, the true renewal of the Church. It seems to me that, fifty years after the Council, we

Translated from the French original by Michael J. Miller.

see that this virtual Council is broken, is lost, and there now appears the true Council with all its spiritual force.[1]

Indeed, the years that followed the Second Vatican Council witnessed a major storm, gale-force winds of madness that devastated whole swaths of the Church. Many things were called into question, treasures of the Church from time immemorial were abandoned for unsubstantial, short-lived novelties; as a result, a large number of vocations were shipwrecked, and a large number of practicing Catholics left the Church. Ven. Paul VI spoke about the self-destruction of the Church, and he uttered this sorrowful cry:

> The smoke of Satan had entered the temple of God through some crack. There is doubt, uncertainty, equivocation, anxiety, dissatisfaction, conflict. . . . It was thought that after the Council would come a day of sunlight for the history of the Church. What came instead was a day of clouds, storm, darkness, searching, uncertainty.[2]

In an address delivered in the same month as the one cited above, Benedict XVI also referred to the phenomenon: "The false optimism was the post-Council optimism, when convents closed, seminaries closed and they said 'but [no matter], everything is fine!' "[3] In a parallel development, those same years witnessed the founding of a large number of new communities, which rediscovered many of those same traditional treasures that were buried and abandoned at the time.

The Key to Reading Vatican II:
The Universal Call to Holiness

What, in my opinion, is the main significance of Vatican II, and what key to reading it should be adopted so as to arrive at a correct understanding and a fruitful reception of the Council? It seems to me that it is the reemphasis on the universal call to holiness. No doubt, this call is nothing new, since it is as old and as new as the Church herself.

---

[1] Meeting with the Parish Priests and the Clergy of Rome (14 February 2013).

[2] Paul VI, Homily for the ninth anniversary of his enthronement (29 June 1972).

[3] Benedict XVI, "*Lectio divina* at the Pontifical Major Roman Seminary" (8 February 2013).

"[B]e holy, for I am holy", we read already in Leviticus (11:44). And the Lord gave this commandment: "You, therefore, must be perfect, as your heavenly Father is perfect" (Mt 5:48). The Church has never lacked saints, in any age whatsoever. But this call had surely been somewhat muted for a large number of Christians, who ended up considering holiness as the business of a small number of "professionals", the monks, nuns, and priests, and so forth, and as something that had no effect on the everyday life of lay people.

This, I think, is one of the great insights of Vatican II, to have highlighted again this call addressed to all the baptized. Incidentally it is more than a call; I dare say that it is a demand on our Lord's part, since Scripture repeatedly tells us that He is a jealous God, jealous of the holiness of the souls that He created, that He redeemed with the Precious Blood of His Son: "that he might present the Church to himself in splendor, without spot or wrinkle or any such thing, that she might be holy and without blemish" (Eph 5:27). Bl. Angela of Foligno heard these words of the Lord one day: "It was not in jest that I loved you; it was not play-acting that I made myself your servant; it was not from afar that I touched you." And she thought then that she would die of sorrow, realizing that her own love was nothing but "a pitiful affectation, an abominable lie".

To take seriously this call to holiness for everyone, in every state of life: this was the insight of several founders of new communities. This is a solid foundation on which to build the house.

No more "anonymous Christianity": daring to proclaim Christ and to propose the Gospel.

It must be acknowledged that the crisis that followed Vatican II had its roots well before the Council. A certain notion of anonymous Christianity, a disdain for the classical methods of apostolate appeared in the years following World War II. It was maintained that non-believers were basically more Christian than those who practiced the Faith, that the latter blocked the non-Christians' view of the Church, that Catholics had to throw out their traditional devotions to the Blessed Virgin, Eucharistic adoration, and frequent confession as though they were old-fashioned. The historian Paul Vigneron has written a remarkable book about the crises of the contemporary French clergy; he sums up the causes of the crisis as follows:

The Catholicism of yesterday was responsible for de-Christianization because of its "iniquities"; practicing parishioners were considered as the main obstacle to the apostolate; the conversion of the masses was to be brought about by the imitation—to the point of mimicry —of the behavior of the social circles of unbelievers; the search for efficiency in the apostolate: these pernicious principles enunciated in 1945 not only oriented the "pastoral approach" of the three priests whose testimony we have just analyzed. So many French ecclesiastics were imbued with them, between the end of the war and the Second Vatican Council, that an actual rupture resulted in the history of the French apostolate.[4]

A certain spirituality of "leavening the dough" ended up not explicitly proclaiming the message of Christ any more. Today is no longer the time for anonymous Christianity, for leaven in the dough; what is urgently needed is to proclaim explicitly the prodigious newness of the Gospel, to propose the Faith explicitly. Imitating Paul VI in the Apostolic Exhortation *Evangelii Nuntiandi*, John Paul II wrote the Encyclical *Redemptoris Missio* to demonstrate what might have appeared to be a truism but had become obscure to many, namely that the Church is essentially missionary, and that it is not possible for her *not* to proclaim the Gospel: "For if I preach the gospel, that gives me no ground for boasting. For necessity is laid upon me. Woe to me if I do not preach the gospel!" (1 Cor 9:16). And Joseph Cardinal Ratzinger wrote the Declaration *Dominus Iesus* (6 August 2000) to affirm what likewise ought to have seemed to all Christians to be a truism, namely that we are saved by Jesus Christ alone. "And there is salvation in no one else, for there is no other name under heaven given among men by which we must be saved", St. Peter declares (Acts 4:12).

Here again, many new communities have reconnected with a traditional spirituality. Whereas in some seminaries candidates to the priesthood were discouraged from the practice of Eucharistic adoration, on the grounds that one must not "reify" the Eucharist, some new communities put this same adoration at the heart of their community life. The same could be said about the reception of the sacraments, especially the abandonment by many of the Sacrament of Penance and the

---

[4] Paul Vigneron, *Histoire des crises du clergé français contemporain* (Paris: Téqui, 1976), p. 266.

corresponding rediscovery thereof by the new communities; it is also true of Marian devotion, especially the Rosary, and of devotion to the saints. And these new communities often have a highly developed missionary spirituality, which leads them to proclaim the Gospel message with great boldness, for one cannot keep to oneself what has experienced profoundly.

Christocentrism and Adoration

One cannot help being struck by the essential place that Eucharistic adoration has in many new communities. This orientation of the heart toward the Eucharist seems to me to be of capital importance.

What enlivened the Church for twenty centuries is the same thing that can enliven it again today. And above all, this is the Holy Eucharist, *fons et culmen totius evangelizationis* (*Presbyterorum Ordinis*, 5), "source and summit of all evangelization", it is the Lord really and substantially present at the heart of His Church. The prophet Zechariah proclaimed: "For I will be to [Jerusalem] a wall of fire round about, says the LORD, and I will be the glory within her. . . . Sing and rejoice, O daughter of Zion; for behold, I come and I will dwell in the midst of you, says the LORD" (Zech 2:5, 10).

The Eucharist plays an important role in nurturing vocations, both to the priesthood and to the consecrated life: "For what is the good thing of [the LORD] and what is his beautiful [gift], but the corn [= grain] of the elect and wine springing forth virgins?" Zechariah also says (Zech 9:17, Douay-Rheims). Wherever Eucharistic devotion diminishes, wherever it becomes impoverished, vocations decrease at the same time or completely dry up. How can we not be seized with great anguish over our traditionally Christian countries, where the number of vocations fell dramatically in the years following the Council and has not increased again appreciably? Put the Eucharist back at the heart of parishes, at the heart of communities: that is the first step, the most important step toward an increase of vocations.

In many communities where this liturgical Christocentrism is found, one observes also a great concern for the poor. Benedict XVI said:

> St. John Chrysostom said, for example, that the sacrament of the altar and the "sacrament of the brother" or "sacrament of the poor man"

are two aspects of the same mystery. Love for one's neighbour, attention to justice and to the poor are not so much themes of a moral society as they are an expression of a sacramental conception of Christian morality.[5]

To put Christ back in the center of the house, especially through Eucharistic adoration, leads correlatively to outreach toward the poorest of the poor, toward those "existential peripheries" that our Holy Father Pope Francis has mentioned many times. As he said—and it is precisely to the ecclesial movements and new communities that he said it—a Church that does not step out of herself to go bring Christ to the poorest, to those who are far away, is an ailing Church.[6] One finds very often in the new communities this evangelizing dimension.

The Last Things

The new communities have also rediscovered the last things. A priest of the Emmanuel Community wrote a book entitled *Osons reparler de l'enfer* [Let us dare to speak again about hell]. Yes, let us dare to speak again about the last things: about death, about the judgment of God that awaits us all, about heaven, and about hell. Let us dare to say to our contemporaries that human life is a choice for or against God, with heaven or hell as its consequence, and that this is what constitutes the greatness and the dignity of the human being. "Man's greatness is great in that he knows that he is miserable", Pascal says. "A tree does not know that it is miserable. To know one's misery is therefore to be miserable, but to know that one is miserable is to be great."[7] And again: "Man is not worthy of God, but he is not incapable of being made worthy of Him. It is unworthy of God to unite Himself to wretched man, but it is not unworthy of God to pull him out of his misery."[8]

Let us never tire of preaching the infinite mercy of God who, until a human being's final breath, offers him salvation and seeks to pull him

---

[5] Benedict XVI, General Audience, 1 July 2009.

[6] Francis, Vigil of Pentecost with the ecclesial movements (18 May 2013), response to the third question.

[7] Blaise Pascal, *Pensées*, n. 397 (Brunschvicg edition) [translated from French].

[8] Ibid., n. 510 [translated from French].

out of his misery; and He offers this to every human being, even to the most hardened sinner. *Abyssus abyssum invocat.* "Deep calls to deep", says the psalm (Ps 42:7).

Yes, let us never tire of preaching the profound abyss of God's infinite mercy. But let us dare also to speak about the terrible demands of Crucified Love who, if he is obstinately rebuffed—obstinately means until the very end, until the very last moment of the life of a human being on this earth—this Crucified Love, then, cannot help but abandon the sinner to his fixed will, which has been crystallized, so to speak, in evil for all eternity. The Council of Trent teaches us infallibly that no one can be assured that he will have the great gift of final perseverance, unless it be by a special revelation (and this special revelation could occur only in an infinitesimal number of cases).[9] We must therefore often ask for this gift of final perseverance, as the greatest of all graces that God can grant us.

St. Thomas asks why it is fitting that the Risen Christ should keep on His glorified body the stigmata of His Passion, and he gives several reasons for it. I cite the last two:

> Fourthly, "that He may convince those redeemed in His blood, how mercifully they have been helped, as He exposes before them the traces of the same death" (Bede, on Luke 24:40). Lastly, "that in the Judgment-day He may upbraid them with their just condemnation" (Bede, on Luke 24:40). Hence, as Augustine says (*De Symb.*, 2): "Christ knew why He kept the scars in His body. For, as He showed them to Thomas who would not believe except he handled and saw them, so will He show His wounds to His enemies, so that He who is the Truth may convict them, saying: 'Behold the man whom you crucified; see the wounds you inflicted; recognize the side you pierced, since it was opened by you and for you, yet you would not enter.'"[10]

---

[9] Council of Trent, Session VI, canon 16; cf. Heinrich Denzinger; Peter Hünermann, Robert Fastiggi and Anne Nash eds., *Enchiridion symbolorum definitionem et declarationem de rebus fidei et morum*, 43rd ed., Latin-English (San Francisco: Ignatius Press, 2012), n. 1566, p. 386.

[10] St. Thomas Aquinas, *Summa Theologiæ*, III, q. 54, a. 4, c.

The Sacred Liturgy

Having rediscovered adoration and also the eschatological orientation of Christian life, via the importance of the prayer *Maranatha* [Come, Lord Jesus!], the new communities are predisposed to rediscover the profound meaning of the liturgy, as the Constitution *Sacrosanctum Concilium* teaches us magisterially. As Pope Benedict XVI often declared, there is something providential in the fact that the first major document approved and promulgated by the Council Fathers was the document on the Sacred Liturgy; this underscored the primacy of God and of adoration in the life of the Church. And he invites us to return to the text itself of this Constitution, notwithstanding the later implementations that have often fallen far short of this fundamental document.

I would like to explore several paths in the field of liturgy and to indicate several points that might help the new communities to make their life more and more Christocentric and to make their apostolate more and more fruitful. Indeed, it seems to me that the insistence of Benedict XVI on the primacy of God and of adoration has made the new communities very receptive to his liturgical teaching and recommendations. I will address the question of Latin, of liturgical song and of obedience to liturgical regulations.

The Rediscovery of Latin
and the Sense of Mystery

It seems to me first of all that it is important to rediscover the Latin language. While opening up the liturgy to the vernacular languages, especially for the readings and the prayers, the Council explicitly prescribed that Latin should still have pride of place in the liturgy:

> The use of the Latin language, with due respect to particular law, is to be preserved in the Latin rites. But since the use of the vernacular, whether in the Mass, the administration of the sacraments, or in other parts of the liturgy, may frequently be of great advantage to the people, a wider use may be made of it, especially in readings, directives and in some prayers and chants. Regulations governing this will be given separately in subsequent chapters. (*Sacrosanctum Concilium*, 36)

The Council furthermore stipulated, in the Decree *Optatam Totius* on the formation of priests, that future priests should learn the language of the Church. "Seminarians . . . should acquire a knowledge of Latin which will enable them to understand and make use of so many scientific sources and of the documents of the Church" (*OT*, 13). On the eve of the Council, St. John XXIII dedicated the Apostolic Constitution *Veterum Sapientia* to an explanation of why the Church owed it to herself to keep Latin as her own language. Benedict XVI also decided to dedicate an Apostolic Letter to Latin, *Latina Lingua*.[11] John XXIII includes this beautiful statement: "The Greek and Latin languages are like the golden attire of the Church's own wisdom." He explains the necessity of a language that will allow the faithful from all the nations of the earth to be united in common praise. In today's world, which is increasingly globalized, this is important. Moreover, a language that is "not only universal but *immutable*", because it has ceased to evolve, is indispensable for the preservation of the truths of the Faith over the centuries:

> The Latin language, which "we can truly call Catholic", because it has been consecrated by the uninterrupted use of the Apostolic See, the mother and teacher of all the Churches, should be considered also "a treasure . . . of matchless price", and a door by which all have access to the Christian truths that have been received from of old and to the translation of documents containing Church teaching; finally it is a precious tie that marvelously binds the present age of the Church with former and with future ages.

Finally, and this concerns the liturgy more immediately:

> Since the Catholic Church, founded by Christ the Lord, is far superior in dignity to all human societies, clearly it is fitting for her to use a language that is *not vulgar* but rather full of nobility and majesty.[12]

We must beware of losing the sense of mystery, the sense of God's transcendence. Although it is veiled beneath the charming features of a little baby, or else beneath the disfigured features of the Suffering

---

[11] Benedict XVI, Apostolic Letter in the form of a Motu Proprio *Latina Lingua* (10 November 2012).

[12] John XXIII, Apostolic Constitution *Veterum Sapientia* (22 February 1962), nn. 2, 6, 8, 7 [translated from Latin].

Servant, the transcendent holiness of God is nonetheless the transcendent holiness of God, the awesome *shekhinâh* of the Hebrews: "I am the LORD, that is my name; my glory I give to no other, nor my praise to graven images" (Is 42:8). "Behold, the nations are like a drop from a bucket, and are accounted as the dust on the scales; behold, he takes up the isles like fine dust" (Is 40:15). This feeling of reverential fear in the presence of the terrible majesty of God is what caused St. Peter to exclaim after the miraculous catch of fish: *Exi a me, quia homo peccator sum, Domine.* "Depart from me, for I am a sinful man, O Lord" (Lk 5:8).

But in the Sacred Liturgy, we no longer see even the sacred Humanity of Christ: *In cruce latebat sola Deitas, at hic latet simul et humanitas.* "On the cross divinity alone was hidden, but here humanity too is hidden", said St. Thomas Aquinas. This is eminently true of the sovereign Majesty present under the Eucharistic species. But it is true too, albeit in a different way, of everything else in the Mass besides the Eucharist, or of any liturgical act that is not the Mass. St. Catherine of Siena, when she went to confession, used to say: "I am going to the Blood." And she wrote:

> This the Divine charity provided in the Sacrament of Holy Confession, the soul receiving the Baptism of Blood, with contrition of heart, confessing, when able, to My ministers, who hold the keys of the Blood, sprinkling It, in absolution, upon the face of the soul.[13]

It is all the more important therefore to safeguard the respect that we owe to this transcendent majesty, given the fact that it is more hidden, and this is where Latin can play a very important and beneficial role. Indeed, Latin has, so to speak, two conjoined effects: it brings the mystery to light, at the same time that it veils its unbearable splendor. It is like an arrow pointing toward the ineffable, which throws it into relief, which brings it to light without staining it; it is also a veil that allows the human mind to perceive it without being stunned, a veil that also makes it possible to avoid touching the precious treasure with bare hands.

The reintroduction of Latin in certain parts of the liturgy, in particular those that are most fraught with mystery, such as the Eucharistic

---

[13] St. Catherine of Siena, *Dialogues*, transl. Algar Thorold (Rockford, Ill.: TAN, 1974), ch. 75.

Prayer, would therefore make it possible to reinforce in the priests and in the faithful the sense of mystery, the sense of divine transcendence, and it would thereby make it possible for the spiritual life and the interior life to grow, which would result in greater effectiveness of the apostolate.

Liturgical Regulations

Everyone knows the beautiful definition of peace that St. Thomas adopts from St. Augustine: *Pax est tranquillitas ordinis.*[14] "Peace is tranquility of order." Order is necessary: indeed, God has arranged everything "by measure and number and weight", says the Book of Wisdom (11:20). *Introduxit me in cellam vinariam; ordinavit in me caritatem.* "He brought me to the cellar of wine, he set in order charity in me" (Canticle of Canticles 2:4, Douay-Rheims). For there to be peace, everything must be in order. No order, no peace. But more than mere order is needed: tranquility of order is necessary, in other words, not order accepted as an unavoidable constraint, an order to which one submits reluctantly; rather there must be order embraced in tranquility of soul, order willed because God wills it, order that is loved. Then there is true peace.

Order is necessary to the utmost degree in the ceremonies of the liturgy, since this is the public worship that is rendered to God. And Holy Church alone has the competence to enact liturgical norms. The rubrics, those regulations in pretty red type, are the instructions given by the Church to safeguard liturgical order. Dom Guéranger said that the definition of a new dogma, far from being a fetter on the human intellect, is on the contrary always a great addition of light for it. By way of analogy, one could say the same about liturgical regulations and rubrics. In the years following the Council, it was considered good form to sweep them aside disdainfully with the back of the hand, while contemptuously labeling them "rubricism". The watchword then was "creativity". In his Letter accompanying the Motu Proprio *Summorum Pontificum*, Benedict XVI mentioned the Lefebvrist split, a reaction against those who failed to obey the Magisterium and its liturgical regulations:

---

[14] St. Thomas Aquinas, *Summa theologiæ*, II-II, q. 29, a. 1, ad 1.

This occurred above all because in many places celebrations were not faithful to the prescriptions of the new Missal, but the latter actually was understood as authorizing or even requiring creativity, which frequently led to deformations of the liturgy which were hard to bear. I am speaking from experience, since I too lived through that period with all its hopes and its confusion (7 July 2007).

Obeying the rubrics is never an iron collar; true freedom is to become fully what God wants us to be. Following the liturgical regulations of the Church is the only way to find peace, liturgical peace, peace of mind, and to spread it around us.

In his discourse on the Bread of Life, our Lord cites this prophecy of Isaiah: *Erunt omnes docibiles Dei.* "And they shall all be taught by God" (Jn 6:45; Is 54:13). To be docile in the etymological sense of the word is to be someone who agrees to allow himself to be taught (*docere*). It is important for us to be able to allow the Church to teach us; it is essential not to set up a customs office at the doors of our heart that filters the teachings of the Church, letting some through and stopping others. We must *sentire cum Ecclesia*, think with the Church, accept everything that she accepts, reject everything that she rejects. That is the true freedom of the children of God.

We should love to appear as poor men and women before our Mother the Church, so as to receive everything from her maternal hand. As soon as we try to draw something from our own resources, instead of receiving it with docility from the Church, we spoil God's work by adding something merely human. "Dead flies make the perfumer's ointment give off an evil odor", says Qoheleth (Eccles 10:1).

The Christian economy is in fact an economy of incarnations and mediations, in the plural. It is the unique mediation of the one Mediator between the Father and us, but this unique mediation is accompanied by multiple mediations that are derived from it and subordinate to it, and these are likewise incarnate. First and foremost, the mediation of the visible Church: "About Jesus Christ and the Church, I simply know they're just one thing."[15] And Bossuet says, "The Church is Jesus Christ, but Jesus Christ spread abroad and communicated."[16] This me-

---

[15] *VIIIe interrogatoire secret* [Eighth secret interrogation], samedi 17 mars [March] 1431. Cited in: *Catechism of the Catholic Church*, 795.

[16] Bossuet, *Pensées chrétiennes*, in: *Œuvres complètes* (Paris: Vivès, 1863), vol. 10, p. 587.

diation of the Church is exercised by her hierarchy, by the Pope, by the bishops in communion with him, and by legitimate superiors. Bossuet also says:

> Bring back Jesus Christ teaching, preaching and working miracles, and I no longer need the Church. But then too, take away the Church, and I must have Jesus Christ in person, speaking, preaching and making decisions with miracles and infallible authority.[17]

Let us never disdain these human, subordinate mediations: they are the authentic channel through which God speaks to us. "He who hears you hears me, and he who rejects you rejects me", the Lord said to the apostles (Lk 10:16).

We must agree to allow ourselves to be formed by the Church, to allow the Church to give birth to us, so as to become completely conformed to Christ: "My little children, with whom I am again in travail until Christ be formed in you", says St. Paul (Gal 4:19). We must agree to let ourselves be formed by the Church, so as to become fully mature, guided entirely by the Spirit of God: *Quicumque enim Spiritu Dei aguntur, hi sunt filii Dei.* "For all who are led by the Spirit of God are sons of God" (Rom 8:14).

Sacred Music and Beauty

When we pray, we unite our voices to that of the Church, "*vox dilectæ*", the voice of the Beloved, the voice of the Bride which alone can move the Heart of the Bridegroom.

The philosopher Étienne Gilson says that of all the transcendentals —that is, the properties that belong to being as being: oneness, truth, goodness—there is one that is often forgotten: beauty.[18] *Domine, dilexi decorum domus tuæ, et locum habitationis gloriæ tuæ.* "O LORD, I love the habitation of your house, and the place where your glory dwells" (Ps 26:8). Benedict XVI wrote in the Apostolic Exhortation *Sacramentum Caritatis*:

---

[17] Bossuet, *Conférence avec le Ministre Claude*, in *Œuvres complètes*, vol. 13, p. 539.

[18] Étienne Gilson, *The Elements of Christian Philosophy* (New York: Doubleday & Co., 1960), ch. 6, "The Forgotten Transcendental: *Pulchrum*".

This relationship between creed and worship is evidenced in a particular way by the rich theological and liturgical category of beauty. Like the rest of Christian Revelation, the liturgy is inherently linked to beauty: it is *veritatis splendor*. The liturgy is a radiant expression of the paschal mystery, in which Christ draws us to himself and calls us to communion. As St. Bonaventure would say, in Jesus we contemplate beauty and splendour at their source. This is no mere aestheticism, but the concrete way in which the truth of God's love in Christ encounters us, attracts us and delights us, enabling us to emerge from ourselves and drawing us towards our true vocation, which is love. . . . The truest beauty is the love of God, who definitively revealed himself to us in the paschal mystery.

The beauty of the liturgy is part of this mystery; it is a sublime expression of God's glory and, in a certain sense, a glimpse of heaven on earth. . . . Beauty, then, is not mere decoration, but rather an essential element of the liturgical action, since it is an attribute of God himself and his revelation.[19]

St. Pius X wanted his people to be able to pray on account of beauty. And the poor and the lowly do not often have access to beauty except through the channel of the liturgy. We must make sure not to deprive them of it. Man does not live by bread alone, and if the Church does not give beauty to the poor, who will?

As for sacred song, the Council reiterated what the Supreme Pontiffs had declared before it: "The Church recognizes Gregorian chant as being specially suited to the Roman liturgy. Therefore, other things being equal, it should be given pride of place in liturgical services" (*Sacrosanctum Concilium*, 116).

Consider the opinions that Ven. Paul VI in a letter addressed to consecrated religious in 1966:

Letters from some of you and reports from other sources . . . have made us aware that . . . your houses or provinces have introduced diverse practices into the celebration of the liturgy. Some of them are deeply attached to Latin while others prefer the vernacular in the choral office; some here and there are in favor of replacing the Gregorian chant with modern music; some have even pressed for doing away with Latin altogether.

---

[19] Benedict XVI, Post-Synodal Apostolic Exhortation *Sacramentum Caritatis* (22 February 2007), n. 35.

We must admit to being quite disturbed and troubled by these demands; they raise the questions of where such an attitude and hitherto unheard of discontent have come from and why they have spread. . . .

It is not a matter merely of keeping the Latin language in the choral office, although this has its own importance since Latin deserves to be safeguarded as an abundant source of culture and a rich treasury of devotion. But the issue is to keep intact the grace, the beauty, and the inherent strength of these prayers and chants. The issue is the choral office. . . .

Even if you are reluctant, allow Us to defend your real interests. The Church has introduced the vernacular into the liturgy for pastoral advantage, that is, in favour of those who do not know Latin. The same Church gives you the mandate to safeguard the traditional dignity, beauty and gravity of the choral office in both its language and its chant.[20]

Of course, these remarks are addressed to men and women religious who are obliged to celebrate the Divine Office in choir in its entirety, and they cannot simply be applied to all the other communities. Nevertheless, it seems to me that one can usefully be inspired by the spirit of these words, *mutatis mutandis*.

Consider what St. John Paul II wrote, citing the words of St. Pius X on sacred song:

Among the musical expressions that correspond best with the qualities demanded by the notion of sacred music, especially liturgical music, Gregorian chant has a special place. The Second Vatican Council recognized that "being specially suited to the Roman liturgy" it should be given, other things being equal, pride of place in liturgical services sung in Latin. St. Pius X pointed out that the Church had "inherited it from the Fathers of the Church", that she has "jealously guarded [it] for centuries in her liturgical codices" and still "proposes it to the faithful" as her own, considering it "the supreme model of sacred music". Thus, Gregorian chant continues also today to be an element of unity in the Roman liturgy.[21]

---

[20] Paul VI, Letter *Sacrificium Laudis* (15 August 1966) in: *Documents on the Liturgy: 1963–1979* (Collegeville: Liturgical Press, 1982), n. 421, pp. 1080–1.

[21] John Paul II, Chirograph for the Centenary of the Motu Proprio of St. Pius X on Sacred Music (22 November 2003), n. 7.

And further on, in paragraph 12:

With regard to compositions of liturgical music, I make my own the "general rule" that St. Pius X formulated in these words: "The more closely a composition for church approaches in its movement, inspiration and savour the Gregorian melodic form, the more sacred and liturgical it becomes; and the more out of harmony it is with that supreme model, the less worthy it is of the temple."

Finally, let us say a few words about the rediscovery by a number of new communities—either as a community or by certain members of these communities—of the treasure contained in the *usus antiquior*, the older form of the Roman rite. This has a contemplative dimension that can fructify spiritual life; it can help to enrich the Missal of Paul VI and to reinstate a more Christocentric *ars celebrandi*.

The Renewal of Our Souls

I would like to conclude with a few considerations on interior renewal, which does not concern the new communities alone, but all Christians and each one of us in particular. *Laus cantandi, est ipse cantator.* "The praise of singing is the singer himself",[22] says St. Augustine. Our praise will be pleasing to God only insofar as it proceeds from the depths of our souls. Dom Delatte, an Abbot of Solesmes, once said: "Adoration is worth as much as the adorer."

There is only one liturgy, the one that St. John saw in the Book of Revelation: the liturgy that the Risen Lord offers to his Father in union with the whole heavenly court and the entire Church Militant. All our earthly liturgies are only participations in this heavenly liturgy, and they have value in God's sight only insofar as they are worthy participations.

St. Thomas poses the question of whether the Mass of a bad priest is worth less than one of a good priest.[23] He answers that with regard to the sacrament, the Mass of a bad priest is worth no less than the Mass of a good priest; in either case the same sacrament is consecrated.

---

[22] St. Augustine, *Sermo* 34, 3, 6 (PL 38:211).
[23] St. Thomas Aquinas, *Summa Theologiæ*, III, q. 82, a. 6.

But with regard to the prayers that the priest offers, a distinction must be made: insofar as they are pronounced by the priest who takes the place of the whole Church, they are fruitful; but insofar as they derive their efficacy from the devotion of the priest who is praying, there is no doubt that the Mass of a better priest is more fruitful. Every Mass—which is the presence among us of the sacrifice of the cross —therefore has the value of this sacrifice, which is infinite, whatever sort of priest may celebrate it. But the application of this effect, which is per se infinite, is measured by the devotion of those who offer the sacrifice and of those for whom it is offered. We must therefore say with the Council of Trent that the Mass is "that clean oblation which cannot be defiled by any unworthiness or malice on the part of those who offer it".[24] But it must also be said, as Charles Cardinal Journet correctly observed, that the efficacy of this prayer varies, not only according to the dispositions of the priest who offers it sacramentally, but also according to the dispositions of those who attend the Mass and who make an interior offering at the same time as the priest:

> It is variable, since at every moment in time it is proportional to the intensity of that charity. It increases when in the Church there is more hope, more co-redemptive suffering, when there are more souls who have entered into the transformative union, through whom the whole Church merits in the strict sense the name of the Spouse of Christ. It was never so high as in the days of the nascent Church, when the Blessed Virgin attended the Mass of the apostles, lifting up their offering by the transport of her desire; and some have remarked that this was the reason for the extraordinary spread of the first preaching of the Gospel.[25]

Just think of the Mass of a Curé of Ars, or closer to our times, of a Padre Pio. But think also of the Masses celebrated by mediocre priests, or even by priests who are not good, which are nevertheless attended by a soul closely united to the Lord who, so to speak, mystically snatches the Sacred Host from the priest's hands to lift it up to the Lord much higher than he himself could have done. Just one soul intimately united

---

[24] Council of Trent, Session XXII, ch. 1; cf. Denzinger; Hünermann *et al.*, *Enchiridion symbolorum definitionem et declarationem de rebus fidei et morum*, n. 1742, p. 417.

[25] Charles Journet, *La Messe: Présence du sacrifice de la croix* (Paris: Desclée de Brouwer, 1958), p. 169.

to the Lord, Mother Cécile Bruyère, the first Abbess of Sainte-Cécile de Solesmes said, is more beneficial to Holy Church than a thousand souls who are only good.

Therefore it is of the utmost importance for us to be renewed in the Lord, to make progress each day in our life of union with God. "Therefore, if any one is in Christ, he is a new creation; the old has passed away, behold, the new has come" (2 Cor 5:17). And in the Book of Revelation St. John tells us: "Then I saw a new heaven and a new earth; for the first heaven and the first earth had passed away" (Rev 21:1). What will be true of material creation only at the consummation of the ages is already true for our souls that have been renewed by Baptism. We have been recreated by the death and Resurrection of Christ, our sins have been swallowed up with Pharaoh's charioteers in the waves of the Red Sea, a new heaven and a new earth have taken their place in the heart of our soul. But this must come true more and more, or else we run the risk of being spiritually bogged down by routine.

The *usus antiquior* of the Roman rite of the Mass opens with Psalm 42 [43], *Judica me*, which in verse 4 says: *Et introibo ad altare Dei, ad Deum qui lætificat juventutem meam.* "I will go in to the altar of God, the God who gives joy to my youth." One of the antiphons at Matins [Morning Prayer] for the Feast of Corpus Christi is a fine commentary on this psalm verse: "I will approach the altar of God, and I will eat Christ, who renews my youth." The Lord alone can make us new, can renew us by interior conversion and by putting off the old man. And the reception of Holy Communion itself is in the final analysis only a means. As Dom Delatte says quite strikingly in some unpublished notes:

> The transubstantiation that is effected on the altar in the hands of each of us priests places our Lord within reach of everyone. Again we must observe that for our Lord the marvelous transformation that is accomplished on the altar is only a means. It is ordered to another definitive transubstantiation, namely this one: "As the living Father sent me, and I live because of the Father, so he who eats me will live because of me" (Jn 6:57). The Lord comes into us only to change us into himself.

Let us approach the altar of God, and above all the altar that is in the center of our heart, on which all of us, priests and laymen, who by our Baptism and our Confirmation have been made sharers in the priesthood of Christ, can offer spiritual sacrifices, τὴν λογικὴν λατρείαν ὑμῶν, "your spiritual worship" or, more literally: "your adoration in conformity with the Logos" (Rom 12:1). We can offer to the Father spiritually the sacrifice of His Son; we can offer ourselves in union with the Lord's sacrifice. Benedict XVI, in the letter that he wrote to priests on the occasion of the Year for Priests, recalls that the Curé of Ars was accustomed to offer the sacrifice of his own life whenever he celebrated Mass: "What a good thing it is for a priest each morning to offer himself to God in sacrifice!"[26] But this applies not just to priests: at every Mass, every Catholic can offer to God the sacrifice of his own life, in union with the sacrifice of Christ on Calvary.

The Blessed Virgin

The Book of Revelation tells us about the Woman, a type of Mary and a type of the Church:

> But the woman was given the two wings of the great eagle that she might fly from the serpent into the wilderness, to the place where she is to be nourished for a time, and times, and half a time. The serpent poured water like a river out of his mouth after the woman, to sweep her away with the flood. But the earth came to the help of the woman, and the earth opened its mouth and swallowed the river which the dragon had poured from his mouth. (Rev 12:14–16)

From this description of the eschatological battle between Hell and the Church, we see that inanimate creation itself comes to the help of the Church by swallowing up the flood spewed out by the Dragon. The Blessed Virgin is at the same time the Mother of the Church and the type of the Church. She is the matchless model of spiritual youth. Because she is the Immaculata, she is the one who teaches us to renew ourselves interiorly. "She is younger than sin",[27] Bernanos said of her. And the liturgy applies to her the words belonging to Wisdom:

---

[26] Benedict XVI, Letter Proclaiming a Year for Priests (16 June 2009), citing *Le Curé d'Ars, sa pensée, son cœur*, Foi Vivante 23 (Le Puy: Xavier Mappus, 1966), p. 104.

[27] Georges Bernanos, *The Diary of A Country Priest* (New York: Macmillan, 1937).

The LORD created me at the beginning of his work, the first of his acts of old. Ages ago I was set up, at the first, before the beginning of the earth. . . . Before the mountains had been shaped, before the hills, I was brought forth. . . . Then I was beside him, like a master workman; and I was daily his delight, rejoicing before him always, rejoicing in his inhabited world and delighting in the sons of men. (Prov 8:22–31)

In order to recover spiritual youth, in order to be renewed interiorly in Christ, we must draw ever closer to Our Lady. Let us resolve to contemplate the youthful splendor of Our Lady, and to do so even now, in the obscurity of faith, so as to be renewed: fixing our sights on her this way purifies us, renews us, and engraves on our souls the features of her Son.

8

Homily at the Solemn Mass on the Solemnity of St. Josemaría Escrivá de Balaguer

Antonio Cardinal Cañizares Llovera

*Prefect of the Congregation for Divine Worship
and the Discipline of the Sacraments*

In this celebration we give thanks to God for the example of holiness that He has granted to the Church for us in the person of St. Josemaría Escrivá de Balaguer, at a time when we have recourse to his intercession so that, like him, we may be docile to the Holy Spirit and may walk along the paths of fidelity to the Lord, accomplishing his will. Sometimes there is widespread discouragement with respect to the times we live in, as though they were shut off from God or prevented the existence of men of God, or as though it were not possible these days to follow the path of the beatitudes, which is the path that Jesus Christ Himself traveled, which He left to us as his self-portrait, and which is the path and the life of holiness. Our era is precisely the era that St. Josemaría belongs to; most of us men and women of today surely knew him. He did not go off and leave our world in order to be a man of God, a holy man, sanctified by the Holy Spirit.

As it has happened throughout history, so too today the Holy Spirit does indeed raise up men of God who have the mission of blazing a trail and making it passable for those who come afterward. These men take the lead in their times and bring them closer to the will of God. One of these men of God was precisely Josemaría Escrivá de Balaguer. He, with God's grace, which he obeyed with simplicity, was able to

---

Translated from the original Spanish by Michael J. Miller.

respond to God's call in our time, a universal call in every age, to become holy, as God is holy and because God is Holy. Furthermore, enriched by a unique charism, he was able to offer a strong response and to prepare a way so that men and women in the world might be sanctified in these times we live in.

A time in need of strong, consistent responses, which require of the faithful Christian, along with the regular reception of the sacraments, a deep ascetical and theological formation, which is an indispensable prerequisite for the profound task of evangelization to which the popes are calling us in this third Christian millennium. Moreover the priests and the lay people now, cooperating as a living unit in the evangelization project, each according to his particular mission, must confront the challenges presented by a de-Christianized society and must give a response consistent with their baptismal faith: the committed and responsible answer of people who live their faith as Christians consistently, twenty-four hours a day. This is one of the points wherein is manifested the profound importance of the charism that Our Lord gave to Josemaría Escrivá to found Opus Dei "by divine inspiration", as St. John Paul II emphasized in the Apostolic Constitution *Ut Sit* (28 November 1982).

Our grateful and joyful celebration of the memory of St. Josemaría on this feast day reminds us of the vocation of all human beings to holiness, the urgent need for sanctity, for divine life, for union with God, for a life that bears witness to our sonship, our spirit of sons and daughters, while placing all our trust in the Father, whose hand is always with us. This splendid example, flesh of our flesh, made of the same clay as we are, which the loving kindness of God has lifted up and enriched, shows us that it is possible, with help from above, to live this life of union with God through the Church, and the sanctifying value of our daily work, of all upright human realities, not just on extraordinary occasions but ordinarily, every day: all this, with the help of grace, is within the reach of everyone.

In *Novo Millennio Ineunte*, when John Paul II, looking at our world and our time and looking ahead to the future to which God is guiding us, sets several pastoral priorities, he does not hesitate to point out that "all pastoral initiatives must be set in relation to holiness" (n. 30). This vocation to holiness, which the Second Vatican Council so vividly highlighted, is something intrinsic and decisive in the life of the Church, of us her members, and of what is and happens in her and for her. There is no renewal of the Church unless this vocation is lived out faithfully; there is no living Church capable of evangelizing by word and deed unless she lives by the gift of the Thrice-Holy God who sanctifies her unceasingly.

"This as it were objective gift of holiness", John Paul II recognizes, "is offered to all the baptized. But the gift in turn becomes a task, which must shape the whole of Christian life: 'This is the will of God, your sanctification' (1 Thess 4:3). It is a duty which concerns not only certain Christians: 'All the Christian faithful, of whatever state or rank, are called to the fullness of the Christian life and to the perfection of charity' [*Lumen Gentium*, 40]" (*Novo Millennio Ineunte*, 30). We need to develop a pastoral ministry of holiness. Let us take care that we priests are outstanding by a holy life and by our witness to holiness; let us foster and strengthen what consecration means as a true sanctification, a total belonging to the Holy God, through the different forms of consecrated life; let us promote the special spirituality of the laity, founded on Baptism, and particularly conjugal spirituality and sanctification in everyday life, through something as basic as the work of each day.

> In fact, to place pastoral planning under the heading of holiness is a choice filled with consequences. It implies the conviction that, since Baptism is a true entry into the holiness of God through incorporation into Christ and the indwelling of his Spirit, it would be a contradiction to settle for a life of mediocrity, marked by a minimalist ethic and a shallow religiosity. (John Paul II, *Novo Millennio Ineunte*, 31)

How well St. Josemaría understood this, and consequently how he inspired others not to be content with half-measures and mediocrity: It will be necessary to aspire to the heights, to perfection, to holiness. Holiness is not for geniuses, for extraordinary minds: it is for everyone, achieved and lived out in ordinary Christian life.

In order to do this it is necessary—and in this St. Josemaría is a master —to overcome the break between faith and personal conduct, between faith and culture, between the supernatural and what is authentically human. It is also necessary, in his opinion, to reestablish the unity of the Christian's life, overcoming that manifold division that disrupts an effective Christian life. Mending these breaks will require many seriously trained Christians who joyously and fully accept Catholic doctrine as it is proposed by the Magisterium, who voluntarily join with the bishops and are integrated into his diocesan pastoral plan, who share, in sincere communion with their brethren, the same Eucharistic Bread. It is necessary that Christians know how to put Christ above all human activities, with personal freedom and responsibility, as those first Christians did who sanctified themselves in the pagan world. Rooted here, in part, is the attraction of the profoundly evangelical message of the Founder of Opus Dei: he taught that the Faith must not lead to a feeble spiritualism—to a "spiritual theory" detached from real life, but rather that it must impregnate even the most hidden recesses of daily life.

May God grant us, through the intercession of St. Josemaría Escrivá de Balaguer, to be holy in these initial years of the third millennium, so that the world may have life and be sanctified. May we be able to turn all the moments and circumstances of life into occasions to love the Church and to serve her simply and joyfully.

9

Sacred Architecture at the Service of the Mission of the Church

UWE MICHAEL LANG

Introduction: The Languages of the Liturgy

The Sacred Liturgy speaks through a variety of "languages" other than language in the strict sense. These "languages" correspond to what the English social anthropologist Mary Douglas has described as "non-verbal symbols", which "are capable of creating a structure of meanings in which individuals can relate to one another and realize their own ultimate purposes".[1] It is my conviction that these non-linguistic or symbolic expressions of the liturgy are, in fact, more important than language itself.

This would seem especially pertinent in today's world, where images are omnipresent: on TV, video, and computer screens, and on the ubiquitous mobile devices. We need to take account of the fact that we live in a "culture of images", as Joseph Cardinal Ratzinger wrote in his introduction to the *Compendium* of the *Catechism of the Catholic Church*, which he later approved as Pope.[2] Today, the image tends to make a deeper and more lasting impression on people's minds than the spoken word.

The power of the image has long been known in the Church's liturgical tradition, which has used sacred art and architecture as a medium of expression and communication. For instance, the (Lutheran) liturgical

---

[1] M. Douglas, *Natural Symbols: Explorations in Cosmology*, 2nd ed. (London and New York: Routledge, 1996), p. 53.

[2] J. Ratzinger, "Introduction", in: *Catechism of the Catholic Church: Compendium* (London: Catholic Truth Society, 2005), p. 15.

scholar Frank Senn writes in his enlightened discussion of the laity's participation in worship during the Middle Ages:

> The laity have always found ways to participate in the liturgy, whether it was in their language or not, and they have always derived meaning from the liturgy, whether it was the intended meaning or not. Furthermore, the laity in worship were surrounded by other "vernaculars" than language, not least of which were the church buildings themselves and the liturgical art that decorated them.[3]

In more recent times Senn observes a tendency to see "liturgy only as text" and to limit participation in it to "speaking roles".[4] I consider this comment very illuminating; it certainly applies to a broad stream of liturgical scholarship that has largely focussed on liturgical texts that are contained in written sources from late antiquity and the early Middle Ages, above all the sacramentaries that have come down to us. This approach is legitimate, at least to a large extent, because the Church's public worship is ordered by the official texts she uses for it. Moreover, documents of the early liturgy are few, and these texts are our primary witnesses. However, even in the best liturgical scholarship of the last century, including that of Josef Andreas Jungmann, author of the magisterial work *Missarum Sollemnia* on the Mass of the Roman rite, it is sometimes forgotten that the liturgy is not simply "a series of texts to be read, but rather a series of sacred actions to be done", as the musicologist William Mahrt notes. "The solemn Mass consists of an integrated complex of words, music, and movement, together with other visual and even olfactory elements."[5] Mahrt published this analysis in 1975; since then progress has been made in the field, and scholars have taken note of the wider perspective of liturgical "vernaculars" evoked by Senn, which spoke so eloquently to worshippers in ages past.[6]

---

[3] F. C. Senn, *The People's Work: A Social History of the Liturgy* (Minneapolis: Fortress Press, 2006), p. 145.

[4] Ibid.

[5] W. P. Mahrt, "The Paradigm: The Musical Shape of the Liturgy, Part I: The Gregorian Mass in general", in *The Musical Shape of the Liturgy* (Richmond, Va.: Church Music Association of America, 2012), (pp. 3–16), p. 5 (originally published 1975).

[6] J. F. Baldovin, *The Urban Character of Christian Worship: The Origins, Development, and Meaning of Stational Liturgy* (Orientalia Cristiana Analecta, 228), (Rome: Pont. Institu-

The tendency to reduce liturgy to text can also be observed on the official level: much of the reform of the Catholic liturgy since the Second Vatican Council has been concerned with producing revised or new texts with insufficient regard for the complexity of ritual. In fact, leading exponents of social anthropology and ritual studies have been critical of the postconciliar reform because of an apparent insensitivity to non-verbal signals and their meaning. Mary Douglas, who was also a faithful Catholic, observes: "This is central to the difficulties of Christianity today. It is as if the liturgical signal boxes were manned by colour-blind signalmen".[7] It was the merit of James Hitchcock's *The Recovery of the Sacred* (1974) to show the significance of ritual studies for understanding the liturgy and for evaluating the contemporary efforts of its renewal. David Torevell has taken up this approach in a systematic manner in his *Losing the Sacred: Ritual, Modernity and Liturgical Reform* (2000).[8]

The Holy See has been largely occupied with the *recognitio* of liturgical texts and translations. This is necessary and important, and some sterling work has been done in recent years, especially the revision of the postconciliar translation of the *Missale Romanum*, most notably in the English language. However, greater attention is needed to the fact that the *lex orandi* expressing the *lex credendi* is much more than just text: it includes gestures and postures, movements and processions, music, architecture, art, and so on.

A striking example of the reductionist tendency can be found in the

---

tum Studiorum Orientalium, 1987) (anastatic reproduction 2002), 35, notes: "Historical understanding of Christian worship cannot rely on the texts of the liturgy alone, as Anton Baumstark realized more than forty years ago. Liturgy is a religious form, but it is also cultural, and as cultural it is subject to the vicissitudes of history. In other words, *context* is as an [sic] important as text for the history of worship". See also the work of E. Palazzo, "Art, Liturgy and the Five Senses in the Early Middle Ages", in: *Viator* 41 (2010), pp. 25–56. "Art et liturgie au Moyen Age: Nouvelles approches anthropologique et épistémologique", in: *Anales de Historia del Arte*, Volumen extraordinario 2010, pp. 31–74; "La dimension sonore de la liturgie dans l'Antiquité chrétienne et au Moyen Age", in: B. Palazzo-Bertholon and J.-C. Valière eds., *Archéologie du son: Les dispositifs de pots acoustiques dans les édifices anciens*, (Supplément au Bulletin monumental, n. 5) (Paris: Société Française d'Archéologie, 2012), pp. 51–58.

[7] Douglas, *Natural Symbols*, p. 44; cf. pp. xii, 1, 53.

[8] J. Hitchcock, *The Recovery of the Sacred* (New York: The Seabury Press, 1974), and D. Torevell, *Losing the Sacred: Ritual, Modernity and Liturgical Reform* (Edinburgh: T. & T. Clark, 2000).

first and second *editio typica* of the *Missale Romanum* of Pope Paul VI. Unlike the preceding editions of the Missal for centuries, it contains only the liturgical texts, with no musical notation at all. This flaw has been addressed in the third *editio typica* of 2002, which has many texts in musical notation, but still not the Prefaces that form part of the *Ordo Missæ*. Hence a solemn celebration of the Ordinary Form of the Roman rite in Latin on a "green" Sunday in the liturgical year still needs to resort to other books at the altar, such as the Solesmes version of the *Ordo Missæ in Cantu*. The institution of a new office within the Congregation for Divine Worship and the Discipline of the Sacraments on 14 November 2012, dedicated to liturgical music and art, is an encouraging sign that more attention will be given to these aspects of the Church's *lex orandi*.

What Is "Sacred Architecture"?

Discussions of sacred architecture often revolve around the concept of beauty and its theological dimension. However, in the context of modernity, the question of beauty has been reduced to a subjective judgment, on which one can reason only to a limited extent. For those who do not share the presuppositions of the classical philosophical tradition, the concept of beauty is elusive.[9] When it comes to church architecture, it will not carry us very far. We may not think that Renzo Piano's church of St. Pius of Pietrelcina in San Giovanni Rotondo works as a church, but how do we respond to someone who finds its architectural forms, or the space it creates for the assembly, "beautiful"?

For these reasons I propose another concept which I believe will provide us with clearer categories for architecture in the service of the Church's mission: the concept of the "sacred". A reflection on the sacred also seems timely, because we customarily speak of "sacred" architecture, art, or music, without giving an account of what this attribute means. And yet for more than half a century theologians in the Catholic tradition have contested the Christian concept of the sacred.

---

[9] See the fine book by Roger Scruton, *Beauty* (Oxford University Press, 2009), who shows how the metaphysical foundations of beauty were eroded in the eighteenth century, when "aesthetics" became a separate philosophical discipline. In the end, Scruton modestly aims at an education of taste.

Ideas have consequences, and it seems evident to me that these theological positions have contributed to a type of buildings dedicated for worship that fail to express the sacred and hence are not adequate for the celebration of the liturgy. As a starting-point for my argument, I should like to draw on the reflections of two well-known architects who designed important church buildings in recent years.

Massimiliano Fuksas: There Is No "Sacred Architecture"

The internationally renowned Italian architect Massimiliano Fuksas in collaboration with his wife Doriana Mandrelli completed in 2009 the church of San Paolo in Foligno, Umbria. This church is one of the "pilot projects" (*progetti pilota*) of the Italian Bishops' Conference and has attracted much attention and controversy.

In a long interview given in April 2009, Fuksas discusses the ideas that guided him in this project.[10] As he makes clear at the beginning of the conversation, he does not believe "that you can do sacred architecture"; what is possible is "architecture that tends to spirituality".[11] Such spirituality is diffusely articulated, above all with reference to the category of light, not only as an architectural element but also as a philosophical idea.

For Fuksas the relationship of a building with its exterior environment is of key importance. The particular character of a church is expressed in the fact that it stands out. Fuksas observes that most contemporary constructions, either for housing or other functional purposes, create urban spaces that lack a centre or point of reference. With his church in Foligno, the architect wants to "return to a structure that is no longer horizontal", a structure that, rightly or wrongly, he associates with the Second Vatican Council, and he sees in his accent on

---

[10] P. Ansideri, La Bottega dell'Architetto. Conversazione con Massimiliano Fuksas sulla chiesa di Foligno . . . ed altro (Roma, 17 aprile 2009) <http://www.oicosriflessioni .it/wp-content/uploads/2011/07/corretto-Paolo-05-10-11-intervista-fuksas.pdf> (accessed 25 April 2013), p. 1.

[11] "La prima cosa da dire è che io non credo si possa fare architettura sacra. Si può fare architettura che tende alla spiritualità. L'architettura sacra o l'architettura profana non vogliono dire nulla . . .". Ibid.

the height of the building a reference to Gothic architecture. In the church at Foligno, this vertical dimension is in fact a striking feature that is realised by the sheer height of the space.[12]

Particular attention is given to the façade and the entrance to the church. Fuksas rejects what the "church of the Counter-Reformation", which he sees exemplified in Vignola's *Il Gesù* in Rome: "you enter after being attracted by a great staircase, a great façade, by the dynamism, by the majesty of the façade and by [its] great power. You enter because it is an act of faith. Once you enter inside, you understand that this faith is something extremely complex".[13] Fuksas' own concept of the façade could not be more different: in extreme abstraction, it presents itself as one side of the cube that is the shape of the building, in plain concrete and without any ornamentation or prominent Christian symbolism. The entrance to the church, which is marked by a front of glass doors and windows on the ground floor and includes a relatively small cross, is reached by means of a large ramp.

Inside the church, the actual liturgical space makes a banal and, in a strange way, dated expression. When I visited the church in Foligno, I was reminded of churches of the 1970s that have aged badly, although this church was completed only three years before. Noteworthy are the attempts (presumably of the parish community) to make the church a "home" to regular worshippers by including a traditional large crucifix, a historical tabernacle and a Baroque statue of our Lady.

The rejection of the idea that a church should distinguish itself as a sacred building in its architectural forms is not original to Fuksas, but rather typical of the modernist movement as such. With reference to his famous chapel of Notre Dame du Haut at Ronchamp (1955), Le Corbusier explained that "the requirements of religion" had little impact on the design; the form was rather intended to stir "the psycho-physiology of the feelings".[14] Likewise Mies van der Rohe, when he

---

[12] See ibid.

[13] "Io non sono per la chiesa controriformista, come la chiesa del Gesù, come la chiesa del Vignola, che tu entri dopo essere stato attratto da una grande scalinata, da una grande facciata, dalla dinamicità, dalla possenza della facciata e dal grande potere. Tu entri perché è un atto di fede. Entrato dentro capisci che questa fede è qualche cosa di estremamente complesso". Ibid., p. 2.

[14] Le Corbusier, *Œuvre Complète: Vol. 6. 1952–57* (Zürich: Les Editions d'Architecture, 1995), p. 52.

designed the chapel at the Illinois Institute of Technology (1952), is said to have been "interested not in the specific solution for the church . . . but in the universal form; an architecture which could accommodate any function".[15]

More recently, when Santiago Calatrava presented his design for the Cathedral of Christ the Light in Oakland, California, which originally won the commission but was then not executed, he stated his ambition to give the building "a universal character independent of the Catholic Church", because of the many different cultures in the city.[16]

Mario Botta: Architecture in Itself a Sacred Work

The Swiss-Italian architect Mario Botta (born 1943) is distinguished not only by the number of significant churches he designed, such as the Cathedral of the Resurrection at Evry near Paris (dedicated in 1995) and the Church of the Holy Face in Turin (2006), but also by his theoretical reflections on the subject of sacred architecture.

In a lecture given at Zurich a few years ago, Botta observes that buildings have the capacity of communicating "values" that transcend their proper function. One such value is the sacred, which he describes as the realisation of a connection that leads us beyond the technical or functional aspects of a building and allows us to recall an experience of a reality that transcends what is immediately perceptible to the senses.[17] Note that the sacred *recalls* this experience: for Botta, the idea of the sacred is linked with a particular history or memory.

It would appear that this memory is constituted in the act of building itself, which he defines as a "sacred act": "it is an action that transforms

---

[15] E. Heathcote and I. Spens, *Church Builders* (Chichester: Academy Editions, 1997), p. 56.

[16] Zahid Sardar, "Cathedral Dreams", in *San Francisco Chronicle Magazine* (18 February 2001) <http://www.sfgate.com/bayarea/article/CATHEDRAL-DREAMS-Celebrated-for-skeletal-2950579.php> (accessed 25 April 2013).

[17] Mario Botta, "Räume des Übergangs", in Mario Botta, Gottfried Böhm, Peter Böhm, Rafael Moneo, *Sakralität und Aura in der Architektur* (Architekturvorträge der ETH Zürich) (Zürich: GTA Verlag, 2010), pp. 10–51, at p. 13: "Eine erste Betrachtung gilt dem Phänomen des Sakralen: Es ist ein Phänomen der Umsetzung einer Spannung, einer Verbindung, die uns über die Fakten, die technischen Nutzungsfunktionen hinausführt und uns dazu bringt, etwas wiederzuerleben, das eine vordergründige Wahrnehmung übersteigt".

a condition of nature into a condition of culture; the story of architecture is the story of these transformations".[18] Botta appears convinced, therefore, that *any* architecture carries with itself the idea of the sacred, in that it is an expression of human work. The first step of "making architecture" begins by putting a stone on the ground, and this action in itself has a sacred meaning, because it transforms a condition that is not controlled by human activity, at least not exclusively, into a living space formed by man. The second step consists in marking a boundary, without which no architecture exists. Thus an "interior and therefore sacred" realm or state is separated from the exterior.[19]

This refers not only to the construction of a church (or synagogue or mosque), but of any edifice. As Botta says in another contribution, a building is an expression of the human labour that created it, with all its joys and efforts, and so communicates sentiments and aspiration that, according to him, "belong to the spiritual sphere". The building thus holds a sacred potential as a memorial to the transforming force of human work.[20] Botta recognises that in the Western Christian tradition, the history of architecture is largely one of church architecture.

---

[18] "Costruire è di per sé un atto sacro, è una azione che trasforma una condizione di natura in una condizione di cultura; la storia dell'architettura è la storia di queste trasformazioni"; Mario Botta, "Lo spazio del sacro" in: G. Cappellato, ed., Architetture del sacro. Preghiere di pietra (Bologna: Editrice Compositori, 2005), (pp. 3–5), p. 3. Cf. Botta, *Räume des Übergangs*, pp. 13–14.

[19] "Sobald man auf dem Boden eine Perimeterlinie einzeichnet, trennt man einen inneren, also sakralen Zustand vom äusseren". Botta, *Räume des Übergangs*, p. 14 (emphasis mine).

[20] "Io credo che l'architettura porti con sé l'idea del sacro, nel senso che è espressione del lavoro dell'uomo. L'architettura non è solo un'organizzazione materiale; anche la più povera delle capanne ha una sua storia, una sua dignità, una sua etica che testimonia di un vissuto, di una memoria, parla delle più segrete aspirazioni dell'uomo. L'architettura è una disciplina dove—più che in altri settori—la memoria gioca un ruolo fondamentale; dopo anni di lavoro mi sembra di capire come il territorio su cui opera l'architetto si configuri sempre più come 'spazio della memoria'; il territorio fisico parla di una storia geologica, antropologica, ma anche di una memoria più umile legata al lavoro dell'uomo. Ecco che allora, da questo punto di vista, l'architettura porta con sé un potenziale di sacro perché testimonia una saggezza 'del fare' con gioie e fatiche che trasmettono sentimenti ed emozioni che appartengono alla sfera spirituale. Di fronte ad una casa o ad una chiesa proviamo un'emozione che non è solo data dal fatto costruttivo in sé ma dai significati simbolici e metaforici". C. Donati, "A colloquio con Mario Botta: le nuove forme della memoria", in: *Costruire in Laterizio* 72 (November/December, 1999), (pp. 40–44), p. 41.

By comparison, he regards the impact of civil and military architecture before the twentieth century as marginal. An architectural historian may well dispute this statement, but this is not our concern here.

This extension of the category of the sacred to architecture as such raises the question what, if anything at all, is added to this in the building of a church? Botta introduces the aspect of durability or solidity, which he defines as "creating an artefact (*manufatto*) as a physical presence between earth and heaven".[21] This would seem to be connected to Botta's conviction that nature should be integrated into architecture and vice-versa, because they are complementing each other—an idea he realized, for instance, in his cathedral of Evry in France, where a crown of trees is set on top of the cylindrical structure.[22]

The noted architect describes a church as "an elementary space for the assembly, where for the faithful the original event of the Christian sacrifice is repeated".[23] This description can serve as a starting point for a conversation on historically formed understanding of a church building. Botta also speaks of the necessity not to subject this space to changing fashions and mentions as his ideal style the Romanesque because of what he perceives as the austerity of its forms. Still, with the extension of the sacred to all architecture, it remains unclear what actually distinguishes a building dedicated to divine worship from any other construction.

It will be instructive also to consider Botta's Cymbalista Synagogue and Jewish Heritage Centre in Tel Aviv. The University of Tel Aviv, anxious to respect the secular tradition of the city as well, decided that the religious building should not dominate the structure and therefore asked the architect to construct a cultural centre next to it. The architect interpreted this request by making both edifices, the sacred and the secular, identical in form and dimensions, in the materials and in the use of light. In his reflection on this project, Botta notes that he

---

[21] "Per esempio, costruire una chiesa vuole anche dire confrontarsi con il tema della durata, della solidità, vuol dire creare un manufatto come presenza fisica fra terra e cielo". Ibid.

[22] The sliced cylinder is a characteristic of Botta's ecclesiastical buildings and also features in his church of San Giovanni Battista, Mogno (1986–1996) and in his chapel of Santa Maria degli Angeli, Monte Tamaro (1990–1996), both in the Swiss Alps.

[23] "La chiesa è comunque uno spazio assembleare elementare dove per il fedele si ripete l'evento originale del sacrificio cristiano". Ibid.

deliberately went against the hailed principle of modern architecture that form should follow function. Here, the same form serves two different functions.[24]

Theological Roots:
the Sacred in Question

The problem I have attempted to sketch is by no means limited to the field of architecture. In fact, the sacred in Christianity has been called into question by a liturgical and sacramental theology that is inspired by the more radical currents in the writings of Edward Schillebeeckx and Karl Rahner.[25] At the risk of oversimplifying matters, it can be said that in this vision the whole created world is regarded as already endowed with or permeated by divine grace. As Schillebeeckx writes in his influential book *Christ the Sacrament of the Encounter with God*, "the whole created world becomes, through Christ's Incarnation and the God-man relationship which is consequent upon it, an outward grace, an offer of grace in sacramental form".[26] While the early Schillebeeckx's sacramental theology is still indebted to a Thomistic Christology and ecclesiology, in his later writings the sacraments appear to be subsumed into the general category of rituals that lead to an existential encounter with God.[27]

Schillebeeckx had a notable influence on the development of Rahner's theology. According to Patrick Burke, Rahner, from the early 1960s, "although never actually denying the grace-nature distinction,

---

[24] See Botta, *Räume des Übergangs*, pp. 36–39.

[25] Cf. D. A. Stosur, *The Theology of Liturgical Blessing in the Book of Blessings: A Phenomenologico-theological Investigation of a Liturgical Book*, Ph.D. dissertation, University of Notre Dame, 1994, who, unlike the present writer, is wholly positive in his evaluation of this development.

[26] E. Schillebeeckx, *Christ the Sacrament of the Encounter with God* (New York: Sheed and Ward, 1963), p. 216. This was published originally as *Christus, Sacrament van de Godsontmoeting* (Bilthoven: H. Nelissen, 1960), which is a shorter version of *De sacramentele Heilseconomie*, published in 1952. For an early critique of this approach, see L. Bouyer, M. J. Costelloe, trans., *Rite and Man: The Sense of the Sacral and Christian Liturgy* (London: Burns & Oates, 1963), pp. 8–10.

[27] See J. Geldhof, "The Early and Late Schillebeeckx O.P. on Rituals, Liturgies, and Sacraments", in: *Usus Antiquior* 1 (2010), (pp. 132–50), p. 140.

stresses ever more their existential unity and [. . .] begins to see categorical revelation as only the posterior explicitization of what man always and originally is".[28] This idea of "transcendental grace" later develops into his theory of the "anonymous Christian"; the consequence Rahner draws for his understanding of grace is that he "sees it coming to categorical expression in any categorical experience, even if not specifically Christian or even religious".[29]

Consequently, the notion of "sacramentality" is extended to such a degree that the Church's sacraments are considered nothing more than manifestations, albeit significant ones, that make explicit what already takes place in the world. In 1970, Rahner writes that:

> The sacraments constitute the manifestation of the holiness and the redeemed state of the secular dimension of human life and of the world. Man does not enter a temple, a fane which encloses the holy and cuts it off from a godless and secular world which remains outside. Rather in the free breadth of a divine world he erects a landmark, a sign of the fact that this entire world belongs to God, a sign precisely of the fact that God is adored, experienced and accepted everywhere as he who, through his "grace", has himself set all things free to attain to himself, and a sign that this adoration of him takes place not in Jerusalem alone but everywhere in spirit and in truth. The sacrament constitutes a small sign, necessary, reasonable and indispensable, within the infinitude of the world as permeated by God.[30]

In other words, unlike classical theology, Rahner no longer takes the sacraments as signs that confer the grace they signify, or instrumental

---

[28] P. Burke, *Reinterpreting Rahner: A Critical Study of His Major Themes* (New York: Fordham University Press, 2002), pp. 47–48. For recent critical reflections on Rahner's theology, see also M. Hauke, "Karl Rahner nella critica di Leo Scheffczyk", in: S. M. Lanzetta, ed., *Karl Rahner. Un'analisi critica. La figura, l'opera e la recezione teologica di Karl Rahner (1904–1984)* (Siena: Cantagalli, 2009), pp. 267–87. M. Gagliardi, *Liturgia fonte di vita* (Verona: Fede & Cultura, 2009), pp. 58–73.

[29] Burke, *Reinterpreting Rahner*, p. 246.

[30] K. Rahner, "Considerations on the Active Role of the Person in the Sacramental Event", in: D. Bourke, trans., *Theological Investigations, vo. 14: Ecclesiology, Questions in the Church, the Church in the World* (New York: Seabury Press, 1976), (pp. 161–84), p. 169. ("Überlegungen zum personalen Vollzug des sakramentalen Geschehens", *Schriften zur Theologie* 10, [Einsiedeln: Benziger, 1972], pp. 405–92, [originally published in 1970].)

causes of grace *extra nos*, but rather as visible manifestations of the inner event of grace that already occurs in man, and is not necessarily linked with Christian Revelation.[31] At this point Rahner introduces Teilhard de Chardin's idea of the (still invisible) "liturgy of the world":

> The world and its history are the sublime liturgy, breathing of death and sacrifice, which God celebrates and causes to be celebrated in and through human history in its freedom, this being something which he in turn sustains in grace by his sovereign disposition.[32]

What is described here is a kind of primordial liturgy, which is reflected in "that which we are accustomed to call liturgy in the more usual sense".[33] Or, as he explains elsewhere, sacramental celebrations symbolise the "liturgy of the world" that is already taking place.[34] From such a theological perspective, the distinction between the sacred and the non-sacred hardly makes sense. Rather, I would argue, the sacred merges into the ordinary or quotidian, which is already permeated by God's grace.

Towards a Reappraisal of the Sacred in Catholic Theology

For a reappraisal of the sacred in Catholic theology I intend to take as a starting point the work of the Belgian religious historian and anthropologist Julien Ries (who was created a Cardinal by Pope Benedict XVI on 18 February 2012). Ries notes the originality of the Christian

---

[31] This idea is already contained in Rahner's article "Sakrament: V. Systematik", in: *Lexikon für Theologie und Kirche*, 2nd ed., vol. 9 (1964), col. 227–30, at 228, and more radically articulated in his "Kleine Vorüberlegung über die Sakramente im allgemeinen", in: *Über die Sakramente der Kirche: Meditationen* (Freiburg: Herder, 1985), pp. 11–21 (originally published in 1974), where he speaks of a "Copernican turn" in the understanding of the sacraments.

[32] Rahner, *Considerations on the Active Role of the Person in the Sacramental Event*, p. 170.

[33] Ibid. Cf. the well-researched if rather uncritical study of M. Skelley, *The Liturgy of the World: Karl Rahner's Theology of Worship*. Foreword by R. G. Weakland (Collegeville: Liturgical Press, 1991).

[34] "On the Theology of Worship", in: E. Quinn, trans., *Theological Investigations, vol. 19: Faith and Ministry* (New York: Crossroad, 1983), (pp. 141–49), pp. 142–43. ("Zur Theologie des Gottesdienstes", *Schriften zur Theologie* 14 [Einsiedeln: Benziger, 1980]), pp. 227–37, (originally published in 1979).

conception of the sacred, which can be understood only in relation to Jesus Christ.[35]

In the Old Testament, the theme of God's holiness appears frequently, for instance, in the *Trisagion* of Isaiah 6:3, "Holy, holy, holy is the LORD of hosts". In fact, God alone is called the "Holy One" (*qadoš*) in the full sense of the word. "Holiness" is a quality that belongs above all to God and describes His being divine; in other words, it expresses His transcendence. In the long discourse that is contained in chapter seventeen of St. John's Gospel and known as His high-priestly prayer, Jesus invokes His "holy Father" (John 17:11) in line with the conception of the Hebrew Scriptures. There is, however, an important difference here, in that the enormous distance between God and man, which is implied in Isaiah's proclamation of God's all-surpassing holiness, is mediated by the communion that is established by the mission of the Son into the world. Holiness, which is rooted in God's transcendence and characterises the unity of the Father and the Son, also constitutes the unity of Christ with His disciples and their unity among one another.

At a significant moment in the high-priestly prayer, Jesus asks His heavenly Father with regard to His disciples: "Sanctify them in the truth; your word is truth. . . . For their sake I consecrate myself, that they also may be consecrated in truth" (Jn 17:17, 19). Earlier in the same Gospel, Jesus speaks of Himself as the one "whom the Father consecrated and sent into the world" (Jn 10:36). In the second volume of his book *Jesus of Nazareth*, Benedict XVI comments on the meaning of "consecrate" or "sanctify" (both words translate the same Greek verb *hagiázein*), which he reads in "connection with the event of atonement and with the high priesthood".[36]

---

[35] J. Ries, R. Nanini, trans., *Il senso del sacro nelle culture e nelle religioni* (Milan: Jaca Book, 2006), pp. 70–79.

[36] J. Ratzinger/Benedict XVI, P. J. Whitmore, trans., *Jesus of Nazareth. Part Two: Holy Week. From the Entrance into Jerusalem to the Resurrection* (San Francisco: Ignatius Press, 2011), p. 85. The Pope presented these thoughts also in his *Homily for the Chrism Mass* (9 April 2009). Benedict XVI relies on A. Feuillet, *Le sacerdoce du Christ et de ses ministres d'après la prière sacerdotale du quatrième Evangile et plusieurs données parallèles du Nouveau Testament* (Paris: Téqui, 1997 [first edition 1972]). Feuillet's reading, while not being generally accepted by biblical scholars today, is already attested in some early Church Fathers;

The meaning of "consecrate" here is rooted in the Old Testament, where God is the "Holy One", and hence means "handing over a reality—a person or even a thing—to God, especially through appropriation for worship".[37] This can happen in preparing and offering sacrifice to God (cf. Ex 12:3; Deut 15:19) or in consecration for priesthood (cf. Ex 28:41). According to Benedict XVI, the process of "consecration" or "sanctification" of which Jesus speaks in the high-priestly prayer comprises two aspects that only appear to be opposed, but are in reality two aspects of the same complex reality. On the one hand, consecration means "setting apart from the rest of reality that pertains to man's ordinary everyday life". The person or object that is consecrated is handed over entirely to God and hence is no longer under human control. On the other hand, such consecration always includes "the essential dynamic of 'existing for' ": precisely because it is handed over into the sphere of God, the consecrated reality exists now for the world and for its salvation.[38] These two aspects of consecration are only seemingly contrary to each other, as is shown by the three moments of consecration, of which Jesus speaks in John's Gospel.

The first consecration, that of the Son by the Father, is identified with the Incarnation. Peter confesses Jesus as "the Holy One of God" in the synagogue of Capernaum (Jn 6:69) and by applying this title, which the Old Testament reserves to God alone, to Jesus, as is done in other New Testament passages as well,[39] Peter professes His divinity.

---

cf. the brief discussion by J. Zumstein, *L'Évangile selon saint Jean (13–21)* (Commentaire du Nouveau Testament. Deuxième série, IVb) (Geneva: Labor et Fides, 2007), p. 180.

[37] Ibid., *Jesus of Nazareth*, p. 86. In the German original only the word "heiligen" is used for *hagiázein* but then its twofold meaning is explained as "*heiligen*" and "*weihen*": Jesus von Nazareth. Zweiter Teil: Vom Einzug in Jerusalem bis zur Auferstehung (Freiburg: Herder, 2011), p. 104. The fact that the same Greek verb is translated differently is significant: the sense of *hagiázein* in John 17 is not restricted to moral holiness, neither to a dedication to a particular mission, but indicates a more profound dimension of consecration.

[38] Ibid. This connection is seen in "the special vocation of Israel: on the one hand, it is set apart from all other peoples, but for a particular reason—in order to carry out a commission for all people, for the whole world. That is what is meant when Israel is designated a 'holy people'. " Ibid.

[39] Mk 1:24, Lk 1:35, Acts 4:27 and 30.

As the Holy One of God, Jesus belongs totally to God, and at the same, in His Incarnation, he is sent into the world and exists for it. His "holiness" is at the heart of His messianic mission.

The second consecration is indicated when Christ speaks of consecrating Himself. In his exegesis of this passage, the highly influential biblical scholar Rudolf Bultmann noted the temporal vicinity of this so-called farewell discourse with the beginning of Christ's Passion. Moreover, this act of consecration or sanctification (the Greek *hagiázein*) is made "for their sake" (*hypèr autōn*), thus giving it a sacrificial dimension. This second consecration anticipates the sacrifice Christ offers of Himself on the Cross. Bultmann also sees in this an allusion to the words of the Last Supper.[40]

In the reading of Benedict XVI, the liturgical background of the high-priestly prayer of Jesus is a hermeneutical key: the great Day of Atonement, which is renewed in the new liturgy of atonement, of which Jesus Himself is the high priest, "sent into the world by the Father"; at the same time he is the sacrifice, "made present in the Eucharist of all times".[41] The meaning of the Day of Atonement is thus fulfilled in the Incarnation of the Eternal Word "for the life of the world" (John 6:51). From the moment that Jesus came into this world in human flesh, He is consecrated priest to offer sacrifice and to intercede for His people, and this consecration is perfected in His Passion and Cross. The messianic mission of Christ thus also has a cultic dimension, and its focal point is the priesthood of Christ, the mediator between God and humanity.

The third consecration consists in the disciples' participation in the consecration of Christ according to the two aspects already mentioned. The disciples are appropriated into God's sphere and, at the same time, they are sent into the world to fulfil a priestly mission. This third consecration of John 17 is important because it presents not only the consecration of Jesus Christ as priest, as does the *Letter to the Hebrews* in

---

[40] R. Bultmann, *Das Evangelium des Johannes* (Meyers kritisch-exegetischer Kommentar über das Neue Testament, 2), 21st ed. (Göttingen: Vandenhoeck & Ruprecht, 1986), p. 391, n. 3; cf. Feuillet, *Le sacerdoce du Christ*, pp. 31 and 38; Benedict XVI, *Jesus of Nazareth*, pp. 87–88.

[41] Benedict XVI, *Jesus of Nazareth*, p. 88.

language that draws on Temple worship,[42] but also includes the participation of the Apostles in this consecration. For this reason Benedict XVI recognises in this Gospel passage the institution of the priesthood of the New Testament, which is nothing else but a participation in the priesthood of Jesus Christ, the one high priest of the New Covenant.[43]

The Sacredness of the Liturgy

These biblical reflections guide us towards re-approaching the theme of the sacred in Christianity. I believe that this is so because the Constitution on the Sacred Liturgy of the Second Vatican Council properly defines the liturgy as "an exercise of the priestly office (*munus*) of Jesus Christ", and goes on to say:

> In the liturgy the sanctification of man is signified by signs perceptible to the senses, and is effected in a way which corresponds with each of these signs; in the liturgy the whole public worship is performed by the Mystical Body of Jesus Christ, that is, by the Head and His members. (*Sacrosanctum Concilium*, 7)

This passage restates a key principle of Catholic worship, formulated by St. Thomas Aquinas,[44] proclaimed in a very similar way by Pope Pius XII in his Encyclical *Mediator Dei*,[45] and resumed in the *Catechism of the Catholic Church*.[46] In these magisterial documents, the liturgy is seen as the exercise of the priesthood of Christ; to be more precise, of

---

[42] Christ is "high priest of the good things that have come" (Heb 9:11) and "the mediator of a new covenant" (Heb 9:15), established in his blood which purifies our "conscience from dead works" (Heb 9:14).

[43] Cf. Benedict XVI, *Jesus of Nazareth*, p. 90; *Homily for the Chrism Mass* (9 April 2009).

[44] *Summa Theologiæ*, III, q. 13, a. 2: "*Totus autem ritus christianæ religionis derivatur a sacerdotio Christi.*"

[45] (20 November 1947), n. 20: "The Sacred Liturgy is, consequently, the public worship which our Redeemer as Head of the Church renders to the Father, as well as the worship which the community of the faithful renders to its Founder, and through Him to the heavenly Father. It is, in short, the worship rendered by the Mystical Body of Christ in the entirety of its Head and members". Ibid., n. 22: "Thenceforth the priesthood of Jesus Christ is a living and continuous reality through all the ages to the end of time, since the liturgy is nothing more nor less than the exercise of this priestly function".

[46] Cf. *Catechism of the Catholic Church* (1992), 1066–70, and, in a very condensed way, *Catechism of the Catholic Church: Compendium* (2005), n. 218.

Christus totus (a favourite phrase of St. Augustine's), that is, the whole Christ, the Head and the members of His Mystical Body, which is the Church. Those who participate in this exercise of Christ's priesthood are the ordained priest, who acts in the person of Christ the Head (*in persona Christi capitis*) by virtue of his priestly ordination, and the baptized faithful as members of the Mystical Body. Note that at *this* point, *Sacrosanctum Concilium* introduces the notion of the sacredness of the liturgy, when it explains:

> From this it follows that every liturgical celebration, because it is an action of Christ the priest and of His Body which is the Church, is a sacred action surpassing all others; no other action of the Church can equal its efficacy by the same title and to the same degree. (n. 7)

In other words, *Sacrosanctum Concilium* considers "sacredness" always derived from the liturgy, which is the presence and action of Christ in His Mystical Body. This principle has also been formulated by St. Thomas Aquinas: "Something is called sacred (*sacrum*), because of its relation to the act of public worship (*ad cultum divinum*)".[47] The German philosopher Josef Pieper, who has written on the subject in an epoch when it was fiercely contested, argues that this concept of the sacred is widely confirmed by ethnology and philosophy of religion, "and no less by the theological interpretation of the Old and New Testaments".[48] He also records a use of language that points to an essential characteristic of the liturgy: it is never simply "done", but "celebrated". Both in classical Latin and in the use of Latin in the Christian liturgy, the verb *celebrare* means "carrying out an action in a non-ordinary manner, on the part of the community".[49] Moreover, unlike personal and interior prayer, the liturgy is an external action, which has its concrete and material forms of expressions, in which the human senses are always involved. Public worship thus is in need of its proper place, its proper time and its proper objects that are specifically

---

[47] *Summa Theologiæ*, II-II, q. 99, a. 1.

[48] J. Pieper, L. Krauth, trans., *In Search of the Sacred* (San Francisco: Ignatius Press, 1991), p. 25; cf. "Sakralität und 'Entsakralisierung' (1969)", in Religionsphilosophische Schriften, ed. B. Wald (Werke, 7), (Hamburg: Felix Meiner, 2000), (pp. 394–419), pp. 403–404.

[49] Ibid., p. 26, with reference to B. Droste, "Celebrare" in der römischen Liturgiesprache (Munich: Hueber, 1963), p. 196.

dedicated to it so that it can be celebrated as a sacred action. It is in relation to this sacred action that we also speak of sacred space, sacred time or sacred objects.

There is another important argument to consider here: from the Christian perspective, the sacredness of the liturgy is based on its sacramental character. When *Sacrosanctum Concilium* affirms that in the liturgy, which is the exercise of the priesthood of Christ, the sanctification of man is signified and at the same time effected by signs perceptible to the senses, (cf. n. 2) it obviously refers to the sacraments. Now, the essential rites of the sacraments—form and matter in scholastic terminology—are distinguished by a stupendous humility and simplicity.

The liturgy, as sacred action, surrounds these essential rites with other rites and ceremonies that illustrate them and help the faithful to a better understanding of the great mystery that is made present.[50] The reality of the sacraments, which is veiled and hidden to the senses, is translated into signs that are perceptible and hence more easily accessible to our understanding. The purpose of this is that the Christian community, "instructed by the sacred actions (*sacris actionibus erudita*)", as an ancient prayer in the *Gregorian Sacramentary* says, be properly disposed to receive God's grace and blessing.[51] The sacred character of the liturgy can thus be seen as part of divine pedagogy.

For St. Thomas Aquinas, the elements of human institution in the sacraments, while not being essential to them, belong to the "solem-

---

[50] Cf. Council of Trent, Session XXII (1562), *Doctrine on the Sacrifice of the Mass*, ch. 5: "On the Solemn Ceremonies of the Sacrifice of the Mass", Heinrich Denzinger; Peter Hünermann, Robert Fastiggi and Anne Nash eds., *Enchiridion symbolorum definitionem et declarationem de rebus fidei et morum*, 43rd ed., Latin-English (San Francisco: Ignatius Press, 2012), n. 1746, p. 419: "And as human nature is such that it cannot easily raise itself up to the meditation of divine realities without external aids, Holy Mother Church has for that reason duly established certain rites . . . she has provided ceremonial, such as mystical blessings, lights, incense, vestments and many other rituals of that kind from apostolic order and tradition, by which the majesty of this great sacrifice is enhanced and the minds of the faithful are aroused by those visible signs of religious devotion to contemplation of the high mysteries hidden in this sacrifice."

[51] *Sacramentarium Gregorianum* (Hadrianum), nn. 308, 895: ed. J. Deshusses, Le Sacramentaire Grégorien. Ses principales formes d'après les plus anciens manuscrits, 3rd ed. vol. I (Spicilegium Friburgense, 16) (Fribourg: Édition Universitaires, 1992) (= Missale Romanum 1570–1962, Collect, Saturday after Passion Sunday): "Proficiat, quæsumus, Domine, plebs tibi dicata piæ devotionis affectu: ut, sacris actionibus erudita, quanto maiestati tuæ fit gratior, tanto donis potioribus augeatur".

nity" (*solemnitas*) that serves to awaken devotion and reverence in those who receive it, especially in the Most Holy Eucharist.[52] Pieper proposes a broad definition of "sacred language", which includes signs and gestures as well as the words used in public worship. In a similar way, the English Dominican Aidan Nichols speaks of "the idiom of worship"; both concepts are by no means restricted to the linguistic aspects of the liturgy and cover more or less the same ground as Aquinas' idea of *solemnitas*.[53] I would therefore propose to see in the sacrality of the liturgy the expression of its sacramentality. Consequently, the question needs to be asked whether Catholic theologians who have endorsed the movements towards a "de-sacralisation" have a strong enough sense of the sacramental principle. It has been Pieper's argument that such theologies "are ultimately rooted" in a "denial of any sacramental reality".[54]

In his book on *The Spirit of the Liturgy*, Joseph Cardinal Ratzinger offers another perspective on the meaning of the sacred in Christianity, when he responds to theological critics of the idea that there should be any such thing as "sacred time" and "sacred space" for Christians. Their critique takes as a scriptural basis Christ's announcement in St. John's Gospel of a worship "in spirit and in truth" (Jn 4:23), a passage also invoked by Rahner in the passage quoted above.

This is correctly taken to mean "the transition from Temple sacrifice to universal worship"; it would be mistaken, however, to draw the consequence that such universal worship is no longer bound by the restrictions of "the sacred". The then-Cardinal recalls that we live in the time of "not yet", that is, we have not yet passed over to the

---

[52] *Summa Theologiæ*, III, q. 64, a. 2 ad 1: "Ad primum ergo dicendum quod illa quæ aguntur in sacramentis per homines instituta, non sunt de necessitate sacramenti, sed ad quandam solemnitatem, quæ adhibetur sacramentis ad excitandam devotionem et reverentiam in his qui sacramenta suscipiunt". See also III q. 83, a. 4: "quia in hoc sacramento totum mysterium nostræ salutis comprehenditur, ideo præ ceteris sacramentis cum maiori solemnitate agitur", and III q. 66, a. 10 resp. on the ceremonies of the rite of baptism. Cf. T. A. Becker, "The Role of *Solemnitas* in the Liturgy According to Saint Thomas Aquinas", in: M. Levering–M. Dauphinais (eds.), *Rediscovering Aquinas and the Sacraments: Studies in Sacramental Theology* (Chicago: Hillenbrand, 2009), pp. 114–35.

[53] See Pieper, *Sakralität und 'Entsakralisierung' (1969)*; *In Search of the Sacred*; A. Nichols, *Looking at the Liturgy: A Critical View of Its Contemporary Form* (San Francisco: Ignatius Press, 1996), pp. 87–114.

[54] Pieper, *In Search of the Sacred*, p. 29; *Sakralität und Entsakralisierung*, p. 406.

New Jerusalem, where God Himself and the Lamb are its Temple (Rev
21:22–23). Certainly, with the revelation of the Son of God, this new
reality has entered our world, but only in an inchoative way, like at "the
time of dawn, when darkness and light are intermingled", as Joseph
Ratzinger explains with reference to the commentary of St. Gregory
the Great on the Apostle Paul's word, "The night is far gone, the day
is at hand" (Rom 13:12). This is the time of the Church, which is an
intermediate state between "already" and "not yet". In this state, the
"empirical conditions of life in this world are still in force", and for this
reason the distinction between the sacred and the quotidian still hold,
even if this distinction is not conceived of as an absolute separation.
With the Church Fathers, this time can be described as "image between shadow and reality" and so the dynamic character of the sacred
is highlighted: through it the whole world is to be transformed into
the worship and adoration of God, but this will be fully realised only
at the end of time.[55] Human existence in this world is structured by
space and time, and so are prayer and divine worship. Therefore the
liturgy needs a place where it can be carried out as a "sacred action".
In the words of Benedict XVI's homily for the solemnity of Corpus
Christi 2012:

> God . . . sent his Son into the world not to abolish, but to give ful-
> fillment also to the sacred. At the height of this mission, at the Last
> Supper, Jesus instituted the Sacrament of his Body and his Blood, the
> Memorial of his Paschal Sacrifice. By so doing he replaced the ancient
> sacrifices with himself, but he did so in a rite which he commanded
> the Apostles to perpetuate, as a supreme sign of the true Sacred One
> who is he himself.[56]

---

[55] J. Ratzinger, *The Spirit of the Liturgy* (San Francisco: Ignatius Press, 2000), p. 54.

[56] Benedict XVI, *Homily at the Holy Mass for the Solemnity of Corpus Christi* (7 June
2012). He also notes the "educational function" of the sacred and warns that "its disappearance inevitably impoverishes culture and especially the formation of the new generations. If, for example, in the name of a faith that is secularized and no longer in need
of sacred signs, these *Corpus Christi* processions through the city were to be abolished,
the spiritual profile of Rome would be 'flattened out', and our personal and community
awareness would be weakened. Or let us think of a mother or father who in the name of
a desacralized faith, deprived their children of all religious rituals: in reality they would
end by giving a free hand to the many substitutes that exist in the consumer society, to
other rites and other signs that could more easily become idols."

Architecture of the Sacred

Following upon this theological reflection, let me consider very briefly the implications this re-appreciation of the sacred has for architecture in the service of the Church's mission. As Pope Benedict says in his 2007 Post-Synodal Apostolic Exhortation *Sacramentum Caritatis*, "the purpose of sacred architecture is to offer the Church a fitting space for the celebration of the mysteries of faith, especially the Eucharist. The very nature of a Christian church is defined by the liturgy" (n. 41).

There is a great richness in the Catholic understanding of the church as a sacred building. Does this mean that architects embarking on such a project will have to be theologians in their own right? I do not think so, but it does require the willingness to enter into a conversation with their clients in order to understand what the *function* of a church is in a profound and meaningful sense. This is a challenge not only for architects, but also for the ecclesiastical clients. The theological currents I have briefly sketched in this paper have contributed much to the de-sacralisation of church architecture in the second half of the last century. While it would be too hasty to claim a direct causal link between this theology and the church architecture I have considered earlier, nonetheless, the weakness or, in some cases, failure in expressing the sacred is not simply a question of architectural styles, but also a question of the theological presuppositions that have gone into these projects, even if they are not always articulated.

When reading the published version of a lecture by Rafael Moneo, I was struck by his comments on one of two essential requirements he followed in his design of Los Angeles Cathedral, namely "the orientation of the apse, which according to ecclesiastic tradition had to face Rome in recognition of the importance of ecumenism for the Catholic congregation".[57] Such a comment betrays an astonishing failure of theological and liturgical consultancy in the planning of a major ecclesiastical edifice. The lack of input on the part of the Church is

---

[57] R. Moneo, "Cathedral of Our Lady of the Angels, Los Angeles, Calif., 1996–2002", in: Mario Botta, Gottfried Böhm, Peter Böhm, Rafael Moneo, *Sakralität und Aura in der Architektur* (Architekturvorträge der ETH Zürich) (Zürich: GTA Verlag, 2010) (pp. 84–105), p. 92. On the "sacred direction" of church buildings see my *Turning Towards the Lord: Orientation in Liturgical Prayer*, 2nd ed. (San Francisco: Ignatius Press, 2009).

a lost opportunity, because many architects, including those who are best known internationally, are still quite keen on building churches, because they realize that here they have the chance to leave a monument of greater and more lasting significance. As Massimiliano Fuksas said in the interview I cited earlier: "But a church is something you must do (*Però una chiesa è una cosa che devi fare*)".[58]

Historically, architects who received important commissions from popes, bishops, or superiors of religious congregations entered into conversations with their patrons, which could at times become difficult. However, such tensions proved to be immensely creative, and opened up depths of artistic expression that otherwise may not have been reached. In other words, the Church has nurtured architects and brought out greatness in them, which may not have manifested itself otherwise. The Church has become too timid in this field, seemingly because of the fear to appear out of touch with modernity.

In the last decade or so, the new classical movement has gained experience and maturity in the field of sacred architecture.[59] Two well-known examples, Thomas Aquinas College Chapel in Santa Paula, California and Our Lady of Guadalupe Seminary Chapel in Denton, Nebraska, were designed by leading representatives of the University of Notre Dame's School of Architecture. While this school is committed to a classical style of building, there is a notable difference between Duncan Stroik's elaborate use of elements from the Italian Renaissance and of the colonial Spanish Baroque at Thomas Aquinas College, and Thomas Gordon Smith's restrained style, indebted to the Romanesque, as was the wish of his client, the Fraternity of St. Peter.

I believe that the recovery of these styles is our best option to renew sacred architecture today. We should not be afraid of imitation, because in this process something new is created, as the historical periods of the Renaissance or of Classicism show us. At the same time, it should be noted that such a renewal is not linked to one particular style. It would be mistaken to conclude that *only* a stark and simple style, or *only* an ornate and exuberant one, is capable of expressing the

---

[58] P. Ansideri, La Bottega dell'Architetto. Conversazione con Massimiliano Fuksas, p. 6.

[59] D. R. McNamara, "A Decade of New Classicism: The Flowering of Traditional Church Architecture", in: *Sacred Architecture* 21 (2012), pp. 18–24.

sacred. However, an architecture that is not ready, or even rejects, to be formed by the Church's liturgy does not work as a church building, as the historical styles of Christianity do. At any rate, the renewal of church architecture that is happening today needs to be supported by a more robust theological reflection on the sacred in Christianity, which will help architects to design apt and indeed beautiful buildings for the Catholic liturgy.

Principles to be Observed in Sacred Architecture

By way of conclusion, I should like to propose four principles that need to be observed in sacred architecture. These suggestions are at an initial stage and made for the purpose of discussion; while they are interrelated, they are not meant to be exhaustive or definitive.

The first principle is *verticality*: a church needs to have a clearly expressed vertical dimension that goes beyond the functional demands on the building. It is not just by accident that historical churches are usually marked by their height. The vertical slant communicates a sense of God's transcendence and leads the worshipper to "seek the things that are above, where Christ is, seated at the right hand of God" (Col 3:1).

The second principle is *orientation*: a church should have a clear sense of directionality. When the Constantinian settlement in the early fourth century permitted the development of a monumental Christian architecture, the type of building that was chosen throughout the Roman Empire was the basilica. While allowing variation in the arrangement of architectural elements, the basic structure of the basilica, with its long rectangular nave ending in a semi-circular apse, was considered singularly suitable for the essential demands of Christian worship and became normative in the Western tradition. The ideal of the Christian church is not a circular building with altar, ambo, and sedilia in the centre; it is not mere accident that samples of this type are hardly found before the second half of the twentieth century.

Historical examples of central-plan churches are usually connected with a specific liturgical use, such as *martyria* (memorial buildings on a venerated tomb or other sacred place) and baptisteries. The clear directionality of this layout expresses the worshipping community's actions of praying and offering to the Lord. The orientation of liturgical space, combined with the first principle of verticality, reaches beyond the visible altar towards eschatological fulfilment, which is anticipated in the celebration of the Holy Eucharist as a participation in the heavenly liturgy and a pledge of future glory in the presence of the living God.

The third principle is the need for *thresholds*. The first such threshold is the entrance to the building, which should not simply be functional but monumental, part of a façade that marks the church as a building set apart. The *Catechism of the Catholic Church* notes the eschatological significance of the church entrance: "To enter into the house of God, we must cross a *threshold*, which symbolizes passing from the world wounded by sin to the world of the new Life to which all men are called".[60] Here is a limit or boundary that separates its ground from the street or square where it stands, but at the same time allows communication and passage between the two worlds. An outside precinct in the form of an atrium or a *sagrato*, as in Bernini's supreme model of the Vatican Basilica, is a particularly felicitous expression of this dynamic.

The second important threshold concerns the sanctuary, which "should be appropriately marked off from the body of the church either by its being somewhat elevated or by a particular structure and ornamentation".[61] A sanctuary raised by a few steps also allows better visibility and so gives a clearer sense of liturgical orientation. In historical churches, the sanctuary is framed by chancel screens or communion rails; thus a shrine is created within the church to highlight the altar, where the sacrifice of Christ is re-presented.

The fourth principle concerns the *connection of sacred art and architecture*. In his book *The Spirit of the Liturgy* then-Cardinal Joseph Ratzinger attempted to formulate criteria for art ordered to divine worship. The first criterion is particularly relevant: "The complete absence of images is incompatible with faith in the Incarnation of God. God has acted in history and entered into our sensible world, so that it may

---

[60] *Catechism of the Catholic Church*, 1186.
[61] *General Instruction of the Roman Missal*, n. 295.

become transparent to him. Images of beauty, in which the mystery of the invisible God becomes visible, are an essential part of Christian worship".[62] In other words, a Catholic church needs art that is figurative. Such figurative art cannot be reduced to naturalism, and in fact the representation of the sacred demands an element of abstraction that will allow it to communicate the reality of the supernatural. This is evident not only from the Byzantine iconographic tradition but also from the masters of Western sacred art, such as Fra Angelico.[63] Moreover, a church also contains space for symbolical and non-figurative expression, as found in the stained glass windows of Cistercian architecture. However, pure abstraction is not adequate, not for aesthetic but for theological reasons.

---

[62] *The Spirit of the Liturgy*, pp. 131–32.

[63] See the somewhat overstated article by T. Verdon, "Anche il Beato Angelico era un astrattista", in: *L'Osservatore Romano*, 12 January 2008, p. 5.

10

"Thoroughly imbued with the spirit and power of the Liturgy"— *Sacrosanctum Concilium* and Liturgical Formation

ALCUIN REID

Introduction

In 1903 the newly elected Pope St. Pius X judged it his "first duty . . . to see the true Christian spirit restored in every respect and be preserved by all the faithful." The "indispensable fount" of this spirit, he asserted, was "the active participation in the holy mysteries and in the public and solemn prayer of the Church."[1]

Over fifty years later, Ven. Paul VI and the bishops assembled in Council would speak of the Sacred Liturgy as the "primary and indispensable source from which the faithful are to derive the true Christian spirit" in the Constitution on the Sacred Liturgy *Sacrosanctum Concilium*, (n. 14). The means by which that source could be accessed, they said, was *participatio actuosa*—conscious and actual participation in the liturgy.

There was nothing startling about this. In the intervening decades the Liturgical Movement had worked long and hard to promote such participation. Whilst a number of its activists' enthusiasms and some of the reforms that were enacted in that period require critical appraisal, the movement's central tenet, that living participation in—or perhaps

---

[1] Pius X, *Tra Le Sollecitudini*, 22 November 1903.

better, "connection with"—the action of Christ in the Sacred Liturgy is fundamental for the Christian life, was utterly sound.[2]

Thus *participatio actuosa* was readily accepted as the cornerstone of the Council's liturgical Constitution. The ensuing decades have seen much done in its name. Some—perhaps a good deal—of liturgical *activity* has had very little to do with *actual* participation, very little to do with being thoroughly *connected* to the action of Christ through the ritual worship of His Church, and more to do with the misconception that as many people as possible must be 'doing things' at the liturgy.[3] Activity, liturgical busyness, or 'activist' participation, are not what St. Pius X called for. That is not what the Liturgical Movement promoted. It is not what the Second Vatican Council mandated.

Participatio actuosa, so rightly laid as the cornerstone of authentic liturgical and ecclesial renewal by these popes itself rests on a foundation and its absence allows the error of activist participation to thrive. Without it liturgical renewal and reform is at risk. *Sacrosanctum Concilium* articulated this danger clearly. It is my concern that in rushing to ensure that everyone 'participates' and in the haste to reform rites to facilitate this, we have perhaps not attended to this precondition for *participatio actuosa*, for a real and fruitful connection with Christ at work in the Sacred Liturgy.

Sacrosanctum Concilium

In order to identify this precondition and address this concern we need to study the first chapter of the Constitution, "General Principles for the Restoration and Promotion of the Sacred Liturgy" (nn. 5–46).

Articles 5–13 present the theological rationale that underpins the

---

[2] Cf. Alcuin Reid, *The Organic Development of the Liturgy*, 2nd ed. (San Francisco: Ignatius Press, 2005).

[3] One only needs to observe the lack of connection with the whole liturgical celebration so often manifested by people asked to participate by reading, announcing the intentions of the prayers of the faithful, or who bring up gifts in offertory processions. Whilst they perform their 'part' as well as they can, for the remainder of the rite they often resemble idle actors before or after performing their role on centre-stage. This is particularly disturbing when it is found in liturgical celebrations in Catholic schools and colleges where liturgical formation should be integral.

pastoral and practical principles that will follow. In this rich theological *exposé* we find the theology of the Paschal Mystery, revived in the twentieth century, in article 5, the differing manners in which Christ is present in the Sacred Liturgy in article 7, and the statement that the Sacred Liturgy is the *"culmen et fons"* ("source and summit") of the life and mission of the Church in article 10. Article 11 provides the reminder that for the liturgy to bear its fruit the faithful must be connected to it by participating in the liturgical action and underlines that facilitating such participation is a duty of all pastors. Articles 12–13 assert the ongoing importance and value of private and devotional prayer in the light of the primacy of the liturgy.

It is in articles 14–20 that we meet the fundamental principle of *actuosa participatio*:

> In the restoration and promotion of the Sacred Liturgy the full and active participation by all the people is the aim to be considered before all else; for it is the primary and indispensable source from which the faithful are to derive the true Christian spirit.[4]

This gives both the clear pastoral rationale (the "why"), and the desired outcome (the "what"), of the liturgical reform desired by the Council; namely facilitating "liturgical piety"—that Christ's faithful would ordinarily find the necessary nourishment for Christian life in the active and conscious contemplation of the Faith of the Church as it is celebrated in the liturgical rites and prayers throughout the annual round of seasons and feasts of the liturgical year, enjoying priority over the practice of an unrelated, however worthy, devotional exercise.

Yet article 14 envisages that this reform requires *a priori* a substantial improvement of the liturgical education and formation of the clergy and through them of the whole of Christ's faithful, stating, perhaps prophetically:

> It would be futile to entertain any hopes of realizing [*actuosa participatio*] unless the pastors themselves, in the first place, become thoroughly imbued with the spirit and power of the Liturgy, and undertake to

---

[4] Art. 14. "Quæ totius populi plena et actuosa participatio, in instauranda et fovenda sacra Liturgia, summopere est attendenda: est enim primus, isque necessarius fons, e quo spiritum vere christianum fideles hauriant."

give instruction about it. A prime need, therefore, is that attention be directed, first of all, to the liturgical instruction of the clergy.[5]

In the redaction of the text of the Constitution the assertion at the heart of this paragraph was present from the first draft distributed to the Liturgical Preparatory Commission in August 1961.[6] By November 1961 this paragraph was in the form that would be approved by the Council.[7] Its self-evident rationale attracted no comment or debate *in aula*.[8]

This paragraph articulates the necessary foundation for what the Council (and St. Pius X and the Liturgical Movement) wished to bring about. It lays down the prerequisite for liturgical reform: the widespread liturgical formation of clergy and through them the liturgical formation of all. The Council not only wished that all should be "thoroughly imbued with the spirit and power of the Liturgy",[9] and thus be enabled to participate fully, consciously and actively in the Sacred Liturgy, it also knew perfectly well that if this precept was not respected, efforts to bring about such participation—to use the Council's own words —"would be futile." Upon this foundation the whole of *Sacrosanctum Concilium*, indeed the liturgical reform of the Second Vatican Council, rests. For what good is a new or renewed liturgical theology, or are

---

[5] Art. 14. "Sed quia, ut hoc evenire possit, nulla spes effulget nisi prius ipsi animarum pastores spiritu et virtute Liturgiæ penitus imbuantur in eaque efficiantur magistri, ideo pernecesse est ut institutioni liturgicæ cleri apprime consulatur."

[6] "Sed quia ut hoc facere recte possint nulla spes effulget nisi prius ipsi spiritu et virtute liturgiæ penitus imbuantur in eaque efficiantur magistri, ideo pernecesse est ut institutioni liturgicæ cleri, præprimis in facultatibus theologicis et in seminariis, apprime consulatur." Pontificia Commissio de sacra Liturgia præparatoria Concilii Vaticano II, *Constitutio de Sacra Liturgia fovenda atque instaurandus*, 10 August 1961, unpublished cyclostated document, xiv+252 pp., n. 20, p. 48, The American Catholic History Research Center and University Archives (ACUA), Frederick Richard McManus Papers, Box 52.

[7] Cf. Pontificia Commissio de sacra Liturgia præparatoria Concilii Vaticano II, *Constitutio de Sacra Liturgia* Schema transmissum Sodalibus Commissionis die 15 Novembris 1961, unpublished cyclostated document, pp. xiii–96, p. 12, (ACUA), McManus Papers, Box 52.

[8] Cf. Francisco Gil Hellín, *Concilii Vaticani II Synopsis: Constituto de Sacra Liturgia Sacrosanctum Concilium* (Rome: Libreria Editrice Vaticana 2003), pp. 56–57.

[9] As this phrase was understood by the Council Fathers in the Aula in 1962. One wonders whether the allusion to Romano Guardini's seminal work *The Spirit of the Liturgy* (London: Sheed & Ward, 1937), is more than coincidental.

reformed liturgical rites, if Christ's faithful, clerical, religious and lay, are unable or ill-equipped to profit from them?[10]

Participatio actuosa and liturgical formation are inseparable, as article 14 itself emphasises and as the following subsidiary articles 15–20 underline. Divorcing them, or allowing one to predominate to the detriment of the other, could not be without severe consequences. Any ritual reform not underpinned by the requisite formation might well be said to be at risk of being built on sand (cf. Mt 7:26–27), just as an activist interpretation of *participatio actuosa* would risk adopting the error of Martha to the exclusion of the indispensable contemplative role of her sister Mary (cf. Lk 10:38–42).[11] Both are essential if we are to read the rest of *Sacrosanctum Concilium* and its consequent principles and policies correctly.

Is this concern unduly alarmist or the setting up of a straw man? Two contemporary liturgists offer evidence that it is not. The first, Keith Pecklers S.J., is clear that "Even today, the kind of liturgical participation and careful preparation envisaged by the Council exhibited in a proper implementation of the new rite is barely visible in some countries", he says. Though, "it is abundantly present in others", he counters.[12]

The second, John Baldovin S.J., laments that "well over half . . . of priests cannot seem to understand how to use the facultative moments of introduction in the liturgy." He adds that his estimate is "very conservative."[13] Furthermore, speaking of the important role of the priest

---

[10] It is instructive that John Paul II would deem it necessary to call this "a most urgent task" in his Apostolic Letter, *Vicesimus Quintus Annus*, 4 December 1988, n. 15.

[11] Cf. Joseph Cardinal Ratzinger's homily "Mary and Martha" in Alcuin Reid., ed., *Looking Again at the Question of the Liturgy* (Farnborough: St. Michael's Abbey Press, 2003), pp. 13–15.

[12] Keith Pecklers S.J., "*Ressourcement* and the Renewal of Catholic Liturgy: On Celebrating the New Rite" in: Gabriel Flynn and Paul D. Murray, eds., *Ressourcement: A Movement for Renewal in Twentieth Century Catholic Theology*, (Oxford University Press, 2012), (pp. 318–32), pp. 331–32. An examination of the prevalent practices where "it is abundantly present" may be instructive. See also Pecklers' enthusiastic assessment in: Keith Pecklers S.J., *The Genius of the Roman Rite: The Reception and Implementation of the New Missal* (London: Burns & Oates, 2009), p. 40.

[13] John Baldovin S.J., *Reforming the Liturgy: A Response to the Critics* (Collegeville: Liturgical Press, 2008), p. 152.

in the preparation of appropriate liturgical music, Baldovin bemoans that "this requires the kind of adequate seminary training (and continuing education) that we are far from achieving."[14]

Sacrosanctum Concilium rightly speaks of the importance of academic formation in the Sacred Liturgy (articles 15–16).[15] Here I would like to return to article 14 where we find what I believe is the kernel of liturgical formation regardless of how many or how few seminars, courses or academic degrees we have completed. I am speaking of the Council's insistence on being "thoroughly imbued with the spirit and power of the Liturgy" ("Spiritu et virtutæ Liturgiæ penitus imbuantur"). That is the liturgical formation desired by the Council. That is where we need to begin.

"Spiritu et Virtutæ Liturgiæ Penitus Imbuantur" at the Council

What did this phrase mean at the Council? Whilst it is an historical fact that from the outset of the work of the liturgical preparatory Commission some individuals sought to push the reform along partisan paths,[16] and whilst we know that later the key individual in the implementation of *Sacrosanctum Concilium*, Archbishop Annibale Bugnini C.M., would feel free to boast the applicability of the saying "fortune favours the brave",[17] there was nothing at all controversial about asserting that clergy should be "thoroughly imbued with the spirit and power of the Liturgy", and that they in turn should thus form others. Although this was an ambitious goal, it was widely accepted as self-evident and essential. This indicates that both the Fathers of the Council and those

---

[14] Ibid., p. 155.

[15] See the paper of Fr. Paul Gunter O.S.B., "Academic Formation and the Sacred Liturgy", ch. 21 below.

[16] See my forthcoming work: *Continuity or Rupture? A Study of the Second Vatican Council's Reform of the Liturgy.*

[17] Annibale Bugnini C.M., *The Reform of the Liturgy 1948–1975* (Collegeville: Liturgical Press, 1990), p. 11. Bugnini used this phrase in reference to his 1948–1949 questionnaire and subsequent article on liturgical reform; cf. A. Bugnini, "Per una riforma liturgica generale" in: *Ephemerides Liturgicæ*, 63 (1949), pp. 166–84.

involved in the work of the reform themselves were at least in some way thus imbued—or beginning so to be.[18]

This was understood and articulated by authoritative contemporary commentators. They took articles 14–20 of the Constitution as a whole, certainly, and devoted much space to their stipulations regarding academic formation. But that alone is not sufficient.

Fewer than eight weeks after the promulgation of *Sacrosanctum Concilium*, Paul VI issued his *Motu Proprio* letter *Sacram Liturgiam* (25 January 1964). In a commentary in *L'Osservatore Romano* the day after its publication the rector of the Liturgical Institute at St. Anselmo, Salvador Marsili O.S.B., observed:

> The liturgy is not the sum total of rubrics, as if all that would be needed would be to make gestures that were different from those made up to now. Instead of being a reform of ritual, the Constitution is a *reform of spirit and of mentality in ritual matters*. This is the reason why it presents us with theological perspectives that, in part, are intended to justify the reform, and, in part, are intended to create a new spirit of Christian worship precisely by means of the reform. In fact, it is not a matter of simply creating new external forms of worship; rather it is one of creating mental categories that were either entirely new in the case of some, or declining or deficient in the case of others.[19]

Marsili concludes: "Unless the spirit of the liturgy is assimilated, the reform movement runs the risk of ending miserably as an external show." And he adds: "It does not follow that because something is modern it has to be better."[20]

In his 1966 commentary Joseph A. Jungmann S.J. observed: "this summons to the 'active participation' . . . has rightly been called the 'refrain' of the Constitution. . . . But in order to ensure this participation, the Council wishes to take precautions in the decisive point: in

---

[18] Many of the Fathers of the Council recall it as a time of profound personal formation.

[19] Published in *L'Osservatore Romano* on 29 January 1964. Cited in: William Baraúna, "Active Participation: the inspiring and directive principle of the Constitution" in: William Baraúna and Jovian Lang O.F.M. eds., *The Liturgy of Vatican II*, vol. I (Chicago: Franciscan Herald Press, 1966), (pp. 131–93), p. 156. Emphasis original.

[20] Ibid.

the education and instruction of the clergy."[21] But beyond this, "the spirit of the liturgy", he insisted, "must penetrate into the entire religious life of the young clergy."[22]

Speaking of the liturgical formation of future clergy, Anton Haenggi, like Jungmann part of both the preparatory commission and of the post-conciliar *Consilium*, insisted in 1965 that:

> Liturgical training does not consist of scientific instruction alone. Knowledge should lead to action, and liturgical science to the celebration of the Liturgy. All . . . must work so that clerics in seminaries and religious houses may acquire a liturgical formation in the spiritual life. . . .[23]

To this end, Haenggi asserted, there needs to be "an integration of the whole religious life through a dignified solemn celebration of the Liturgy with active participation and the observation [sic: read 'observance'] of liturgical laws." "Thus", he concluded, "what they learn and live through this 'proper direction' and the 'very celebration of the sacred mysteries' they will be able to communicate to the faithful committed to their pastoral care later on."[24]

In 1964 Frederick R. McManus, another preparatory commission and *Consilium* expert, noted the importance of the "broad spiritual formation of the seminarian in the celebration of the liturgy" and, with reference to article 13 of the Constitution which speaks of popular devotions, underlines "the requirement by the Council that the other exercises of piety in seminaries, such as retreats, devotional exercises, etc., should be 'imbued with the spirit of the liturgy.' "[25]

---

[21] Joseph A. Jungmann S.J., "Constitution on the Sacred Liturgy" in: *Commentary on the Documents of Vatican II*, vol. I (London and New York: Herder, 1967), (pp. 1–87), p. 17.

[22] Ibid., p. 18.

[23] Cf. Antonius Haenggi, "The Liturgical Education of the Clergy" in: A. Bugnini C.M. and C. Braga C.M., *The Commentary on the Constitution and on the Instruction on the Sacred Liturgy* (New York: Benziger, 1965), (pp. 79–83), p. 82.

[24] Ibid.

[25] Frederick R. McManus, *Sacramental Liturgy* (New York: Herder, 1967), p. 24. His commentary originally appeared in *Worship*, vol. 38, in three parts, commencing in the May 1964 issue.

Bishop Henri Jenny, who made a significant contribution to the preparatory and conciliar liturgical commissions, and who was a member of the *Consilium*, introduced a commentary in 1966 with the caveat:

> The liturgical renewal, as is foreseen, cannot be accomplished by the mechanical observance of a certain number of requirements. It was understood that it requires, on the contrary, a state of mind, a mentality, which requires constant formation. Many hopes will be disappointed if we assume, consciously or not, that it would suffice to make external changes for to bring about an efficacious reform.[26]

William Baraúna O.F.M., a Council *peritus*, underlined this in his 1965 commentary on *participatio actuosa* which appears in two volumes graced with a Foreword by Giacomo Cardinal Lercaro, the President of the *Consilium*. Baraúna writes:

> Before announcing the principles that should lead to a reform of the liturgy, and the ways and means that by which that reform should be effected, the Constitution . . . speaks about the theological nature of the same . . . and . . . of the primary necessity of a solid liturgical formation of the clergy and the laity. It is evident, therefore, that in the mind of the Fathers, guided by the assistance of the Holy Spirit and by their own pastoral experience, the reform will be of little or no value unless we give first place to the effort to enable the laity to grasp the authentic liturgical spirit—for this spirit is a stranger to the people of our day, because they have little appreciation for anything that savours of symbolism, the community life, living in the spirit of the mystery of the liturgy. Even if all the liturgy of the future were in the vernacular, it would avail nothing unless people were first prepared by a deep and persevering indoctrination into [formation in] the *spirit* of the liturgy.[27]

---

[26] "Le renouveau liturgique, tel qu'il est prévu, ne peut s'accomplir par l'observation, comme mécanique, d'un certain nombre des prescriptions. On a compris qu'il demande, au contraire, un état d'esprit, une mentalité, qui requièrent une incessante éducation. Bien des espoirs seraient déçus, si l'on supposait, consciemment ou non, qu'il suffirait de changements extérieurs pour une réforme efficace." "Introduction" in: Bernard Marliangeas O.P., *La Liturgie: Constitution Conciliare et Directives d'Application de la Réforme Liturgique* (Paris: Centurion, 1966), (pp. 25–47), p. 41.

[27] Baraúna, "Active Participation: the inspiring and directive principle of the Constitution", p. 148. Emphasis original.

Baraúna provides an insightful exposé of liturgical formation as an essential precondition, drawing on a number of sources which demonstrate clearly the widespread contemporary understanding that being "thoroughly imbued with the spirit and power of the Liturgy" was *the* place to start the work of liturgical renewal as desired by the Council. By way of example he warns:

> Those who today pray their breviary with haste and without devotion, with no thought of obtaining from it the vital strength that should support their spiritual life and ministry, would take the same attitude tomorrow, even if the Church were to reform the breviary, authorise the use of the vernacular in it, and reduce to half an hour the time required to recite it.[28]

Later, Cyprian Vagaggini O.S.B. asserted that:

> The reform of structure, of language, of chant, the very creation of new liturgical forms cannot be anything more than an aid, important though it may be, toward introducing people into the world of the liturgy. A certain French priest showed that he did not overestimate the effectiveness of this when he observed, in a discussion about the liturgical language, "Whether the liturgy is done in Latin or in French, for my people it will always be in Hebrew!"
>
> And even today, after the Council, with the liturgy happily almost all in the vernacular, it remains substantially "in Hebrew", not only for the people but also for the clergy. And if the clergy do not first master this Hebrew and then explain it to the people, the liturgical reform will not have done much toward Christianizing the world.[29]

These commentators were committed to the Constitution and to liturgical renewal. Today rites ancient and new daily immerse Christ's faithful in all that the Sacred Liturgy makes available to us, but both can be celebrated in a manner estranged from that spirit. For *Sacrosanctum Concilium* ritual reform is secondary to the work of formation in

---

[28] Ibid., p. 151. Baraúna is drawing on: F. Vandenbrouke O.S.B., "Problèms du Bréviare" in: *Questions Liturgiques et Paroissiales*, 37 (1956), pp. 169–72.

[29] Cyprian Vagaggini, *Theological Dimensions of the Liturgy: A General Treatise on the Theology of the Liturgy* (Collegeville: Liturgical Press, 1976), p. xxiii. This English translation by Leonard J. Doyle and W. A. Jurgens is of the fourth Italian edition of *Il senso teologico della Liturgia* (Rome: Edizioni Paoline, 1965).

order to enable all to benefit from the spiritual and apostolic fruits that being "thoroughly imbued with the spirit and power of the Liturgy" unlocks.[30]

Another commentary, whilst not contemporary, is important—that of Archbishop Bugnini. Speaking in his memoirs of article 14 he too insists on the primacy of liturgical formation, stating that:

> Everything is presented with an eye on the conscious and devout participation that should result from the properly organised instruction of the faithful and, even before that, from the development in priests and seminarians of a strong and comprehensive sense of liturgy.[31]

And yet we know that following the Council this was not what occurred. As one Council Father who was enthusiastic about the liturgical debate at the Council and the progeny that it was made to bear reflected in the Epilogue to his Council diary: "One mistake that may have been made . . . was to allow changes, both on the part of the celebrant as well as the participants, without providing sufficient education and preparation."[32]

Because of this it is necessary today to rediscover precisely what it means to be "thoroughly imbued with the spirit and power of the Liturgy."

The Meaning of *"Spiritu et Virtutæ Liturgiæ Penitus Imbuantur"*

What, then, does it mean?

In the part of Provence, France, in which I live the annual *Bravades* —the festivals in honour of the patron saints of the villages—are an important tradition. This year, before the customary procession, our mayor greeted the Curé and the deacons assisting him and remarked enthusiastically on the beauty of the cope and dalmatics.

---

[30] It remains an interesting question whether the reformed rites promulgated by Paul VI are not, perhaps, too ritually and psychologically evacuated in their *editiones typicæ*, as well as in their application, to facilitate this, and indeed whether the reformers were not too optimistic or even significantly naïve in this respect.

[31] Bugnini, *The Reform of the Liturgy*, p. 41.

[32] Marion F. Forst, *Daily Journal of Vatican II*, privately published, Olathe, Kansas, 2000, p. 180.

Uncomfortable at such attention to vesture the Curé retorted that 'true beauty is found in the heart.' His *riposte* was not wrong. For one (as he) formed in a counter-reformation tradition influenced by some of the liturgically minimalist if not quietist strands of the *devotio moderna* —which in our day, combined with a misinterpretation of *Sacrosanctum Concilium*'s desire for "noble simplicity", has too frequently resulted in simplicity being ignobly visited upon the liturgy[33]—for such people, his reply conveys all that needs to be said: what is interior is all that matters. Liturgical vesture and ceremonial, liturgical language, music, art and architecture, the orientation of the altar, and so forth, are not important. Paying attention to them is seen as a distraction from more important things.

But the Curé had missed the point. When the Church celebrates the Sacred Liturgy, the Holy Sacrifice of the Mass, the sacraments, the sacramentals and, in this case, a procession, Christ's sacred ministers are not displaying *their* interior beauty—heaven forbid! As Joseph Cardinal Ratzinger wrote in 2004, "the Liturgy is not about us, but about God."[34]

The Sacred Liturgy is not about the clergy: rather, their liturgical actions and comportment serve to reflect the beauty and splendour of Christ made present through their sacred ministry. The putting on of worthy and beautiful vesture to reflect this, including those riches of ecclesiastical art that are the fruit of the faith, prayer and generosity of previous generations—indeed the employment of the best of all of created things in the Sacred Liturgy—is not an exercise of self-exaltation or indulgence on the part of the clergy, but their humble ministration of Christ in and to our world—a world of material things and corporeal beings to whom such signs and symbols speak and with whom they connect, as indeed they did with my mayor.

The Sacred Liturgy makes present Almighty God's indulgence towards man: it is a feast of His incarnate and saving love realised sacramentally in our midst by means of created things. This is why, as Pope Benedict XVI insisted, everything associated with this feast ought to

---

[33] Cf. Alcuin Reid, "Noble Simplicity Revisited" in: D. V. Twomey SVD and Janet E. Rutherford, eds., *Benedict XVI and Beauty in Sacred Art and Architecture* (Dublin and New York: Four Courts and Scepter, 2011), pp. 94–111.

[34] Joseph Cardinal Ratzinger, "Preface" in: Reid, *The Organic Development of the Liturgy*, (pp. 9–13), p. 13.

be marked by beauty.[35] That is why the Sequence of the feast of *Corpus Christi* sings "quantum potes tantum aude", urging us to dare to do as much as we can as we feast upon the divine present in our midst. Here we begin to grasp the spirit of the liturgy.

The liturgy is not an idea, the product of a meditation, a personal feeling or conviction arising from some devotion or spiritual enthusiasm howsoever worthy such things may be. Let us not forget that according to the first commandment of the Decalogue worship is our first duty and that, as St. Thomas Aquinas articulates, rendering true worship is the primary response of man demanded by God's justice.[36] The liturgy is not one optional spiritual practice amongst others, or a peculiar method of devotion promoted by seemingly obsessive people called "liturgists." It is normative for Christian life.

Being imbued with the spirit of the liturgy is first and foremost about wholly immersing ourselves in this ritual worship of Almighty God. It is about diving into the great reservoir of Christ's action in His Church, as it were, and learning to swim and rejoice in her currents. It is about the entire body-soul being that each one of us is encountering Christ by entering into and submitting to the requirement *that* we worship and to the demands of the *ritual* worship of our tradition.

This encounter is essentially ecclesial—and I use the word advisedly, in place of "communal", which conveys but one aspect of its true nature. None of us worships as an isolated individual; rather we take our rightful places in the liturgical assembly as members of the Church. This encounter is objective: it is not something made up for the occasion according to the gifts or desires of individuals. It is the Church's liturgy, the richly laden orchard ripe with fruit cultivated in the centuries of her Tradition, into which we enter. Thus the Church, our Mother, feeds and nourishes us on Christ's Word and sacraments according to her wisdom throughout the seasons and feasts of her annual cycle, and according to our particular needs as the circumstances of life require.[37]

A most beautiful appreciation of this reality comes from Cardinal

---

[35] Cf. *Sacramentum Caritatis*, (2007), n. 41.

[36] Cf. Robert Jared Staudt, *Religion as a Virtue: Thomas Aquinas on Worship through Justice, Law and Charity*, Doctoral dissertation presented at Ave Maria University, 2008.

[37] See further: Romano Guardini, *Formazione liturgica* (Brescia: Ed. Morcelliana, 2008).

Ratzinger who wrote about his becoming captivated by the liturgy as a youth. He describes this awakening, occasioned by the gifts of bilingual missals as he grew older:

> Every new step into the liturgy was a great event for me. Each new book I was given was something precious to me, and I could not dream of anything more beautiful. It was a riveting adventure to move by degrees into the mysterious world of the liturgy which was being enacted before us and for us there on the altar. It was becoming more and more clear to me that here I was encountering a reality that no one had simply thought up, a reality that no official authority or great individual had created. This mysterious fabric of texts and actions had grown from the Faith of the Church over the centuries. It bore the whole weight of history within itself, and yet, at the same time, it was much more than the product of human history. Every century had left its mark upon it. . . . Not everything was logical. Things sometimes got complicated and it was not always easy to find one's way. But precisely this is what made the whole edifice wonderful, like one's own home. Naturally, the child I then was did not grasp every aspect of this, but I started down the road of the liturgy, and this became a continuous process of growth into a grand reality transcending all particular individuals and generations, a reality that became an occasion for me of ever-new amazement and discovery. The inexhaustible reality of the Catholic liturgy has accompanied me though all phases of life, and so I shall have to speak of it time and time again.[38]

This boy was shown and willingly entered a small gate into the Church's richly laden orchard. I think it is true to say that as a priest, bishop and pope his eyes, widened with excitement and delight at the first discovery of these riches, never narrowed. Benedict XVI never tired of the process of becoming more thoroughly imbued with the spirit and power of the liturgy. This discovery introduced him to Christ Himself, alive and at work in His Church through her sacred rites. When we have entered into such a relationship how can we tire?

This is the spirit of the liturgy: a spirit which makes demands of us certainly, and which requires our conformity to established—sometimes

---

[38] Joseph Cardinal Ratzinger, *Milestones: Memoirs 1927–1977* (San Francisco: Ignatius Press, 1997), pp. 19–20.

seemingly antiquated—paths and practices; a spirit whose disciplines and language I must learn and to which I must humbly submit; yet a spirit whose paths lead to the joyful discovery and celebration of Christ alive and working in His Church and which nourishes us at the very source of all that we can need for our daily Christian life and mission in the diverse and changing circumstances our particular vocations; a spirit which gives us a foretaste of and an appetite for the eternal and which shapes us and sustains us here on earth until we are called to share together in the unending joy of the heavenly liturgy.

This is a spirit more easily 'caught' than 'taught:' caught by hands joined in a way only used for prayer, by knees bent in adoration, by voices raised in the discipline of the Church's chant, through the body bowed profoundly, by signs of the cross made, in ashes accepted on our foreheads, through water sprinkled on us, and in many other ways besides.

This is a spirit which every altar server once imbibed imperceptibly when, after perhaps arriving in youthful haste, he put on his surplice before Mass and then assisted the priest vesting, witnessing silent prayers that humbled the priest and daily recalled to but a man his high calling: all this in a sacristy enveloped in a silence which could be interrupted only in case of urgency. This silence, present also in our churches before the Sacred Liturgy, radiated the fact that we were about to engage in sacred acts. It bridged our own haste, filtered distractions, and enabled us to enter more fully and more fruitfully into the liturgical act.

Such practices are sometimes regarded today as relics of a bygone age. The bodily gestures we use, our odd use of holy water or ashes, the putting on of a surplice, the praying of vesting prayers: none of these are commanded by Divine Law—nor is maintaining a reverential silence. But they are cherished and tested means to a more-than-worthy end. These and so many other little customs serve as small but powerful steps in initial and ongoing liturgical formation: and it is thus that they achieve their importance. They bespeak, radiate and protect the spirit of the liturgy and, by conforming us to and immersing us in the action of Christ in and through His sacred rites, they facilitate the power of the Sacred Liturgy—the power of Christ Himself—working more efficaciously in our lives and thereby in our world.

It is when we discover this and open ourselves to its multivalent dynamic that we too start down the road of the liturgy. It is then that we begin to become thoroughly imbued with its spirit and power.

Liturgical Formation in the Twenty-first Century

But how do we facilitate this discovery, this formation, now, fifty years after the Council, when so much water—and perhaps also a good deal of liturgical 'capital'—has long since flowed under the bridge?

In 1968 Louis Bouyer, an enthusiastic promoter of liturgical renewal made a most astonishing claim:

> There is practically no liturgy worthy of the name today in the Catholic Church. *Yesterday's liturgy was hardly more than an embalmed cadaver. What people call liturgy today is little more than this same cadaver decomposed.* . . .[39] Perhaps in no other area is there a greater distance (and even formal opposition) between what the Council worked out and what we actually have. Under the pretext of 'adapting' the liturgy, people have simply forgotten that it can only be the traditional expression of the Christian mystery in all its spring-like fullness. I have perhaps spent the greater part of my priestly life in attempting to explain it. But now I have the impression, and I am not alone, that those who took it upon themselves to apply (?) the Council's directives on this point have turned their backs deliberately on what Beauduin, Casel and Pius Parsch had set out to do, and to which I had tried vainly to add some small contribution. . . .[40]

Bouyer may well have been given to provocation, but he had a point. Certainly, there are parishes and religious communities, especially monasteries, where the spirit and power of the liturgy has breathed freely these past decades (at times not without difficulty or considerable cost), but they have been far fewer than they ought to have been. It is, nevertheless, a great sign of hope that now "the question of the

---

[39] Emphasis added. "La liturgie catholique n'était plus guère qu'un cadavre embaumé. Ce qu'on appelle aujourd'hui « la liturgie » n'est pas plus de ce cadavre décomposé." Cited in Louis Bouyer, *Le métier de théologien* (Geneva: Ad Solem, 2005), p. 63.

[40] Louis Bouyer, *The Decomposition of Catholicism* (Chicago: Franciscan Herald Press, 1969), p. 105. See also: Alcuin Reid, "The Reformed Liturgy: A 'Cadaver Decomposed'? Louis Bouyer and Liturgical *Ressourcement*" in: *Antiphon*, 16 (2012) n. 1, pp. 37–51.

liturgy" is very much in the minds of younger Catholics, particularly clergy and seminarians, and is increasingly a concern for seminary and diocesan liturgical formators.

Yet Bouyer's criticism was not isolated. Writing in 2004 of the Neoscholastic reductionism and theological disconnection with the living form of the liturgy that the liturgical movement had attempted to overcome, Cardinal Ratzinger asserted that: "Anyone who, like me, was moved by this perception at the time of the liturgical movement on the eve of the Second Vatican Council can only stand, deeply sorrowing, before the ruins of the very things they were concerned for."[41]

And in 2002 the then Professor Gerhard Ludwig Müller asserted that "in many countries the euphoria of the liturgical movement has given way to disillusionment." "Modern man, formed by secularism and by an environment both immanentist and secular", he observed, "no longer understands the individual rites and gestures of the liturgy", and insisted that nothing less than "a *sanatio in radice*" (a healing in the very roots of the matter) is necessary.[42]

Bouyer laments deviations in the reforms following the Council. Müller highlights a profound cultural crisis. Cardinal Ratzinger, I think it is fair to say, shares both concerns whilst underlining the profound theological nature of the Sacred Liturgy as ritual.

Bouyer continued with a suggestion that may provide a route to a *sanatio in radice.* "When one has thrown everything out, people will have to return to these sources", he said.[43] Whether or not "everything" has in fact been thrown out, I would like to suggest some fundamentals of a much-needed *ressourcement* in the spirit and power of the liturgy.

In the first place we need to dust off some seminal publications of the classical Liturgical Movement. Dom Lambert Beauduin's *Liturgy the Life of the Church*, first published one hundred years ago,[44] is the

---

[41] Preface to: Reid, *The Organic Development of the Liturgy*, p. 11.

[42] Gerhard Ludwig Müller, "Can Mankind Understand the Spirit of the Liturgy Anymore?" in: *Antiphon*, 7 (2002) n. 2 (pp. 2–5), pp. 2, 3.

[43] Bouyer, *The Decomposition of Catholicism*, p. 105.

[44] Lambert Beauduin O.S.B., *La Piété de L'Église: Principes et Faits*, Abbaye du Mont-César and Abbaye de Maredsous, Louvain 1914. It was published in English in 1926 by the Liturgical Press as *Liturgy the Life of the Church*. The most recent edition, edited by the author, was published in 2002 by St. Michael's Abbey Press, Farnborough.

place to begin. It remains a sound theological and practical charter for liturgical renewal. So too is Dom Maurice Festugière's *La Liturgie Catholique: Essai de Synthèse*, unfortunately only available in French.[45] Then there is Romano Guardini's small, powerful work *The Spirit of the Liturgy* and his beautiful meditation *Sacred Signs*.[46] His book on liturgical formation, only ever published in German and Italian,[47] is also of importance, as is his 1964 letter on "the liturgical act."[48]

Bouyer referred to the work of Pius Parsch and Dom Odo Casel. Whilst their writings are valuable they are perhaps not those with which to begin again today. However two less well known works, *The Spirit of the Liturgy* by Abbot Emmanuele Caronti,[49] and Abbot Ildefons Herwegen's *Liturgy's Inner Beauty*,[50] deserve attention.[51] And to this list of classical treasures one must add that of the Father of the New Liturgical Movement: Joseph Cardinal Ratzinger's *The Spirit of the Liturgy*.[52]

With the obvious exception of Ratzinger's book these works formed the background to *Sacrosanctum Concilium*—paragraph 14 practically borrows their words. Those who drafted the Council's provisions and implemented them were not lacking the foundation they gave. Indeed, it is an interesting historical question to ask whether, without this foundation—as many find themselves today—the reforms enacted can be as fruitful as these men and the Council Fathers had hoped? Can the modern rites, celebrated without a thorough formation in the spirit and power of the liturgy be as effective (I am not speaking of validity)

---

[45] Maurice Festugière O.S.B., *La Liturgie Catholique: Essai de Synthèse*, Abbaye de Maredsous 1913.

[46] Romano Guardini, *The Spirit of the Liturgy* (London: Sheed & Ward, 1930); *Sacred Signs* (London: Sheed & Ward, 1937).

[47] Romano Guardini, *Liturgische Bildung* (Burg Rothenfels am Main: Deutsches Quickbornhaus, 1923); *Formazione liturgica*, 1988.

[48] "A Letter from Romano Guardini" in: *Herder Correspondence*, Special Issue, 1964, pp. 24–26.

[49] Emmanuele Caronti O.S.B., *La pietà liturgica* (Torino: Libreria del Sacro Cuore, 1920); *The Spirit of the Liturgy* (Collegeville: Liturgical Press, 1926).

[50] Ildefons Herwegen, *Das Kunstprinzip in der Liturgie*, Paderborn 1912; *Liturgy's Inner Beauty* (Collegeville: Liturgical Press, 1955), published as *The Art-Principle of the Liturgy* by the same publisher in 1931.

[51] A more popular classic that retains its value is Virgil Michael O.S.B.'s *The Liturgy of the Church: According to the Roman Rite* (New York: Macmillan, 1938).

[52] Joseph Cardinal Ratzinger, *The Spirit of the Liturgy* (San Francisco: Ignatius Press, 2000).

in respect of the mission and life of the Church as was intended? But I digress.

I do not propose these classical texts primarily as textbooks. Rather, they are witnesses. From their pages we can hear the hearts of men thoroughly imbued with the spirit and power of the liturgy beating still. We close them only to find ourselves with a thirst for the divine refreshment from which their authors have drunk. These are texts more for *lectio divina* than for study. They are invitations to discover, or re-discover, both our need for the liturgical life and its true spirit.

In 1912 Abbot Herwegen wrote:

> Whoever lives the liturgical life of the Church according to her venerable and hallowed ordering, will find therein all the grades of perfection; his life will become a work of beauty, and will attain its everlasting value in its progressive transfiguration.[53]

This is the second fundamental element of any *ressourcement*: to live the liturgical life of the Church, as fully as possible. For it is by *living* the liturgy that we become imbued by its spirit and power: it is this which forms us—before ever we read, study, talk or write about it.

In this we are confronted by two difficulties. The first is that alluded to by Bouyer: the liturgy following the Council has, at best, been full of what one might call "issues", and living it, "issues and all", may not be as formative in the spirit and power of the liturgy as *Sacrosanctum Concilium* had desired. In this case, where do we turn for our *sanatio in radice*?

Certainly, this raises the large and valid question of a reform of the reform which must be addressed by authority as well as scholars as a matter of justice to the Council and indeed to liturgical tradition itself.[54] But we cannot necessarily wait for that—the matter is too important. What then are bishops, formation staff, pastors and those who work for the preparation of liturgical celebrations and ministers to do?

---

[53] Herwegen, *Liturgy's Inner Beauty*, p. 44.

[54] Here we must consider the issues raised by the theological changes made to the liturgical texts in both the Latin original and in vernacular translation. See in particular the scholarship of Lauren Pristas, *Collects of the Roman Missals: A Comparative Study of the Sundays in Proper Seasons before and after the Second Vatican Council* (London: T. & T. Clark, 2013).

I believe that Pope Benedict XVI provides the answer in his 2007 Apostolic Exhortation *Sacramentum Caritatis*, in the five paragraphs on the *ars celebrandi* (nn. 38–42). The *ars celebrandi* is the "fruit of faithful adherence to the liturgical norms *in all their richness*", he teaches (n. 38; emphasis added). He underlines the role of the bishop as "chief steward of the mysteries of God in the particular Church" (n. 39), of respect for the liturgical books and of fostering "a sense of the sacred and the use of outward signs which help cultivate this sense" (n. 40), of the importance of liturgical art and architecture (n. 41) and of liturgical singing (n. 42).

These components of the *ars celebrandi* reflect the fact that the Sacred Liturgy is not primarily a cerebral or intellectual experience—it is not a text to be studied (though its texts are capable of study). No; it is a sensual, ritual experience, involving our mind, body and spirit and we must allow the riches of our liturgical tradition to form us by connecting us to Christ by means of these portals. This is one area in which our modern, literate and rational culture has impacted adversely: a mentality (educated and perhaps somewhat middle-class) that treats the liturgy as a discourse and reduces its forms to the prosaic rather than respecting its nature as multifaceted ritual radically reduces the possibility of such connection.

In the light of this I would like to make some observations on living the liturgical life today. Firstly, Benedict XVI speaks of observing the liturgical norms "in all their richness." Let it be said clearly: liturgical minimalism is the enemy of the spirit of the liturgy and is a cancer to true liturgical formation.[55] Certainly, some circumstances limit how much we can do, but even then we are called to give all that is possible as did the widow at the treasury (cf. Mk 12:41–43). Less is not more when celebrating the Sacred Liturgy.

Secondly, in the Church's wisdom and tradition the sung liturgy is the norm—a truth our Eastern brethren have never forgotten. Yet for centuries the liturgical formation of far too many has been grounded

---

[55] This is, perhaps, most apparent with the liturgically minimalist approach often found to Exposition and Benediction of the Most Blessed Sacrament in many parishes and communities which ignore the requirements of the modern *Ordo Expositionis et Benedictionis Eucharistiæ* that incense and particular vesture be used whenever the Sacred Host is exposed; cf. *Rituale Romanum: De Sacra Communione et De Cultu Mysterii Eucharistici Extra Missam* (Rome: Typis Polyglottis Vaticanis, 1973), nn. 93–100.

in the read liturgy, the *missa lecta* or low Mass. Before we rest content that "Vatican II changed all that"—and we should note that the modern Mass read just like an old, rushed low Mass lives still—I would ask us to consider whether we have in fact achieved what the Council desired: the singing *of* the liturgy, rather than singing *at* the liturgy?[56] The answer is that, on the whole, we have not. Decades of widespread liturgical malformation are not going to be easy to undo.

Thirdly, following the Council the Divine Office has been prayed in common far more frequently. But let us ask how this is done—liturgically, with the ministers, vesture, postures and other rites and chant foreseen in the liturgical norms? Or is the celebration of the Divine Office more often the experience of a text read through together? If our praying of the Divine Office in our cathedrals, churches, seminaries and religious houses is liturgically deficient, what formation does this impart? How will this sustain those whose vocation includes the duty to pray it privately? And if our parishes *never* celebrate the Divine Office liturgically, in all its richness, how will our people imbue the spirit and power of the liturgy?

Finally, an essential element of formation by living the liturgy is familiarity with the riches of the *usus antiquior*—of the older liturgical rites. Formation as desired by the Council cannot conceivably exclude the liturgical Tradition that *Sacrosanctum Concilium* itself assumed. These rites celebrated according to their own integrity, in all their richness, are a powerful means of formation. Many clergy and faithful find that the older rites fruitfully inform their participation in and celebration of the modern rites and enable them to approach them seeking continuity with rather than rupture from the Church's bi-millennial liturgical tradition. In the Church of the twenty-first century, it is hard to see how any formation programme could exclude these living treasures.

Other ways of formation in the spirit and power of the liturgy will become clear if we examine our liturgical practices in the light of the principles outlined in *Sacramentum Caritatis*: faithful adherence to the liturgical norms in all their richness is our aim. We must allow the

---

[56] See Alcuin Reid, "*Ut mens nostra concordet voci nostræ:* Sacred Music and Actual Participation in the Liturgy", in: Janet E. Rutherford, ed., *Benedict XVI and Beauty in Sacred Music* (Dublin and New York: Four Courts and Scepter, 2012), pp. 93–126.

power of the Sacred Liturgy work for itself. We must facilitate its connectivity.

In addition to the post-conciliar "issues", the second difficulty that confronts us in seeking to live the liturgy is cultural. Our cultures are increasingly post-Christian and aggressively secular. The Sacred Liturgy is so very, very different, even foreign, to all that is about us. Modern man does not understand it. How do we deal with this reality?

I think that it needs to be said clearly that the project of adapting the liturgy to the supposed needs of 'modern man' has failed. We have not filled our churches, seminaries, religious houses—or perhaps even heaven—by making the liturgy reflect middle-class modernity. There are many causes for the widespread statistical decline in Catholic practice, but the changes to the liturgy as experienced at the local level feature amongst them. Some might argue that this necessitates ongoing reform, adaptation and inculturation at the local level.[57] In my opinion opening such paths would endanger the "substantial unity of the Roman rite" the Council required (cf. *Sacrosanctum Concilium*, 38), and would risk utterly subjectivising the Church's liturgy.

No, the answer is not the imitation of the spirit of the world, but reviving the spirit of the liturgy. For the faithful who frequent the Sacred Liturgy we need to attend to the elements of *ressourcement* we have spoken of above. Thorough catechesis is necessary in order to bridge the cultural gap or that created by liturgical malformation. We must be patient and charitable: we cannot be guilty of scandalising people again with the drastic imposition even of better practices. Yes, pastors must lead, and lead decisively. But they must also bring their flock with them.

And here it must be noted that 'modern man' can indeed connect with the Church's liturgy. The churches, communities and seminaries whose liturgical life is faithful, rich and beautiful—those that celebrate the older rites and those that celebrate the new—are not empty today, at the beginning of the twenty-first century. They are alive with the spirit and power of the liturgy. Their successes are worthy of study and imitation.

For those who rarely if ever encounter the Church's liturgy we need

---

[57] See Anscar Chupungco O.S.B., "Inculturation and the Organic Progression of the Liturgy" in *Ecclesia Orans*, VII (1990) n. 1, pp. 7–21.

two things; firstly, an awareness that the Sacred Liturgy is not primarily a missionary or catechetical tool. It is the Church's worship of Almighty God, not a means of propaganda. We do violence to its nature, and perhaps even to Christ, when we make use of it as a direct instrument of evangelisation.

And yet, we know from the lives of St. Augustine of Hippo, Paul Claudel and others that the liturgy can indeed convert the heart of man. We should not be ashamed of its counter-cultural impact, especially in an age where media transmit its sounds and images so widely. Let the mortal hearts of post-Christian secular mankind be confronted by the spirit and power of the liturgy, by the reality of the Church drinking from the very source of life itself in her worship!

Cardinal Ratzinger asserted that: "Forgetting about God is the most imminent danger of our age. As against this, the liturgy should be setting up a sign of God's presence."[58] In this way, certainly, the Sacred Liturgy is an evangelical witness *ad intra* and *ad extra*. Neither Claudel nor St. Augustine stumbled across liturgy self-consciously fashioned to speak to the peculiarities of their times: they encountered the worship of Christ by His Church in all its richness. Thus they found Christ. It is perhaps instructive to ask what those like them who have found themselves in our churches in recent decades have encountered, and to what effect?

Conclusion

In mandating ritual reform the fathers of the Second Vatican Council, drawing on the best of the classical Liturgical Movement, insisted on the necessity of the *a priori* work of formation in the spirit and power of the liturgy. It is true to say that in the haste to reform and translate rites and have everyone 'do something' at the liturgy, this precondition was widely bypassed and that this necessary foundation was not securely laid.

Today we can speak of a new Liturgical Movement, and in doing so we must acknowledge our profound debt to Pope Benedict XVI.

The primary task of the New Liturgical Movement is one of *ressourcement*, of reviving the spirit of the liturgy and living from it in all its

---

[58] Ratzinger, "Preface", *The Organic Development of the Liturgy*, p. 13.

richness, of becoming imbued with the spirit and power of the Sacred Liturgy as the Second Vatican Council, the classical Liturgical Movement and St. Pius X so ardently desired.

Thus formed we shall be able to read *Sacrosanctum Concilium* correctly. From this basis we shall be able to evaluate the reforms and pastoral policies enacted in its name. Enlightened by this spirit the right paths to take in the future shall become clear.

According to the vocation that Almighty God has given to each one of us, this task is yours as it is mine.

11

Liturgy, Ritual and Contemporary Man—
Anthropological and Psychological Connections

ABBOT CHRISTOPHER M. J. ZIELINSKI O.S.B. OLIV.

Abbot of Lendinara, Italy

Status Quæstionis

The role of ritual in the Sacred Liturgy of the Roman Catholic Church has not been consistently appreciated or fully understood. Aside from the work of Raymond Leo Cardinal Burke, *Divine Love Made Flesh*,[1] my considerations here are largely influenced by Anton Usher's book, *Replenishing Ritual: Rediscovering the Place of Ritual in the Western Christian Liturgy*.[2] Usher's work presents the results of advanced research into ritual studies since the 1960s, expounding on both the dynamics of ritual and its inherent interplay between the body, the soul, and the mind.

A friend of mine, an Italian psychologist, who has dedicated several years to play therapy, once remarked, "No ritual, no liturgy!" This remark provides an appropriate segue into the zealous goal of this presentation, namely, to engage in a historical comparative study of this

---

I wish to thank Dr. William F. E. Mahoney for his assistance and prayers in the preparation of this work. I also would like to acknowledge a debt of gratitude to Raymond Leo Cardinal Burke for his excellent book, *Divine Love Made Flesh*, which has influenced my own reflections both generally and particularly in this paper. His work is an extraordinary read which provides an excellent meditation on the beauty and power of the Holy Eucharist in light of the profound teachings of both John Paul II and Benedict XVI.

[1] R. Burke, *Divine Love Made Flesh: The Holy Eucharist as the Sacrament of Charity* (San Diego: Catholic Action for Faith and Family), 2012.

[2] A. Usher, *Replenishing Ritual: Rediscovering the Place of Rituals in Western Christian Liturgy* (Milwaukee: Marquette University Press, 2010).

religious phenomenon by considering some of the key contributions in the fields of psychology and anthropology in order to demonstrate that ritual is both a constant given and, more significantly, a vital necessity. Ritual is fundamental to the human person. It is ingrained in the very fibers of the human person's being. The rituals found in the Sacred Liturgy are not stagnant and, as Pope Francis notes regarding the sacraments of Easter, for example, the grace offered "is an enormous potential for the renewal of our personal existence, of family life, of social relations" (*Regina Cæli*, Easter Monday, 1 April 2013).

Some scholars, priests and religious as well as lay men and women, have in the past exhibited a certain allergic reaction to psychological and anthropological studies in the area of religion. However, while an allergic or even violent reaction to such studies is not always unwarranted, it is nevertheless important not to anathematize every psychological and anthropological venture *a priori*. The human sciences are not without merit any more than reason is without merit when enlightened by faith. Indeed, faith even presupposes reason.

It is necessary to emphasize here that the aim is to locate "trustworthy connections" in the fields of psychology and anthropology and not to canonize any particular author or provide some kind of implicit ecclesiastical approval to any particular human theory in its whole or in its parts. The purpose is to extract those ideas which are more universal in nature, that is, those ideas which expound on the essence of ritual itself in both the fields of psychology and anthropology, and incorporate them into the discussion in order to evoke a fuller understanding —albeit a limited and imperfect one—of the mysteries of faith as expressed primarily in the Sacred Liturgy.

To this end, I would like to consider the work of Carl G. Jung and his exposition of analytical psychology as expressed in his controversial theory of symbols, myths, and archetypes. This approach allows for an important connection to be made with the school of comparative religions which began in the University of Chicago with its well-known co-founder, Mircea Eliade. Based on some notions originating from these two prominent personages in the fields of psychology and anthropology respectively I will attempt to shed some light on the themes of liturgy, ritual, and contemporary man.

To impress on our minds the innate reality of ritual, it will be worth recounting a revealing and even humorous reality about Sigmund Freud. Freud and many of his followers, who were no great lovers of Christian truth, had a form of suspicion which skimmed the dangerous edges of paranoia despite their treatment of most forms and expressions of ritual as being primitive, infantile, and neurotically obsessive and compulsive. Freud, who reveled in the adulation of all by his title, Herr Professor, and who was so focused on the alleged sexual undertones of all human actions—a focus which eventually cost him his friendship with Jung—never analyzed his own compulsions which tormented him like "old and grumpy gods."[3] His obsessive behavior had something of a mystical, spiritual, and ritualistic nature to it and, had he confronted this behavior honestly, he most likely would have discovered the sublimating and transformative forces which rites, rituals, and rituality provide.

Rituals can harness this irrational energy which can so easily overwhelm individuals or groups and transform that energy into creative and cohesive relations. Ritual, which tames the over creative and stimulates the under creative, has the power to create community and teach individuals to share time and space in a loving and patient manner by fostering the use of a common language and vision in preparation for participating in a common meal. Thus, contrary to Freud's words but more or less in harmony with his actions, we can observe that ritual is not a kind of regression, that is, a return to the mother's womb, but rather a containment, rebirth, and authentic liberation of the entire person.

Studying some of the main tenets of these psychological and anthropological contributions, it should become apparent that ritual in itself tames the passions, transforms fear, and provides a wider and more inclusive vision of reality. My commentary here is grounded on both personal experience and private study. These have helped me meditate and reflect, coming to a more profound understanding of the human condition, that is, the existential malaise and sickness of the human soul. However, my outlook is optimistic, since my experience and study have also led me to realize that there is an exit from this sad state and that exit is simultaneously the entrance into a saner state of being

---

[3] A full account of what is being discussed here regarding Sigmund Freud can be found in J. Burke's informational and entertaining book, *The Sphinx on the Table: Sigmund Freud's Art Collection and the Development of Psychoanalysis* (New York: Walker & Company, 2006).

as well as a constantly growing personal relationship with Christ. It is God who is the center of all liturgical life with its spiritual processes. It is the action of his unconditional love and gratuitous provision of grace which is both the beginning and the end of liturgy and ritual. Said more colloquially, some of the insights of psychology and anthropology, which will be examined here, might lead us to the porch, but only Christ has the ability to grant us entrance into the building.

Liturgy and Ritual: *Homo Liturgicus*

A. Bodily Gestures and Postures

David Jaspers notes that, "It is in the body that we worship God."[4] Regarding this, Anton Usher states, "Being predominantly 'bodily,' ritual forms a canvas on which the mind is freed up in order to pray and contemplate."[5] Thus, ritual involves the body, the mind, and the soul. Ritual teaches the individual and the community how and when to act, speak, and move. Böntert states that: "Every liturgical expression therefore remains dependent on signs, symbols, speech, and other forms of expression that participants can grasp and to which they can assent."[6] This allows for the establishment of the *homo liturgicus*, namely, the liturgical man. Liturgical ritual is, therefore, the basis for fulfilling the Church's desire "that all the faithful should be led to that fully conscious, and active participation in liturgical celebrations which is demanded by the very nature of the liturgy" as expressed in the Constitution on the Sacred Liturgy, *Sacrosanctum Concilium* (n. 14). This participation is an expression of the Christian people as "a chosen race, a royal priesthood, a holy nation, a redeemed people" (1 Pet 2:9). It is both the right and the duty of all the baptized (cf. *Sacrosanctum Concilium*, 14).

---

[4] D. Jasper, *The Sacred Body: Asceticism in Religion, Literature, Art, and Culture* (Waco: Baylor University Press, 2009), p. 184.

[5] Usher, *Replenishing Ritual*, p. 30.

[6] S. Böntert, "Liturgical Migrations into Cyberspace: Theological Reflections", in: Teresa Berger, ed., *Liturgy in Migration: From the Upper Room to Cyberspace* (Collegeville: Liturgical Press, 2012), (pp. 279–95), p. 289.

The bodily gestures found in the liturgy promote unity and are "signs" or "symbols" of the realities which they express. For example, the kiss of peace "is a liturgical gesture which expresses agape in a visible manner, the reciprocal love of the faithful, the peace of the Lord which He gives us and which we share with the brothers."[7] This is most evident with the Eucharistic Body and Blood, which "are the gift *par excellence* that Christ has left for the Church."[8] This is a mystery which—as Bishop Athanasius Schneider highlights—"must be made manifest even in external gestures."[9] St. John Paul II also underscored this by saying, "the mystery of the Eucharist has found historical expression not only in the demand for an interior disposition of devotion, but also in outward forms meant to evoke and emphasize the grandeur of the event being celebrated" (*Ecclesia de Eucharistia*, 2003, 48). This, naturally, applies to all the gestures found in the Sacred Liturgy. They are ultimately signs of charity and unity and thus the General Instruction of the Roman Missal observes that "This unity is beautifully apparent from the gestures and bodily postures observed together by the faithful" (n. 96).

B. Sacred Space and Time

Carl Jung defined ritual in general as "the practice and repetition of the original experience."[10] Ritual can be of "extraordinary importance"[11] and serve as way to achieve "mental hygiene."[12] It can also serve as a means to experience something which one does not anticipate.[13] These general observations can be applied to the Sacred Liturgy at least by way of appropriation. The original experience, for example, could be the Last Supper, which is practiced and repeated as an obligation and

---

[7] P. Christophe, L. Marino, trans., *La Bellezza dei Gesti del Cristiano* (Bose: Qiqajon, 2009), p. 33.

[8] A. Schneider. *Dominus Est—It is the Lord! Reflections of a Bishop of Central Asia on Holy Communion* (Pine Beach, N.J.: Newman House Press, 2008), p. 28.

[9] Ibid.

[10] C. G. Jung, "Psychology and Religion" in: *The Collected Works of C. G. Jung*, vol. 11 (Princeton University Press, 1969), p. 9.

[11] Ibid., p. 44.

[12] Ibid., p. 44.

[13] C. G. Jung, "Commentary on 'The Secret of the Golden Flower'" in: *The Collected Works of C. G. Jung* (Princeton University Press, 1969), p. 25.

sublime privilege based on the Lord's tender command, "Do this in memory of me" (Lk 22:19). As Cardinal Burke notes, "In a certain sense, the whole history of the Church may be described as the story of the Apostles' obedience to our Lord's commission to them at the Last Supper."[14] Consequently, the ritual is clearly of "extraordinary importance" and, at the very least, assists in obtaining "mental hygiene." Even more than that, however, Pope Francis proclaims, "The Eucharist is the sacrament of communion that brings us out of individualism so that we may follow him together, living out our faith in him" (Homily on the Solemnity of Corpus Christi, 2013, n. 2).

These rituals, such as the Mass, occur in a particular place, usually a church. Here a distinction between sacred and profane space, as elucidated by Mircea Eliade, can be useful for arriving at a fuller comprehension of the Sacred Liturgy. According to Eliade, "a sacred space possesses existential value for religious man: for nothing can begin, nothing can be *done*, without a previous orientation."[15] Whereas with "profane experience, on the contrary, space is homogenous and neutral; no break qualitatively differentiates the various parts of its mass."[16] Here the concept is differentiated from the experience. This experience of sacred and profane space is a constitutive part of the human person's reality and no matter how much one might try to rid himself of this experience, that is, of this religious impulse, he will never be fully successful. Thus, Eliade further states, "To whatever degree he may have desacralized the world, the man who has made his choice in favor of a profane life never succeeds in completely doing away with religious behavior."[17] In other words, the drive to act religiously and to observe ritual is innate to the human person. Modern man's *rationalism* cannot make this reality disappear. Regarding modern man in this context, Jung states, "He has freed himself from "superstition" (or so he believes), but in the process he has lost his spiritual values to a positively dangerous degree."[18] Notwithstanding the exact nature of the particular "spiritual values" to which Jung refers, it should be evident

---

[14] Burke, *Divine Love Made Flesh*, p. 49.

[15] M. Eliade, W. R. Trask, trans., *The Sacred and the Profane: The Nature of Religion* (New York: Harvest, 1959), p. 22.

[16] Ibid., 22.

[17] Ibid., 23.

[18] C. G. Jung, *Man and His Symbols* (New York: Dell, 1964), p. 84.

that whether he wishes it to be so or not, man is oriented to something spiritual which drives him to engage in some religious behavior and ritual. The gift of faith informs us that this "something spiritual" is actually "someone", in fact, the only one who exists eternally as the ineffably inexplicable *ipsum essens subsistens*, that is, the most mysterious and wonderful "I Aм."

In this sacred space, the *homo liturgicus* follows a set of instructions and directives which allow him to perform the rituals like actors and actresses perform their parts in plays and films. Michael Kunzler highlights this by writing, "In the re-sacralization of the world remote from God the distinction between sacred and profane is even more emphasized: the signs, the significant actions, the gestures, the attitudes, the words, the objects of nature and of art, vestments and liturgical spaces, become 'epiphany of the sacred' ",[19] where creatures are returned "to their full reality and supreme dignity."[20]

Christ the Lord commanded that a large, furnished upper room be prepared for the celebration with His disciples of the paschal supper (cf. Lk 22:22). The power of place is here demonstrated by the Master to be very important for the performing of a sacred rite. Sacred space should be as free as possible from any conditions which might be distracting, making the people of God feel uncomfortable, unimportant, or unprotected. It is important to consider the effects of light, color, temperature, sounds, smells, proximity to others, and so forth when delineating the boundaries of a sacred space.

One's physical surroundings certainly affect one's emotional reactions and mental disposition. Consider the dining atmosphere at restaurants of the fast-food chain McDonald's. The red and yellow color scheme can hardly be considered pleasing either aesthetically or emotionally. The environment creates a sense of urgency and agitation. After ordering a "value meal", you must proceed to an austere countertop for some condiments, napkins, and straws. If, by this point, you are not notably traumatized by the impersonal treatment somewhat reminiscent of how livestock are fed, there is always the seating arrangement to complete this distressing dining experience. Yes, after sitting, you realize that you are a bit far away from the table and, despite your desperate

---

[19] M. Kunzler, *The Church's Liturgy* (Munster: Lit, 2001), p. 30.
[20] Ibid.

attempts to move closer, your ugly, uncomfortable chair goes nowhere since it is permanently bolted to the floor. So, thinking yourself quite clever, you reach to move the table closer to you, but come to the sad realization that it too is irrevocably bolted to that uninviting floor which, by now, you cannot help but imagine is mocking your efforts to enjoy yourself. Clearly, the atmosphere for this dining experience is an engineered one. The purpose is to make you quite uncomfortable so that you are encouraged to take your food "to go", or—if you must stay to eat—ensure that you do not stay long. After all, this is *fast food* intended to make *fast money*. The designers of McDonald's understood well the importance of space and its psychological effects and anthropological consequences.

Recognizing this importance in relation to Christian liturgy, Usher writes that "ritual furnishes a carpet on which the liturgy takes place— a special time and space, a special atmosphere within which the community can enter into communion together, as a community, with God —a sacred public square."[21] This last part, "a sacred public square", is interesting in light of a *Regina Cæli* address Pope Francis gave on the Solemnity of Pentecost 2013. The Holy Father stated that the Solemnity "was a renewed Pentecost that transformed St. Peter's Square into an Upper Room beneath the open sky." He realized that St. Peter's Square had become a *sacred space* due to the solemn occasion and gathering of the faithful.

The reality of sacred space is accompanied by the reality of sacred time. In *The Spirit of the Liturgy*, Benedict XVI, then Cardinal Ratzinger, expressed the interconnection between space and time in the following words:

> Thus time and space are interconnected in Christian prayer. Space itself has become time, and time has, so to speak, become spatial, has entered into space. And just as time and space intertwine, so, too, do history and cosmos. Cosmic time, which is determined by the sun, becomes a representation of human time and of historical time, which moves toward the union of God and world, of history and the universe, of matter and spirit—in a word, toward the New City whose light is God himself. Thus time becomes eternity, and eternity is imparted to time.[22]

---

[21] Usher, *Replenishing Ritual*, p. 30.
[22] J. Ratzinger, *The Spirit of the Liturgy* (San Francisco: Ignatius Press, 2000), p. 94.

This is an insightful exposition of a great mystery which is reflected in the Sacred Liturgy. The liturgy with its rituals admits of both sacred space and sacred time. The book of Ecclesiastes declares that "There is an appointed time for everything, and a time for every affair under the heavens" (3:1). This extends to the liturgy which observes both space and seasons. The rituals are accomplished in sacred spaces at designated sacred times and—as Usher notes—"This has psychological, practical and mystical implications."[23] It is important to remember that the Lord often designated sacred times of prayer in His own earthly life. Silver highlights this when writing, "We would do well to remember how often Jesus regularly (and sometimes abruptly) withdrew from the demands of his ministry to spend time in prayer alone or with his disciples."[24]

C. Silence

I would like now to say a few words on silence. A German proverb says: *Schweigen ist ein Zaun für die Weisheit,* that is, "Silence is a fence around wisdom." The *Liturgical-Monastic Directory* for the Abbey of Santa Maria di Monte Oliveto states that silence "is the essential dimension of hearing profoundly."[25] Thus, the Constitution on the Sacred Liturgy advised that "at the proper times all should observe a reverent silence" (n. 14).

It is important that both the individual and the community share in this wonderful gift to the spirit by becoming silent in spirit. This is both the proper spirit and tone that should precede and accompany the entire liturgical celebration. The Church exhorts that "Even before the celebration itself, it is a praiseworthy practice for silence to be observed in the church, in the sacristy, in the vesting room, and in adjacent areas, so that all may dispose themselves to carry out the sacred celebration in a devout and fitting manner" (*General Instruction of the Roman Missal,* 45).

Our fear of silence and of being alone drives us to make noise and

---

[23] Usher, *Replenishing Ritual*, p. 30.

[24] A. W. Silver, *Trustworthy Connections: Interpersonal Issues in Spiritual Direction* (Cambridge, Mass.: Cowley Publications, 2003), p. 89.

[25] Congregazione Benedettina: Santa Maria di Monte Oliveto, *Direttorio Liturgico-Monastico* (Monte Oliveto: Edizione Monte Oliveto Maggiore, 2012), n. 8.

sometimes to seek anonymous crowds recklessly. Our minds are overcome with a storm of ideas, images, thoughts, and words until we reach an almost wild state of sound and fury. We are even unconscious slaves to our cellphones and prisoners of the world which tracks us down everywhere: at home, at Mass, in the confessional, and even in the bathroom. The world is constantly present, but never the "presence"! Wayne Muller observes that "There comes a moment in our striving when more effort actually becomes counterproductive, when our frantic busyness only muddies the waters of our wisdom and understanding."[26] He further states, "When we become still and allow our life to rest, we feel a renewal of energy and gradual clarity of perception."[27]

The liturgy and its ritual help us understand in the depths of our being that we need not choose between a false dichotomy of loneliness or clatter. Consequently, we need to cultivate an inner solitude and silence that frees us from loneliness and fear. It is important to understand that loneliness is inner emptiness, but solitude is inner fulfillment. Societies, which have abandoned their rites and ceased to practice common rituals, nomadically wander throughout a lonesome and desolate wilderness.

Silence is the real test of the *homo liturgicus*. It is fear which often drives us to use words endlessly for we fear not being in control or, reprehensibly worse, not being able to control others. In a word, we are not at peace and have established barricades which block us from receiving that divine peace which this world cannot give (cf. Jn 14:27). It is in silence that we can hear and receive Christ's gentle admonition, "Do not let your hearts be troubled and do not be afraid" (Jn 14:27). Thus, Guido Marini observes that: "Silence in the liturgy is the moment in which one listens with greater attention to the voice of God and internalizes His word, so that it bears the fruit of sanctity in daily life."[28]

---

[26] W. Muller, *Sabbath: Restoring the Sacred Rhythm of Rest* (New York: Bantam Books, 1999), p. 26.

[27] Ibid.

[28] G. Marini, *Liturgical Reflections of a Papal Master of Ceremonies* (Pine Beach, N.J.: Newman House Press, 2011), p. 87.

D. Monastic Reminiscences

Here I would like to discuss monastic art and architecture as well as provide a few personal reflections from my life as a monk. First, however, I would like to begin with a story. Once in a medieval monastery, the monks were rigorously engaged in producing paintings of sacred art. After weeks of prayer and contemplation, as each monk labored meticulously, the Abbot noticed one monk who had hidden himself in the corner and who was clearly guarding his work from any peering eyes. The Abbot, who was impressed with this monk's intense and guarded labors, asked him, "What is it you are painting, my son?" The monk whispered to the Abbot, "I am depicting God as He is in His essence." The Abbot was visibly amused by this response and said, "But son, God dwells in inapproachable light and thus the realization of your endeavor is impossible. After all, nobody knows what God looks like!" To this, the monk responded abruptly and confidently, "Patience, Father Abbot. They will in just a few more minutes!"

As noted in the work, *Defining the Holy: Sacred Space in Medieval and Early Modern Europe*, "Churches, and the sacred spaces around them, were not only distinguished from the surrounding physical landscape, but also by more sensory distinctions."[29] These sensory distinctions, found in monastic art, architecture, and music, were not merely attestations to the talent of the various artists, but rather were statements of theological significance.[30] The monastic architecture of the middle ages is a witness to truth.[31] Every detail represents a part of the whole, helping the monk to stay on track and not to lose his way. Both the whole and the details form one sublime reality in which every detail is connected by a hidden thread of grace, transforming the multitude into a miracle of utter plenitude. One such miracle is the Abbey of Le Thoronet, a twelfth-century Cistercian monastery nestled in a valley in Provence, in the south-east of France.

The essence of monastic life is the assiduous following of Christ

---

[29] A. Spicer and S. Hamilton, eds., *Defining the Holy: Sacred Space in Medieval and Early Modern Europe* (Burlington: Ashgate, 2005), p. 7.

[30] Cf. D. Stancliffe, *The Lion Companion to Church Architecture* (Oxford: Lion Hudson, 2008), p. 142.

[31] For a further and fuller discussion of this see: L. Hervé, *Architecture of Truth: The Cistercian Abbey of Le Thoronet* (London: Phaidon, 2001).

through prayer and encountering God. This establishes both a physical and spiritual movement which can be witnessed and observed in the particular framework which seeks to embody the life and spirit of the monk. Medieval monastic architecture is, therefore, fresh and deeply inviting as it speaks less about the period in which it was created and more about the daily life of the monks who have passed through the corridors in ages past and who continue to pass through them to this day. They are "living stones" (1 Pet 2:5), who tell the enduring story of what it means to seek God.

St. Benedict was solicitous that his monks understand and embrace temperance, quality, humility, and respect for the sacred. He desired that these virtues guide the prayers and labors of the monk. St. Benedict wished that his Rule assist the monk in embracing and loving only what was necessary for the journey. When considered from an epistemological point of view, the Holy Rule of St. Benedict teaches the monk that too much is absolutely unnecessary, since the unnecessary hides truth. Monastic architecture was constructed to aid and support the monks in their search for God. It was an embodiment of the quest for God and taught the monk to be a monk while providing an appropriate ambiance for this to occur.

St. Bernard of Clairvaux taught his monks that moving about the monastery was not a merely physical venture, but rather a spiritual journey in which the soul seeks light by following light. Thus, in the pilgrimage of faith, the monk's bodily movements became spiritual ones in which shadows were dispersed by light and the darkness of the night surrendered to the brilliance of the day. As Gilbert of Swineshead wrote, "The roughness of regular observances and the stone of discipline frequently bring forth abundant streams of oil, and the rigidity of our order like that of stone makes the soul to feel the sweetness of prayer."[32]

This architecture of truth provides a truly healing experience for those who connect with the truth it conveys, as well as the entire world. How the monk's spiritual life unfolds depends largely on how he embraces the art and architecture of the monastery. It is clear to me, as a monk, that both the liturgy and these sacred spaces deeply affect our inner life. This clarity is based on my personal experience

---

[32] Cited in: ibid., p. 47.

as well as many conversations I have had with others who have gladly witnessed to me how the quiet beauty of the architecture of a church helped them overcome dissatisfaction, distress, and unease.

I would like to note that where the *Catechism of the Catholic Church* situates some commentary and instruction on sacred art is not without reason. This commentary and instruction can be found in the section of part III which concerns the eighth commandment of the Decalogue, namely, "You shall not bear false witness against your neighbor." We see clearly that sacred art is included under the Church's commentary on the divine commandment concerning the communication of truth. Monastic art, architecture, and music tell the truth. The Catechism offers a profound reflection on sacred art in the following words:

> *Sacred art* is true and beautiful when its form corresponds to its partic-
> ular vocation: evoking and glorifying, in faith and adoration, the tran-
> scendent mystery of God—the surpassing invisible beauty of truth
> and love visible in Christ, who "reflects the glory of God and bears
> the very stamp of his nature", in whom "the whole fullness of deity
> dwells bodily." This spiritual beauty of God is reflected in the most
> holy Virgin Mother of God, the angels, and saints. Genuine sacred art
> draws man to adoration, to prayer, and to the love of God, Creator
> and Savior, the Holy One and Sanctifier.[33]

Where is this truer and more evident than within the walls of the monastery? Monastic architecture is designed to draw monks to ado-ration, to prayer, and to the love of God.

Monastic meditation is similar to a ritual and emphasizes a set of ex-periences and techniques conceived as a "way" that is to be followed in a spirit of discipleship.[34] Here the behavior is patterned according to the norms, teachings, and examples by which thought is "crafted" and the mind, body, and soul are prepared for an experience of God should one be granted. Monastic art, architecture, and music have been actualizations of such meditations. Ritual, which educates the mind and which transforms the emotions, the imagination, and cognition, stirs the creative process and provides the basis for a concrete expression of

---

[33] *Catechism of the Catholic Church*, 2502.

[34] For a deeper and detailed discussion of this, please see: M. Carruthers, *The Crafts of Thought: Meditation, Rhetoric, and the Making of Images, 400–1200* (Cambridge Studies in Medieval Literature, 34, 2000).

transcendent truths through the arts, architecture, and music. This is as true today as it was in the Middle Ages.

Our churches, like the sacred liturgies which they house, should be witnesses to the Truth which saves. Every single detail is part of the creative principle, which designs and animates, allowing both the details and the whole to be one. Order and harmony emanate from this, making beauty visible. In this beauty, there is a certain kind of justice whereby we honor both the Creator and His holy people.[35] This architectural truth is a living presence of that beauty and justice which lovingly incorporate all of creation. Its stones and the liturgical life therein make for this unending hymn of prayer and work, holy actions including positive gestures, economy along with skill and quality, and all this is for the glory of God and the salvation of God's people.

Contemporary Man and *Acedia*

Contemporary man lives in the midst of great transition. Confused and stressed, he is confronted with a change not so much in what one believes, but rather in how one believes. There is an ubiquitous eruption of cultural chaos and rampant pluralism. This elusive revolution entails a changing mentality regarding faith. Many do not seem to understand what is happening, though they hope for the best. Constantly bombarded with sensations and emotions, this global transition impedes any time for reflection and so many are left asking the simple and obvious question, "What is happening?"

This shift in mentality is a shift in belief about belief. Timeless truths are often considered to be mere products of culture or constructs of man. Rather than viewing revelation as God finding man, it is viewed as man's attempt to find God, or gods, or the force, or whatever. In the dark shadow of this confusion, one happily attends any church, synagogue, temple, or even attempts to worship on a stroll through nature. This change feels like liberation for some and a grievous loss for others. Nobody can doubt the effects of a certain syncretism which has been promoted in the worst of ecumenical and inter-religious cir-

---

[35] For a fuller discussion of this see: L. Zoja, *Giustizia e Bellezza* (Torino: Boringhieri, 2007).

cles where a *laissez faire* spirit dominates. Belief systems are mutated into mere fables in need of endless interpretations which comment on everything without ever reaching the core of anything.

At the risk of being politically incorrect, we are living in an age of overexposure to otherness and becoming ever more incapable of distinguishing differences even in solid belief systems, such as Catholicism and Orthodoxy. There is an erroneous and destructive idea that all values and beliefs are equal. This is a strange world which cannot define itself with its own current terms, but only in terms of what it has ceased to be. We are surrounded by bizarre innovations and strange new variations, such as: Free Market Communism, New Age Science, and Feminist Christianity. In an attempt to "find themselves" in this chaos, many have turned to psychotherapists. Unfortunately, however, the mental health field is not currently enjoying good mental health.

For me, a symbol of what we are discussing is a Bedouin sitting on a camel and dressed in traditional robes. Underneath these robes, he is wearing a pair of jeans and holding a cell phone in one hand and a soda in the other. I am neither ridiculing this nor shedding an intellectual tear over the destruction of local cultures in the wake of the multi-national West's commercial expansion. Yet, I see clearly the spiritual malaise which this multicultural era creates. There is no unifying thought or belief to hold people together since sensations and emotions have become the basis of determining and understanding reality and truth. This indefinable and bizarre state of affairs is incapable of holding people and things together. Even in our own sacred liturgies, cell phones ring, people excuse themselves, gum is stuck under the pew, and some even go so far as to drink their soda during liturgical celebrations. There is much self-assertion, but little self-grounding. This is a sure sign that we need to look seriously at rites, ritual, and rituality.

It is certain that the "death of God" has not freed man from his need to have some kind of belief and/or holy alliance. No longer believing in God has led many to believe in anything. This is evident in the rise of neo-paganism, witchcraft, yoga, new age movements, and the shops of fortune tellers and tarot card readers sprinkled everywhere over the landscape. Recently, I was browsing the English section of a Catholic bookstore. I was searching for a book recommended for spiritual reading and was informed that the main readers of this volume were religious sisters. In the book, I came across the following words: "A

solution to spiritual problems common to all of us." The text continued with writings, quotations, references to Zen Buddhism, artistic
illustrations from Goya to Picasso, writers from Teresa of Avila and
John of the Cross to Dostoevsky and Joyce, and texts from the Bible
to the Bhagavad Gita. There were also thinkers ranging from Plato
to Nietzsche. What should one make of this spiritual salad? We recall
from the nursery rhyme that Humpty Dumpty, who sat on the wall,
found himself broken on the ground without any possibility of recovery. If you sit on the wall, then you are neither here nor there. In this
sense, being everywhere will ensure that you are nowhere. Humpty
Dumpty paid a high price for living on the edge!

Many more examples could be provided, but the main point is that
this contemporary sickness of the soul is symptomatic of that dreadful disease which fuels an utter sense of meaninglessness, namely, *acedia*. *Acedia* comes from a Greek word which refers to a "non-caring
state."[36] *Acedia*, or *accidie*, is "the lazy sullenness and despairing indisci-
pline of not caring about anything."[37] Joseph Pieper even goes so far
as to call *acedia* a "perverted humility."[38] He further notes that this
spiritual sickness is also seen in psychology, stating, "The psychiatrist
frequently observes that, while a neurotic individual may have a superficial will to be restored to health, in actuality he fears more than
anything else the demands that are made, as a matter of course, on one
who is well."[39] The focus here is not the moral culpability of individuals, (that is not for us to decide), but rather the general confusion
and malaise which has led many men and women of good will to the
frightening precipice of indifference. Not knowing where to turn and
being encouraged by an obfuscated world to try any and every journey
without a map, people—even those of good will—are led to the brink
of a certain despondency. Without rites, rituals, and liturgies, which
bring the human person into direct contact with the God of love and
mercy, man is condemned to follow shadows.

---

[36] J. Raddan, ed., *The Nature of Melancholy: From Aristotle to Kristeva* (Oxford University Press, 2000), p. 69.

[37] B. C. Lane, *The Solace of Fierce Landscapes* (Oxford University Press), pp. 192–93.

[38] J. Pieper. *Faith, Hope, Love* (San Francisco: Ignatius Press, 1997), p. 119.

[39] Ibid., p. 119.

Conclusion

In conclusion, I would like to leave our priests with a few thoughts. Rites, ritual, and rituality include rubrics, directives, rules, and also episcopal suggestions. Of course, on the day of our ordination, we make a solemn promise to perform the sacred rites in total fidelity to the received texts and rituals. Fr. Peter Stravinskas underscores this in *The Rubrics of the Mass*. He writes, "Fidelity to the rubrics is not an end in itself—although a priest does make a solemn promise at his ordination to perform the sacred rites in total fidelity to the received texts and rituals—but is intended to bring the entire People of God (clergy and laity alike) to the most profound experience possible of God's entrance in our world and of our gaining a glimpse of His."[40]

The liturgical norms protect our liturgical worship from arbitrariness, banality, the imposition of idiosyncrasies, and material heresy. These norms ensure everybody that we are celebrating the greatest gifts as a true treasure for the entire Catholic community and not as the private possessions of any one person. The signs and symbols inherent in the rituals and rites are an expression of divine charity communicated to humanity and humanity's response of adoration, contrition, thanksgiving, and ultimate petition for God's Kingdom to come in all the fullness and splendor of its glory. The Sacred Liturgy of the Catholic Church is a participation in the Heavenly Liturgy and as close as we can come to Heaven while here on earth.

This is a participation in the divine love which transforms us and conquers our exaggerated sense of individualism, replacing it with a noble sense of our unity as many individual members of the same body. From the symbol and sign of Christ's washing the feet of His disciples, for example, we learn that God is at our service and so we must be at His. Commenting on this washing, therefore, Pope Francis reminds us of the communal aspect of such service, namely, "That all of us must help one another" (Homily, Mass of the Lord's Supper, 2013).

In a word, the Liturgy of the Catholic Church is a school of love. The *ordo amoris* in this school of love both commands us to love and teaches

---

[40] P. J. Stravinskas, *The Rubrics of the Mass* (Pine Beach, N.J.: Newman House Press, 2002), p. 8.

us how to do so. This, the *ordo amoris*, is the real answer to the malaise of contemporary man. It is the proper response to contemporary man who has lost his soul and is in search of meaning. Rediscovering the role of ritual in our liturgical actions has the power to guide all of us back to the truth and to the healing force of the Lord's Eucharistic Love. This is the necessary medicine for healing both the disturbed individual and the ailing world. The Liturgy is a call to conversion and it brings salvation to the world. By lovingly and eagerly obeying the liturgical rituals of the Church, we receive the fire of divine charity and all the graces necessary for loving one another.

In his classic book, *Liturgy and Personality*, Dietrich von Hildebrand communicates a notion akin to the one being articulated here. He states, "The person formed by the liturgy has absorbed in his flesh and blood the notion that he owes a suitable response to every value." The *homo liturgicus* becomes saturated with the things of God and thus— von Hildebrand continues—"He will rejoice in every exalted spectacle of nature, the beauty of the starlit sky, the majesty of the sea and mountains, the charm of life, the world of plants and animals, the nobility of a profound truth, the mysterious glow of a man's purity. . . . The man formed by the liturgy will affirm this as a reflection of the eternal glory of God."[41] In other words, the true *homo liturgicus* overflows with divine charity and cannot help but spread that charity everywhere. This becomes ever clearer as one continues to advance in the school of love which is the Sacred Liturgy. We come to an ever greater understanding as we grow in love, since—as St. Augustine skillfully and beautifully states—"We understand perfectly only that which we perfectly love."[42]

---

[41] D. von Hildebrand, *Liturgy and Personality: The Healing Power of Formal Prayer* (Manchester, N.H.: Sophia Institute Press, 1986), p. 64.

[42] St. Augustine, *De Diversis Questionibus*, 35.2.

12

The Bishop: Governor, Promoter and Guardian of the Liturgical Life of the Diocese

ARCHBISHOP ALEXANDER K. SAMPLE

Archbishop of Portland in Oregon

Introduction

This topic is very close to my heart and at the center of my attention as a diocesan bishop. The promotion and safeguarding of the liturgical life of the local Church should be one of the diocesan bishop's highest priorities and is a matter worthy of his careful reflection and attention.

Here, firstly, I hope to illustrate what I have just said concerning the importance of this topic in the ministry of the diocesan bishop. This will be accomplished by exploring what official Church teaching and law have had to say on this topic, beginning with the Second Vatican Council. In the second part I will explore on a practical level how this care for the liturgical life of the diocese might be accomplished by the bishop in the exercise of his ministry as the high priest of the portion of the people of God entrusted to his pastoral care.

An Appraisal of Conciliar and Post-Conciliar Sources

I chose to start with examining what the Second Vatican Council had to say on this matter for two reasons. First and most important is that this is the Year of Faith, which has been proclaimed to coincide with the fiftieth anniversary of the calling of the Council by St. John XXIII. Pope Benedict XVI asked that we read and study anew the Council documents themselves as an integral part of our observance of the Year of Faith.

Secondly, an exhaustive historical study of the role of the bishop in regulating the Sacred Liturgy would be well beyond my scope here. It would be a fascinating study. However, I must leave that for another scholar.

So, let us turn to the documents of Vatican II to help us begin to see how the Church in our own time envisions the role of the diocesan bishop in regulating the liturgical life of the local Church. We begin, of course with the first document produced by the Council, *Sacrosanctum Concilium*, the Constitution on the Sacred Liturgy. There we read:

> The bishop is to be considered as the high priest of his flock, from whom the life in Christ of his faithful is in some way derived and dependent.
>
> Therefore all should hold in great esteem the liturgical life of the diocese centered around the bishop, especially in his cathedral church; they must be convinced that the pre-eminent manifestation of the Church consists in the full active participation of all God's holy people in these liturgical celebrations, especially in the same Eucharist, in a single prayer, at one altar, at which there presides the bishop surrounded by his college of priests and by his ministers. (n. 41)

This text firmly established the important role that the bishop has within the local Church as the high priest of the flock entrusted to his care. While not specifically addressing his role in moderating the Sacred Liturgy, the text does highlight the esteem that should be given to his central liturgical role within the diocese.

Earlier in the Constitution on the Sacred Liturgy, we see more specific references to the bishop's role in the regulation of the liturgy:

> Regulation of the Sacred Liturgy depends solely on the authority of the Church, that is, on the Apostolic See and, as laws may determine, on the bishop. (n. 22)

> Liturgical services are not private functions, but are celebrations of the Church, which is the "sacrament of unity", namely, the holy people united and ordered under their bishops. (n. 26)

For a further reference to the bishop's responsibility in moderating the Sacred Liturgy, we turn to the Dogmatic Constitution on the Church, *Lumen Gentium*, where we read:

Every legitimate celebration of the Eucharist is regulated by the bishop, to whom is committed the office of offering the worship of Christian religion to the Divine Majesty and of administering it in accordance with the Lord's commandments and the Church's laws, as further defined by his particular judgment for his diocese. (n. 26)

We find the first clear and direct reference to the bishop's responsibility to "govern, promote and guard" the liturgical life of the diocese in the Decree concerning the Pastoral Office of Bishops, *Christus Dominus*:

In exercising their office of sanctifying, bishops should be mindful that they have been taken from among men and appointed their representative before God in order to offer gifts and sacrifices for sins. Bishops enjoy the fullness of the sacrament of orders and both presbyters and deacons are dependent upon them in the exercise of their authority. . . . Therefore bishops are the principal dispensers of the mysteries of God, as well as being the governors, promoters, and guardians of the entire liturgical life in the church committed to them. (n. 15)

This phrase, "governors, promoters and guardians of the liturgical life" of the local Church, will come to be the phrase used to describe the role of the diocesan bishop in this area. It actually is what has given the title to this presentation.

One of the fruits of the Second Vatican Council was the revision of the Code of Canon Law, which sought to update the Code and incorporate the teachings and insights of the Council. With regard to the regulation of the Sacred Liturgy by the diocesan bishop, the relevant canons are as follows:

Can. 392 § 1. Since he must protect the unity of the universal Church, a bishop is bound to promote the common discipline of the whole Church and therefore to urge the observance of all ecclesiastical laws.

§ 2. He is to exercise vigilance so that abuses do not creep into ecclesiastical discipline, especially regarding the ministry of the word, the celebration of the sacraments and sacramentals, the worship of God and the veneration of the saints, and the administration of goods.

Can. 835 § 1. The bishops in the first place exercise the sanctifying function; they are the high priests, the principal dispensers of the mysteries of God, and the directors, promoters, and guardians of the entire liturgical life in the church entrusted to them.

These principles derived from the Council and developed over the ensuing years became further enshrined in the *General Instruction of the Roman Missal* (2002) and in the *Directory for the Pastoral Ministry of Bishops* (2004).

From the *General Instruction of the Roman Missal*:

> For the diocesan bishop, the prime steward of the mysteries of God in the particular Church entrusted to his care, is the moderator, promoter, and guardian of the whole of liturgical life. In celebrations that take place with the bishop presiding, and especially in the celebration of the Eucharist by the bishop himself with the presbyterate, the deacons, and the people taking part, the mystery of the Church is manifest. Hence, solemn celebrations of Mass of this sort must be exemplary for the entire diocese.
>
> The bishop should therefore be determined that the priests, the deacons, and the lay Christian faithful grasp ever more deeply the genuine significance of the rites and liturgical texts, and thereby be led to the active and fruitful celebration of the Eucharist. To that end, he should also be vigilant in ensuring that the dignity of these celebrations be enhanced and, in promoting such dignity, the beauty of the sacred place, of the music, and of art should contribute as greatly as possible. (n. 22)

> The celebration of the Eucharist is the action of Christ and of the Church, namely, of the holy people united and ordered under the bishop. It therefore pertains to the whole Body of the Church, manifests it, and has its effect upon it. (n. 91)

> Every legitimate celebration of the Eucharist is directed by the bishop, either in person or through Priests who are his helpers. (n. 92)

One of the strongest statements concerning the importance of the role of the bishop in regulating the Sacred Liturgy comes from the *Directory for the Pastoral Ministry of Bishops*:

> The bishop should consider his responsibility for divine worship to be his pre-eminent role: his other activity as teacher and pastor is ordered to this sanctifying function. Although closely united by nature to the ministries of teaching and governing, the sanctifying role is distinguished from the others insofar as it is specifically exercised in the person of Christ, Eternal High Priest, and insofar as it constitutes the source and summit of the Christian life. (n. 142)

This strikes me as a remarkable statement. The Directory calls the bishop's responsibility for divine worship, which obviously and principally means the Sacred Liturgy, his "pre-eminent role." Everything else he does as Pastor of the flock and as teacher is ordered and directed to his role as sanctifier of the local Church.

But perhaps such a bold statement should not surprise us, since the Second Vatican Council emphasized the centrality and supreme importance of the Sacred Liturgy in the life of the Church. From the Decree on the Ministry and the Life of Priests, *Presbyterorum Ordinis*, we read: "The other sacraments, as well as with every ministry of the Church and every work of the apostolate, are tied together with the Eucharist and are directed toward it" (n. 5).

More clearly and emphatically than anywhere else, perhaps, we see this point emphasized in *Sacrosanctum Concilium*: "every liturgical celebration, because it is an action of Christ the priest and of His Body which is the Church, is a sacred action surpassing all others; no other action of the Church can equal its efficacy by the same title and to the same degree" (n. 7).

Further on in *Sacrosanctum Concilium*, after mentioning the other important works and apostolates of the Church, especially the preaching of the Gospel in order to bring people to Christ, the Council says, in a text very familiar to us:

> Nevertheless the liturgy is the summit toward which the activity of the Church is directed; at the same time it is the font from which all her power flows. For the aim and object of apostolic works is that all who are made sons of God by faith and baptism should come together to praise God in the midst of His Church, to take part in the sacrifice, and to eat the Lord's supper. (n. 10)

Hence the pre-eminent responsibility that the bishop has for the Sacred Liturgy in his diocese naturally flows from the Church's understanding of the supreme place that the liturgy itself occupies in the life of the Church and in the lives of her individual members.

Returning to the *Directory for the Pastoral Ministry of Bishops*, the Directory goes on to make an important point, quoting from the *Ceremonial of Bishops*. This is a point to which I will return: "[The bishop] should be mindful that the celebrations at which he presides are to set an example for all other celebrations" (n. 144).

The Directory also takes up the terminology which we have already seen beginning with *Christus Dominus*, adding a particular concern for fidelity to the liturgical norms:

> As High Priest responsible for divine worship in the particular Church, the bishop has the task of ordering, promoting and safeguarding the entire liturgical life of the diocese. He should, therefore, be vigilant that the norms established by legitimate authority are *attentively observed*. In particular, he should make sure that clergy and lay faithful carry out all those tasks and only those tasks which are proper to them, without changing the sacramental rites or liturgical celebrations according to personal taste or preference.
>
> In liturgical matters, it pertains to the bishop to *issue appropriate norms* that are binding throughout the diocese, while always respecting what has been established by higher authority. (n. 145)

The Directory further explicates the ways in which the bishop fulfills these responsibilities. It speaks of diocesan offices for divine worship, diocesan liturgical commissions, commissions for sacred music and sacred art, vigilance concerning the decorum of the Sacred Liturgy and ways to promote the "full, conscious, and active" participation of the faithful in the Sacred Liturgy.

Practical Application of the Bishop's Responsibility for the Sacred Liturgy

It should be clear from what has been said, that the diocesan bishop has the principal, important and irreplaceable role of governing, promoting, and safeguarding the celebration of the Sacred Liturgy within his own diocese. Now we must turn to the equally important question of the practical application of this responsibility. How does the diocesan bishop fulfill this serious mandate?

As the one who ministers *in persona Christi capitis* in an eminent way for the clergy and faithful entrusted to his pastoral care, the diocesan bishop shares in the threefold ministry of Christ as Priest, Prophet and King. He is to sanctify, teach and govern the flock over which and for whom he has been appointed chief shepherd.

One might be tempted to conclude that his role in regulating the celebration of the Sacred Liturgy is exclusively or principally a part of the *munus sanctificandi* of the diocesan bishop. I would like to propose that the promotion and regulation of the Sacred Liturgy by the diocesan bishop involves all three of the *munera* attached to his sacred office. By this I mean that it involves the *munus docendi* and the *munus regendi* as well. Let us examine this more closely.

The *Munus Sanctificandi*

In his own celebration of the Sacred Liturgy and the sacraments of the Church, the diocesan bishop sanctifies the clergy, religious and faithful of the diocese as the high priest of the local Church entrusted to his pastoral care. This is the primary way in which he exercises the *munus sanctificandi* entrusted to him through sacred ordination.

But his celebration of the Sacred Liturgy and the sacraments also helps promote, regulate and safeguard the proper celebration of the same throughout the entire diocesan Church. His example, as he personally exercises the *munus sanctificandi*, must also serve as the model, or exemplar, for the rest of the clergy and faithful. How he celebrates the Sacred Liturgy must "teach by example."

This is especially true of the pontifical liturgies celebrated at his cathedral church in the presence of his priests, deacons and the lay faithful from all over the diocese. The cathedral liturgies, even when not celebrated personally by the diocesan bishop, must serve as the model for the parishes and missions of the diocese. This is clearly indicated in the ecclesial documents we have been examining, especially *Sacrosanctum Concilium*.

When poor liturgical practice, inappropriate sacred music, or even more serious liturgical abuses are justified on the parish level by saying, "But that's the way we saw it done at the cathedral", we are a long way from achieving the best in diocesan liturgical renewal and reform. This is especially true when the less than stellar liturgy was celebrated by the bishop himself. Sadly, this is the case more often than we might like to admit.

But the opposite is also true. When the cathedral liturgies, especially pontifical liturgies, are celebrated well, faithfully adhering to the liturgical norms and with as much beauty, reverence, decorum and prayerfulness as possible, it serves as an inspiration and model for the whole diocesan Church. Those in attendance at pontifical liturgies at the cathedral are taught by a living example what is possible, even if it needs to be scaled down or simplified on the local parish level due to more limited resources.

On these occasions, when something truly noble is imitated in the parishes, what a joy it is to hear, "That's how they do it at the cathedral" or "That's what the bishop does." Much good can be accomplished in this way in the ongoing work of the reform and renewal of divine worship in the diocese.

But the diocesan bishop's liturgical example in the exercise of his *munus sanctificandi* must also extend beyond solely cathedral liturgies. As we might say in the United States, he must take his example "on the road" to his parish visitations. As much as possible he must bring to the local level sound and beautiful liturgical practices as he visits and celebrates the Sacred Liturgy with the parish communities under his pastoral care.

This can be more challenging because the bishop does not have as direct and frequent presence in the local parishes as at his cathedral church. Nevertheless, there is still much that can be done as he seeks to bring certain expectations when visiting parishes.

The bishop must make good use of the opportunities local pastors or parish personnel provide him when he is asked, "This is the way we typically do it here, Your Excellency, but how would you like to do it?" These are great moments to teach proper and sound liturgical practice. The bishop should clearly state his preferences (always the Church's preferences) and readily provide an explanation (a form of brief catechesis) on the proper and fitting liturgical practice.

The *Munus Docendi*

Speaking of catechesis, this will be absolutely essential to the bishop's effectiveness in bringing about renewal and reform in the diocese's liturgical life. Where poor and improper liturgical practice has taken root, we must acknowledge that we did not get there overnight. It is usually the result of years, if not decades, of poor catechesis, bad liturgical practice and improper formation.

We must also acknowledge that our clergy, religious and lay faithful, although they may be poorly or improperly formed with regard to liturgical practice, are generally of good will in this regard. They typically want to do what is proper and the best, but they may simply not know what that entails. They need sound catechesis and formation.

This is where the bishop must take a strong lead in exercising his teaching office, the *munus docendi*. Much can be accomplished through a patient and consistent effort to teach and form the clergy and faithful in a deeper understanding of the Sacred Liturgy which will bear fruit in sound and beautiful liturgical practice.

I am more and more convinced that a very significant part of the problem with the celebration of the Sacred Liturgy in our day, especially the holy Mass, stems from a profound and general lack of understanding of the very nature and inner meaning of the Sacred Liturgy itself. Pope Benedict XVI wrote of this in his book *The Spirit of the Liturgy*.[1] Because far too many do not know the inner meaning of the Sacred Liturgy, they are tempted to impose other meanings on it, resulting in poor liturgical practice, trying to make the liturgy do something it was never intended to do.

We must reverse this trend, beginning with the principal catechist and teacher of the local Church, the diocesan bishop. He must personally teach through his homilies, pastoral letters, columns in the local Catholic newspaper and every other means personally available to him. He must teach the true spirit of the Sacred Liturgy consistently and systematically, always reflecting, of course, the mind of the Church. My personal experience would indicate that a pastoral letter on some aspect of divine worship can have influence and effect even beyond diocesan boundaries.

Diocesan offices for divine worship and sacred music and diocesan liturgical commissions must assist the bishop in his task as teacher. Through newsletters, diocesan workshops, and colloquia and through diocesan web-based media, solid, consistent, and clear catechesis and formation must be given to the clergy and lay ecclesial ministers. A sustained and consistent effort over time will begin to reverse some

---

[1] Joseph Cardinal Ratzinger, *The Spirit of the Liturgy* (San Francisco: Ignatius Press, 2000).

of the unfortunate trends of the past several decades. This once again relies on the good will and desire of the clergy and faithful to do what is correct, that is, what the Church asks.

Such sound catechesis and liturgical formation must focus on the theology of the Sacred Liturgy as well as liturgical practices and methods themselves. Such teaching accompanied by the bishop's own example as discussed above will eventually bring about the liturgical renewal and reform needed in our own time on the diocesan level.

Catechesis and liturgical formation can and should also take place on regional, national and international levels as well. I would like to bring to your attention an initiative by an archbishop on a local level that has had international influence on liturgical formation.

In the year 2000, Francis Cardinal George, Archbishop of Chicago, founded the Liturgical Institute in order to prepare Catholics for a "new era in liturgical renewal." It serves a diverse international student population of laity, religious and clergy.

The Liturgical Institute prepares its students in a context of prayer and scholarship with the Church's future priests, deacons, pastors and lay ecclesial ministers to bring solid theological knowledge, critical reasoning and practical skills to bear on the challenges opened by the phase of liturgical renewal emerging in recent years.

The Institute offers an integrated program for the advancement of the renewal promoted by the Church, rooted in the ideals of the twentieth-century liturgical movement, the writings of recent popes, including St. Pius X, St. John Paul II and Benedict XVI, and the authentic achievements of the post-conciliar era. To this end, students enjoy a mix of intense study and research; lectures and discussions; and active, intelligent participation in the Institute's liturgical life with the daily celebration of Mass and the Liturgy of the Hours.

In establishing an Office for Divine Worship in my former diocese, I sent one of the permanent deacons of the Diocese of Marquette to obtain a Master's Degree from the Liturgical Institute in order to equip him for the important work of liturgical renewal in the diocese. Having well educated and properly formed staff in the diocese to assist the bishop can be invaluable in helping him fulfill his primary responsibility for the Sacred Liturgy.

In this regard it is extremely important for the bishop to choose the right persons to assist him in liturgical reform and renewal. He must choose persons who are very much of the mind of the Church concerning liturgical theology and practice. He must ensure that they are educated at schools and institutes that truly seek to further the Church's vision for authentic liturgical renewal. A priest recently said to me that "policy is people." We need to have the right people in place to accomplish the mission entrusted to us.

Special mention must be made of the seminaries where the future priests of the Church are being formed and trained. I am of the firm mind that "as goes the head, so goes the body." If the priests in pastoral charge over the local parishes of the diocese lead well by good and sound liturgical practice, the parish will follow suit. That is why the bishop must exercise due diligence over seminary formation programs to whatever extent possible. This is especially true for the bishop who is canonically responsible for the seminary within his own diocese. The future leaders of the local Church, and therefore the future leaders of the liturgical life of the diocese are being educated and formed there. The same basic philosophy would apply also to formation programs for the permanent diaconate, over which the bishop must exercise personal vigilance as it regards liturgical formation.

Before moving on to the topic of the bishop's office of governance exercised in his vigilance over the liturgical life of the diocese, one more thing needs to be said concerning the bishop's own liturgical formation. It seems we often speak about the need for ongoing formation for priests, deacons and lay ecclesial ministers. We recognize that the process of learning and keeping up to date on theological, pastoral and liturgical matters does not end with ordination or completion of a degree program or a program of lay formation. We actively encourage the clergy and laity to continue to study and receive further and updated formation.

The same must hold true for the bishop. His need for further study, reflection and formation also did not come to an end on the day he received the ring and the miter. If he is going to be effective in leading liturgical reform and renewal in the diocese, he must do so from a solid and strong theological foundation. He too must continue to read, study and receive updated formation in liturgical matters, always according to the mind of the Church.

He must pay particular attention to the papal magisterium and the information that comes from the Congregation for Divine Worship

and the Discipline of the Sacraments. He must read and study periodicals and journals dedicated to liturgical reform and renewal in the authentic spirit of reform according to the mind of the Church. He must
also take advantage of conferences and colloquia where pastors and
scholars come together in a united and concerted effort to bring about
the liturgical renewal for which we all work, hope and pray. Properly
formed, educated and updated himself, the bishop can be confident in
exercising his responsibility for the liturgical life of his diocese.

The *Munus Regendi*

Finally, we must examine the role of the diocesan bishop in governing the local Church entrusted to his pastoral care as it concerns his
responsibility to regulate, promote and safeguard the liturgical life of
the diocese. This involves the *munus regendi*. Here the bishop seeks to
both ensure the observance of the liturgical norms of the Church and
to establish particular norms within the diocese, as the universal law
allows, regulating the Sacred Liturgy on the local level.

It is clearly the responsibility of the diocesan bishop to do all in
his power to ensure that the priests, deacons and lay ecclesial ministers within the diocese observe carefully the liturgical discipline of the
Church. This should be very clear from the texts that we examined in
the first part of this presentation. I am convinced that what we might
call "good liturgy" begins with an unswerving fidelity to the liturgical
norms established by competent authority. It does not end there, as
there is much that can be accomplished through sacred art, sacred music, and the general decorum of the liturgy in order to enhance it. But
it begins with what the Church has given us in the proper celebration
of the liturgy.

The question becomes, of course, how does the bishop ensure such
fidelity to the liturgical norms? This is not easy, especially in places
where there is an ecclesial culture that prefers liturgical experimentation and celebrating the Sacred Liturgy in its own way. Again, presum-
ing the good will and good intentions of those on the local parish level,
the bishop needs to consistently and patiently point out the failure to
observe liturgical norms and call those involved to fidelity to those
same norms. Often it is not a willful violation of liturgical norms, but

a simple lack of awareness of what is proper. I have found this to be so most of the time.

The bishop should take careful note of what he observes in the celebration of the Sacred Liturgy as he visits the parishes of his diocese. He can gently correct things as he observes them locally. But he can also, from time to time, issue corrective guidance on the diocesan level for things he has observed on a larger scale. I have seen this done as a "liturgical examination of conscience." In doing so he can call the whole local Church back to careful observance of what the liturgy requires. Doing so publicly in this way also lets the faithful in the parishes also know what is correct, and this can lighten the burden on the pastor when making the necessary adjustments.

The universal liturgical law also leaves many things to be determined on the local level by the diocesan bishop. The bishop should make good use of these options to help form the way the Sacred Liturgy is celebrated in the diocese. Good catechesis accompanying these local norms, a form of particular law, will also go a long way toward good liturgical formation of the local Church. The bishop, with the assistance of his office of divine worship and the diocesan liturgical commission, should issue diocesan policy with regard to liturgical matters. These should be made readily and widely available to both clergy and the lay faithful.

If these efforts to hold everyone faithful to the liturgical norms of the Church, both on the universal and local level, are done with consistency and patience, much can be accomplished over time to correct any liturgical aberrations or abuses in the local Church and to promote sound liturgical practice. Only in serious matters and when all else fails must the bishop resort to disciplinary measures to bring about a reform of liturgical abuses. Again, the vast majority of the clergy and faithful want to do what is correct and best for the Sacred Liturgy.

A Personal and Practical Example on the Diocesan Level

Without seeming to be self-serving, I would like to share my own recent experience regarding a pastoral letter I issued just before being moved from my former diocese of Marquette to the Archdiocese of

Portland. It was entitled "Rejoice in the Lord Always" (21 January 2013), and dealt with the matter of sacred music in the liturgy, specifically the holy Mass. I use it as a personal example of how a bishop can bring together both the office of teaching and the office of governing to help achieve liturgical renewal. I leave judgment of the quality and effectiveness of my small effort to others. I only seek to illustrate the point I have been making.

The pastoral letter attempts to do two things. In the first part, I have attempted to lay out a sound catechesis on the nature and purpose of sacred music, faithful to the teaching and practice of the Church. I drew from historical and more recent teaching of the Church's Magisterium. I attempt to answer the question, "What does the Church ask of us regarding music for the Sacred Liturgy?"

I received some criticism from some of the liturgical blogs on the internet, claiming that I was being narrow in my focus and promoting my own agenda and view on the matter. In reading some of the comments, I noted that, although many did not like what I had to say, no one could point to where I had gone wrong in representing the Church's teaching on the matter. That has been the problem for too long in liturgical matters, especially on sacred music. We have too often focused on our own personal tastes and perceptions rather than go to the source of sound principles found in the primary sources.

In any case, the letter moves from a catechesis on sacred music to practical application of those principles on the local level. This took the form of directives from the bishop to the priests, deacons, and laity of the diocese. These should be considered liturgical norms for the diocese, completely consistent with the universal liturgical norms. In fact, my attempt was to incarnate those universal norms on a diocesan level, recognizing that time and patience would be needed as we move toward achieving the ideal called for by the Church.

Again, my point in discussing this is to illustrate how teaching and governing can come together to further the mission of liturgical renewal. It would be largely ineffective to simply lay down particular law without preparing the local Church through catechesis.

The *Usus Antiquior* and Diocesan Liturgical Reform

Before drawing my presentation to a conclusion, I wish to say a word about the *usus antiquior*—the older form of the Roman rite. Let me begin by saying that, in my humble opinion, the 2007 *motu proprio* of Pope Benedict XVI, *Summorum Pontificum*, is one of the greatest gifts that could be given to the Church in the service of liturgical renewal and reform. Why do I say this?

I think it is fairly safe to say that the liturgical reform that was called for and envisioned by the Second Vatican Council became derailed ("went off the track") not very long after the Council itself. It is my concerted opinion that the post-conciliar liturgy as it is celebrated and experienced in most churches today is sadly not what the Council Fathers envisioned. I will not bore you with the liturgical horror stories we all experienced in the wake of the Council. I was formed as a young Catholic in the late 1960s and the 1970s, so I know of what I speak.

If we are going to bring about an authentic and fruitful renewal in the liturgical life of the Church, we need to be open to almost "starting over", taking into account all of the good fruit achieved in the wake of the Council. Pope Benedict XVI often spoke of a need for a "reform of the reform." I am solidly in that stream of thought.

But if we are going to accomplish what the Council envisioned, we need a reference point in re-appreciating that to which the Council Fathers called us. That reference point is the *usus antiquior*. The older rites are our "touchstone" in moving forward with the reform of the reform. All that we do, as authentically called for by the Council, must be measured against the ancient liturgical tradition of the Church embodied in the pre-conciliar liturgy. That is not at all to say that the Council Fathers did not have legitimate concerns regarding the need for the renewal and reform of the liturgy as expressed in the conciliar texts themselves. I am not at all calling into question the Council's call for reform. But many of us believe that the reform that actually came about in the wake of the Council lost much of what is truly the genius of the Latin Rite.

This is what Pope Benedict XVI spoke of in *Summorum Pontificum* when he tells us that there can be no rupture with what has gone before, but that a hermeneutic of reform in continuity must guide us, not just in liturgical matters but in theological matters as well. Allowing for a more generous use of the *usus antiquior* is not meant only to reconcile individuals and groups who have been disaffected by recent liturgical reform, but also to reconcile the whole Church with her past.

The most powerful statement in this regard, in my opinion, can be found in the letter of Pope Benedict XVI to the bishops of the world which accompanied the *motu proprio*. Here Pope Benedict wrote: "What earlier generations held as sacred, remains sacred and great for us too, and it cannot be all of a sudden entirely forbidden or even considered harmful" (Letter, 7 July 2007).

All of this is why I would urge bishops to familiarize themselves with the *usus antiquior* as a means of achieving their own deeper formation in the liturgy and as a reliable reference point in bringing about renewal and reform of the liturgy in the local Church. Speaking from personal experience, my own study and celebration of the older liturgical rites has had a tremendous effect on my own appreciation of our liturgical tradition and has enhanced my own understanding and celebration of the new rites.

I would further encourage bishops to be as generous as possible with the faithful who desire and ask for the opportunity to worship in the *usus antiquior* in their dioceses. Allowing for is natural flourishing will have its own effect on the liturgical life of the whole diocesan Church. It must never be seen as something out of the mainstream of ecclesial life, that is, as something on the fringes. The bishop's own public celebration of it can prevent this from happening.

The bishop should also encourage his seminarians to familiarize themselves with the *usus antiquior*, not just for the possibility that they may one day be called upon to celebrate this form of the Mass for the benefit of the faithful, but indeed for the future priest's own appreciation of the deep and rich liturgical tradition from which the reformed rites flow. I know of one bishop in the United States who has required his seminarians to learn how to celebrate the *usus antiquior*. Since it is a fully legitimate expression of the one Latin rite, every seminarian should at least study and familiarize himself with these rites, and if possible eventually learn to celebrate them. I guarantee that this will have a profound effect on how he celebrates the modern liturgy.

Conclusion

In conclusion, then, we can say that there is no doubt about the seriousness with which the diocesan bishop must carry out his primary responsibility for the Sacred Liturgy and divine worship in his local Church. This should be abundantly clear from the texts we examined earlier. He is the first governor, promoter and guardian of the Sacred Liturgy.

But this heavy burden of responsibility placed upon the shoulders of the bishop need not cause him any anxiety or needless worry. Through the sacred ordination he has received, the Church endows the bishop with the necessary grace and office to fulfill this responsibility. As teacher, sanctifier and shepherd of the flock entrusted to his care, he possesses the authority and means to accomplish so awesome a responsibility. He must teach clearly, lead by his own example, and govern wisely and patiently so that the Sacred Liturgy in his diocese will truly give glory to Almighty God and be for the sanctification of his people.

May Jesus Christ, our eternal High Priest, inspire in the hearts of all bishops a great love and care for the mysteries of our redemption which they celebrate in the Sacred Liturgy. May holy Mary, Mother of the Word Incarnate and Ark of the Covenant intercede for us! Amen.

13

Pastoral Liturgy and the Church's Mission in Parishes— The Dangerous Hermeneutic of a Concept

GUIDO RODHEUDT

Among the concepts that have established themselves as standard vocabulary in the Church over the last fifty years, the term "pastoral" is one of the most scintillating. Alongside *aggiornamento, participatio actuosa* and "lay apostolate", "pastoral" is omnipresent in the jewel box of ecclesiastical language in the period after the Second Vatican Council. Of course it is also just as ambiguous in its application.

Originally it described a simple truism. Etymologically it means everything that is necessary for the care of souls. The concept is modeled on the Good Shepherd, Jesus Christ, Who goes ahead of His flock and leads them to green pastures. Its derivation from the image of the shepherd already rules out one thing entirely: namely that the flock knows better than the shepherd what is good for it. Ultimately, the care of a shepherd—that would probably be the best way to paraphrase the term "pastoral" ministry—always proceeds from the shepherd's superior knowledge about good pasturelands, the dangers of hostile animals and the time to change location. And in every case this shepherd's care —if it is to be genuine and not the disinterested management of a hired official—must be exercised with one's lifeblood. This is true also in the case where the sheep rebel and in their laziness refuse to follow, or in the smugness typical of a herd animal think that they themselves have the full perspective. A shepherd is "pastoral", then, only when

---

Translated from the German original by Michael J. Miller.

he leads his flock with knowledge and courage, with fidelity and far-sightedness toward the goal of their path. Pastoral ministry therefore will be needed precisely when the sheep start to forget the goal and the path and either absent-mindedly or mischievously go astray. This decisive, essential feature of pastoral ministry, namely goal-directed leadership, is indispensable if one does not want to risk the welfare of the flock. Therefore the task of leading toward a good, worthwhile goal, and all the care, rigor, passion and love necessary to do so, make up the inner core of the concept "pastoral".

Since it is derived from the image of the Good Shepherd, "pastoral care", as a commission for the Church as a whole, can be understood only as follows: to form the faithful as Christ's flock and not just to accompany them along their path to eternity, but to lead them, to make accessible to them the sources of strength on the green pastures of the sacraments, and occasionally to keep them from going astray with a stern demeanor and by raising a shepherd's voice in warning, and if they do stray to go after them—of course, never just to pay them a visit in the foreign country of their separation from the flock, but to bring them back.

Thus "pastoral care" is something completely and utterly educational in the literal sense of that word—of leading others towards an end that is clearly in view by the "pastor", something that deliberately intervenes in the everyday routine of the flock in order to train it, something that forms and shears, when necessary, that rewards and punishes, a pedagogy that actively proceeds with knowledge about the flock and with prudence in its choice of methods. "Pastoral care" furthermore serves a purpose, namely to move the flock toward its happiness.

Therefore at first glance it seems contradictory to speak about "pastoral liturgy". For the liturgy does not intend to be something pedagogical at all; it is not something that could be repurposed for some other use that lies beyond itself. Liturgy is by its very nature something entirely free of purpose; it is an encounter with Almighty God, Who in His proximity cannot tolerate any distraction for the benefit of anything that is not He Himself. When you have entered the space of God's presence in the liturgy, then all training comes to an end, then you can no longer feed on explanations or instructions, for then you are no longer in the antechamber—you are with the Lord Himself. The sacred theater allows no audible stage directions, it does not intend to teach; it intends to dissolve completely and utterly into the sacred action and to unfold for its own sake. In this respect theater and liturgy are closely related.

"Regietheater", a method of staging a drama that was invented in Germany in the 1960s, among other things also robbed many liturgists of their sense of this relatedness. "Regietheater" replaces the play with explanation. It stages a literary work, not with a view to its content, but rather with a view to the understanding of its spectators. The audience is supposed to be able to follow intellectually what takes place on the stage, it is supposed to see through and understand and apply it, in other words, it is supposed to change itself.

This is of course a concern in ancient tragedy as well, but—and this is an important difference—the theatrical pedagogy of Greek antiquity tries to purge the spectator morally by bringing him along into the realm of the unusual and extraordinary through the form in which it is clothed. In its productions "Regietheater" is guided essentially by the currently prevailing everyday morality and therefore bends every play so that it becomes a part of today. The spectator is not supposed to adapt to the moral of the play, but rather vice-versa: the moral of the play is adapted to the present.

In this way of treating theater there is more than an accidental or perhaps merely chronological parallel to the changes in liturgical life in the post-conciliar period.

One characteristic of this period was that it tried on many levels to turn life into a pedagogical exercise and above all made what is objective and self-evident the object of criticism. Nothing stood on its own any more; now everything could be questioned and had to be questioned. Art was not spared by this trend; it mutated completely from the contemplation of nature to an agenda-driven method of education. Everyday art no longer tried to portray beauty; it tried to reshape the present, to set itself up over against it like a mirror and thereby lead it to self-reflection. No longer was anything to speak for itself; everything was supposed to be drawn into a process of world progress, so as to put an end to man's alleged immaturity and dependence [*Unmündigkeit*] through which old ties to outmoded things had crippled him and taken away his true freedom—so they said.

It is no accident then that the dissociation of man from the objective realm and the collapse of the arts fall into the hemisphere occupied by a kind of abstract art that springs from the subjective needs of the artist or the spectator and by the sort of "applied art" that serves the transformation of society or merely decorates it as design. Accordingly, works of art that are "merely" beautiful remain museum pieces and thus bits of art history because of their uselessness. There lie, as though in a cemetery, the depictions of what was once held to be true.

This twentieth-century cultural revolution in the 1960s could not pass by the Church's liturgical development without leaving its traces, at least given the *aggiornamento* as it was misunderstood. For in a tragic mistake about the real intention of St. John XXIII, the unfortunate concept was understood, not as the Church's age-old effort to encounter the present day appropriately and effectively so as to permeate it with the eternal, but the other way around, so as to make a clean sweep of the eternal and its burdensome requirements. All that mattered was what was happening today!

The conviction that truth is changeable and essentially embedded in history had blazed a trail in this regard at a sensitive place in ecclesiastical life. The about-face in modern thought, which had made the subject the point of departure for grasping the world, was now grasping also a realm that hitherto had remained untouched. The purpose-free game in the presence of the Most High mutated into a multi-purpose event. Explanations were added to the rite that were supposed to make it transparent. This dealt it a death-blow. What had to happen on its own and not as the active expression of the celebrating group, what is invisible to the eye and was created for God alone, like the decorative carving on the capstone of a Gothic vaulted ceiling, became obsolete, because it seemed too far away, too high, too unrelated to everyday life to "make anything out of it". The uselessness that is characteristic of all liturgical art was suddenly turned into a reproach against it. From now on the rite was supposed to be not just the rite, but something to be staged, something that requires interpretation and must be made relevant and needs commentary as it is being celebrated, so that the congregation can participate and find itself again therein.

The result was that the congregation was thereby incited to engage in an external activity that paradoxically took away the interior celebration and—far more tragically—that the desire to find oneself again in the forms of the liturgy drove the search for God (whom these forms depict), into the background. The attempts to understand the mystery better made it quite incomprehensible precisely for that reason and at last caused it to vanish.

The call for the accessibility of liturgical forms to the participant, for comprehensibility of the action and for an interior participation in it turned into a detachment from the intrinsic core of the liturgy, the worship of God. Man, who is never more beautiful than when he worships,[1] unexpectedly lost his real relation to the liturgy precisely through that new movement. It suppressed worship through the well-intentioned but dangerous turn of its attention to man. Examples of this are the flattery of his "maturity" through the distribution of Communion at eye level into the hand of *homo faber* [man the artifact-maker], the effort to make the liturgical action "comprehensible" in commentaries and stage directions, which are the death of ritual as well as of theater, the "lightening" of difficult or less agreeable Scripture readings through ad-libbed abridgments, and finally the attempt at intellectual formation by constantly interrupting the course of the liturgy with homilies, introductions and readings of every sort, with which the ears of the body and the antennae of the understanding are served, but the ears of the heart and the tentacles of the soul are no longer reached.

The attempts of the post-conciliar liturgical reform to explain the liturgy begat a praxis which—even though it may be an illegitimate child—cited Vatican II as the "pastoral Council" and caused the destruction of the rite by turning it into a pedagogical exercise. The concern about understanding the liturgy better, which had already been on the minds of popes such as Pius X or Pius XII, was turned upside down: the celebration was not brought closer to the faithful through better practicing of customs, singing, rituals and prayers, more solemn execution of them and greater efforts to cultivate them; instead the rite became encrusted with everyday occurrences and was pushed farther away by simplified explanations. What the rite actually is, namely the physical side of God who is present in a hidden way, from now on became even more incomprehensible, because the counterfeit of a staged version preoccupied with comprehensibility and the commonplace was offered to the faithful as a substitute. Just like a Gothic Madonna, that has been put in a museum so as to rescue it from decay, dies because

---

[1] Cf. Arnold Rademacher, *Religion und Bildung* (Bonn: Hanstein, 1935).

it is taken out of the immediate setting of worship and no one ever thinks to pray in front of it.

Thus in the post-conciliar development we described a trajectory that insidiously departed from the worship of God, not by any conscious act of turning away, but rather through the retirement of the rite and its replacement by an anthropocentric event that makes the great liturgical Tradition of the Church seem incomprehensible (instead of comprehensible) to anyone who grows up in this new form. Every sober assessment of the situation must admit that an operation was being undertaken after all, when they clinically dissected what had been handed down organically.

Consequently the alleged success of the liturgical reform is a Pyrrhic victory, in which the victor ends up being the vanquished. Instead of opening men's hearts to God, making His majesty shine forth more clearly and intimately (something that our era could have used in order to survive), access to the sanctuary was barred. Those who were seeking were not led to the timeless liturgical oases whose waters consist of the forms preserved and tenable in Tradition, which make God's grandeur shine forth as the only consolation in this finite world, but rather they offered the people a new "liturgy" as the satisfaction of their current needs for cultural entertainment, political consciousness-raising or intellectual activity. Formation of the heart along the lines of a childlike immersion in the mystery was condemned as simpleminded. Whatever we do not understand has to go! According to this motto the whole grand liturgical building was downsized and cleared out in favor of intelligibility and humanity.

The priest is supposed to have stage presence and a subjective tone of voice. Above all he should speak the language heard in the street. That would make it easier to follow the celebration—these are the sorts of things you used to hear. The rites should be less complicated, should be liberated from old collections of incomprehensible, archaic elements that hitherto have remained untouched; the whole storeroom filled with centuries of liturgical junk should be cleaned out, so as to leave behind a clear liturgy corresponding to the demands of the present.

This demand feeds on the spirit of an age in which society as a whole was shaking off the dust of the centuries, and in all departments of life —from architecture to manners and clothing—preferred clear lines in which there no longer was or should be room for anything mysterious.

With a no-frills attitude that reduced everything to what was apparently essential, the 1960s carried out a gigantic purge of traditional treasures that people had ceased to understand.

Astonishingly, it never occurred to anyone to attempt to encounter what had been forgotten by remembering or to regain the lost understanding, or with the devotion of a child for his grandparents to have the past recounted anew so as to understand it or to learn to love it, because in the tales told by the elderly we have a guarantee that what once was must never sink into oblivion, because it is vitally necessary for today. Especially when—as with liturgical treasures—it is a question of forms that developed in this way and only in this way, so that they might timelessly unite man with the eternal, regardless of where and how he lives.

Therefore we observe that the recent development with regard to the liturgy has something to do with a fundamental forgetting of Tradition and furthermore with a loss of understanding for what is inexplicable, for mystery. The demythologization of the world goes hand in hand with the demythologization of worship. Under the pretext of improving access to the world, it distorts that very access by explaining the world in places where it cannot be explained. Consequently the Enlightenment, in its impulse to make all of reality parade past the tribunal of reason, has achieved its final and at the same time most destructive victory when it divests the absolutely unattainable mystery of worship of its appropriate covering of sacred forms in order to bring it closer. This closeness, however, is what destroys the mystery. Distance from the numinous, in contrast, helps us to recognize that a human being knows nothing but can only marvel at what exists.

The liturgy, with its various forms of veiling things from sight with the icon screens of the Eastern Church, and with its inaudible recitation of the liturgical word in the Church of the West, allowed adequate room for the mystery. Man, who wants to meet God in the liturgy, must restrain his objections and his boundless desire to understand and enter the sacred place in wonder and humility with the attitude of a silent listener. There he is close to God when he does nothing productive, when he does not speak and behave in an everyday manner, but rather steps out of the everyday routine and finally out of himself too. He has to become free for what is hidden and true, free from the compulsion to want to be useful—however noble and intent on improving the world he may be. Only when he adores in silence and astonishment does a human being come closest to his purpose of becoming blessed in the service of God. Only then is he of any "use", if you will, to himself and to the world.

It is therefore quite obviously the duty of pastoral care to help human beings to do this very thing, not only to show them the way, as a Good Shepherd does, but also to equip them with the means that make it possible for them to find and worship God as God. For the essential thing is to take a human being by the hand, to lead him out of the narrowness of his everyday life and to open up for him the horizon of truth.

Pastoral care therefore, if it deserves the name, will first and foremost keep in mind the essential purpose of a human being: to adore God. A not insignificant part of this, however, is a basic liturgical attitude, which in the image-like forms of worship makes it possible even this side of heaven for a human being to draw near to God in a holistic way, and by no means merely intellectually or symbolically. The real presence of God in the liturgy challenges the one who participates in it to set aside everyday business and to be exclusively in the presence of the Lord, to listen to Him, to sing and to play for Him. This emptying-out of everything useful and functional is the first step into the sanctuary, without which a real encounter with God will not succeed. The person who celebrates must have no reservations and set no conditions if he is to be filled with the presence of the Hidden One.

To understand and to practice this and to call it to mind again and again is the object of pastoral care when it is concerned with the liturgy. Indeed, it is even the central object, because in this life nothing brings one closer to God more intimately than the celebration of worship. The entire endeavor of pastoral care must serve to make the faithful capable of liturgy in this sense. The shepherd who guides the flock to good, nourishing pastures must exercise definite leadership, so that along the way the sheep do not stuff themselves with the wrong plants, which fill them up in an unhealthy way and might rob them of their appetite for fresh grass.

Applied to pastoral care this can only mean that the shepherd misleads his flock if he does not urge them to seek what is holy. He must lead them to the sources and—regardless of whether he is prompted by his own convenience or by unenlightened philanthropy—must not feed them with counterfeits that still the hunger of the sheep for truth and beauty by satiating them with trivialities. Therefore everything that is apt to make people capable of worship can rightly be described as "pastoral" in the literal sense, especially with regard to the liturgy. For in the cultic encounter with God is found the real preparation for eternity. In ritual activity, which is not driven by any agenda, the human being comes closest to his destiny.

For the sake of the salvation of human beings it is essential to lead them to the worship of God; from this perspective the expression "pastoral liturgy" takes its real meaning and at the same time reveals its weakness. It offers an occasion for a dangerous misunderstanding. This is because the term "pastoral", on account of its pedagogical dimension, can make it seem as though the liturgy served some purpose found outside of itself, that it could be applied, so to speak, as an educational device that can be formed and shaped to that end. There is no disputing the fact that the liturgy as such has an educational effect, because it makes God present in visible forms. To that extent it brings the participants along into the majestic grandeur of the Most Holy. But it never does this as a strategic method; rather, it sings and plays before God and thus is the earthly court of the invisible God, in which He shows Himself in sounds, words and ritual gestures.

It is self-evident that this cannot be a means, but rather is a self-contained event that cannot be drafted into the service of something else. Hence "pastoral liturgy" can exist only inasmuch as the liturgy *per se* is a guide for souls, but never in such a way that it becomes the place for implementing pastoral methodologies (as catechesis, conversation, or discussion groups might be).

Furthermore something has generally crept into the notion of "pastoral" that is actually contrary to the real care of a shepherd. For the term is not infrequently applied in an attempt to make things easier, to avoid exacting demands, or in an effort to characterize something else as too "dogmatic". As though it were beneficial for a flock to dispense with guiding them to green pastures just because it requires effort to get to them. Or as though it were really helpful to the sheep not to demand of them the discipline of staying together and to give them the option, through laxity and by renouncing the exercise of authority, of being devoured by wild animals.

It goes without saying that this interpretation of the term "pastoral" is doubly dangerous when it is applied to the liturgy. Not only is imposing a pastoral agenda on the sacred action inherently a way of destroying it; above and beyond that there is also the widespread, erroneous understanding of the term "pastoral" that implies easing demands and explaining away mysteries, which make it unsuitable for describing what is really necessary.

What does the liturgical reality look like in the parishes, that is, in the places where the faithful normally practice their faith? Has not the destructive potential of a misconceived "pastoral ministry" long since obliterated a true understanding of the liturgy and any celebration of the rites accordingly? Aside from a few laudable exceptions that have been maintained only with a difficult struggle in the context of the various local Churches, where is there a parish in which the liturgy acknowledges its obligation to an unswerving Tradition? Where, for example, are the parishes that have kept Gregorian chant alive, which Vatican II described as the authentic singing of the liturgy of the Latin Church? In what parish do the priests and the faithful forgo the usual profane mannerisms with which the Holy Mass is decked out nowadays? In order to find out the liturgical status of a parish, you can easily run a test yourself, by demanding all the things that Tradition considered indispensable (which is why the Council did not abolish them either): communion on the tongue as a rule, the celebration of Mass with the priest and people facing the same direction, pride of place given to Gregorian chant and the regular performance of classical polyphonic works, and the prohibition of the sorts of informality that in the Anglo-Saxon world have appropriately been termed "happy-clappy". As a rule, if these demands were made, a storm of indignation would be unleashed, because this set of essential components was disposed of long ago. And this was done—unfortunately it must be said—for "pastoral" reasons.

In order to start the healing process of these same cultic sicknesses at the heart of the Church, it would be necessary to stop overlooking the fact that officially the current practice can in every case find support in what is spelled out in the Missal of the liturgical reform of Ven. Paul VI. For that is where the blank checks for those "pastoral" adaptations and options can be found. They are not really "pastoral", though, because they are carried out by priests who as a rule are not dramaturgically equipped to select profitably from among the options or to apply the adaptations sensibly, and thus they destroy the rite. For a rite that wants to be a rite will never conform in its singing, readings, prayers, comments and gestures to the needs, the preparation and the peculiar character of the participants, as the *General Instruction of the Roman Missal* demands. And a rite cannot tolerate it if "the texts of the readings, the prayers, and the liturgical songs correspond as closely as possible to the needs, spiritual preparation, and culture [*or* educational level] of those taking part" (*General Instruction of the Roman Missal*, 352). The rite conforms instead to what it makes present: the God of mystery. Thereby it protects the treasure of the Faith that is being celebrated and at the same time trains the participants to let themselves be formed by the liturgy.

Here—in the formation of the faithful—lies the meaning of all "pastoral" ministry, however. "The care of souls is the whole function of a parish priest", says Vatican II in its Decree on the Pastoral Office of Bishops, *Christus Dominus* (n. 31)—nowadays an oft overlooked statement that would again set many things that got out of line in the arbitrary interpretation of the provisions of the last Council.

Therefore it should be a central concern in the present to restore this order in our thinking. For when we lose sight of *why* there is pastoral care of souls, then it remains unclear furthermore *what* pastoral care is and what means it should therefore employ, both for "pastoral ministry" and also for the liturgy—so too the meaning of "pastoral liturgy" is unclear.

It is no less important to define clearly the nature of a parish before reflecting on the place that liturgy occupies in it or on the concrete forms that it takes. For here the life of the faithful becomes concrete under the direction of the ministry. "A parish is a certain community of Christ's faithful stably established within a particular Church, whose pastoral care, under the authority of the diocesan bishop, is entrusted to a parish priest as its proper pastor" (Code of Canon Law, 515 §1)—thereby adopting the traditional idea that pastoral care needs a structure within which it must be exercised and received.

Regardless of how the individual parish is structured, whether as a territorial parish or a personal parish, one thing is important: namely that it is the place where the sanctification of the faithful occurs in an orderly fashion under the direction of the pastor. In this connection the idea of order is quite decisive. For pastoral interests should not come into their own in amorphous structures but rather should develop in a regulated interaction of shepherd and flock; not insignificantly, besides individual formation, this development has a universal ecclesiastical dimension. For the parish is a part of the Universal Church and is essentially bound up with it—as its smallest institutional unit, so to speak.

Thus the parish is actually the most privileged place in which the formation of the faithful through the liturgy occurs. As the Church documents see it, the celebration of the Sacred Mysteries should be embedded in the overall context of pastoral ministry, and concretely that means in the life of a parish, which is regarded as the place of instruction in the Faith and as the guarantor of the continuity of ecclesiastical life. Parishes "in some way . . . represent the visible Church constituted throughout the world" (*Sacrosanctum Concilium*, 42). In them the liturgy should be the place of the encounter with God, unsurpassed by anything else. The Eucharist, according to the will of the Second Vatican Council, should be the source and summit of all ecclesiastical life. The faithful who are assigned to a parish, in addition to receiving catechesis and direction in all questions about Christian life, should be immersed in the real presence of the Redeemer. They should sense the guiding hand of the priest, who as their shepherd leads them to that same source about which the Council speaks. In the liturgy he causes them to participate in what is above. The shepherd (in Latin: *pastor*) consequently occupies a key position. He must lead and therefore—before he himself leads others—he himself must lead a completely and utterly liturgical life.

To remedy this situation, the Church's mission must therefore, in the sense of that true reform, courageously address the roots of the problem. And, as Pope Benedict XVI observed in the conclusion to his reflections on a "reform of the reform", these lie in the destruction of the rite.[2] Therefore if we want to renew the liturgy—also and precisely in the parishes—then this will not work without a unified, prescribed and binding rite that has been purged of all facile accommodating options. Then—and only then—would the desolate liturgical situation in the parishes come to an end. Because then the temptation

---

[2] Cf. Joseph Cardinal Ratzinger, "Assessment and Future Prospects" in: Alcuin Reid, ed., *Looking Again at the Question of the Liturgy with Cardinal Ratzinger* (Farnborough: St. Michael's Abbey Press, 2003), pp. 145–53.

to engage in "planning" and "creativity" would be banished, and priest and lay people would again abide by the law of prayer, instead of reinventing the liturgy constantly and considering this "do-it-yourself" celebration as something "pastoral". On the contrary: a "pastoral" liturgy will always be a non-adapted liturgy, and the liturgy that educates will always be a liturgy that renounces everything that is pedagogical.

In order for this insight to prevail, we need priests, and thus ministers of worship, who have noted this and understood it. Then the parishes would have priests, and thus pastors, who lead their flock into the sanctuary which they themselves love and where they know their way around. What matters is love for the liturgy and the resulting love of the faithful for the encounter with God in the earthly forms of worship, which are a this-worldly participation in the Heavenly Liturgy. Only liturgically sensitive priests can enable the faithful through the most varied pastoral methods—from the homily via catechesis to liturgical instruction properly speaking—to prepare themselves for the celebration of the Sacred Liturgy in the sense of a genuine *participatio actuosa*. In this connection it ought to be clear that these instructions are not to take place during the liturgy—as stage directions, so to speak—and certainly not as running commentary on it, but rather outside of the liturgy, before the actual celebration, with the possible exception of a homily on a liturgical theme.

Vatican II conversely sees no hope "of realizing this unless pastors of souls, in the first place, themselves become fully imbued with the spirit and power of the liturgy and capable of giving instruction about it. Thus it is absolutely essential . . . that steps be taken to ensure the liturgical training of the clergy" (*Sacrosanctum Concilium*, 14). For ultimately:

> With zeal and patience pastors of souls must promote the liturgical instruction of the faithful and also their active participation, both internal and external, taking into account their age, condition, way of life and standard of religious culture. By so doing pastors will be fulfilling one of the chief duties of a faithful dispenser of the mysteries of God, and in this matter they must lead their flock not only by word but also by example. (*Sacrosanctum Concilium*, 19)

Judging by this requirement, the fact that the example of pastors in recent decades, with regard to the significance and the celebration of the liturgy, has not corresponded to the demands of the Church is a shortcoming that can be observed universally. Therefore if we are looking for reasons for the general decline of liturgical forms or for the arbitrariness with which the liturgy has been transformed from a schoolmistress into a slave girl, they are to be found first and foremost among the ministers of worship. It is obvious that the example and the personal attitude of celebrants are altogether decisive for the liturgical formation of the faithful and consequently for the pastoral significance of the liturgy as the place of a purpose-free encounter with God. It must immediately be added that the renewed form of the liturgy does not make it exactly easy for priests either to perform their task as celebrants, since after all—in contrast to the ritually fixed classical liturgy of the Roman Church, which was largely exempt from subjective tinkering —the *Novus Ordo* to a much greater extent requires that someone who celebrates it be a liturgical artist.

Whereas formerly celebrating the liturgy beautifully and worthily was primarily a matter of obeying the rubrics, today the liturgical *ordo* demands a greater measure of dramaturgical abilities. Before the reforms following Vatican II, the oft-cited *ars celebrandi* consisted essentially of carrying out the existing regulations consistently and according to form, whereas today, without specially detailed regulations, it makes the celebrant himself the inventor of a dignified creation. He must now make use of options empathetically and inventively, recognize situations and adapt to them liturgically; he no longer is ruled by an iron law but—just as modernity would have it in all departments of life—must become the *homo faber* who produces liturgy.

In doing so one may find something altogether positive in the fundamental concern about enriching liturgical life through flexibility at many places in the ritual proceedings; after all this concern is the result of a mystagogically aligned liturgical movement in the first half of the twentieth century, and means to root the liturgy more deeply in the faithful—a concern, therefore, that can rightly be called "pastoral".

Nevertheless—and here a deep pit yawns between theory and practice—all this presupposes that the celebrant also has the ability to deal with the aforesaid flexible options and to make out of them a new wealth of worship and not its devastation. Precisely herein, however, the "pastoral" reform of the liturgy is exposed in the life of an ordinary parish to those dangers which almost never allow what would be possible in theory to bear fruit in practice. Instead of keeping to the rules, the liturgy now relies on the celebrant's ability and accepts as part of the bargain the fact that dramaturgically untrained celebrants, for instance, notwithstanding the great piety that they may have personally, are unable to carry out in the celebration itself the things that are necessary for a dignified proceeding. In other words, even those who theoretically know how it could go, in some circumstances cannot manage to celebrate "beautifully", because of many personal defects in the area of aesthetics and in their sense of style and form.

To exploit the liturgy with a view to pastoral concerns and to turn it into a means of pastoral care is a fundamentally dubious undertaking, because it repurposes something that is purpose-free; even apart from that, however, whether it is pastorally successful will depend entirely (even in the case of legitimate adaptations and the use of options) on whether the one who makes the decision, namely the liturgist, has had enough practical training in the area of the *ars celebrandi*.

Just as it is not enough for a host who is entertaining to know about the beauty of a table that is appropriately set for a dinner party, but also has to practice setting the table for various occasions, so too the liturgist must reflect on his liturgical decisions and make them according to the laws inherent to the liturgy. Just as one must "know how" to set a table—starting with considerations as to how the occasion of a meal should be taken into account in designing the table, down to practical, creative know-how with regard to the arrangement of the objects that are part of a festive table—so too in the context of the revised liturgy that has been freed from minute prescriptions, the celebrant himself must carry the whole burden of the individual decisions in implementing the liturgical options.

Now on the other hand, if the liturgist is someone who even in everyday life is less gifted as far as his aesthetic and creative abilities are concerned, he will most certainly fail in carrying out the liturgical proceedings as the Missal of the post-conciliar reform demands of him without the help of detailed rubrics, and with him the liturgy will run aground. And then too there is the breakdown of what is termed "pastoral" liturgy, because ultimately what has prevailed is not the immutability of the mystery, but rather the mutability of the forms, which in the end are not binding. It must be pointed out, despite all the insistence to the contrary, that mutability of form is correlated with mutability of contents. If this is to be the result of a "pastoral liturgy", then it is not "pastoral" at all but rather seriously misleading and does not train the faithful to draw closer to the mystery.

There are numerous examples of this tragedy, which the Church brought on herself through a misconceived liberalization and deritualization. No one who has preserved a remnant of aesthetic sensibility can miss them. The only way to escape from this trap of subjectivism and ugliness would be a return to a stricter reliance on rubrics, through the guidance of which—also and precisely in their minute details—the liturgy would be delivered from the hands of the tinkerers who, by overdoing it, demystify it and adapt it to their own bad taste. To return to the image of designing a festive table: if a host does not know instinctively how to arrange a beautiful table, and if he has not really learned how either, but now it is his turn to be the host, who has to perform the service of designing and arranging, then the only thing that can help him is the book on etiquette, a "primer" that he can rely on unconditionally, so as to arrange a beautiful and tastefully prepared table in this particular way—and only in this way. The word "creativity" does not apply here, since the result would not come about through the host but rather solely by carrying out instructions. In this way he would succeed through "blind" obedience, so to speak, and this outcome could be attained even if he personally had no sense for such things.

Pursuing the analogy with the liturgy, this can only mean that those dimensions of the liturgy that the papal master of ceremonies, Msgr. Guido Marini, formulated in Rome on the occasion of the First International Conference for Eucharistic Adoration, which are indispensable for the liturgical life of the Church, must be safeguarded with the help of rubrics. Besides the dimensions of catholicity, historical continuity and participation in the heavenly liturgy, he also mentions the dimension of non-arbitrariness, that is, the prohibition of destructive subjectivism.[3] This will not succeed, however, unless this non-arbitrariness is secured by a new and detailed obligatory ritual. And unless, furthermore, the training of liturgists is conducted with great care so that the immutable character of the divine is no longer at the mercy of the often unenlightened creative urges of priests who have

---

[3] Cf. Guido Marini, "Celebrating the Feast of *Corpus Christi*" in: Alcuin Reid, ed., *From Eucharistic Adoration to Evangelisation* (London: Burns & Oates, 2012), pp. 71–82.

not learned to disappear behind the iconostas of the rite and to become the *alter Christus* that Holy Orders made them, so that they might serve the people of God through this sacramental identity. This is true especially of the smallest "biotope" of ecclesiastical life, the parish. Here it is an immediate pastoral concern that the liturgy should again become holy, formally beautiful and objective. If this is overlooked or ignored, there is no more protection against the invasion of those wolves that approach the flock in the sheep's clothing of pastoral endeavors, in order to confuse them and to replace their faith in Christ with the counterfeit of something human but otherwise undefined.

A lot will depend therefore on priestly formation, if a healing process is to begin and the Church is to be able to carry out her mission of leading people into the mystery of God's hidden presence. In any case the ecclesiastical authorities have to want a renewal, in the sense of a reacquisition of fixed rites, and to set the example. For every reform needs cover from "above"; otherwise it will unravel "below".

High-ranking pastors and the Chief Shepherd of the Church must resolve to show the flock that the way to the inviolable sanctuary is one of the most important ways of all; unfortunately thus far only timid initiatives are evident. That being the case, these thoughts about the issue of a "pastoral liturgy" must end not so much with concrete plans as in a hopeful stage. But finally in the Church's mission hope has always been—contrary to all expectations, as a rule—the thing that in the end has led to the goal.

14

Liturgical Catechesis and the New Evangelization

NICOLA BUX

The Meaning of the Sacred Liturgy

The basis for the relation between catechesis and liturgy is the fact that through the liturgy Revelation is transmitted "in its solemn or ordinary form", (John Paul II, *Catechesi Tradendæ*, 52), making it possible to encounter Jesus Christ, that is, to have the experience of faith; a human being cannot encounter Him merely through the word, but also in gestures laden with His divine presence.[1] Just as the words and the gestures in Sacred Scripture cannot be divided, so too the Word cannot be separated from the Eucharist, catechesis from the sacraments, adoration from communion, because that would mean separating Christ's divine nature from His human nature, as though the Word had not been made flesh. The Catholic Faith is proposed in the sacramental encounter, which is made up of gestures and words, of signs, beauty, lights, images and splendor, as is particularly evident in the Eastern liturgies. The encounter with the Lord occurs in the mysteries according to times and manners that are different for each person—an experience that Paul describes as a process of perceiving the form and of rapture, we might say of aesthetics and ecstasy: "And we all, with unveiled face, beholding the glory of the Lord, are being changed into

---

Translated from the Italian original by Michael J. Miller.

[1] Cf. Romano Guardini, *The Spirit of the Liturgy* (New York: Crossroad, 1998), pp. 53–60; see also: Nicola Bux, "L'itinerario per la costruzione dell'identità cristiana mediante la catechesi e la liturgia", in: *Catechesi e catechismi*, *Communio* [Italian ed.] 67 (1983): pp. 10–22.

his likeness from one degree of glory to another; for this comes from the Lord who is the Spirit" (2 Cor 3:18).

The constant search for the sacred delineates the ample extent of the mystery: man can be caught up and transported to it through contemplation or more simply can adhere to it with his intellect and will, thanks to revelation. There are some signs of the marvelous exchange between heaven and earth, between the divine and the human that was inaugurated by the Incarnation of the Word. Jesus Christ, "the fairest of the sons of men" (Ps 45:2), the paradox of the one who is the fairest and at the same time "had no form or comeliness that we should look at him" (Is 53:2): he is, according to the famous remark by Dostoevsky, the "beauty [that] will save the world".[2]

Nothing succeeds better in establishing this contact than the art created by faith and the face of the saints which is to be sought every day, as the *Didache* exhorts us. For the purpose of learning to see and to know the divine beauty, according to John Damascene, "gnosis" or concepts that create idols are useless; what is necessary is wonder: one can say that the understanding of the Christian mystery begins with adoration. Mystical theologians from Dionysius the Areopagite to John of the Cross started with the form of being so as to arrive at the interior spirit, according to the method of the Incarnation of the Word: "the true light that enlightens every man was coming into the world" (Jn 1:9); they showed the convergence, in a certain way, of mysticism and aesthetics. God revealed Himself, manifested His form to mankind; we, through what is visible of Him in the liturgy, are drawn to participate in the glory of God: "In [Jesus Christ] we see our God made visible and so are caught up in love of the God we cannot see" (*Roman Missal*, First Preface of Christmas). Indeed, in the Creed we profess our faith in God, the creator of all things visible and invisible: note the adjective "invisible" modifying the noun "things", which usually refers to material reality, whereas here it also designates the realm of the invisible.

To clarify: the reality in which we live is not virtual, of course, but it is not all that exists, either. If I believed that the reality in which I live is the only one possible, people might worry about me. . . . That

---

[2] Fyodor Dostoevsky, Richard Pevear and Larissa Volokhonsky trans., *The Idiot* (New York: Knopf, 2002), p. 382.

is not the case. Albert Einstein reached the conclusion that the most beautiful thing that we can experience is the sense of mystery. It is the source of all true art and of all science. To know that something that we cannot fathom really exists and manifests itself as the most sublime wisdom and the most radiant beauty, which our poor faculties can perceive only in its most primitive forms—this knowledge, this sense is the core of true religiosity.[3] If a non-Catholic or an agnostic can attain this insight, *a fortiori* [with greater reason] we can understand the meaning of a set (or of just one) of the gestures through which Jesus Christ willed that His Incarnation and Paschal Mystery should continue to communicate His own life to mankind: the sacramental mode. This mode is not abstract but concrete in the matter of bread and wine, oil, water, in other words, by means of the matter formed by His word. In short, He redeemed and now saves in the same way in which He created, by His word, united with His flesh, or as the Council of Trent defined with regard to the Eucharist, He willed to "leave to His beloved spouse the Church a visible sacrifice (as the nature of man demands) by which the bloody sacrifice which He was to accomplish once for all on the Cross would be re-presented."[4]

St. Bonaventure describes the mystical passage required by the liturgy: "all intellectual activities ought to be relinquished, and the loftiest affection transported to God and transformed into Him."[5]

The Second Vatican Council's Constitution on the Liturgy prescribes that the liturgy should be understood by the method *per ritus et preces*, through rites and prayers (cf. n. 48); unfortunately this is (all too often) replaced by a flood of words: the priest thinks that if he does not explain, the rites will not function effectively. But can we expect the liturgy to become catechesis? That way, we are immersed in banality. Children are prevented from participating in solemn liturgies under the

---

[3] The scientist speaks about this at length in "How I See the World", an essay originally published in *Forum and Century*, vol. 13 in the series Living Philosophies (New York: Simon & Schuster, 1931). Also reprinted in Albert Einstein, Carl Seelig ed., *Ideas and Opinions: Based on Mein Weltbild* (New York: Bonanza Books, 1954), pp. 8–11.

[4] Session 22, "Doctrine concerning the Sacrifice of the Mass", ch. 1; DS 1740; see also *Catechism of the Catholic Church*, 1366.

[5] St. Bonaventure, *Itinerarium mentis ad Deum*, 7, 2 *Opera omnia*, 5:312; *The Journey of the mind into God*, transl. Philotheus Boehner O.F.M. (Indianapolis: Hackett Publishing, 1990), p. 38.

pretext of special psychological needs; supposedly they do not under-stand, whereas actually they are being deprived of an encounter with the divine mystery through wonder, silence, listening, sacred music, prayer and thanksgiving, as it happened to us when we were little, and we grew up in the Faith through our participation in the Catholic liturgy of the Church, with its universal breathing. Do not the little ones want to become big and to be with the grown-ups?

How to Understand the Liturgy

We must ask ourselves: is modern man capable of grasping the Catho-lic liturgy? Of understanding that in it "heaven comes down to earth" and the mystery allows itself to be encountered and touched? Romano Guardini doubted the ability of modern man to understand it.[6] Mod-ern man is surrounded by immanentism and materialism, yet at the same time feels dissatisfaction and the need to escape from their vise-like grip, to find a solution to this situation, and then it is necessary to make him see some possible way of answering the question that he carries within him. The liturgy is the answer to the need to en-counter the meaning of life, in some way to draw near to the mystery, as though to perceive it and to be somehow implicated in it, involved in the mystery: this is what touches a human being, what evokes in the human mind a longing for the absolute, the divine. Jesus revealed to Nicodemus his divine and human natures: "No one has ascended into heaven but he who descended from heaven, the Son of man who is in heaven" (Jn 3:13). At the same time he revealed the purpose of His coming into the world: to give eternal life and salvation (cf. Jn 3:15–17), to make it possible for human beings and the cosmos to reach God; in order to do that, therefore, he had to open a passage, to offer a stairway to climb, so as to accomplish the ascent to God.

The purpose of the Word's descent is to share the life of human beings; hence the mystery was made flesh and entered into our every-day routine, and therefore we do not have to be afraid. The angel said to Mary: Fear not, be not afraid. Jesus said this to His disciples: Be not afraid, it is I. A human being is afraid when he does not open his

---

[6] R. Guardini, *Liturgie und liturgische Bildung* (Würzburg: Werkbund, 1966), pp. 9–18.

eyes to the fact that the mystery was made flesh and became one of us. Indeed, as St. Augustine says, although what was promised to us is great, what happened is even greater: the unheard-of event of God coming down to earth and taking on our humanity, sharing in it totally and hence revealing to history its meaning and imprinting its final direction upon it. History, considered in itself, has neither a meaning nor a direction; it appears to be a series of courses and recurrences. Its one true meaning and one true direction is the one imprinted on it by God the creator and redeemer, because everything is recapitulated in Christ, who is precisely the *alpha* and the *omega*. The meaning of the liturgy is specifically to make man capable of recognizing the [divine] mystery that comes to meet him. If the liturgy is not an encounter with the mystery but rather a crude replica or caricature of what happens every day in our routine, it is not clear why a human being should feel attracted to it.

This adoring, "cosmic" concept of God who is present in the sacramental mystery was typical of Church Fathers such as Augustine, of monks such as Nicodemus of Mount Athos, and of theologians such as Thomas Aquinas. They therefore felt responsible for introducing the faithful to the mystery and saw the priest as the administrator of the mysteries, and hence the interpreter or the mystagogue of the divine-human mystery, which is the light of truth that has come into the world. The light is itself a mysterious reality, and it is humble, because it wants people to see not itself but everything else; it is transparent to reality; it is made up of all colors so that effectively it is transparent. St. Ambrose masterfully teaches that "the light itself of the Mysteries will shed itself with more effect upon those who are expecting they know not what, than if any discourse had come beforehand."[7] Gregory Palamas centers his meditations on the mystery of the Transfiguration of the Lord to establish his mysticism of the *lumen taboricum*, the light of Mount Tabor, where according to Tradition the Lord showed His glory to the dearest disciples.

The Lord said: "Behold, I am with you always, to the close of the age" (Mt 28:20); therefore He is the one who makes himself present permanently, the Risen, Living One who makes all things new (cf.

---

[7] Ambrose, *On the Mysteries*, in: *Nicene and Post-Nicene Fathers*, Second Series (Peabody, Mass.: Hendrickson Publishers, 1995), 10:317a.

Rev 21:5), whenever His death is commemorated and His coming is awaited, because He comes into the Church which, as it raises the chalice, acclaims: Blessed is He who comes.

So that they might enter into the mystery of His presence, the faithful are formed through catechesis for the catechumens and through the *mystagogia* or post-baptismal catechesis for the initiates; in either case catechesis cannot be separated from the liturgy. Combining the Alexandrian and Antiochene patristic traditions, the liturgy, like Scripture, should promote the elevation of man from the visible mysteries, the sacraments, to the invisible mystery by imitating (*mimesis*) or commemorating (*anámnesis*) the saving gestures of the life of Jesus. All this takes place through the [ascension and] entrance of the Risen Lord "at the right hand of the Father". Even before this, catechesis should help priests and believers to understand and to put into effect the answer to the question "who celebrates the Eucharist", as well as the answers to the questions "how, when and where is it celebrated" (cf. *Catechism of the Catholic Church*, 1135–86). Therefore there is a relationship of continuity between initiation and mystagogy, although they are different things; a relationship which, by being adapted to the different contexts, can help human beings to enter into the mystery.

We are surrounded, however, by a new gnosis: some "initiates" possess the ultimate meaning of things and can decide what is real and what is not; this is an ancient tendency that is nevertheless influential in many and various ways, even in ecclesiastical circles. In contrast, the Christian method is a journey of conversion, unlike the tendency to rely on the interpretation of intellectuals, which replaces a reality that is considered hostile and inimical. If this were not the case, catechesis and mystagogy would be reduced to a set of instructions, which paradoxically ignore the experience of the personal relationship with the mystery, with the Being who establishes us, and brings into being and upholds reality, satisfies our desire for truth and mobilizes our freedom and responsibility as a response to life.

All this cannot be done without a faith *encounter* with the Lord, which according to Catholic teaching occurs by sheer *grace*; this cannot happen without creating a friendship with the persons whom we meet, who are drawing closer to the Church, so as to lead them to the Eucharist, to His presence; this cannot happen without the attraction that Jesus exerts through the Eucharist. Do not the gospels tell of Jesus' encounters with men and women of every sort, sincere and hypocritical, curious and docile? Those who asked Him: "where are you staying? . . . stayed with him" (Jn 1:38–39).

The "sober inebriation" of the Spirit is mysteriously and unforeseeably communicated to the heart, making use of the sacramental words and gestures. There is no need to add other words to comment on the liturgical symbols. We need to trust the invisible Mystagogue, the Holy Spirit, who makes us understand the words that Jesus revealed. The revelation that the Spirit accomplishes does not have a specific content of its own, but refers back to the Trinitarian work.[8]

Subordinate to the Spirit is the visible interpreter of the mystery of the Eucharist, the ordained minister. The priest is someone who does not speak in his own name, who does not come on his own account, but who represents the entire Church, of all places and of all times. One example of *sacerdos* is John the Baptist, who wanted to decrease so as to bring about the increase of the Lord, to whom was "given all power in heaven and on earth". For the priest, to act *in persona Christi* means to make Christ live (cf. Gal 2:20); He is given to the community, indeed He "is a gift which the assembly receives through episcopal succession going back to the Apostles" (John Paul II, *Ecclesia de Eucharistia*, 2003, 29); for these reasons he must celebrate the Eucharist with dignity and humility (cf. *General Instruction of the Roman Missal*, nn. 60 and 56g). Joseph Cardinal Ratzinger observed:

> This service, in which we are made the entire property of another, this giving of what does not come from us, is called sacrament in the language of the Church. . . . Sacrament means: I give what I myself cannot give; I do something that is not my work; I am on a mission and have become the bearer of that which another has committed to my charge. Consequently, it is also impossible for anyone to declare himself a priest or for a community to make someone a priest by its own *fiat*.[9]

This is why the celebrant and the community cannot control the liturgy as if it were their "private property" (cf. *Ecclesia de Eucharistia*, n. 52).

---

[8] Cf. St. Basil, *The Holy Spirit*, V, 10; PG 32:84, *Nicene and Post-Nicene Fathers*, Second Series, 8:7a.

[9] Joseph Cardinal Ratzinger, *Called to Communion* (San Francisco: Ignatius Press, 1996), p. 115.

The priest is a "bridge" for the purpose of establishing relations. If this bridge is broken down, God forbid, because of a sub-standard *ars celebrandi*, he ends up not accomplishing his mission, which is to facilitate man's encounter with the mystery. The old adage *melius prodesse quam præesse* ("better to be useful than to be in authority over others") applies to him as well, because the "success" of the liturgy is not something external but concerns the heart of the human being; he is not producing a drama and must not inspire fear with invective and admonitions, but above all must give witness, by his adoring prayer and recollection, to the fact that the Eucharist is for the life of the world. Today instead there is a widespread tendency to make the liturgical action spectacular through the exhibitionism of some "ministers" in the celebration, the infantilizing of the gathering, the emphasis on applause, *et cetera*, things that tend to obscure the *proprium* (the distinctive character) of the Eucharist, which is the mystery made present, the gift of the Real Presence. One consequence is the abandonment of the traditional signs of veneration, sometimes with a contradictory admiration for the signs of the Eastern Churches. What an impact the celebrant's attitudes have on the faithful!

Faith lived out in grace is the precondition for an "effective" Eucharist, or a fruitful Eucharist, as Ignatius of Antioch would say. If the priest who presides changes the rite or invents a liturgy to his own liking—and this is the current notion of "creativity"—the congregation is faced with a manipulation of the Catholic faith, which may make the celebration invalid. The 1947 Encyclical *Mediator Dei* of Pius XII teaches that "The entire liturgy . . . has the Catholic faith for its content, inasmuch as it bears public witness to the faith of the Church"; also that the liturgy is hierarchical, in other words, not belonging to an individual, whether priest or layman, but to the entire Church. (n. 47)

One cannot humiliate the people of God with overbearing abuses and arbitrary rites, because they have the right to the liturgy of the Church. The one who presides must abstain from any and all theatricality in the various parts of the Mass: the homily should be sober, clear, pertinent, discreet, courteous and if possible elegant in its expression; it should avoid long digressions, which are best reserved for private devotions, but on the other hand it should avoid haste; the *oratio fidelium* or prayer of the faithful should not be distorted with petitions that sound like mini-homilies; time should be devoted to silence and not just to comments, which are often invasive and make the celebration unbearable. The priest cannot change the liturgy as he pleases.[10] Perhaps priests should go back to reflect on the *munus sanctificandi* or "power" of sanctifying that was entrusted to them at ordination,[11] because "the authority of the priest must in the end be adoration, must spring from adoration and culminate in adoration."[12] This is why Cyril of Alexandria can declare: "Peace will be given to every builder, either someone building up the Church and appointed spiritual guide [mystagogue] for the house of God, or benefiting his own soul . . . such a one succeeding in saving his own soul without the slightest difficulty."[13]

Educate the Faithful to Adore so that They Can Evangelize

A lay Christian sketched this compassionate diagnosis:

> The sacraments used to educate the faithful to look at life in a profound way: baptism is birth; communion is the mystery of friendship in which Christ dwells; confession is the request for mercy as the law of life; confirmation and holy orders exist in order to fight the good fight in the world; the anointing of the sick—so as to sanctify illness and not curse it, as the pagans do. These actions, especially the liturgical celebration, were not only and most importantly "word", they were not in the first place "discourse". They were rich actions in which, with all their senses, the people were educated to see, hear and touch. Music, liturgical gestures, formulas, movements by the people: everything was part of one single event. Nowadays everybody goes to church distracted, listens very little and does not sing. The colors and the liturgical vestments are more or less parts of an outfit; the rites— a tiresome, meaningless hustle and bustle, "things that always are and

---

[10] Cf. M. Thurian, *Passione per l'unità e contemplazione del mistero* (Vatican City: Libreria Editrice Vaticana, 1997), p. 73.

[11] Cf. A. Garuti, *Il Mistero Della Chiesa: Manuale di Ecclesiologia* (Rome: Ed. Antonianum, 2004), p. 334f.

[12] Joseph Cardinal Ratzinger, *God is Near Us: The Eucharist, the Heart of Life* (San Francisco: Ignatius Press, 2003), p. 97.

[13] Cyril of Alexandria, Commentary on Haggai, 14; PG 71:1050; English translation in *Commentary on the Twelve Prophets*, Fathers of the Church, vol. 124 (Washington, D.C.: Catholic University of America Press, 2012), p. 80.

never occur", as Saturninus, the fourth-century pagan philosopher, once said.[14]

It is almost as if St. John Paul II responded to it first, by proclaiming the Year of the Eucharist and convoking the Synod of Bishops on the Eucharist; then Benedict XVI, with the Year of Faith. We need to turn our attention now to education for the mystery, starting with "being in church": what to do when you enter the church; genuflection or profound bow to the Blessed Sacrament; an atmosphere of recollection; guidelines to help interior participation during Mass, especially in certain moments (times of silence, personal prayer after communion), and to educate the people in external participation (how to declaim or recite the common parts in unison) (cf. *Sacrosanctum Concilium*, 55; *General Instruction of the Roman Missal*, 281–87; *Redemptionis Sacramentum* 100–107). All three discuss communion under both kinds.

It must be admitted that, often, Jesus Christ is just an excuse to speak about something else: peace, solidarity, and so forth. He is not regarded with adoration, nor does anyone give a thought to His central words: "Do this in memory of me", that is, the Eucharist, His abiding presence, the fact that he willed that we should sit at table with Him, a sorrowful table with the cross looming over it. Unfortunately, not a few theologians and priests contribute to this situation. Opinions circulate in the theological faculties and the seminaries, and even revealed truth and the Magisterium of the Church are considered mere opinions: many pastors are incapable of telling the difference, or worse, they may teach debatable theories instead of "proclaiming the truth openly" (2 Cor 4:2) (cf. John Paul II, *Fides et Ratio*, 6).

It is necessary to return to the sacrament. The sacrament is not *esoterikós*, that is, a book, a language or a teaching reserved for a select few within the Church, although according to the Fathers the Church does have a language of initiation and foresees instruction that is reserved for the catechumens and also a mystagogy in faith and doctrine, an "arcane discipline", but this is not reserved for the elect. In fact the Church does not forbid Christians to reveal to non-initiates the principles and rites of the Christian doctrine or religion, provided that they are not curious individuals who want to exploit it magically or worse.

---

[14] G. Vittadini, "La bellezza donata", *Notiziario Meeting*, Rimini 2004, Anno XXIV, 2, pp. 33–36.

The Italian bishops recognized that one of the problems is the trans-mission of the true meaning of the liturgy, because it is evident that the sacrament is not being understood, and hence they ask for a lit-urgy that is capable of introducing people to the mystery.[15] Priority should be given to the regeneration of the Christian individual. Two theoretical dangers interfere with this: the danger of neo-Gnosticism, whereby what is spiritual cannot become incarnate, and hence one can lead a full life without Christianity; the other danger consists of a sort of primacy of a "least-common-denominator ethics" for all peoples. Another snare in practice is the separation of faith from life, which is supposedly resolved by a commitment to peace and the poor, while bioethics and marriage have to fend for themselves. According to the "weak thinkers" today, there can be only interpretations of reality,[16] about which it would be impossible to make value judgments, since they do not refer to any objective meaning.

Faced with the nihilism that surrounds us, we learn from the sacra-ment to be in the presence of Being and to fight against nothingness by exalting It; this is the profound meaning of Eucharistic exposition. His resurrection and His Presence have overcome nothingness; the result and the sign of His victory is His people, the Church. There is no ed-ucation of a human being without adoration, that is, an interpersonal relationship with God. Do not forget that on the one hand faith is for-mally an act of the faculty of reason, while on the other hand reason needs faith if it wants to be faithful to itself. Plato noted the necessity of a divine revelation to assist the raft of reason. Someone who adores the Lord is capable of guiding young people into the enigma of reality with the key of the sacrament: it opens up and reveals a reality that possesses a primordial intelligibility and goodness that our reason is capable of grasping and loving.

To adore, praise and thank God and to delight in Him. What a beau-tiful and pleasant occupation it is to adore God! It unites the Creator to the creature with a strong, joyful love, and removes the barriers

---

[15] Italian Episcopal Conference, *Comunicare il Vangelo in un mondo che cambia*, 2001, §49.

[16] Cf. F. Nietzsche, *Frammenti postumi* [*Posthumous Fragments*], in: *Opere*, vol. 5/1 (Mi-lan: Adelphi, 1964), p. 299. The same idea can be found in *The Birth of Tragedy*, in: Wal-ter Kaufmann, ed., *On the Genealogy of Morals and Ecce Homo* (New York: Vintage Books, 1967), (pp. 270–76), p. 272.

between heaven and earth, between time and eternity. Adoration is inevitably drawn by the sacrament to its center in the Eucharistic species, which brings about in the Church a meeting of heaven and earth, man with God and with all the saints. The many strands of the life of the Church converge on it—both the present-day Church with her separations and also the future Church with her tendencies to unity and to perfect communion.

Adoring Christ leads us to make courageous choices: it calls some to the priesthood and to the consecrated life, but above all to live out one's baptism in holiness, and this leads us to proclaim to others our own experience, to those who do not know Him or who go after substitutes. We need to ask the Lord for at least a spark of love for the Church, the *Catholica*, Mother of the saints. He wants us to be a people transformed by our encounter with Jesus: adoration is this encounter. Only saints can renew humanity and, while awaiting His coming, prepare it by adoration for eternal life.

Therefore liturgical catechesis means understanding the "priority" of bringing man to God: this is the ever-new evangelization of the world.

The "I" and Worship

The Hebrew thinker Abraham Joshua Heschel observes:

> It is customary to blame secular science and anti-religious philosophy for the eclipse of religion in modern society. It would be more honest to blame religion for its own defeats. Religion declined not because it was refuted, but because it became irrelevant, dull, oppressive, insipid.[17]

This judgment cannot be generalized, but it should make us Christians reflect; for example, whether by giving priority to social concerns we have healed the division produced within the "I" between its faith and the reality in which it lives; whether we have first evaluated the culture surrounding us and then kept what is valuable. Indeed, religion is what man does in his solitude, but it is also the activity in which he discovers his essential companionship, the necessity of saying "Thou"

---

[17] A. J. Heschel, *God in Search of Man: A Philosophy of Judaism* (New York: Farrar, Straus and Cudahy, 1956), p. 3.

to God: "O God, you are my God, I seek you. . . . So I have looked upon you in the sanctuary, beholding your power and glory" (Ps 63: 1–2). The liturgy nowadays does not stimulate a yearning for the divine Thou, does not help an "I" to emerge in this way, because it is deprived of His presence which fills souls with silence—the tabernacles are removed from the center and placed in a corner or even outside the church—and therefore to whom can we say: "O LORD, we wait for you; your memorial name is the desire of our soul" (Is 26:8)? The *Desired of the nations* cannot be found, because he is no longer in church. Then, the excessive insistence on what is "communal", especially in the celebration of the sacraments, has obscured what is "personal": thus the desire that urges every human being to seek God cannot survive, is not transformed into a question, that is, into prayer.

"If you do not want to be afraid", says St. Augustine, "examine your conscience. Do not probe the surface, but go down into yourself and enter the innermost recesses of your heart."[18] But a great deal of what is deepest in human beings remains buried because they have distanced themselves from God: only Christ incarnate and risen can waken it, because He is continually seeking it. Benedict XVI explains why God set out in search of man: "He comes to meet the unrest of our hearts, the unrest of our questioning and seeking" (Homily at the Chrism Mass 2011). Therefore the liturgy must show its ability to reawaken the "I": if it succeeds in doing so, it will prove its truth and effectiveness. Indeed, only what is divine, the presence of the sacred, He who is the ultimate meaning of things, can save mankind, that is, preserve and defend its essential dimensions and its destiny.

What the "I" is cannot be understood outside of Christianity. Because Christ corresponds to what I am, and when I encounter Him, especially in the mystery of the liturgy, I understand what I lack: the Mystery, Someone who tells me: "I am the Mystery that is missing in everything that you enjoy, in every promise that you live. Whatever you desire and seek to attain, I am the Destination of everything that you do. You seek me in everything whatsoever."[19]

The "I" is reborn from an encounter in this way and generates an affinity with the person encountered and a companionship with others

---

[18] Augustine, *Sermons*, 348, 2; PL 38/1:1527 [translated from Latin].
[19] Cf. L. Giussani, *Avvenimento di libertà* (Genoa: Marietti, 2002), p. 149.

who have encountered him;[20] this is how the new liturgical movement
is being born. No power can totally prevent the encounter from taking
place, but it seeks nevertheless to prevent it from becoming history;[21]
many are unwilling to see freedom: this is proof of the lack of a real
experience of faith, according to the axiom of St. Ambrose: *Ubi fides,
ibi libertas.* ("Where there is faith, there is freedom."). If there is freedom, which is the most precious and powerful sign of faith, it can be
verified that we are having an experience of faith capable of resisting
anything. But freedom is God Himself, and hence man's freedom to
be true and sound is dependence on God. In the atmosphere of the
"civil religion of self-determination" surrounding us, it is necessary to
proclaim freedom as a responsibility and a limit.

Even today it happens that the secular government, and sometimes
the ecclesiastical authority as well, does not tolerate true religiosity,
true devotion according to St. Francis de Sales, because it sees that
as a limit to its ownership. Faith remains the gesture of fundamental
freedom and prayer is continual education in freedom. This is the importance of the tabernacle, so that human beings might learn to adhere to the Mystery on which they are dependent. Thus it becomes
possible to experience the Mystery and we visit It, because with Jesus
the Mystery has become "an emotionally attractive presence".[22] The
present Mystery is discovered in an encounter, as the beloved person.
He is the Incarnate Word and the hinge of our salvation (*caro salutis
cardo*).[23] The fact that He abides is the sign of His truth: without the
continual reoccurrence of the Christ-Event there is no possibility of
any freedom or of any real communion.

But several erroneous doctrines are making the rounds: for example,
some maintain that *the subject that celebrates the liturgy is the assembly.*

In truth, only Christ is the protagonist and acting subject of the Mass
in which He is present; He is the One Who joins to Himself "the hier-
archically ordered people of God", that is, the Catholic Church, which
lives also in the local gathering of two or three persons that is called a
celebration, based on the Latin term *celeber* (which means "frequented,

---

[20] Cf. L. Giussani, *L'io rinasce da un incontro (1986–1987)* (Milan: BUR, 2010), p. 364.

[21] Ibid., p. 247.

[22] Ibid., Giussani, *L'autocoscienza del cosmo* (Milan: BUR, 2000), p. 247.

[23] Tertullian, *On the Resurrection of the Flesh,* VIII, 10; PL 2:806. ("The flesh is the very
condition on which salvation hinges"). *Ante-Nicene Fathers,* 3:551a.

well attended"); other terms in use are *rite* (from the Greek *arithmós* and from the Sanskrit *rtám*, "order") to designate the sacred action that is performed according to an order in keeping with what the religion demands, and *ceremony*, derived from Latin, which means "cult", a broader term than "rite" or "liturgy". In the Mass the priest acts in the person of Christ, the Head of the Body which is the Church.

The fact that the Mass can be celebrated by a priest alone is quite consistent with this personification which culminates in self-offering: however few or many we may be, if there is no offering of my body as a sacrifice, there is no spiritual worship (cf. Rom 12:1). On Golgotha were not Mary and John the only ones left? And in Emmaus were there not only two disciples? Some have gone so far as to say that a "Mass without the people" is a *monstrum*: but if we found ourselves in the midst of a persecution would not a priest have to celebrate alone so as not to be discovered? And therefore the individual believers? Although persecution is the ordinary condition of the Church, the exception confirms the rule. The "Mass with the people" has been made an absolute: but if "people" means a "crowd of persons", then only Sunday Masses would be preserved, where attendance was still good. If the "people" are presupposed, Mass would have to be celebrated rarely, given that there are few people at weekday Masses. Not even monastic communities would be preserved. If the Church is the Mystical Body, then it lives even in one believer and in only one priest. Is it not true that by opposing individualism in the liturgy one ends up denying the primacy of the person over the community? Hence the "Mass with the people" should not be considered superior to a Mass not attended by the people or at which a few persons are present. The Constitution on the Liturgy establishes that any Mass has a public and social nature (cf. n. 27). Ven. Paul VI declares that "it is not permissible to extol the so-called 'community' Mass in such a way as to detract from Masses that are celebrated privately" (*Mysterium Fidei*, 11).

Finally, the truth and validity of the celebration—terms that some try to apply to the faithful, according to the Protestant idea that priestly mediation is exercised by the people as well—does not depend on everyone going to Communion: even today, as in antiquity, the Mass envisages the presence of the "excommunicated", penitents and catechumens who cannot receive Communion. Therefore the subject who celebrates is not the assembly, but the Lord.

Moreover, some claim that *Christ's presence is mediated by the reunited assembly, by the priest celebrant, by the word proclaimed.*

The presence of the Lord is not merely mediated, as the Constitution on the Liturgy explains: "Christ is always present in his Church, especially in her liturgical celebration": hence He precedes the means by which He is mediated (even in a special way) and through which He makes Himself visible, "especially under the Eucharistic species" of bread and wine (n. 7). This presence is described as real by Paul VI, who cites the Council of Trent, which is "not to exclude the idea that the others are 'real' too, but rather to indicate presence par excellence, because it is substantial and through it Christ becomes present whole and entire, God and man" (*Mysterium Fidei*, 39). Not even the divine Word proclaimed in the Church is on a par with this.[24] And he also recalls that "it is not permissible . . . to concentrate on the notion of sacramental sign as if the symbolism . . . fully expressed and exhausted the manner of Christ's presence in this Sacrament" (*Mysterium Fidei*, 11). Therefore the presence of Jesus Christ precedes the visible signs and is not merely mediated by them.

Conclusion

Certainly the ecclesial crisis manifested in the post-conciliar years is dependent on the collapse of the liturgy. Several websites have posted a discourse of Ven. Paul VI at the consistory of May 24, 1976, which censured those who were dividing the Church, because they refused to respect the liturgical norms. It is necessary to explain the whole situation: he, *in the name of Tradition*, asked that the renewed liturgy be celebrated with dignity, recalling that "the adoption of the new *Ordo Missæ* is certainly not left up to the arbitrary decision of the priests or of the faithful" (he said this in reference to those who wanted to continue in the older *Ordo*, although he had conceded that privilege to old or infirm priests, only when they celebrated *sine populo*). The point is that later on the very same *Novus Ordo* that he had promulgated became the object of abuses, offenses and violations of liturgical law;

---

[24] Cf. the asterisk and the note referencing paragraph 21 of the Constitution *Dei Verbum*.

hence the forecast [*auspicio*] that the *Novus Ordo* had been promulgated in order to replace the old one—in the name of Tradition—was off the mark, inasmuch as the presupposition for it was being denied: the *ritus servandus*, the observance, in other words the principle of the *ius divinum* (divine law) from which the *ius liturgicum* (liturgical law) is derived. Paul VI spoke on this subject several times.

Ferdinando Cardinal Antonelli, when Secretary of the Sacred Congregation of Rites and a member of the *Consilium ad exsequendam Constitutionem de Sacra Liturgia* (the Consilium for implementing the Constitution on the Sacred Liturgy), wrote about the progress that the reform was making (1968–1971) and commented: "Up to the Council, liturgical law was regarded as something sacred, for many it no longer exists. Everyone now takes it that they are authorised to do what they like, and many of the young do just that."[25]

So it happens today that many Christians who participate in the liturgy find themselves constrained not by the law of the Universal Church, but by the "creative liturgy" of a particular diocese, parish or group that goes against the norms of the Constitution on the Liturgy. Now, as Benedict XVI candidly recalled: "For bishops, who are the 'moderators of the Church's liturgical life', the rediscovery and appreciation of obedience to liturgical norms is a form of witness to the one, universal Church, that presides in charity" (Address to the Bishops of Brazil, 11 May 2007).

Concretely, what is to be done? The guidelines drawn up by then-Cardinal Joseph Ratzinger are still valid: First: Promote the correct celebration of the *Novus Ordo*, according to what is prescribed in the liturgical books—this is the reason why John Paul II promulgated the Encyclical *Ecclesia de Eucharistia* and the Instruction *Redemptionis Sacramentum*—Second: Promote the correct celebration of the Mass according to the *Vetus Ordo*, as the Instruction *Universæ Ecclesiæ* now prescribes. Third: Complete the revision of the new liturgical books, making sure to reintroduce some of the treasures that were formerly discarded.[26] The Congregation for Divine Worship and the Discipline

---

[25] N. Giampietro, *The Development of the Liturgical Reform as seen by Cardinal Ferdinando Antonelli from 1948 to 1970* (Fort Collins: Roman Catholic Books, 2009), p. 191.

[26] Cf. Joseph Cardinal Ratzinger, "La Teologia della Liturgia" in: *Davanti al Protagonista* (Siena: Cantagalli, 2009), pp. 129–48; *Dio e il mondo* (Milano: San Paolo, 2001), pp.

of the Sacraments, together with the Pontifical Commission *Ecclesia Dei*, are the ordinary instruments for promoting these guidelines.

Therefore, the then-Cardinal had to observe, "We shall also be able to persuade the bishops that the presence of the old liturgy does not disturb or break the unity of their diocese, but is rather a gift destined to build-up the Body of Christ, of which we are all the servants."[27]

The Holy Father, Pope Francis, declared two days after his election:

> The Paraclete creates all the differences among the Churches, almost as if he were an Apostle of Babel. But on the other hand, it is he who creates unity from these differences, not in "equality", but in harmony. I remember the Father of the Church who described him thus: "*Ipse harmonia est.*" The Paraclete, who gives different charisms to each of us, unites us in this community of the Church, that worships the Father, the Son, and Him, the Holy Spirit (Audience with the College of Cardinals, 15 March 2013).

Liturgical catechesis and the new evangelization need both the variety of charisms and ministries, and also their unity and communion.

379–80; ET: *God and the World* (San Francisco: Ignatius Press, 2002), pp. 415ff.; "Assessment and future prospects" in: A. Reid, ed., *Looking Again at the Question of the Liturgy with Cardinal Ratzinger* (Farnborough: St. Michael's Abbey Press, 2003), pp. 145–53.

[27] J. Ratzinger, Address on the occasion of the Tenth Anniversary of the Motu Proprio *Ecclesia Dei*, 24 October 1998.

15

Homily at the Solemn Votive Mass
of the Most Blessed Eucharist

Walter Cardinal Brandmüller

*President Emeritus of the Pontifical Committee
for Historical Sciences*

Memoria, Repræsentatio, Applicatio

Ever since Christ the Lord, on the evening before His passion, offered Himself, hidden under the appearances of bread and wine, to God the Father as a sacrifice to redeem the world and administered His Body and Blood to the Apostles, His words have reechoed through the millennia: "Do this in memory of me."

And we, gathered around this altar, reverently obey His command. It is good, my dear brothers and sisters, to remind ourselves of this again and again, for experience unfortunately proves the saying, *Quotidiana vilescunt,* "Routine things lose their splendor."

Therefore let us ask ourselves once again today what happens when we approach the altar during the celebration of the Holy Sacrifice.

The Apostle Paul—as we have just heard—is the one who reminds the Christians in Corinth and us too of what it is about (cf. 1 Cor 11:23–29).

There is a term that expresses this: παράδοσις, *traditio*, tradition. "Brethren . . . I received from the Lord what I also delivered to you." So says the Apostle. By that he means that the Eucharistic celebration is not his creation, not a ritual invented by human beings. What he, Paul, experienced as the celebration of the Lord's Supper, after his

---

Translated from the original German by Michael J. Miller.

experience at Damascus, had its origin in that upper room in Jerusalem, where Jesus had spoken these words: "Do this in memory of me." He is the Lord who gave this command and determined the essential form of the celebration. Paul himself received what he then handed on to the Christians in Corinth and elsewhere.

The other Apostles, who once in the Cenacle had experienced the breaking of the bread and the sharing of the cup by Jesus Himself, did no differently. "Do this", He had said, and they obeyed His command. Since then this tradition was carried on by them and by those who followed them, from one generation to the next—down to the hour in which we have gathered here.

Tradition—παράδοσις—is the essential law of the Church generally speaking. Through it every generation of Christians knows that it is united with the source of salvation. Through the sacred imposition of hands which occurs in the administration of the Sacrament of Holy Orders, the command and the authority to celebrate the Tradition come down to us from the Lord.

In this way we, though "fragile vessels", receive and hand on the Redeemer's truth and grace to future generations.

The most precious thing that we receive thereby and have to hand on is the Eucharistic Mystery, the Holy Sacrifice of the Mass.

On December 4, 2013, 450 years will have passed since the conclusion of the Council of Trent. This is the Council that expresses for us briefly and precisely the nature of Holy Mass in the three concepts: *memoria, repræsentatio, applicatio*: memory, re-presentation, application. Let us dwell for a while on these three momentous concepts.

We just spoke about *memoria*—memory. Jesus commissioned the Apostles to celebrate in memory of Him, after His return to His Father, precisely what He Himself did on the evening before His passion. "Do this in memory of me." His salvific work must never be forgotten until He comes again at the end of time.

In fact we read the Passion narrative again and again in church. Moreover, great composers have set it to impressive, deeply moving music; painters and sculptors have depicted it in thousands of images or sculptures. In many places to this day the passion, death and resurrection of Jesus is performed onstage. Then too: are not the impressive processions in Holy Week a fulfillment of this command to remember the event of Holy Thursday, Good Friday and Easter? Certainly! But the memorial cannot be exhausted in that alone.

In the Holy Sacrifice of the Mass what happens is not mere memorial, a remembrance of things long past. The Council speaks instead about *repræsentatio*. In the liturgical celebration, the event of Holy Thursday and Good Friday steps out of the past of two thousand years ago into the present moment, out of the Cenacle in Jerusalem in the year 30 into this Basilica of Sant'Apollinare this evening.

The question, "How is that possible or conceivable in the first place?", has fascinated the most enlightened minds of Christendom for two thousand years, yet despite all their intellectual effort it has proved to be ultimately insoluble. The exceedingly bright, dazzling, light of the mystery blinds the eye of reason. St. Thomas Aquinas experienced and sensed this as no one else ever did: *Tibi se cor meum totum subjicit, quia Te contemplans totum deficit.* ("My heart submits to you totally, for in contemplating you it completely falls short.") The experience of the failure of our understanding on the verge of the mystery simply causes us to sink to our knees and to worship wordlessly. For the Holy Sacrifice of the Mass is not an event that takes place only in our thoughts, as memory does. It is—let it be said again—the re-presentation, the making-present-again in a mysterious divine manner, with the fullest possible reality, of the event in the Cenacle and on Golgotha.

The third term that that Council of Trent uses to describe the nature of the Holy Sacrifice of the Mass is "*applicatio*", which could be translated "application" or "allocation". But what does that mean? For me what comes to mind is the system of aqueducts with which Rome was supplied with water in antiquity. Streaming down from the mountain springs, it came through the aqueducts to the many fountains from which the citizens could draw this vitally essential element.

In a similar way, we might say, the vital stream of grace, which springs from the once-and-for-all sacrifice on Golgotha, is conducted through the countless celebrations of the Mass to individual believers who gather around altars everywhere.

Thus the sound of the bells that call the people to Holy Mass is each time an echo of those words that the Lord Himself exclaimed in the Temple on the Feast of Booths: "If any one thirst, let him come to me and drink."

But the drink that he offers is eternal life. Now it is up to us to drink from this well that never runs dry.

"Do this in memory of Me", the Savior had said on the evening before His passion, and St. Paul continues: "As often as you eat this bread and drink the chalice, you proclaim the Lord's death until he comes." Indeed, the celebration of the Holy Eucharist takes place with a view to the Last Day; it is the celebration of hope in the Lord who is to come again. After all, the crucified and risen Christ who is present in the Eucharistic celebration is at the same time the one about whom we profess: *Et iterum venturus est cum gloria judicare vivos et mortuos. . . .* ("He will come again in glory to judge the living and the dead. . . .")

This is what the Church of Jesus Christ has done for two thousand years now "from the rising of the sun to its setting". She does not ask about the day on which the Lord will come again; it is enough for her, day by day, to draw strength from the faithful celebration of the *memoria* and *repræsentatio* and *applicatio* of the redemptive sacrifice. In this way she and every individual Christian can endure in this cold, harsh, godless world, until—as St. Peter says—"the day dawns and the morning star rises in your hearts".

Mortem tuam annuntiamus, Domine, et tuam resurrectionem confitemur donec venias. ("We proclaim your death, O Lord, and profess your Resurrection, until you come again.")

At the conclusion of the reading that we have just heard, the Apostle draws from what has been said a rather unexpected conclusion. What he now expresses is a very serious admonition, indeed a warning: "Let a man examine himself, and so eat of the bread and drink of the cup. For anyone who eats and drinks without discerning the body [of the Lord] eats and drinks judgment upon himself. . . ." In fact—as we have already said—there is an all-too-present danger that our daily celebration of the Mass will become something routine: *Quotidiana vilescunt.* Routine things lose their splendor. Precisely because the presence of Jesus Christ in the sacrament is so completely hidden and profoundly mysterious, the divine majesty of the Eucharist all too easily disappears from our field of vision. It may even happen that many people do not reflect that they must first obtain the forgiveness of their sins before they can receive the Lord's Body.

The Apostle's admonition is extremely relevant today: "Let every man examine himself. . . ."

We celebrate this Holy Mass at a moment when the Year of Faith has already passed its zenith. *Mysterium Fidei*, the mystery of faith purely and simply is the Most Holy Eucharist. It is the sacrament that challenges our faith in a special way. In its presence not only do our senses fail; against it our concepts and categories of thought are shattered too; our hearts and minds can get a glimpse of it only from a great distance. This is the experience that St. Thomas expresses when he says: *Tibi se cor meum totum subjicit, quia Te contemplans totum deficit.*

What remains is faith, that conviction about a reality that one does not see—so the Letter to the Hebrews puts it. And this conviction is based solely on the words that our Lord spoke on the evening before His passion: This is My Body, this is My Blood; Do this in memory of Me.

Our answer, once again, can only be that of St. Thomas: *Credo quidquid dixit Dei Filius, nil hoc verbo veritatis verius.* (I believe whatever God's Son has said; nothing is truer than this word of truth.) When we bend our knee before the tabernacle in this way, it should be each time a new *credo* [I believe].

16

The Contribution of English Liturgical Patrimony to Continuing Renewal in the Roman Rite

Andrew Burnham

The Apostolic Constitution of Benedict XVI, *Anglicanorum Cœtibus* (4 November 2009), brings to our attention "the liturgical books proper to the Anglican tradition" and speaks of the "liturgical, spiritual and pastoral traditions" as "a precious gift nourishing the faith of the members of the Ordinariate and as a treasure to be shared".[1] Having grown up with the English liturgical books, I want to explore some of what is problematic, as well as what is richly resonant, in the traditions and then reveal, briefly, something of how *Anglicanæ Traditiones*, the interdicasterial working group of the Holy See, has set about producing an Order of Mass.

The communicant at the Lord's Supper, according to the Second Prayer Book of Edward VI (1552), would be attending the rite which most closely conforms to the mind-set of its compiler, Archbishop Thomas Cranmer. That communicant, in order that the Communion Service would be quorate, would signify his name "to the Curate over night or else in the morning, afore the beginning of Morning Prayer,

---

[1] III. Without excluding liturgical celebrations according to the Roman rite, the Ordinariate has the faculty to celebrate the Holy Eucharist and the other Sacraments, the Liturgy of the Hours and other liturgical celebrations according to the liturgical books proper to the Anglican tradition, which have been approved by the Holy See, so as to maintain the liturgical, spiritual and pastoral traditions of the Anglican Communion within the Catholic Church, as a precious gift nourishing the faith of the members of the Ordinariate and as a treasure to be shared.

or immediately after".[2] As the service began, with the Lord's Prayer
and Sarum Collect for Purity, he would see the Curate, standing in
surplice at the North side of a table, set lengthwise in the chancel. He
would hear the Decalogue read, and, after the Collect for the King
and the Collect of the Day, the Epistle and Gospel pericopes as set for
the Sunday in the Use of Sarum. He would join in saying the Nicene
Creed, and then either listen to the one sermon prescribed by the
Prayer Book or hear an authorised homily read. He would be invited
to give generously, and hear the Prayer for the Church "militant here
in earth". One or other exhortation would then follow. He would be
invited to examine his life, make confession of his sins, sins which provoke the "wrath and indignation" of God's "divine majesty", hear a
declaration of absolution for those "which with hearty repentance and
true faith turn unto" God, now re-imagined as "our heavenly father".
Comfortable Words would follow, drawn up by Archbishop Hermann
of Cologne, who, excommunicated in 1546, died a Lutheran in 1552.

The communicant, assured of forgiveness, is now almost ready to
play his part in the Eucharistic action, though, after *Sursum corda*, Proper
Preface, and *Sanctus*, the Priest on his behalf, kneels and prays the Prayer
of Humble Access: "we be not worthy, so much as to gather up the
crumbs under thy table". In what 100 years later the Laudian rubrics of
1662 would call "the Prayer of Consecration", the Priest would plead
the sufficiency of Christ's sacrifice and pray that those receiving the
Sacrament be "partakers of his most blessed body and blood". As he
recites the Dominical words, the Priest breaks the bread, and, immediately the words are complete, the ministers and people receive the
Sacrament, each being urged to "take and eat . . . in remembrance that
Christ died for thee", and "drink . . . in remembrance that Christ's
blood was shed for thee". What might then be regarded as the rest of
the Canon, the Prayer of Oblation, as it became known, could follow,
though instead, ensuring that "oblation" is not integral, there might
be a Prayer of Thanksgiving. As J. H. Srawley puts it, in the Prayer of
Oblation:

> The worshippers, who have cemented their union with Christ in the
> act of Communion, ask God to accept their "sacrifice of praise and

---

[2] *The First and Second Prayer Books of Edward VI*, Everyman's Library (London and
New York: Dent, 1910). Spelling has been modernised.

thanksgiving", and pleading Christ's death as the ground of "remission of sins and all other benefits of his Passion", offer themselves as a living sacrifice to him. The effect of this rearrangement of the prayer is, however, weakened by the unfortunate compromise which allowed the second of the post-communion prayers to be used . . . for in this second prayer there is no reference to the Church's sacrifice of praise.[3]

The taking and breaking, the communion, and the oblation or thanksgiving having been enfolded in a smooth progression, for the first time music becomes possible: the communicant is caught up in the worship of heaven as the *Gloria in excelsis* is sung or said. Finally the priest gives the blessing: "the peace of God which passeth all understanding . . ." (Phil 4:7) and presumably people greeted one another with what we would now regard as a sign of peace as, reconciled with one another, they left the church. At the end of this 1552 Order we notice that "it shall suffice that the bread be such, as is usual to be eaten at the Table with other meats", that "if any of the bread or wine remain, the Curate shall have it to his own use". Finally, in the "Black Rubric", we read that, though communicants receive the Sacrament kneeling, they need to know that "as concerning the Sacramental bread and wine, they remain still in their very natural substances, and therefore may not be adored, for that were idolatry to be abhorred of all faithful Christians".

We have looked at this cameo because it shows us most clearly what Cranmer, in his ingenious way, set out to do. In Elizabeth I's Prayer Book of 1559, and in the 1662 book, there would be some damage limitation—the restoration of unleavened bread and vestments, the reintroduction of the 1549 words of administration,[4] and the consuming of what remains after Communion being the principal repairs, and also some fine-tuning of the Black Rubric—but the problem for many Anglicans these last 450 years has been a Communion Order which is, at best eccentric, and at worst defective. Anglicans notoriously sit light to doctrine but, of the three sub-sets identified by Aidan Nichols

---

[3] J. H. Srawley, "The Holy Communion Service" in: Lowther Clarke and Harris, *Liturgy and Worship* (London and New York: SPCK, 1932), (pp. 302–73), p. 344.

[4] "The Body of our Lord Jesus Christ which was given for thee [the Blood of our Lord Jesus Christ which was shed for thee], preserve thy body and soul unto everlasting life." The combining of the 1549—literalist—and 1552—receptionist—formulæ is a classic example of the Anglican *via media*.

in *The Panther and the Hind*,[5] the largest group from the middle of the nineteenth century to the middle of the twentieth, the Anglo-catholics, has been severely challenged, as were their seventeenth- and eighteenth-century High Church predecessors, by the language and shape of the Cranmerian Communion Order. An axiom of the High Churchmen has always been that, after 1559, or perhaps 1662, everything that needs to be there is there and there have been scholarly expositions of the importance of the 1549 Rite—the First Prayer Book—in which Cranmer's language and layout more closely follows the mediæval Mass. Indeed the 1549 Rite was sub-titled "commonly called the Mass". But, as Diarmaid MacCulloch puts it, "The very great liturgist F. E. Brightman did his Anglo-catholic best to misunderstand Cranmer's outlook in general, and in particular his intentions in 1549; it has taken the work of Geoffrey Cuming and others to disentangle subsequent confusion".[6] Meanwhile we can agree with Procter and Frere in general that "such was the revolutionary revision of 1552: each revision since has done something to undo some of its effects"[7] and, in particular, that "the present position of the prayer of oblation is the main blot upon the English Liturgy, a blot which has carefully been removed in both the Scottish and the American liturgies".[8]

There is no space here for—and few need reminding of—the subsequent history of the English Prayer Book rites. What I have set out, however, makes it unsurprising that there has been, generally speaking, a restlessness over what one might call "shape". The greatest Anglican liturgist of the first half of the twentieth century was Dom Gregory Dix

---

[5] Aidan Nichols O.P., *The Panther and the Hind* (Edinburgh: T. & T. Clark, 1993). The other sub-sets are Broad Church Erastians (for whom dogma remains necessarily opaque) and *sola scriptura* Evangelicals.

[6] Diarmaid MacCulloch, *Thomas Cranmer: A Life* (Yale 1996), p. 412. He refers to Geoffrey Cuming, *Godly Order*, A.C.C. 65, 1983, and to Colin Buchanan, *What did Cranmer think he was doing?* (Nottingham: Grove Liturgical Study, 1976). For F. E. Brightman's outstanding work, see his *English Rite*, two vols. (London: Rivingtons, 1915).

[7] Francis Procter and W. H. Frere, *The Book of Common Prayer*, revised ed. (London: Macmillan, 1901), p. 474.

[8] Procter and Frere, *The Book of Common Prayer*, p. 473. The commentary goes on to say (p. 474) "the English Liturgy still lags behind its Scottish and American daughters, and its best friends are those who would most desire some amendment and reform".

the title of whose *magnum opus*, *The Shape of the Liturgy*, reveals his own preoccupation with "shape".[9] His pioneering work was primarily about the early evolution of what he thought was the "seven-action shape" of the Last Supper—taking, breaking, giving thanks, and distributing the bread before Supper and taking, giving thanks, and sharing the chalice after Supper—into the "four-action shape" of the Eucharist, (offertory, thanksgiving, fraction, and communion). After some 600 pages, he eventually turns his attention to the idiosyncratic "shape" of the Prayer Book liturgy, having sought, in his words, "to avoid the specifically Anglican interests of the paper from which it began".[10] Yet, seeing clearly how Cranmer had cosmetically adapted the language of the mediæval Canon for his own purposes, he was critical of the solution of simply changing the order of things.

The 1927/1928 Deposited Book, defeated in Parliament, and opposed by Anglo-catholics because of the Antiochene shape of the Eucharistic Prayer,[11] was the first attempt to deal with "shape". The "Interim Rite", first proposed in 1911 by W. H. Frere,[12] became the informal way forward after 1928. Here the Prayer of Oblation was appended —often silently—to the Prayer of Consecration, with the Prayer of Thanksgiving then used invariably after Communion. The "Interim Rite" came to fruition in 1966, when it formed part of the provision of *Alternative Services, Series I*, the Church of England having gained more control of its liturgy from Parliament by way of the "Prayer Book (Alternative and Other Services) Measure 1965".

It is necessary to take note that the controversy over "shape" would never be resolved. English Evangelicals, under the leadership of Roger Beckwith, campaigned against the drawing into the Eucharistic Prayer of the language of oblation, and saw this as a fatal flaw in both the "Interim Rite" arrangement and the conservative Eucharistic Prayer which

---

[9] Gregory Dix, *The Shape of the Liturgy*, first published by Dacre Press, Westminster 1945; New edition with Introduction by Simon Jones (London and New York: Continuum, 2005). The underlying thesis is explained on p. xv.

[10] Ibid., p. xxxvii.

[11] The Antiochene shape, as in the Byzantine Rite, has the *epiclesis*—the invocation of the Holy Spirit—on gifts and people after the Institution Narrative (which, in Catholic spirituality, is the dramatic moment of consecration).

[12] Cf. *Some Principles of Liturgical Reform* (London: Murray, 1911), p. 133.

was formed from it.[13] Thus in the 1980 English *Alternative Service Book* revision and in *Common Worship* 2000, Evangelicals have been granted a Communion Order which allows the use of contemporary language, praying within the 1662 (essentially the 1552) shape. Meanwhile, if cautious High Churchmen were content with such adaptations, not every Anglo-catholic was. Dom Gregory Dix thought that:

> If the prayer were put back *before* communion . . . it would not only be an obvious piece of Pelagianism to offer "ourselves . . . to be a reasonable, holy and lively sacrifice"; but taken in conjunction with the lack of any explicit offering of the sacrifice of Christ in our rite, it would lay a most unfortunate emphasis on its substitution of the oblation of the sons of men for that of the Son of Man.[14]

Dom Gregory Dix was an Anglican Benedictine who, day by day, offered Mass in Latin, according to the *Missale Romanum*. His community at Nashdom was Anglo-papalist.[15] The Anglo-papalists believed that the English Church had been savagely separated from the Holy See by Henrician *coup d'état* and that it behoved them to practise the Catholic Religion as if that separation had not taken place. The more daring of the Anglo-papalist clergy therefore either simply used the Roman rite (with the prayers prescribed to be said aloud, at least, in translation), or, for practical and pastoral purposes, used as much of it as possible, for example, reciting most of the Canon under the singing of *Sanctus* and *Benedictus*, but reading Cranmer's Prayer of Consecration in place of the *Qui pridie*. Most were content with the accident that the English Church has the vernacular—it was surely the theological polemic of the Reformation which had interrupted the otherwise natural evolution of the European languages for liturgical use—and Dix himself said that "we have an immense advantage over the dissenters in that we have a liturgy, and over the Roman Catholics in that it is

---

[13] This prayer is found as the Fourth Eucharistic Prayer in Rite A (contemporary language) and as the First Thanksgiving in Rite B (traditional language) in the *Alternative Service Book* (London: SPCK, 1980). It appears too in a more conservative form as Prayer C (contemporary and traditional language) in: *Common Worship* (London: Church House Publishing, 2000), Order One.

[14] Dix, *The Shape of the Liturgy*, p. 666.

[15] Cf. Michael Yelton, *Anglican Papalism* (Norwich: Canterbury Press, 2005). See also John Shelton Reed, *Glorious Battle: The Cultural Politics of Victorian Anglo-Catholicism* (Nashville: Vanderbilt University Press, 1996; London: Tufton, 1998), p. 260 and *passim*.

in the vernacular".[16] Many were content also to enjoy the benefits of clergy marriage, as practised in the Reformed tradition, and the passing down through the clerical gene pool of the gentle introversion and dutifulness of the parish clergy.

With this particular English history in mind we are now in a position to sum up what might be the contribution of English liturgical patrimony to continuing renewal in the Roman rite, as envisaged by Pope Benedict XVI. On the one hand, there are indubitably pages and pages of beautiful prose, prose that has been prayed for centuries. Cranmer's translation of the Sarum collects are a particular example. The psalter of Myles Coverdale is another. There is the English Bible tradition, expressed in the ecumenical consensus of the Revised Standard Version, now the Lectionary of the Ordinariates.[17] There is the vast Anglo-catholic industry of translating and bringing into anthology the writings of the Fathers and the thesaurus of hymnody, from Ambrose to the Oratorians. There is a plainsong tradition and a hymn-singing tradition, no older than the Tractarian revival, but nowadays expressing something of the Wesleyan tradition too. There are marriage and funeral rites which, not least through royal occasions, are part of the warp and woof of national life.

All of this, especially the Anglican Divine Office, the resources for which remain available to the Ordinariates through the *Customary of Our Lady of Walsingham*,[18] seems to have been understood and embraced by Pope Benedict XVI, not only as fertile ground for ecumenism but also as part of the great project of theological *ressourcement* and liturgical renewal. Hence the reference in *Anglicanorum Cœtibus* to maintaining "the liturgical, spiritual and pastoral traditions of the Anglican Communion within the Catholic Church, as a precious gift nourishing the faith of the members of the Ordinariate and as a treasure to be shared" (n. 3). In a new pontificate, with Franciscan simplicity the watchword, there is a danger that commentators will confuse beauty with opulence. The liturgical reforms of Pope Benedict XVI, yet to be fully realised,

---

[16] Ibid., p. 732.

[17] Cf. *The Lectionary*, 2 vols., Revised Standard Version, Second Catholic Edition (San Francisco: Ignatius Press, 2006). *The Holy Bible*, Revised Standard Version, Second Catholic Edition (San Francisco: Ignatius Press, 2006).

[18] A. Burnham and A. Nichols, eds., *Customary of Our Lady of Walsingham: Daily Prayer for the Ordinariate* (Norwich: Canterbury Press, 2012).

are about seemliness and solemnity, the vital link between contemporary celebration and the treasury of Tradition.

Here something further needs to be said, first, about the *Customary* and, then, about hymnody. The *Customary*, authorised by the Ordinary's *Nihil obstat* is a *Vade mecum* through the Divine Office. The Prayer Book Offices and Psalter in course are combined with the Office Lectionary of the *Divine Office*, with the traditional collects, slightly amended, and a rich treasury of devotional writing from the English spiritual tradition, drawn together by Fr. Aidan Nichols O.P. It is very much a book "for the time being" but experience is already teaching us that the clergy who use it to fulfil the canonical requirement to say the Office, and the laity who experience it for Solemn Evensong and Benediction, or for the Festival of Nine Lessons and Carols at Christmas, have a strong, and new, sense of the coming together of traditions within the full communion of the Catholic Church.

Hymn-singing, at least in the popular understanding, is one of the hallmarks of Anglicanism. Generations of schoolchildren were brought up singing a hymn at morning assembly in Church of England schools and, whether the main Sunday services are Morning and Evening Prayer, a Family Service, or the Parish Communion, hymn-singing remains integral. To those outside the Anglican tradition, it comes as a surprise, perhaps, to discover that this has not always been the case. The Book of Common Prayer includes no hymns and no provision for hymns. The Ordinals, bound with the Book of Common Prayer, include *Veni, Creator*—since 1662 in John Cosin's[19] beautiful translation "Come, Holy Ghost, our souls inspire"—but, in the first centuries, there would have been no hymns, apart from the metrical versions of the Psalter,[20] which were often also bound with the Prayer Book and extensively used as a vehicle for the psalmody at Morning and Evening Prayer. The belief among Protestants—excluding Lutherans —was that, unless verse paraphrased Holy Scripture, it had no place in public worship. In the late eighteenth century, this understanding

---

[19] John Cosin (1594–1672) was Bishop of Durham and one of the Divines responsible for the preparation of the Book of Common Prayer 1662.

[20] The principal metrical psalters were Robert Crowley's *The Psalter of Dauid* (1549), the Sternhold and Hopkins Psalter (1549), expanded in 1621 by Thomas Ravenscroft (and, in one form or other, reprinted 200 times between 1550 and 1640), and Brady and Tate's *A New Version of the Psalms of David* (1696).

was challenged by the Methodist revival with their vigorous hymn singing at meetings, and the Tractarians, in the nineteenth century, then saw their opportunity. Hymn singing was a way of re-introducing the mediæval Office Hymn, and the devotional melodies of the centuries, Catholic, Genevan, and Lutheran, became a particular enthusiasm of the musical editors, notable amongst whom was the agnostic Ralph Vaughan-Williams. For the priests, it was a way of solemnising the Eucharist and introducing (and re-inforcing by constant repetition) Catholic teaching on the Eucharist. Many a twentieth-century Parish Communion congregation would sing the following *memento* of the living and the departed at the end of the Prayer of Consecration:

> Wherefore, O Father, we thy humble servants
> Here bring before thee Christ thy well-beloved,
> All perfect Offering, Sacrifice immortal,
> Spotless Oblation.
>
> See now thy children, making intercession
> Through him our Saviour, Son of God incarnate,
> For all thy people living and departed,
> Pleading before thee.[21]

And, as they queued up for Communion, they would sing hymns about the Real Presence—"Let all mortal flesh keep silence", "Sweet sacrament divine". It is, in one sense, a form of the *alius cantus aptus* practice, what the late Lazlo Dobszay called "the anthrax in the envelope",[22] and most Anglo-catholics have indeed used hymn singing as a substitute for singing the Propers of the Mass, but there has been, historically, one important difference. Whereas the Anglo-catholics were adding value to the Cranmerian Communion Service by introducing

---

[21] *The English Hymnal*, n. 335; words by W. H. H. Jervois, 1852–1905.

[22] Laszlo Dobszay, *The Bugnini-Liturgy and the Reform of the Reform* (Front Royal: Church Music Association of America), 2003, p. 86. Paragraph 32 of the Instruction *Musicam Sacram* (5 March 1967) says: "In some places there exists the lawful practice, occasionally confirmed by indult, of substituting other songs for the Introit, Offertory and Communion chants in the *Graduale Romanum*. At the discretion of the competent territorial authority this practice may be retained, on condition that the songs substituted fit in with those parts of the Mass, the feast, or the liturgical season. The texts of such songs must also have the approval of the same territorial authority;" *Documents on the Liturgy: 1963–1979* (Collegeville: Liturgical Press, 1982), n. 4153, p. 1299. This provision later formed part of the *General Instruction of the Roman Missal*.

Catholic teaching through hymnody, the post-conciliar Roman Catholic song writers seemed to have had a different agenda. They were setting aside the Propers (often for very sensible practical reasons) and, at best, exploring some of the Scripture themes of the new Lectionary, and, at worst, indulging use of the ditty as diversion. Little seemed to be learned—and less than one might have imagined imported—from the very solid experience of hymnody as teaching aid and exuberant doxology, which the Wesleyans, then the Anglicans, and now the Ordinariates, bring to the feast.

What the Ordinariates do not bring—because the theological consensus has never been there in Anglicanism, especially in English Anglicanism with its polarities of churchmanship—is a robust, unambiguous Eucharistic rite. The Church of England Liturgical Commission has always recognised this, as an initial statement from 1965 makes clear:

> We have also, where matters of Eucharistic doctrine are involved, tried to produce forms of words which are capable of various interpretations. In the Prayer of Consecration, for instance, we ask that the bread and wine "may be unto us" the body and blood of Christ. This phrase can be used by Anglicans of all schools of thought to express their views of the Eucharistic presence. Only by using such language as does not require any one interpretation can we produce a liturgy which all will be able to use, and which each will be able to interpret according to his own convictions.[23]

This ambiguity underlay the dialogue between the Holy See and Anglicans, following the first Anglican-Roman Catholic International Commission (ARCIC I: The Final Report 1982).[24] The clarifications issued by ARCIC II (1993)[25] scarcely resolved some of the anxieties raised, for example, by the theological position of the Open Letter of the Executive Committee of the Evangelical Fellowship of the Anglican Communion (1988).[26] One of the major players in that Open Letter and in the late twentieth-century liturgical debates was Colin Buchanan. The very title of his booklet, *The End of the Offertory: An*

---

[23] *Alternative Services: Second Series* (London: SPCK, 1965), p. 146; *An Order for Holy Communion* (London: SPCK, 1966), p. viii.

[24] C. Hill, and E. Yarnold, eds., *Anglicans and Roman Catholics: The Search for Unity* (London: SPCK & CTS, 1994).

[25] Ibid., p. 197.

[26] Ibid., p. 283.

Anglican Study,[27] indicates that, once we are into the Liturgy of the Eucharist, there can be no clear and unambiguous Anglican expression of the Catholic understanding of the Eucharistic transaction. All suggestions of a viable Anglican Eucharistic Prayer are thinly based in experience or otherwise problematic. William Laud's Scottish Prayer Book of 1637, with its *epiclesis*[28] and its "memorial or prayer of oblation" added on to the end of the Prayer of Consecration,[29] expressed the theology of the Caroline Divines but did not prevail twenty five years later, when King Charles II indicated that the Prayer Book of 1662 should not diverge too far from that of 1559, the Use before the Commonwealth, during the reign of his father. It remains important nevertheless not least because it formed the basis of the American rite of 1789, and thereafter of the revisions of 1892 and 1928.[30]

---

[27] Colin Buchanan, *The End of the Offertory: An Anglican Study* (Nottingham: Grove Liturgical Studies, 1978).

[28] "Hear us, O merciful Father, we most humbly beseech thee, and of thy almighty goodness vouchsafe so to blesse and sanctify with thy word and holy Spirit these thy gifts and creatures of bread and wine, that they may be unto us the body and blood of thy most dearly beloved Son; so that we receiving them according to thy Son our Saviour Jesus Christ's holy institution, in remembrance of his death and passion, may be partakers of the same his most precious body and blood."

[29] "*Immediately after shall be said this memorial or prayer of oblation, as followeth.* Wherefore, O Lord and heavenly Father, according to the institution of thy dearly beloved Son our Saviour Jesus Christ, we thy humble servants do celebrate and make here before thy divine Majesty, with these thy holy gifts, the memorial which thy Son hath willed us to make, having in remembrance his blessed passion, mighty resurrection, and glorious ascension, rendering unto thee most hearty thanks for the innumerable benefits procured unto us by the same. And we entirely desire thy Fatherly goodness, mercifully to accept this our sacrifice of praise and thanksgiving, most humbly beseeching thee to grant, that by the merits and death of thy Son Jesus Christ, and through faith in his blood, we (and all thy whole church) may obtain remission of our sins, and all other benefits of his passion. And here we offer and present unto thee, O Lord, ourselves, our souls and bodies, to be a reasonable, holy, and lively sacrifice unto thee, humbly beseeching thee, that whosoever shall be partakers of this holy communion, may worthily receive the most precious body and blood of thy Son Jesus Christ, and be fulfilled with thy grace and heavenly benediction, and made one body with him, that he may dwell in them, and they in him. And although we be unworthy, through our manifold sins, to offer unto thee any sacrifice: yet we beseech thee to accept this our bounden duty and service, not weighing our merits, but pardoning our offences, through Jesus Christ our Lord; by whom, and with whom, in the unity of the holy Ghost, all honour and glory be unto thee, O Father almighty, world without end. Amen."

[30] Cf. Alan Dunstan, "The Eucharist in Anglicanism after 1662", in: C. Jones, G. Wainwright, E. Yarnold, and P. Bradshaw, eds., *The Study of Liturgy*, rev. ed. (Oxford University Press, 1992), (pp. 318–24), p. 320.

More recent attempts at a classically argued Eucharistic Prayer have been problematic in terms of the Latin rite, for example, by being Antiochene in shape. There has been a plethora of Eucharistic Prayers from the various churches of the Anglican Communion but, emerging as they have mostly during the last thirty years, they have as yet had no real grounding in the worshipping life of the Church, and are largely not part of the experience of those who have joined the Ordinariates.[31]

Gregory Dix's fellow Anglo-papalists, active in the parochial ministry, and rejecting piecemeal amendments of the Prayer Book, knew exactly what to do about all this. Whether the *Anglican Missal*, published in England by the Society of St. Peter and St. Paul in 1921,[32] or the *English Missal*, the pre-conciliar missal in English, in its 1958 edition,[33] could be regarded as "liturgical books proper to the Anglican tradition" (cf. *Anglicanorum Cœtibus*, 3), is a moot point. Some of the Provinces of the Anglican Communion, inaugurated by Anglo-catholic Missionary Societies, used this kind of resource but they were never authorised for use in the Provinces from which the Ordinariates have so far emerged. But the Anglo-papalists used them confidently and defiantly to give expression to the Catholic Faith, not only of pre-Reformation times, but as practised throughout the Catholic world. There were some ironies here, as pointed out by John Shelton Reed.[34] Here is liturgical anomy, using resources, which in their proper context, are tightly reg-

---

[31] Cf. Colin Buchanan, ed., *Anglican Eucharistic Liturgies from Around the World, 1985–2010* (Norwich: Canterbury Press, 2011). This is the fifth in a series of such books. Details of the earlier four (beginning with Bernard Wigan's *The Liturgy in English*, [Oxford University Press, 1962, 1964]) are given on p. xi.

[32] The *Anglican Missal* was brought to the United States, Canada, and other English-speaking countries over the course of the last century. In the United States, it was produced by the Frank Gavin Liturgical Foundation, which has sold to the Anglican Parishes Association the rights to its publication. The newer American version is not substantially different from the Gavin editions except that some typographical errors have been corrected.

[33] Canterbury Press reissued the 1958 edition of the *English Missal* in 2001. The 1958 edition was the latest of a series of editions, each closer to the Roman Missal.

[34] Cf. Shelton Reed, *Glorious Battle*. See p. 259 where Cardinal Manning describes "Ritualism" as "private judgment in gorgeous raiment, wrought about with divers colours". In his Introduction (p. xxiv) Shelton Reed confesses that, when he began, he "did not think of Anglo-catholicism as a countercultural movement" but gradually he was left "wondering how it could be so impolitic, so indifferent to the offense it gave in so many ways to so many people whose goodwill would seem to have been desirable". Eventually he "had to conclude that the offensiveness was not just accidental. . . . Anglo-catholicism, in other words, thrived on opposition".

ulated by liturgical law. Here are Anglo-catholic priests, ministering in parishes formed during the Industrial Revolution—mostly neo-Gothic churches in newly built-up areas—using the liturgies of another Communion, whereas, in the mediæval parish churches, up and down the land, conscientious clergy in Sarum cassocks and Canterbury caps rang the church bell day and night and laboured to bring to life the liturgy and pastoral practice of mediæval times. These clergy were known as "Prayer Book Catholic" and, for many, Percy Dearmer's *Parson's Handbook*,[35] setting out "the English Use" (as against the ultramontanism of the Anglo-papalists), was their guide. Here too was essentially the cathedral tradition, where the Canon Precentor could be relied upon to be well-versed in the principal mediæval Use, the Use of Sarum.

These two traditions in a sense were less disparate than they seemed. Despite superficial differences—the Baroque "big six" on the gradine as against the English altar with riddell posts and curtains—and the crucial question of textual fidelity—there were many similarities. There was a shared Eucharistic faith: the Anglo-papalist at Benediction and the Prayer Book Catholic at Devotions before the aumbry or hanging pyx. There was a shared devotion to the Mother of God: the Anglo-papalist reciting the Marian anthems aloud, the Prayer Book Catholic, with Tractarian reserve, saying the *Angelus Domini* to himself whilst the parish thought he was simply ringing the bell for Evensong. There was a shared hymnody too:[36] in the *English Hymnal* (1906) were not only the ancient words of the office hymns, recreated by J. M. Neale, and set to the Sarum plainsongs by Dr. Arnold, but also the words for the propers of the Mass,[37] with the music as found in the *English*

---

[35] *The Parson's Handbook, containing Practical Directions both for Parsons and Others as to the Management of the Parish Church and its Service according to the English Use as set forth in the Book of Common Prayer, with an Introductory Essay on conformity to the Church of England by the Rev. Percy Dearmer, M.A.* (London: Grant Richards, 1899).

[36] The Anglo-papalist had a supplementary collection, the *English Catholic Hymn Book*, privately published and revised, augmented, and published by Knott and Sons, London 1955. Numbered from 801 it was intended to supplement the *English Hymnal*. Its first part is intended to be a more correct—more Roman—collection of Office Hymns than the (Sarum) collection in the *English Hymnal*. There is also a collection of exuberant Marian anthems, devotions, and hymns, which would be too "advanced" for many, except when visiting the Shrine of Our Lady of Walsingham, where normal reserve was cast aside.

[37] Listed in *English Hymnal* under "Part XII, Introits and Other Anthems", and numbered from 657 onwards. The collection was not quite complete: the feasts of the Blessed

Gradual,[38] available in diverse forms to suit *schola* and cantor. The Sarum series of Advent Antiphons, starting a day earlier than the Roman series, might be sung before the *Magnificat* and sung from the *English Hymnal*. The Anglo-papalist found this material in his *English Missal*, the Prayer Book Catholic in his hymnbook. Both relied on the publications of the Plainsong and Mediæval Music Society for the music for Holy Week, there being very little liturgical provision for that week in the Book of Common Prayer.

The scene changed in England with the Second Vatican Council. The Anglo-papalists adopted the 1970 Sacramentary and the Prayer Book Catholics the liturgical revisions of the Church of England.[39] With shared ecumenical texts—this was the heyday of ICET and ELLC[40]—there was little difference between the Roman Mass and the Anglican Eucharist, and parishes peacefully placed themselves somewhere on the continuum between the two. The visit of St. John Paul II to the United Kingdom in 1982, and the high hopes entertained for the Anglican-

---

Virgin (n. 725) include the Purification and the Annunciation (both of which would now be regarded as feasts of the Lord) and do not include the Conception or Assumption. The propers do not include music. Other liturgical resources (e.g. 735 Advent Prose) do. Nos. 741 to 743 are the texts of *Benedictus, Agnus Dei,* and *Agnus Dei* for Requiems, texts which were in use in moderate Catholic parishes but which were not in the Book of Common Prayer.

[38] Francis Burgess, ed., *The English Gradual,* The Plainchant Publications Committee, 1871 (Seventh Edition 1961), is in two parts. Part I is The Ordinary and Part II is The Proper for the Liturgical Year. Simple psalm tones are used but the editor draws "attention to the collection of Introits for Sundays and Festivals, edited by the late Dr. Palmer, and published at St. Mary's Convent, Wantage. To that book may be added the collection of Graduals, Alleluia and Tracts, obtainable from the same source". It will be of interest that a dozen sisters from Wantage, including the Reverend Mother, joined the Ordinariate of Our Lady of Walsingham on January 1, 2013 and are nowadays known as Sisters of the Blessed Virgin Mary. Also of interest will be adapted C. David Burt, *The Anglican Use Gradual* (Mansfield: Partridge Hill Press, 2007), which is in continuity with *The English Gradual.*

[39] A very accessible account of the revision of Anglican Eucharistic liturgies, in historical context, and of what are now *Common Worship* Orders One and Two is: Paul Bradshaw, Gordon Giles, and Simon Kershaw, "Holy Communion" in: P. Bradshaw, ed. *Companion to Common Worship,* vol. 1 (London: SPCK, 2001), pp. 98–147.

[40] The English Language Liturgical Consultation (ELLC) promotes common liturgical texts in English. It is the successor body to the International Consultation on English Texts (ICET). ICET was formed in 1969 and completed its work in 1975. ELLC published revisions of the ICET texts in 1988. Some of these texts were used for the Ordinary of the Mass in the 1970 Missal and within the various Church of England liturgies in contemporary language. The *Roman Missal* 2010 does not use ELLC versions.

Roman Catholic International Commission, brought even those Anglo-catholics who were most distrustful of Rome to the point of accepting, in theory, the Petrine primacy, and the remaining differences among Anglo-catholics became increasingly unimportant.

The working group, *Anglicanæ Traditiones*, at work on the Order of Mass, looked first at the experience of England. Would it be sufficient, as Anglo-catholics have done, to supplement the Roman Sacramentary with some of the beautiful prayers of the Cranmerian tradition—the collects, the communion devotions—and some of the Anglican practices, such as the exchange of the peace before the Liturgy of the Eucharist, the practice in Milan and a practice which the Holy Father had commended for further study in *Sacramentum Caritatis* (2007)?[41] This was discounted at an early stage as not being close enough to the North American experience of Anglican liturgy, where traditional language and traditional ceremonial were particularly valued. (The prevailing British pattern—and here one describes rather than passes judgment —has been to use contemporary language at Mass and to celebrate the *Novus Ordo* with full ceremonial, and attentive to the *General Instruction of the Roman Missal*, but not usually in a way which would be regarded as old-fashioned.)

The second line of enquiry by the working group, *Anglicanæ Traditiones*, led us, under some pressure from the academic community, to look at the Sarum Use. It matched the criteria laid down by the Council of Trent for the preservation of existing Uses in that it clearly had several hundred years' established history. It was finally suppressed at the death of Queen Mary in 1558, though in the chapel of Bishop Richard Challoner, who was active in the eighteenth century, one still finds, alongside his vestments, his Sarum altar missal.[42] The problem

---

[41] Cf. n. 150 to para. 49: "Taking into account ancient and venerable customs and the wishes expressed by the Synod Fathers, I have asked the competent curial offices to study the possibility of moving the sign of peace to another place, such as before the presentation of the gifts at the altar. To do so would also serve as a significant reminder of the Lord's insistence that we be reconciled with others before offering our gifts to God (cf. Mt 5:23ff.); cf. *Propositio* 23". It will be of some regret to many former Anglicans that the Ordinariate Order of Mass (unlike the *Book of Divine Worship*) does not permit the exchange of the Peace before the Offertory, even at the main Sunday Mass. It would have been a small, yet distinctive piece of liturgical patrimony.

[42] Bishop Challoner's chapel is at Milton Park, which is within the Catholic parish of East Hendred in which the author of this paper lives and works. Originally buried at Milton in the parish vault, Bishop Challoner's body is now in Westminster Cathedral.

with Sarum was both its distinctiveness—the joint offering of bread and wine, the intense personal devotional language used by the priest as he addresses the newly-consecrated host—and its strangeness. Here is a Use which no one in recent history has used. Powerful though the historical and liturgical arguments, the relevance of the Sarum Use to the pastoral mission of the Ordinariates made this seem an unnecessarily antiquarian option. It is good though that the discussion took place and that we were able to look at what the Sarum Use in English might be like. [43] It did not seem to match the needs of either the British congregations, raised on variants of the *Novus Ordo*, or congregations in America and Australia, for whom the Sarum Use was a remote historical connection.

The third exploration provided a way forward. Here, broadly, we took the work already done under the Pastoral Provision, 1980, whereby former Episcopalians in the U.S.A. became Catholics but maintained their own liturgical Use. Within the *Book of Divine Worship*, authorised in 1983 and published in book form in 2003, [44] was "The Holy Eucharist: Rite One", the traditional language rite based on the corresponding rite in (the Episcopalian) Book of Common Prayer 1979. Here was a rite which had been used within the Catholic Church for a generation and one which corresponded with what many former Episcopalians would expect to encounter in an Ordinariate rite. The choice of this way forward has not been entirely unproblematic. For one thing, there is a privileging of the Scottish-American history of the Book of Common Prayer over the English, suggesting that the daughter is fairer than the mother whereas, from an English perspective, the daughter has certainly adopted some strange ways of expressing herself.

The strength of the revision of the Order of Mass, the Use of the Ordinariates, will gradually reveal itself. It includes the Propers that the Anglo-catholics always valued—whether they derived them from

---

[43] A. H. Pearson, trans., *The Sarum Missal in English* (London: The Church Press, 1868, reprinted Eugene: Wipf & Stock, 2004.)

[44] The Pastoral Provision of 1980 permitted the establishment of Anglican Use parishes in the United States and created a missal using liturgical elements from the Anglican tradition (cf. Paul VI, *Sacerdotalis Cælibatus*, n. 42). This liturgy was approved in 1983 by the Congregation for Divine Worship and the U.S. Committee for the Liturgy of the National Conference of Catholic Bishops. It was published in book form as the *Book of Divine Worship* (Mt. Pocono, Pa.: Newman House Press, 2003).

missal or hymnbook. It includes the classical Cranmerian prayers—collects and devotions—and his translation of the Ordinary. Contrary to the flow of opinion amongst English Anglicans, where the emphasis this last thirty years has been on restoring Penitence to the beginning of the Mass, it restores the Reformation logic of Scripture and preaching leading to repentance and Communion.[45] It gives us, in two forms of the Offertory Prayers, the Gallican prayers of the pre-conciliar Mass and the *Berakhot* of the modern Roman Missal in traditional language.

I suspect that too much detail, at this point, might be confusing or tedious, but, in order to convey an accurate sense of the new Order, here is a summary of the other, mostly minor, changes to the *Book of Divine Worship* version. There are eight appendices. Appendix 1 has the so-called Hippolytan Eucharistic Prayer, Roman Eucharistic Prayer II in traditional language, as an alternative to the Roman Canon for weekdays, masses with children, and other less solemn occasions. Appendix 2 begins with *Veni, Creator Spiritus*, in the Cosin translation. This devotion is in the Sarum Use as the Priest prepares for Mass, and it is here for use in the sacristy. Following on is the traditional Preparation of ministers, in the sacristy or at the foot of the altar ("I will go unto the altar of God") still in widespread use. Appendix 3 is the Rite of Sprinkling Holy Water—*Asperges* or *Vidi aquam*. Appendix 4 is the Decalogue, with the division of Commandments implying the Catholic numbering, instead of the Protestant order of the *Book of Divine Worship*.[46] Appendix 5 gives seven forms of the Intercession, three of which are from the *Book of Divine Worship*, one is the Prayer for the Church from the English 1927/1928 Deposited Prayer Book, and three of which are from modern English liturgical revisions,[47] including a

---

[45] *The Book of Divine Worship* permits an earlier and a later position for the Penitential Prayers.

[46] In the Protestant order, "Thou shalt not make to thyself any graven image" is the second commandment and the tenth commandment covers all aspects of coveting. In the Catholic order, "Thou shalt not make to thyself any graven image" is part of the first commandment and, as regards coveting, coveting thy neighbour's wife is forbidden by the ninth commandment and coveting "thy neighbour's house" and "any thing that is his" is forbidden by the tenth commandment.

[47] Form V, with addition of Pope and President, is Form 1 in *Common Worship 2000* (p. 281), a form which emerged in *Alternative Service Book 1980* (p. 125). Form VII similarly is Form 4 in *Common Worship* 2000 (p. 284), a form which emerged in *Alternative Service Book 1980* (p. 167).

light revision of the splendid seventeenth-century Prayer for all Conditions of Men, probably composed by Peter Gunning.[48] The principal amendment in these forms, as compared with their sometimes Erastian originals, is that pope and ordinary come before monarch or president. Seven forms may seem profuse but the rite does not permit either *ex tempore* or home-composed versions of the Prayers of the People. Appendix 6 gives ten collects for use at the end of the Prayers, five of them are additional to the selection on pages 325–26 of the *Book of Divine Worship*.[49] The remaining Appendices—the Last Gospel (Appendix 7) and Pontifical Variations (Appendix 8)—though technically additions to the rite, catch up with what already happens in some places, as do some ceremonial directions within the main text. The genuflection at the *Incarnatus* in the Creed was there in the *Book of Divine Worship* but the sign of the cross, at the end of both *Gloria* and Creed, are now also made explicit.

Also provided are the blessing of incense and of the deacon before the Gospel. The Communion Rite now has the traditional embolism restored to the Lord's Prayer, the Peace in its Roman position, the words for the commixture, the Requiem petitions in the *Agnus Dei* for Masses for the Dead, the restored Prayer Book text of the Prayer of Humble Access, and the words of administration found both in the traditional Mass and in the 1549 Communion Rite. The egregious grammatical error in the *Book of Divine Worship*—"the Lamb of God . . . that takest away"—is corrected—"Behold the Lamb of God, behold him that taketh away"—and the Prayer of Thanksgiving, though still a clause shorter than Cranmer, is an expanded version of what is there in the *Book of Divine Worship*. Finally, in this inventory of minor changes, we note the change of the rubric "From the Easter Vigil through the Day of Pentecost, 'Alleluia, alleluia' may be added to any of the dismissals" to "From the Easter Vigil through the Octave Day and on the Day of

---

[48] Peter Gunning (1614–1684) was successively Bishop of Chichester and Ely. The version of this prayer in *Common Worship 2000* (Form 2, p. 282) is in contemporary language. Another version of this prayer is set for Wednesday Week 4, Evening Prayer, of *The Divine Office* (Australia, England and Wales, Ireland edition) (Sydney: E. J. Dwyer, 1974).

[49] Four of these extra prayers are from Church of England sources, the last, most immediately, is a prayer of the seventeenth-century divine, Jeremy Taylor, from the Visitation of the Sick of the 1928 American Book of Common Prayer.

Pentecost Alleluia, alleluia, shall be added to the dismissal." With that change of wording we have a clear sense of a move from the gentle permissiveness of Anglican liturgy to the rubrical precision of the Roman rite, from the minimal consensus of common law in Anglo-Saxon Northern Europe (where traffic lights are regarded as mandatory), to the more highly regulated culture of sunny South Europe (where, however, traffic lights seem to be regarded as advisory).

We finish with the Canon of the Mass. In the main text is the Roman Canon, the Old English Translation of the *Book of Divine Worship*,[50] but with the Institution Narrative and acclamations conforming to the Roman Missal of 2010. In the Use of Sarum, the Canon of the Mass was the Roman Canon, albeit with the name of the monarch inserted after the names of the pope and bishop. The Roman Canon—whether they were following the Use of Sarum or not—is what the British prayed in the long centuries between the coming of the first Archbishop of Canterbury, St. Augustine, in A.D. 597, and the brilliant, stylish, but heretical sixty-ninth Archbishop, Thomas Cranmer, author of the Second Prayer Book of King Edward VI, burnt at the stake nearly 1,000 years later.

That was a time of terrible rupture in the life of the Church. Pray that we have now a time of continuity, not least in an increasing awareness of the way in which throughout all ages, in the Catholic Mass, we continue to encounter the awe-inspiring eternity and perfection of the Lord Jesus Christ, who, with the Holy Spirit, is the Most High in the glory of God the Father. Amen.

---

[50] No one quite knows where this translation came from. It has been attributed to Myles Coverdale but equally it has been attributed to unknown American Anglo-catholic sources.

Some Remarks

*Ordinary of the Personal Ordinariate
of Our Lady of Walsingham*

Anglican patrimony has been discussed at length since the announcement of *Anglicanorum Cœtibus*, Pope Benedict's Apostolic Constitution, in November 2009. Those who have joined the Ordinariate of Our Lady of Walsingham, and the other Ordinariates, and are now in the full communion of the Catholic Church, continue to wrestle with this question: what is it that we bring?

Anglicanorum Cœtibus speaks about two main elements of Anglican liturgical, spiritual, and pastoral patrimony which we are being asked to bring into the Catholic Church as "a treasure to be shared" (*Anglicanorum Cœtibus*, 3). First, we are being asked to bring something of our pastoral structures, including the proper involvement of the lay faithful in the work of the apostolate or parish, and much could be said about that. But it is the second area highlighted by the Apostolic Constitution, the Sacred Liturgy that concerns us here. The Constitution says that "Without excluding liturgical celebrations according to the Roman rite, the Ordinariate has the faculty to celebrate the Holy Eucharist and the other Sacraments, the Liturgy of the Hours and other liturgical celebrations according to the liturgical books proper to the Anglican tradition, which have been approved by the Holy See" (n. 3). Thus, whilst fully part of the Latin rite, we are granted the particular privilege of using certain Anglican liturgical texts—not simply music —to maintain "the liturgical, spiritual and pastoral traditions of the Anglican Communion within the Catholic Church, as a precious gift nourishing the faith of the members of the Ordinariate and as a treasure to be shared" (n. 3).

Msgr. Andrew Burnham was prevented by ill-health from delivering his paper in person. It was read by Msgr. Keith Newton who was invited to offer some remarks of his own, which we publish here.

Most of the priests and faithful of the Personal Ordinariate of Our Lady of Walsingham—I cannot speak, of course, for America and Australia—have come from parishes that have placed a high value on celebrating the modern Roman rite well and with proper solemnity. We are used to traditional vestments, good congregational (if not choral) music, the priest singing his part, and a full ceremonial for the principal Mass on Sunday. We are being reminded, furthermore, to rediscover the riches of our own tradition—a hieratic vernacular and the public and sung recitation of the Office—some of which, especially Cranmerian material, we, in England, had tended to discard, in our eagerness to be as close as possible to the modern Western rite. And yet it has been to safeguard this very tradition and to gather in its riches into the full communion of the Church that generosity and flexibility has been shown to us in the past few years, as we have seen some of our clergy given dispensations from clerical celibacy, and many ordained at the beginning of their formation as Catholic priests, rather than at the end. And it is worth saying, in passing, that almost all former Anglicans in the U.K.—whether they have been incardinated into dioceses or the Ordinariate, and whether they have been ordained at the end of formation or earlier, have had to undergo at least two years' formation, on top of their often very considerable theological education and pastoral experience as Anglicans.

With all this in mind, it is vital that we acknowledge the generosity shown to us, and the interest shown in our patrimony, by establishing a rich, distinctive liturgical life and I hope that you—and all who look kindly on our work—will help us to value those parts of our heritage which are worthy of recovery and preservation. The inter-dicasterial working party, *Anglicanæ Traditiones* has already produced Marriage and Funeral Rites, a Calendar, the basic Order of Mass, and the Rite of Baptism. Meeting here in Rome this week they have been hard at work on the rites of Initiation and on the Propers of the Mass. All of this work, to borrow an image from our liturgist, Msgr. Andrew Burnham is like beginning to glue back a fragment of a very precious vase, a vase broken at the Reformation. The mediæval vase was not so damaged as to be unusable, these last 450 years, but it will be all the more splendid when the beautiful fragment which was broken off is finally restored. That restoration has begun.

17

Liturgy, Liturgical Music
and the Internet Apostolate

JEFFREY TUCKER

Introduction

Ten years ago, one could not hear Gregorian chant on a cellphone or watch the unfolding beauty of the traditional Roman rite liturgy on a desktop computer. You could not receive training in the rubrics of the liturgy with an internet search and a few clicks of the computer mouse. You could not read the great works of the past, look at the earliest missals from all over the world, or read the complete archives of the liturgical periodicals of the past. There were no applications running on tablet computers that allowed you to browse the propers for the entire liturgical year in English and Latin. You certainly could not tweet out news of your forthcoming liturgy to interested parties, and you could not watch Papal Masses in real time from your pocket device while sharing this experience through a Facebook "embed".

All of this is possible today. Indeed, thousands and hundreds of thousands do all of this daily. And they do it all without a thought to the remarkable contribution that the digital revolution has meant for the cause of Sacred Liturgy.

Perhaps it is an implausible marriage: liturgical forms from the first millennium together with technological forms from the third. The irony is obvious but so are the results. This medium, combined with the passionate and mostly volunteer work of tech-savvy enthusiasts, has led to an unprecedented spread of knowledge about Catholic Liturgy. Indeed, this medium has been central to the progress we have seen and it will continue to be in the years ahead.

Universal Liturgical Education

Evangelism for the *ars celebrandi* depends on the capacity of those who know to teach and inspire those who do not know. In an open society in which information can so easily be universalized through digital media, knowledge and practice can be one. As Pope Benedict wrote in *Sacramentum Caritatis* (2007): "the primary way to foster the participation of the People of God in the sacred rite is the proper celebration of the rite itself. The *ars celebrandi* is the best way to ensure their *actuosa participatio*" (n. 38).

For the people to participate in the unfolding beauty of truth, liturgical knowledge must not be the exclusive province of an educated elite; it ideally must be available to the whole of humanity. The more availability, the better. This is precisely what the internet has brought to the cause of good liturgy. As a technology, it is morally neutral, a tool in our hands, and what it produces reflects our values. But as a tool, history has never seen anything like it. It is best characterized as the world's most spectacular copier, one that never needs ink or paper to be replenished. It can produce copies unto infinity, and those copies can be changed or adapted and reloaded to the internet cloud to be copied again unto infinity. What is produced and copied and consumed is entirely in the hands of the users themselves. We have seen the effects of this in a series of political revolutions, new modes of friendship and association among the young, an economic upheaval all over the world that has led to unprecedented declines in infant mortality and hunger. The low cost of production on the internet has led to more inclusive economic and communications environment all over the world.

For those who are dedicated to the celebration of the Roman rite in both its modern and more ancient forms, in continuity with liturgical Tradition, the internet provided a ray of hope amidst the liturgical turbulence of recent decades. Digital media provided an opportunity to get the message out even as conventional channels of opinion and ideas continued to ignore this concern. As a result, the internet has given us images of sacred spaces that might otherwise not be seen in our highly secularized and noisy world. It has provided videos of liturgy from all over the world and presented them to people who might otherwise never encounter such sacredness and beauty.

Digital communications have enabled this new form of evangelization. It has educated millions on architecture, vestments, readings, Church interiors, liturgical controversies, and so much more. For decades during the great liturgical upheaval, Catholics outside of major cities were unable to see or observe solemn liturgy and their expectations of what should be were shaped by that lack of access. They could only know what they themselves experienced, and they were often told that there was no choice but to go along without question. The same was true for priests. They were told that these are new times and that everyone has changed and that there was no going back.

But the new availability of historic texts, videos, images, and discussions changed everything for millions. It opened up knowledge of new possibilities. In effect, the internet is what shattered the cartel of 'established' liturgical opinion and poor praxis. It demonstrated that in other places around the world and sometimes as near as the next town, there was a different opinion and a different praxis. Several sites in particular are worthy of mention as regards the English-speaking world: NewLiturgicalMovement.org, ChantCafe.com, and MusicaSacra.com, among many thousands of individual blogs, parish websites, and uncountable numbers of social media connections. All these have become virtual gathering places for Catholics to learn, share, and build a virtual library and resource center for all matters.

This is especially true of the music of the Mass, which serves a crucial role in framing the aesthetic and cultural ethos in which the faithful experience Catholic liturgy. It is the responsibility of musicians to provide this music, but there must be more: their knowledge and understanding is crucial to achieving the ideal.

This is not possible without access to both music and to liturgical education and formation. It must reach the widest possible audience and be accessible to anyone with the tiniest spark of interest. Today, teaching and inspiration very much depend on the internet as an outreach tool, a creative force, and hyper-effective delivery system. Just as the internet has given rise to global networks focused on a billion particular niche interests, it has played an enormous role in getting out the word and musical resources on the song that is integral to the Roman rite: Gregorian chant.

The End of Isolation

In the past, priests would finish their years in seminary and then face a very different situation at the parish level. They lacked musical resources. They lacked beautiful buildings, altars, and even basic liturgical items and vestments. Many of these parishes were built after so many traditional items were either thrown out or considered to be old fashioned and outdated. The seminaries are bringing them back but the parishes are behind the times. New priests can feel themselves to be cut off from all their friends and even from the Faith itself. Sites such as the New Liturgical Movement have enabled these priests to see how others have handled similar problems and gave them colleagues, friends, a sense of identity that extended beyond their immediate parish environment. They gave them the confidence to act and reform, and provided the intellectual basis for doing so.

The internet gave assurance to otherwise isolated priests that there are others out there facing east, others using chant, and others acquiring new vestments, adopting the "Benedictine" altar arrangement by placing the crucifix at the center of *versus populum* altars, and re-reordering their churches to repair the iconoclasm of previous decades. These priests discovered that even if their own bishop was not offering overt support for such changes, there were bishops leading the way in the liturgical revival in different parts of the world. Crucially, live broadcasts from Rome demonstrated that the center of Roman rite activity was very much swinging in the direction of serious reform. And this information about real-time liturgical reform came unfiltered, through people with YouTube channels and personal cameras hooked into the digital cloud, rather than filtered through the lens of the mainstream media.

The same sense of enlightenment affects the laity as well, who come to expect liturgical change at the local level that is a keeping up with the documents and practices at the cathedrals, larger parishes, and papal liturgical events. People in the pews are inspired to work for a more dignified and solemn celebration, knowing that it is possible and achievable with certain steps. If people could not find these at their most local parish, they could discover information about other parishes within driving distance that were attentive to liturgical concerns. Also, counter-examples of particularly bad liturgical presentations can be equally instructive, and the internet and liturgical blogging venues have provided a troubling look at those as well. Indeed, there have been several cases in which unusually abusive practices have been disparaged so much by online commentators that their organizers have repudiated them after the fact.

From the opening of the traditionalist and "reform of the reform" digital venues, as well as chant-based websites, many writers have carefully chronicled the growing momentum all through the 2000s to recover what had been lost. This helped people who had a sense that something has been wrong and that change is possible, and realize that others felt the same and were working toward that end and successfully so. Whereas the mainstream press, and the entrenched voices within the diocesan bureaucracies, made people who expressed such concerns feel marginalized and even heretical for desiring a more continuous relationship between the past and the present. The growth of digitized societies helped people realize otherwise; that this notion was not wrong or regrettable. Indeed, it was a sign of a possible future, one that could be more deeply integrated with our longer tradition.

For organizers of conferences, art displays, liturgical demonstration projects, seminars, teaching programs, and much else, the advent of digital media of universal reach provided an unprecedented opportunity. In the past, it would have been necessary to pay for ads in print publications. With the free tools of the internet, organizers could reach people at little to no cost, people who attend the programs and learn from them, all accessible within a few search terms. For the Church Music Association of America, this meant that we could plan events that otherwise would never have been planned, and we could reach people who otherwise would not know about such training events.

Our annual Sacred Music Colloquium had typically attracted thirty to forty people before promotion and registration went online, few of whom were actual directors of music in parishes. Seven years later, the same event attracts 250 and this in turn supports an additional two to three programs throughout the year. Many other organizations can report the same effect. The commercial aspect of the internet and its book-buying services radically reduced the costs of publishing and permitted new publishers to reach consumers and thereby recover the costs of investment. This has led to a notable publishing renaissance that can compete with even the largest publishers. The main publisher of Benedict XVI's books in English, Ignatius Press, reached an entirely new audience through its website and through the new market for ebooks.

And it is not only about new programs, new books, and new opportunities. The world-wide web allowed for the distribution of the archives of journals and books written decades ago, even as far back as a century. What had been long ago thrown out by libraries now has a new life online. We uploaded 100 years of *Sacred Music*, *Cæcilia*, the *Catholic Choirmaster*, and many other publications that dealt directly with great liturgical problems of the day. These publications also provide insight into what happened in that mysterious period between 1963 and 1968. They help to make sense of those times and show how so many wonderful hopes turned into near chaos by the end of the decade. To read about these times gives us a special appreciation for the emerging orderliness and coherence of our own. I often think what it must have been like in the early 1970s to struggle and labor on an article that explained why dismantling the Roman rite is not a very good idea, and to publish it in a journal where it was read by a few hundred people at best. Well, all of these writings today have been given new life and can be read by potentially millions and billions of people until the end of time itself. This is the special power that the internet has to offer.

It was the internet that gave voice to so much new scholarship and the changing of the ethos of disruption to an ethos of continuity. A good example of this is the controversy that surrounded the introduction of the new English translation of the Roman Missal in 2011. The major media described this as an attempt by reactionary conservatives to turn back the clock and impose a hated new language on progressive Catholic people. Had online resources not been available, this might have been the sensibility that stuck. Instead, the pro-revision blogosphere got to work and posted the parallel versions of the old translation, the new translation, and the Latin—just to provide an objective comparison. From this it became very obvious that this was not about politics, or imposition, or reaction. What was really at issue were values like beauty, solemnity, accuracy, and ritual tradition. The opportunity to post and examine these texts made it impossible for mainstream media caricatures to carry the day. All these activities provided an important counterweight to the conventions coming from the usual media, and built crucial support for the new translation when it was most necessary.

We also posted the music from the new missal and circulated it widely. As we frequently pointed out, these chants for the new missal were being made *gratis* by the International Commission on English in the Liturgy. This was the official music of the new missal, as we constantly insisted. It was not necessary for parishes to pay large amounts of money to conventional publishers using conventional copyright in order to have beautiful music at Mass. The authentic music of the Mass was being circulated without charge and with built-in permissions to sing in every parish environment.

Distribution of Music for the Roman Rite

The internet has forever changed music distribution for the liturgy, restoring it to its first-millennium status as part of the open culture of the Church. It was through free sharing and the oral tradition that chant grew and spread—not through large capitalistic institutions relying on government-protected grants of "intellectual property", but through human energies, love, passion, and charity.

Two thousand years since the earliest emergence of music for the Mass, the methods of chant distribution have been truly universalized. The entire body of music is now available for rich and poor, no matter what geographic space a person may inhabit, and it is available in many archival and new editions, in formats like PDF, ePub, smartphone apps, and thousands of YouTube videos. Most importantly of all: it exists in common, which is to say that law does not constrain its distribution in any way. Now we even have online chant classes that anyone can take from a laptop or tablet, while lounging at the beach or walking on a treadmill at the gym.

Today there are many commercial publishers of Gregorian chant, probably more than have existed in many decades, but the corpus of the chant itself is also freely available to all as a complementary good to the commercial products, all within a click. They are working together: internet and print, free and paid, original and derivative works, digital works and high-quality liturgical books, not to mention every

manner of application for digital devices such as iPads. There are probably more people alive today who have heard chant and know about
it than at any other point in human history.

The major part of this progress is due to technological innovation, an
underappreciated feature of the liturgical apostolate. In the latter part
of the first millennium, there were the first attempts at writing music down, a process which required physical materials and intellectual
achievement. There were editions copied by hand on durable vellum
(made only through an expensive and time-consuming process). There
was the innovation of the staff in the eleventh century by the great
monk/genius Guido D'Arezzo. There was printing. We benefit today
from the internet and the liberation it provides for any idea, including
the musical idea, to be made infinitely malleable, instantaneously re-
producible unto infinity, and immortalized so that it can be made to
last in this form for as long as time exists into the future.

Chant as "Free Culture"

During this entire period, from the beginnings all the way to the twentieth century, the chant was part of what is called today "free culture"
—free as in "libre", meaning unfettered, unimpeded, unrestricted. The
information is not just "gratis" that is, available at no cost—materials
and delivery are rarely without cost—but, more importantly, it is unrestricted by laws and regulations that seek to restrain its spread. The
texts were not held in proprietary arrangement but were available to
all. They were part of the treasure of civilization itself. No permission
was ever necessary to print them. Their source or authorship neither
required nor asked for attribution. This was the status of the chant for
the whole of Church history and it was crucial to its spread throughout
Europe and the world.[1]

The world-wide web—first made accessible to private interests in
1995 but only developing sophisticated content and download methods at the turn of the millennium—allowed the chant and all genuinely

---

[1] The restored chant books were intended to be published without any copyright
restrictions but a dispute between competing interests changed that. See Dom Pierre
Combe O.S.B., *The Restoration of Gregorian Chant: Solesmes and the Vatican Edition* (Washington, D.C.: Catholic University of America Press, 2003), p. 241.

liturgical music to have a fresh start. The chant has again entered the common realm from whence it came. This, I believe, is a major reason for its astonishing revival over the last several years.

In fact, I would judge one of the most significant events in the revival of Gregorian chant to be the public posting of the 1961 edition of the *Liber Usualis* on MusicaSacra.com. This was the event that turned the tables. I would speak more on the specifics of how this came about.

Twenty years ago, long before the internet became the primary delivery system for liturgical music education, I began to look into making a contribution in my own parish to improving the presentation of the music for the (modern) Roman rite. I spent countless hours, days, and weeks in the library trying to find the answer to a simple question: what should be sung at Mass? The answer was never clearly stated anywhere, at least in what I could find. Even if the information had been available, the music itself would not have been easy to access.

It's true that I had a *Liber Usualis* and had a vague understanding that this book pertained to a form of the Mass said long ago, but I had no notion of how to make that apply in our times, and no notion of whether it should apply or not. The *General Instruction of the Roman Missal* is helpful in this regard but it presumes a level of knowledge that I did not have, and I would suggest that most Church musicians were in the same position. We had no idea what the "entrance antiphon" or the "offertory antiphon" really was, much less how to sing it—for this music had long been replaced by hymns in modern notation that make up the bulk of our liturgical materials.

As regards the chant itself, I could not read this old notation, despite a lifetime of musical training. It was not even clear to me that the clef sign on the four line staff represented the "do" or the "fa" in the scale, below which the half step could be identified. I did not understand that the clefs were movable. I could not point a psalm and there was no one around to teach me how. Knowledge that every Catholic musician once possessed had nearly evaporated from memory to the point that I could not discover it no matter what I did. Regardless, even if I had a sense of what to do at this basic level, and where to obtain such music for the new rites, I could not have read the music much less known how to sing it well.

In retrospect, this whole period seems like an authentic version of the mythical Dark Ages. Yet it was not that long ago. Fortunately, this is something no living person and no person in the future will ever face again. There is no need to wallow in ignorance. We now have unlimited access to knowledge and inspiration that had been unavailable in this quality or quantity.

The book had already been reprinted in the United States by St. Bonaventure Press. At the time, I had grown ever more curious about the current copyright status of the chant. For example, in the United States many books that had been in printed in the 1950s by the Gregorian Institute of America (now known as GIA) had since fallen into public domain. We put those editions online in complete compliance with the copyright law.

But these laws can be enormously complicated. It is not as clear as people imagine. Often there is no clear dividing line between: "this is available" and "this is infringement." According to the law, copyright can cover the full text, the melody, the engraving, the signs and symbols and edits of a free edition, the introductory matter, the art—any one of which can cause an entire edition to be considered controlled. Then there are different laws in different countries and different statuses based on the date of renewal or nonrenewal. The case of the chant itself is particularly intriguing because the texts date from the earliest Christian centuries and the melodies are mostly from the first millennium—and no state in the world protects copyright that long because no state has actually lasted that long.

I began my research to discover that the melodies themselves were open to the public. The typography had been largely carried over from nineteenth-century editions. The text was available as well. The editions had long been printed in the United States, thereby subjecting them to a more liberal copyright law domestically than internationally. What seemed to be the Abbey of Solesmes' claim to proprietary rights came down to the rhythmic markings. That is when I got the U.S. copyright office involved. I had several conversations with experts, who completely dismissed the idea that one could claim any proprietary rights over a tiny dash or line. It was their judgement that the chant book *Liber Usualis* was already in the public domain. I secured a letter from the office to that effect and embarked upon the great mission. I was not the first to discover this but the others who already knew had been interested in the reprinting of the book, not the posting of the book online for all to download, and so these institutions were not incentivized to reveal the source of their permissions.

What we were contemplating was far more radical. We intended to introduce the world to chant through a free download. Not entirely knowing what the results would be, we decided to forge ahead. The *Liber* upload I have recorded as having taken place on July 16, 2007—a mere six years ago. It was a momentous occasion. This one action took a book that had previously depended on physical access and made it something that entered the internet cloud. Previously, if you borrowed my book, I no longer had it and you had to return it to me. But after posting, I could have the book and you could have it too. We could experience simultaneous ownership. And this simultaneity extended from two people to two thousand people to potentially seven billion people. And this would remain true if I suddenly got hit by a car, our server crashed, or everyone who downloaded it lost the file.

Within hours of posting, the book became available on hundreds of download sites. And this availability will extend beyond our present age to all future ages. The great book had entered that magical, beautiful, mystical space called the digital cloud that affords previously physical things the status of unlimited reproducibility, malleability, and immortality. This was the moment that all previous work in the world of chant had headed toward. The efforts of thousands and thousands, dating back even to the earliest years of the Church—the singers, the scribes, the archaeologists, the printers, the scholars, the typesetters, the choirmasters, the theologians and liturgists—were accumulated and packaged into one gigantic and permanently valuable gift to humanity. It was all made possible with one scanning machine and an FTP upload that took fewer than three minutes.

I initially faced some serious threats from anonymous people through email. I was told that I would soon find myself fined and maybe in jail, that I had violated some dreadful taboo, that I was ruining the chant by making it available. The prohibition against putting chant in the common domain was so strong that it created more shock and astonishment than anything else. But this upload was just the beginning. Soon we had the 1908 Vatican edition of the *Graduale Romanum* online. We posted the *Antiphonales*. We posted books from various orders. We began to post books that no one had ever heard of but had taken many thousands of hours a hundred years ago to make possible. That process continues.

We grew more bold with each upload. We posted our own books, even those we had for sale, such as the *Parish Book of Chant* and a book of communion antiphons with printed verses. We posted every book we could find, in easy-to-use editions. Our goal was to flood the world with chant, to become the equivalent of Napster (the first music download site) of liturgical music editions. We've continued this seemingly reckless practice of giving away as much music as possible—as much as anyone wants.

Are there risks associated with this practice? Yes. Here is one amusing story. I had run across a copy of the pre-Solesmes Ratisbon/Medici edition of the chant from the mid-nineteenth century. This was the old "corrupt" version of chant that Solesmes had struggled mightily and successfully to displace. It has no presence at all in any modern liturgical context. It was the kind of book that even the enthusiast would be unlikely ever to possess. But a priest/scholar kept writing me and he was very interested in getting it online. I was reluctant because I feared my posting would give this antiquated Gradual new life. I did it anyway for historical and archival interest. I even posted a warning on the file itself: this is a historical curiosity only. After the upload, within a week I received several messages of excitement about the beautiful new chant that had been posted. People were busily looking through liturgical law to examine whether anything would really prevent these old editions from being used. After all, people were saying, "these chants are simple and beautiful, so why not sing them?" What had I done? You see, it really does matter what you put on the internet! Nonetheless, I see no evidence of the imminent return of the Ratisbon chant editions.

That still left the problem of the modern Mass and its music. The book that would open this up to Americans was the *Gregorian Missal*, a Solesmes publication that included translations. Not one in a thousand (or ten thousand) musicians working in the English-speaking world in the Catholic church knew that there was a chant assigned to each major liturgical action. This book was the best for demonstrating this. Inspired by the new interest that had been generated by previous uploads, Solesmes generously granted us permission to post this book in the common domain (the answer to my query came in the form of one word: "*oui*"). It was the book that settled all argument: the chant pertained to the modern Mass too. With one link, one person could enlighten a generation of priests and musicians.

Some very visible effects came about from these efforts. Adam Bartlett discovered the chant for the first time and dedicated himself to the cause. By 2011, we had the first English Gradual of simple chant for the Mass available—something that should have happened decades ago but we needed the "hands on deck" to make it happen. Many new databases and digital applications started to appear based entirely on the editions we posted. Because we shared the documents, new websites opened that provided tutorials in the old Mass, in chant singing for the new Mass, and also many blogs and YouTube videos.

As I began to prepare this paper, I wondered how I might document the importance of this change for liturgical music, so I asked the question on the MusicaSacra.com forum: how did you discover the chant? Dozens of answers came that confirmed my intuition.

Here is one example among many:

> I was in the process of switching career paths from University administration (Environmental Health and Safety) to being a Director of Music. (I was always involved as a pianist/musician/cantor in part-time/ volunteer positions on the side). From my previous line of work, I was used to looking up the regulations to determine how something should be done, so I began to dig into the GIRM to understand the instructions for music in the liturgy. I looked at the first choice for Entrance, Offertory and Communion and wondered what the *Graduale Romanum* was. A Google search led me to the MusicaSacra website, which opened up a whole world of resources.

In addition, many commentators mention how digital access also alerts them to physical and geographic events they would otherwise not know anything about. In the old days, you had to subscribe to specific publications to discover the existence of a teaching conference. To register took a stamp, physical check, and envelope. Today you can do it all from your tablet device or phone using a credit card or digital wallet.

The teaching apostolate never ends. Those of us at MusicaSacra (the Church Music Association of America) began to face a barrage of daily questions, so many that we could not answer them all. So we put up a forum—an online space for a community to gather where we could all explore answers to the ongoing questions. The results were spectacular. It now has many thousands of registrants and a complete archive for any Church musician to use. It is also the leading job placement portal, music upload site for preliminary versions of new compositions, and a place where directors can seek out singers. Every hour of the day, this portal serves as a place for information and inspiration.

Let me say a few words about the CMAA's publishing model. We attempt to upload and make everything we publish freely available, using the license called Creative Commons Attribution Only. This means that anyone can download our material for free, print it, sing it, and even publish it at a profit. We also print the books and sell them, supposing that there is an interest in both digital and physical. I can't really imagine that we would face any demand for the physical books at all if they were not also available for free in digital format. Our goal is to push chant out there as widely as possible, using every means we have at our disposal. This method also comports with an ethical ideal of permitting the music to realize what music is capable of becoming: owned and used simultaneously by the whole of humanity.

This is all an effort to restore chant to its status as part of the "free culture" movement. The chant should achieve universal reach, be available to the poorest of the poor, and freely shared among all members of the human race forever. This was precisely the status the chant had between its origin and the twentieth century. This was precisely the same status as the "folk" music that took over the liturgical scene in the 1960s even as chant had become restricted by a legal thicket of competing proprietary claims.

Additional Musical Resources

Many other sites have contributed to the digital liberation of liturgical music and changed the entire landscape. The Choral Public Domain Library (CPDL.org) is responsible for letting the world know about and download the masters of Renaissance polyphony. This site opened in 1998 and now hosts 12,750 musical scores. It is the Wikipedia for polyphony and saves parishes countless amounts of money. It allows choirs to try among thousands of pieces to find the ones that work for their choirs and their skill level. The difference from the past is amazing to consider. We know more today about the variety of music available than any previous generation, excepting perhaps highly skilled musicologists. What was once specialized knowledge is now generally accessible to the whole world, along with the actual music. A site like this does not entirely negate the point of publishing houses that specialize in printed editions but it does open up the world of liturgical choral music in a way that had never been possible in the past. DiLasso, Obrecht, Tallis, Palestrina, Josquin, Isaac, Vittoria—they have all been made universally ownable and immortal by the internet.

In 2011, when the new English translation of the Roman Missal was being prepared for publication, the International Commission on English in the Liturgy took the highly sophisticated step of putting all the chants from the missal online for free download. This was an amazing decision, one that flew in the face of the proprietary nature of all the keeping music. Suddenly the average parish could have its music for free. Anyone could record it. Anyone could print and sing it. This gave English chant the best possible start. Long before the missal made its final appearance, there were editions of this music circulating in all parishes, so that choirs and priests could learn it. It was part of the "free culture" movement—a highly progressive and intelligent decision on the part of ICEL. It made the margin of difference. Finally, in the English-speaking world, we have chants that can legitimately be called common to us all.

Let me make a comment about blogging—now an old-fashioned art of which I am still a practitioner at the ChantCafe.com. Blogging is a means to share ongoing information and reactions to news. There is an endless stream of things to blog about today, unlike the past. It is an open model that extracts spontaneity from us and elicits our emotional sense. This is very attractive to people and keeps people engaged on a daily basis in the great enterprise of restoring Gregorian chant to its proper place within a larger liturgical framework of authenticity, solemnity, and seriousness.

In a similar way, social networking such as Facebook and Twitter provide opportunities to offer real-time coverage of activities in sacred music, posting videos, images, homilies, and commentary. These venues permit people to express their enthusiasm for the cause and effectively evangelize. I might add that there is, so far, no comparable digital infrastructure emerging from the advocates of pop music in liturgy or the opponents of solemn liturgy. In addition, there are practical matters of job seeking for directors of education, organists, directors of music, and singers that have been beautifully solved through sites such as LinkedIn and the jobs marketplace at MusicaSacra.com. Priests looking for competent employees have been able to use these free tools to find employees who match their needs.

Today the chant has been freed from its fetters and the world has been invited to sing. I like to think that Dom Mocquereau is looking down and smiling—perhaps not at our meager talents but at our radical and paradigm-breaking methods. He fought for years to use the best technology available to push the chant sources and highest scholarship out to the world in every way he had available to him. We are able to continue this side of his work, and thereby give his life's mission— and those of tens of thousands of others—new life. The internet has allowed us to follow up on this evangelical mission and bring liturgical music within the possession of the whole of humanity.

There is also an important lesson in this history as regards the question of whether liturgical materials should be "possessed" by one institution or individuals, or whether the liturgical material should be permitted to achieve the aim of departing from the physical world and freely entering that beautiful realm of the infinite, in which there is no need to distinguish mine from thine, but instead allow everyone with desire to partake equally and inexhaustibly without taking from anyone else. Chant can be like the loaves and fishes at the great miracle of our Lord, removed from the realm of scarcity and made an abundant feast for all who come. But in order for this to happen, we need to embrace its potential as part of our "free culture" and be inspired to share it—abundantly and without fear.

In particular, the great paleographic work of the late nineteenth century, interposed on modern chant editions in the masterful work *Graduale Triplex*, needs to become universally available for singers and scholars, along with the modern *Graduale Romanum*. Uploads of these would represent a fantastic culmination of the progress made over the last six years in reversing the errors of the past.

Conclusion

In the last few decades, until very recently, many Catholics had sensed a prevailing ethos in which our past has been covered up, if not banned outright. This was not a result of legislation. It was not instituted by any one group in particular. Even so, it had become woven into the fabric of Western Catholic life in subtle and deeply dangerous ways. In the tumult of the age, Catholics were not entirely sure what it is we were supposed to believe and do, but we were sure of this much: whatever we believed and did was different from what our ancestors in the Faith did and believed.

All Catholics have felt a grave form of discomfort all these years. The older form of the Mass that was displaced and then nearly suppressed was the center of Catholic life in the past. It made appearances everywhere in art, music, theology, and spiritual writings. We would stumble upon an old holy card with a high altar and wonder whether it is really of any use today. We would find children's books in used book stores and decide not to buy them because they featured priests facing liturgical East. The writings of the saints on the Mass did not seem as relevant to us since they seemed to be talking about something we did not know or experience in our time. We would look at great musical compositions and wonder why the Sanctus is separated from the Benedictus and we would be tempted with the idea that this timeless music just is not viable in our day.

But with new information pouring out to us through digital sources, together with the great liberalization of the older rites achieved by Pope Benedict XVI in *Summorum Pontificum* (2007), much of that tendency to hide and apologize for having a historical interest or for desiring continuity of practice changed. The Mass of the past was renewed again, it became completely licit for every Roman rite priest. It was being taught in seminaries. It was making appearances in cathedrals and even in our parishes. The objections you would have heard ten years ago have nearly vanished, as ever more bishops and priests feel free now to embrace this heritage and even celebrate it.

Just as striking has been the progress toward the "reform of the reform" in the many ways in which that phrase is being used. I personally know of no young priest who is not liturgically sophisticated in ways that the previous generation was typically not. They have a wonderful curiosity about the past and a burning desire to recover the beauty and liturgical forms from previous ages, bringing into new times. Online communities are the sources for ideas and plans. And I sense this even in my own parish, where my experiences parallel those of so many others: our musical and liturgical program is no longer seen as the hobby horse of a faction but rather an expression of a fuller and richer experience of the liturgy than we have seen in the past decades.

When you consider the history and the current institutional layout, we can see that a major inhibitor to progress in the last 50 years has been a simple lack of knowledge and a lack of immediately accessible resources. This has changed dramatically with history's greatest and most fruitful copy machine at work to not only distribute but to inspire and build whole communities. The fruits of that change are all around us.

Pope Benedict XVI gave a beautiful reflection on the internet in his June 5, 2011 message for World Communications Day. In this message, he celebrated the changes wrought by this technology but also said that the digital means must give rise to a new demand for personal connection to others and for genuine encounter with God. Toward this end, he urged that:

> The new communications technologies must be placed at the service of the integral good of the individual and of the whole of humanity. If used wisely, they can contribute to the satisfaction of the desire for meaning, truth and unity which remain the most profound aspirations of each human being.

Further, he said:

> I would like then to invite Christians, confidently and with an informed and responsible creativity, to join the network of relationships which the digital era has made possible. This is not simply to satisfy the desire to be present, but because this network is an integral part of human life. The web is contributing to the development of new and more complex intellectual and spiritual horizons, new forms of shared awareness. In this field too we are called to proclaim our faith that Christ is God, the Saviour of humanity and of history, the one in whom all things find their fulfilment.

18

The Social Aspects of the Sacred Liturgy

MIGUEL AYUSO

Introduction

Taking as a point of departure several truths of social philosophy, focusing particularly on the family and its role, I will try to offer some
simple reflections on the role of the liturgy in relation to familial and
social life. This will be articulated through five interrelated defenses:
of the Christian people, of Christendom, of religious practice, of the
sacraments, and of the liturgy per se—defenses that are necessary and
even indispensable. The first four are based on various texts by Fr. Jean
Daniélou, S.J., later a cardinal of the Holy Roman Church.

The Spanish writer Ramiro de Maeztu, who was assassinated during
the religious persecution that broke out in 1936, coined the expression "to be is to defend oneself."[1] This close connection, between the
ontological reality of the very existence of being and the necessity of
defending it, concisely illustrates the truths expounded by St. Thomas
Aquinas in elaborating on the cardinal virtue of fortitude.[2]

Translated from the Spanish original by Michael J. Miller.

[1] Ramiro de Maeztu, Gonzalo Fernández de la Mora, ed., *Ideario* (Madrid: Asociación
de Amigos de Maeztu, 1957). Followed by the standard biography by Vicente Marrero,
Maeztu (Madrid: Rialp, 1955).

[2] St. Thomas Aquinas, *Summa Theologiæ*, I-II, 123–40. See in particular the study
by Marcel de Corte, *De la force* (Bouère: Dominique Martin Morin, 1980), pp. 23–24,
where he underscores the fact that the principal act of fortitude is to resist and that all
resistance includes a reaction to this evil and, consequently, an attack.

Defense of the Christian People

In the 1960s, during the proceedings of the Second Vatican Council and in the years immediately after its conclusion, and regardless of the fact that the character of his work fell within the polemics that accompanied the condemnation of the *nouvelle théologie* by Pius XII,[3] Fr. Daniélou valiantly took up the banner of the fight against secularization, above all beginning with a remarkable book, the title of which was in itself a program and a provocation: *Prayer as a Political Problem.*[4]

Secularization, like all modern culture, originated in a Protestant context. So did Europe, a by-product of Christendom, as traditional Spanish thought clearly saw, while it opposed a movement for European unification that was synonymous with de-Christianization. So did the State, an artifact that replaces the faith-based political community. The same goes for capitalism, which is connected with consumerism and the abandonment of the traditional prohibition against usury. Likewise, finally, subjective law, the basis of what were later called "human rights", which separates authority from the norm and destroys the *ius* as an objective statute.[5] But perhaps secularization, which is present in all the other areas just listed summarily, is the core element of them all, even where this Protestant pedigree is most plainly evident.[6]

In it there are three different facets that must be carefully distinguished.[7] The first is an opposition to religion, which is considered to be a cultural fact that has ceased to be valid in the world of science:

---

[3] Santiago Ramírez, O.P., *Teología nueva y teología* (Madrid: O crece o muere, 1958).

[4] Jean Daniélou, S.J., *L'oraison problème politique* (Paris: Fayard, 1965). ET: J. R. Kirwan, trans., *Prayer as a Political Problem* (New York: Sheed and Ward, 1967).

[5] Cf. Álvaro d'Ors, "Retrospectiva de mis últimos XXV años" in: *Atlántida* [Madrid] 13 (1993), pp. 90–99. Since it is common to all the themes, let this one reference suffice, so as to avoid duplicating the footnotes.

[6] The reader may consult my book, *La constitución cristiana de los Estados* (Barcelona: Scire, 2008). Italian ed.: *La costituzione cristiana degli Stati* (Naples: Edizioni Scientifiche Italiane, 2010).

[7] Jean Cardinal Daniélou, "Secularismo, secularización y secularidad", in: J. Daniélou and C. Pozo, *Iglesia y secularización* (Madrid: BAC, 1973), pp. 4–14. This volume includes the papers read by then-Cardinal Daniélou and Fr. Cándido Pozo, S.J., during the *"II Semana de Estudios y Coloquios sobre problemas teológicos actuales"* ["Second Week of Studies and Colloquia on Current Theological Problems"] held in Burgos from August 25–30, 1969.

religion corresponds to a mentality that had its heyday at a particular stage of humanity's evolution; whereas today we have entered into the scientific era, in which science is inexorably called to replace religion, just as technology replaces ritual and humanism replaces mysticism. The second facet presupposes a rejection of the idea that there is a sphere belonging specifically to the sacred: those who hold this thesis believe that Christianity boils down to a manner of living worldly life, but that it lacks any specific expressions. Finally, the third facet, which poses the most classical problem, manifests itself as a demand for a radical separation between Christianity and civilization, that is to say, from the Christian perspective, the problem of the existence of a Christian civilization.

Confronted with this threefold secularization, Daniélou sets out to defend the Church, an ambit belonging to the sacred within the sphere of human realities, and the existence of Christian peoples supported by institutions that are also Christian. In short: to defend the Church but also Christendom, which are combated respectively by the heralds of "religion without God" and by the proponents of a mere "Christianity in public life".

Indeed, he writes in the prologue of the abovementioned book:

> What will make the existence of a Christian people possible in the civilization of tomorrow? The religious problem is a mass problem. It is not at all the problem of an élite. At the mass level religion and civilization depend very much on one another. . . . [N]or . . . can there be a religion of the masses which is not supported by civilization.[8]

Nevertheless, he continued, in actuality too many Christians accept the juxtaposition of personal religion and secular society, and this notion is nothing if not disastrous both for society and for religion.

Since the terms of the issue had been framed so clearly, too clearly to remain without a response, the Dominican theologians Jossua and Geffré gave one. The debate concluded in the dialogue between Daniélou and Jossua that was published in book form with a title that sums it all up: *Christianity of the masses or of the elite?*[9]

---

[8] Daniélou, *Prayer as a Political Problem*, p. 7.

[9] Jean Daniélou, S.J. and Jean Pierre Jossua, O.P., *Christianisme de masse ou d'élite* (Paris: Beauchesne, 1968).

The question could and still can be considered in two ways. First of all, a consideration at the level of facts, whereby it may be necessary to reflect that in the future the Church might end up being reduced to a little flock within a massively atheistic world. However there is also the consideration of the principles, whereby it will be necessary to ask what is desirable, a Church of the multitudes or a little group of authentic Christians.[10]

Daniélou's fundamental concern was that Christianity should be able to continue to reach all the people, without being confined to minorities.[11] Moreover, this search for a large Christian populace should not be absolutely incompatible with the importance of forming Christians who are truly committed.[12]

Defense of Christendom

The adversaries of Christendom object, in the first place, that the existence of Christian peoples is closely connected with the existence of a Christian civilization, and the latter can definitely be said to have no future. As a second argument, they add a critical and negative evaluation of what is commonly called "cultural" Christianity, using a term that is rooted in the fact that, in countries where Catholicism is very extensive, there are large numbers of people who are Catholics because they belong to a Christian society and not out of any personal conviction. Finally, they completed their critical picture with a consideration —which we do not have to go into—of an ecclesiological nature about varying conditions for salvation.

The real reason behind those who objected to Christendom at that time, and likewise the basic motive of those who, among other theories, support the idea of the "Christian minority",[13] is not so much an option for stiff requirements—a difficult, heroic Christianity, the heritage of only a little flock—as it is the acceptance of the paradigm of secularization. This is clearly evident in the writings of the Dominican Jean-Pierre Jossua when he rebukes his opponent, who regards the

---

[10] Jean Cardinal Daniélou, "La Iglesia, ¿pequeño rebaño o gran pueblo?", in: *Iglesia y secularización*, p. 23.

[11] Daniélou, *Christianisme de masse ou d'élite*, p. 15.

[12] Daniélou, *Iglesia y secularización*, pp. 24–30.

[13] Rafael Gómez Pérez, *La minoría cristiana* (Madrid: Rialp, 1976).

dismantling of the sociological scaffolding of the Faith as the result of a pastoral approach, when actually it is merely an irreversible phenomenon of civilization.[14] About a decade later, however, and from a significantly different ecclesial perspective, a Spanish writer wrote: "The logic of democracy leads society today to satisfy the requests that are thought to come from the majority. This logic, however, is not a political problem, but rather a moral one." So that, faced with the panorama of empirically observable moral deterioration, "neither could a strong government prevent this degeneration in the long term by decree, not even if it decided to do so."[15]

Even conceding that the problem is moral rather than political—which of course is not to exclude the political as if it were a somewhat exaggerated component that sprang up outside of the area under consideration—the interesting thing is not that a strong government by itself (that is, in the exclusively political arena) is incapable of slowing or preventing this degeneration. The truly interesting question—to which there is no answer—is whether any method that truly could prevent it (within the field of morality to which we alluded before) will be effective without a "strong" government—understood in terms of the virtue of fortitude, without necessarily overlooking prudence—that is willing to do so. That is to say, whether the moral solution of the problem can be attained "without" politics and "against" politics. I sincerely believe that we are compelled to answer in the negative.[16] And I seem to find an identical solution in the words of Daniélou, for whom "freedom is not absolutely something abstract and independent of the conditions in which it is exercised"; since for most human beings the exercise of freedom is not determined but is conditioned by the environment in which said freedom operates. This implies, consequently, "that it is not possible for most people to respond to certain needs that they have except to the extent that the environment within

---

[14] Jossua, *Christianisme de masse ou d'élite*, p. 20.

[15] Pérez, *La minoría cristiana*, pp. 28–29.

[16] Miguel Ayuso, *La política, oficio del alma* (Buenos Aires: Nueva Hispanidad, 2007), pp. 49ff. (There is a French edition entitled *Appel de l'âme et vocation politique*, [Paris: Muller, 2011], pp. 57ff.), where I comment on a very interesting passage from Jacques Maritain, *Une opinion sur Charles Maurras et le devoir des catholiques* (Paris: Plon, 1926), pp. 20–21. The original edition, incidentally, contains several obvious errors, since the editor-in-chief translated on his own several texts that were originally in French, with results that are sometimes grotesque.

which they live makes it possible for them to do so."[17] The example of certain peoples with very special histories—and it seems to me that we do not have to fill more paragraphs to point out the Spanish people in particular, among others—is sufficiently enlightening. And it would be unfair to classify it under the derogatory headings of cultural Christianity or social conformism.

This leads directly to the idea of Christendom, which is situated at the center of the debate: "There is no Christianity of the masses without Christendom." This goes a step further. It is no longer about affirming the need for a Christianity of the masses, but rather about emphasizing that Christian peoples cannot exist without Christian institutions. And this consideration inevitably collides with the phenomena of secularization and its corollary, pluralism. This pluralism, which furthermore is thought to be inexorable and irreversible—somewhat pretentiously, since the only processes proven to be irreversible are those of aging, which lead to the death of every human being—can turn out to be favorable for outstanding personalities, challenging them to form an independent judgment, but for the average person it is completely destructive. The pluralistic atmosphere, moreover, leads to the disappearance among most people of the sense that there "can" be any truth, in other words, to the disappearance of the "possibility" of affirming something with conviction and certainty.

Daniélou, on this point, adheres to a steadier doctrine and, refusing to admit radical pluralism as something inevitable, expresses the wish that reflection might lead human minds to the insight that there are things that "can" be imposed, that there "can" exist a consistent universe that is supposed to be inherited by mankind as a whole as a valid tradition.[18]

If we want a Christian people, Daniélou concludes, it is essential to create the conditions that make it possible. To claim to detach faith from a definite framework—to consider that endeavor along with Jossua as "the very act of faith"[19]—is precisely to make this Christian people impossible. It is at the same time an attack on the natural virtue of *pietas*. . . .

---

[17] Daniélou, *Christianisme de masse ou d'élite*, pp. 14–15.

[18] Daniélou, ibid., pp. 28–29.

[19] Jossua, *Christianisme de masse ou d'élite*, p. 20.

Defense of the Practicing Christian

He argues along these same lines in his defense of "religious practice".[20] Many contemporaries have denied the value of any practice which is unattainable without a "religious façade" made up of a set of habits (Sunday Mass, confession and communion during the Easter season, fasts and abstinence—which incidentally have practically disappeared) and based on family traditions, social conformism and emotional loyalties. Challenging this view, the French Jesuit affirmed the necessity of some external expression of the Faith and the importance of worship and the sacraments. Without these, Christianity is reduced (and this was the objective) to a philanthropic morality detached from any act of worship.

But in attacking in this way what seemed to them to be a merely formalistic practice, they were thereby fundamentally compromising the visible, sacramental, cultural (and cultic) aspect of the Catholic Church. The point is that religious practice, even in its most elementary form, signifies a certain intention not to break up with God, staying in contact with Him in the midst of one's frailties.

Note that until now we have not stopped arguing at a human or, if you prefer, a pre-Christian level. This is because human beings have always felt the need to sanctify the essential acts of life: the birth of a child, the union of a man and a woman, death. . . . Events which, even for the most cloistered or hermetic lives are crevices through which seeps a ray of light and love. At its most elementary level, Christian practice increases the believer's solidarity with human nature. And even though it is clear that we are not talking about reducing Christianity to these acts, why should anyone despise them and reject them? How can we fail to mention, in this regard, the Lord's words: He will not break a bruised reed, or quench a smoldering wick (Mt 12:15-21)? The reed can always straighten up; the wick is still smoking. . . . If the one is broken or the other is extinguished, this produces spiritual death instead, and civil marriages and funerals spread everywhere, as

---

[20] Jean Daniélou, S.J., *Le chrétien et le monde moderne* (Tournai: Desclée, 1959, 1961); ET: Kathryn Sullivan, R.S.C.J., trans., *The Christian Today* (New York: Desclee Company, 1960), pp. 97ff., esp. p. 100.

we see today. And the poor, the weakest and the neediest are the ones who suffer the consequences. Yet these consequences do not affect the supposedly "pure" Christians, whom Guitton castigated from another perspective, whose faith—they say—does not need institutional or sociological support structures.[21] And so we enter into a world where there can be sacrifices for the sake of humanity, progress or science, but where these sacrifices—to use Daniélou's expression—immolate human lives "to the monstrous idol which is their collective pride".[22]

It does not cease to be paradoxical that in a world like ours, in which "sociological conditions today still have considerable importance", whenever the religious problem is addressed, many people try to reduce it to "the personal dimension."[23] On the other hand, it turns out to be an extremely debatable idea that the importance of social conditions was greater in the past than it is today, when the powerful resources of the mass media far surpass the media of yesteryear.

Although interaction with the media prevails everywhere as a methodological requirement, although we seem to be more sensitive to the influence of sociology, the one area that resists this trend is the relation between nature and the supernatural, forgetting the maxim of St. Thomas Aquinas: *Gratia non tollit naturam, sed perficit eam.*[24] ("Grace does not abolish nature but rather perfects it.") If nature is not a stratum over which grace spreads but rather what is elevated by it, there would be much to think about in the functions that Saint-Exupéry attributed to the human community, starting with the family but extending also to political society, the home in space and ritual in time.[25] The Church, with her sacraments and her Sacred Liturgy, on a strictly human or pre-Christian level which is indeed naturally Christian, is also a home and a ritual that welcome people.

---

[21] Jean Guitton, *L'impur* (Paris: Desclée, 1991).

[22] Daniélou, *The Christian Today*, p. 101.

[23] Daniélou, *Christianisme de masse ou d'élite*, p. 24.

[24] St. Thomas Aquinas, *S. Th.*, I, q. 1, art. 8, ad 2.

[25] Antoine de Saint-Exupéry, *Citadelle* (Paris: Gallimard, 1948). The reader may consult the profound commentary by the Spanish philosopher Rafael Gambra, *El silencio de Dios* (Madrid: Prensa Española, 1968). There is a French edition, *Le silence de Dieu* (Perpignan: Artège, 2012).

Defense of the Sacraments

If we turn our attention now from the previous topic to the Church's sacraments, strictly speaking, this perspective becomes concrete and stands out. To begin with, the sacraments are essential to Christianity, which is, yes, a *re-ligio*, that is, a "binding together", but above all a life, the life of Christ communicated through His Church through several channels, which are the sacraments; one cannot be Christian without participating in them. It is unfair, therefore, to regard them disdainfully as things belonging to an external, collective or secondary religion, or to contrast sacramental religion to a sort of Christianity in spirit and in truth, from which worship (among other things) would be excluded. At the same time, however, it is still somewhat useful to consider this view, even though it is erroneous, since it allows us to understand better the meaning and importance of the sacraments in the Catholic Church.

First of all, the opposition between interior Christianity and social religion does not happen to be a completely baseless prejudice. Then we must not forget that sociability is natural in a human being, running through all his ontic levels and opening him up to the supernatural. Society, indeed, is a projection of man, so that his entire nature is reflected in this projection. Hence the basic human society is not the product of an agreement, pact or constitution, as political rationalism claimed; neither can it result from technological planning, as socialism in its various forms claims. Natural impulse, instinct and intellect collaborate in society, as well as feelings and emotions, whose function as social cement runs very deep. Even reason, which presides (or ought to preside) over the government and progress of the human City, is not pure reason, disincarnate from reality, but rather *wisdom about life*, that product of prudence and of a particular rooting that should also guide the life of every human being.[26]

It is certain that the divine constitution of the Church, to which Christ entrusted the task of dispensing salvation to the whole world, distinguishes her from all other organizations. As the LORD remains in

---

[26] Rafael Gambra, *El exilio y el Reino: La comunidad de los hombres y sus enemigos* (Barcelona: Scire, 2010), p. 19.

the meeting tent in the midst of the Hebrew people, from the Church
we receive even more the riches of Christ. So then, in the first place, the
sacraments, being acts through which we enter into communication
with the Church, have a social character. Fr. de Lubac, S.J., and later—
like Daniélou—a cardinal of the Church, and likewise connected with
the *nouvelle théologie*, managed to discuss "the social aspects of dogma"
with some language that could perhaps be theologically nuanced yet
in any case useful for the purpose that interests us here:

> Baptism initiates into the ecclesiastical community and by this initi-
> ation introduces souls into the communion of Christ's life; penance
> reconciles with the community, which delegates [*sic*] this job to the
> priest and, consequently [*sic*], reconciles with Christ; the Eucharist is
> the very expression of membership in the ecclesiastical community:
> the glorified Christ makes himself present in the midst of the com-
> munity gathered in large numbers [*sic*]; marriage situates the husband
> and the wife in their proper mission with a view to building up the
> body of Christ. . . .[27]

Well, we can go further. Christianity is the religion of the Incarnation, since God became man: *"Et Verbum caro factum est"* (Jn 1:14).
And the Church prolongs the Incarnation: only someone who comes
into contact—says Daniélou—with her flesh [*sic*], with her visible appearance, with her structure and her sacraments, can have access to the
riches of the spirit. What Chesterton said about the moral order can
be applied also to the dogmatic order. I am referring to the two circles
that he distinguishes in Christianity, or more exactly, in the Catholic
Church, which he had not yet joined, though, when he wrote these
words. In the first, exterior circle we find a rigid defense made up
of ethical renunciations and professional priests; the second, interior
circle, however, guards the dances of the children and the wine of the
adults. Consequently this is the opposite of modern civilization, where
the appearance is enchanting and attractive while despair writhes inside.[28]

---

[27] Cf. Henri de Lubac, *Catholicisme: Les aspects sociaux du dogme* (Paris: Cerf, 1938). ET:
Lancelot C. Sheppard and Elizabeth Englund, trans., *Catholicism: Christ and the Common
Destiny of Man* (San Francisco: Ignatius Press, 1988).

[28] Gilbert Keith Chesterton, *Orthodoxy* (London: John Lane, 1908), pp. 292–93.

Here, then, is the essence of the sacraments: sensible signs of an invisible grace. Péguy admirably expressed this poetically: the supernatural becomes carnal.[29] And just as there is a way of building the city of men (however much they follow God's plans) in which what man has created glorifies man (however much it may glorify God also), more profoundly there is a way of building the city of God in which what God has created glorifies God. This building of the City of God is sacred history, that is, the ultimate contents of history. Of which the sacraments constitute, according to Daniélou, the present form: they are the presence in our midst of the great works of God.[30]

Defense of the Liturgy

The Sacred Liturgy occupies a central place in the panorama that we have described. And, if we may copy the expression of the oft-cited Fr. Daniélou, which is as daring as it is correct, to the political problem of prayer we could add the political aspect of the liturgy. In addressing this we will examine first the unique dimension that corresponds to the family.

The connection between the family as community and politics is more complex than the one that is somewhat trivially expressed by what we might call, with Augusto del Noce, "clericalism", that is, the submission—common among ecclesiastics and clericalized laymen— to the playbook imposed by the enemy, occasionally attempting to baptize his categories and, at best, modifying their own in the service of the fight against the prevailing ones.[31] This strategy, however you may like it to be, always proves to be a losing one.

With regard to this clericalism we should emphasize—as the Italian philosopher Danilo Castellano has explained subtly—that the political community is a natural society, firstly, similar to the family, secondly,

---

[29] Cf. "Eve", in: Charles Péguy, *Morceaux choisis: Poésie* (Paris: Gallimard, 1927), pp. 176ff.

[30] Daniélou, *The Christian Today*, p. 107.

[31] Cf. Augusto del Noce, "Giacomo Noventa: dagli errori della cultura alle difficoltà in politica" in: A. del Noce; F. Mercadante, A. Tarantino and B. Casadei, eds., *Rivoluzione Risorgimento tradizione* (Milan: Giuffré, 1993), (pp. 97–119), pp. 103ff.

contemporaneous with it (meaning that it does not come *after* but rather *with* the family) and thirdly, the guarantee of its existence, which is ordered to achieve its proper end.[32] The preceding does not exclude that there should be—as the famous Spanish jurist Álvaro d'Ors has pointed out—an inflexible link between the form of government and familial legitimacy. In a monarchy the family has political importance, whereas in a democracy only individuals attain it, and thus its aristocracies distinguish those families that preserve that importance from the others that have lost it.[33]

The Church has usually emphasized this political importance of the family, which is consistent with its preference for the monarchic form; for proof of this, just look at n. 408 of the *Catechism* of St. Pius X, which states that civil society is made up of families. Compare this with the new *Catechism*, which in paragraph 2213 says instead that "Human communities are made up of persons", although it states immediately at the outset of the discussion in paragraph 2207 that the family is "the original cell of social life". This is also sympathetic with a certain democratic turn that the Church has made, although it proves to be not totally extraneous to the most essential feature of the structure of the Church, which is composed of baptized persons.[34] Yet it has some harmful consequences, since personalism dilutes the communitarian aspect as much as it reinforces the societal aspect, and the Church is a community, the Mystical Body of Christ, and not a society that came about through voluntary membership.[35]

The liturgy, for its part, as the worship due to God, reflects these

---

[32] Danilo Castellano, *La naturaleza de la política* (Barcelona: Scire, 2006), pp. 49ff. The chapter cited was originally a conference paper read in Barcelona during the *Reunión de Amigos de la Ciudad Católica* in 1995, published in Spanish in *Verbo* in 1996 and then in the original Italian in the author's book, *L'ordine della politica* (Napoli: Edizioni Scientifiche Italiane, 1997).

[33] Álvaro d'Ors, *Forma de gobierno y legitimidad familiar* (Madrid: O crece o muere, 1960).

[34] Álvaro d'Ors, *Nueva introducción al estudio del derecho* (Madrid: Civitas, 1999), pp. 151, 162.

[35] For a critique of personalism, see Danilo Castellano, *L'ordine politico-giuridico "modulare" del personalismo contemporaneo* (Napoli: Edizioni Scientifiche Italiane, 2007). Regarding the distinction between community (*Gemeinschaft*) and society (*Gesellschaft*), coined in the early twentieth century by Ferdinand Tönnies, cf. Rafael Gambra, *El exilio y el Reino*.

communitarian aspects in terms of a vertical, hierarchical arrangement. And this has important didactic repercussions. In instituting the liturgical feast of Christ the King, Pius XI explained it specifically in terms of this arrangement, but with reasons that serve generally to stress the value of the liturgy (cf. *Quas Primas*, 20ff.).

Thus, in the first place, feast days are experienced intimately and periodically by most of the faithful over the course of the liturgical year:

> For people are instructed in the truths of faith, and brought to appreciate the inner joys of religion far more effectually by the annual celebration of our sacred mysteries than by any official pronouncement of the teaching of the Church. Such pronouncements usually reach only a few and the more learned among the faithful; feasts reach them all; the former speak but once, the latter speak every year—in fact, forever. The Church's teaching affects the mind primarily; her feasts affect both mind and heart, and have a salutary effect upon the whole of man's nature. Man is composed of body and soul, and he needs these external festivities so that the sacred rites, in all their beauty and variety, may stimulate him to drink more deeply of the fountain of God's teaching, that he may make it a part of himself, and use it with profit for his spiritual life. (cf. *Quas Primas*, 21)

Feast days, moreover, were instituted at opportune moments:

> [I]n the course of ages . . . one after another according as the needs or the advantage of the people of Christ seemed to demand: as when they needed strength to face a common danger, when they were attacked by insidious heresies, when they needed to be urged to the pious consideration of some mystery of faith or of some divine blessing. (*Quas Primas*, 22)

A glance at history proves this:

> Thus in the earliest days of the Christian era, when the people of Christ were suffering cruel persecution, the cult of the martyrs was begun in order, says St. Augustine, "that the feasts of the martyrs might incite men to martyrdom." The liturgical honors paid to confessors, virgins and widows produced wonderful results in an increased zest for virtue, necessary even in times of peace. But more fruitful still were the feasts instituted in honor of the Blessed Virgin. As a result

of these men grew not only in their devotion to the Mother of God as an ever-present advocate, but also in their love of her as a [heavenly] mother bequeathed to them by their Redeemer. Not least among the blessings which have resulted from the public and legitimate honor paid to the Blessed Virgin and the saints is the perfect and perpetual immunity of the Church from error and heresy. We may well admire in this the admirable wisdom of the Providence of God, who, ever bringing good out of evil, has from time to time suffered the faith and piety of men to grow weak, and allowed Catholic truth to be attacked by false doctrines, but always with the result that truth has afterwards shone out with greater splendor, and that men's faith, aroused from its lethargy, has shown itself more vigorous than before.

The festivals that have been introduced into the liturgy in more recent years have had a similar origin, and have been attended with similar results. When reverence and devotion to the Blessed Sacrament had grown cold, the feast of Corpus Christi was instituted, so that by means of solemn processions and prayer of eight days' duration, men might be brought once more to render public homage to Christ. So, too, the feast of the Sacred Heart of Jesus was instituted at a time when men were oppressed by the sad and gloomy severity of Jansenism, which had made their hearts grow cold, and shut them out from the love of God and the hope of salvation. (*Quas Primas,* 22–23)

Finally, this explains the institution of the Feast of Christ the King:

If We ordain that the whole Catholic world shall revere Christ as King, We shall minister to the need of the present day, and at the same time provide an excellent remedy for the plague which now infects society. We refer to the plague of anti-clericalism, its errors and impious activities. This evil spirit, as you are well aware, Venerable Brethren, has not come into being in one day; it has long lurked beneath the surface. The empire of Christ over all nations was rejected. The right which the Church has from Christ himself, to teach mankind, to make laws, to govern peoples in all that pertains to their eternal salvation, that right was denied. Then gradually the religion of Christ came to be likened to false religions and to be placed ignominiously on the same level with them. It was then put under the power of the state and tolerated more or less at the whim of princes and rulers. Some men went even further, and wished to set up in the place of God's religion a natural religion consisting in some instinctive affection of the heart. There were even some nations who thought they could dispense with God, and that their religion should consist in impiety and the neglect of God. The rebellion of individuals and states against the authority of Christ has produced deplorable consequences. We lamented these in the Encyclical *Ubi Arcano*; we lament them today: the seeds of discord sown far and wide; those bitter enmities and rivalries between nations, which still hinder so much the cause of peace; that insatiable greed which is so often hidden under a pretense of public spirit and patriotism, and gives rise to so many private quarrels; a blind and immoderate selfishness, making men seek nothing but their own comfort and advantage, and measure everything by these; no peace in the home, because men have forgotten or neglect their duty; the unity and stability of the family undermined; society in a word, shaken to its foundations and on the way to ruin. (*Quas Primas*, 24)

If we look at "the liturgical devastation" today, which Cardinal Ratzinger spoke about before his elevation to the papal throne,[36] accelerated by an *ordo* that has become worse in practice, and examine more closely what Bishop Schneider called "the five wounds of the present liturgy", we find detached elements that develop the topic that we are discussing.

"In the liturgy, as in the Church"—the latter author said—"the human element must be oriented (and subject) to the divine, and likewise what is visible to what is invisible, action to contemplation and the present to the future city to which we aspire." He continues:

The rite and every detail of the Holy Sacrifice of the Mass must center on glorifying and adoring God by insisting on the centrality of Christ's presence, whether in the sign and representation of the Crucified or in His Eucharistic Presence in the tabernacle, and especially at the moment of the Consecration and of Holy Communion. The more this is respected, the less man takes center stage in the celebration, the less the celebration looks like a circle closed in on itself. Rather, it is opened out on to Christ as in a procession advancing towards Him with the priest at its head; such a liturgical procession will more truly

---

[36] Cardinal Joseph Ratzinger, "Vorwort" to: Klaus Gamber, *Die Reform der römischen Liturgie* (Regensburg: Pustet, 1981). ET: *The Reform of the Roman Liturgy: its problems and background* (San Juan Capistrano: Una Voce Press, 1993).

reflect the sacrifice of adoration of Christ crucified; the fruits deriving from God's glorification received into the souls of those in attendance will be richer; God will honor them more. The more the priest and the faithful truthfully seek the glory of God rather than that of men in Eucharistic celebrations and do not seek to receive glory from each other, the more God will honor them by granting that their soul may participate more intensely and fruitfully in the glory and honor of His divine life.[37]

Starting from this general consideration, Bishop Schneider explains what these five wounds are, namely: celebration *versus populum*, communion in the hand, the new prayers that are recited at the offertory, the *de facto* suppression of Latin and the admission of women to the ministries of lector and acolyte. His study goes beyond the scope of our competence, to which we have deliberately restricted our analysis.

Yet all of them correspond to the wounds of the modern "world", which is opposed to the supernatural in the deepest sense, since it fails to recognize either grace or nature.

---

[37] Athanasius Schneider, "La nouvelle évangélisation et la sainte liturgie", conference paper read in Paris on 15 January 2012, on the occasion of the "IV Rencontre pour l'Unité des Catholiques" (Fourth Meeting for Unity among Catholics), published as "Guérir la sainte liturgie", in: Claude Barthe, ed., *Propositions Pastorales* (Paris: Collection Hora Decima, 2012), pp. 86–100.

19

Sacred Liturgy and the Defense of Human Life

IGNACIO BARREIRO CARÁMBULA

Introduction

We do not conduct a struggle for what is evident, and shared by all. Regrettably things that were evident for previous generations are no longer evident today. Sixty years ago the natural human desire to spread life and to have children did not need to be defended, but today it seems to have dried up in most of the industrialized countries. We can see how the fertility rates are dropping at concerning levels in many countries in the south of the world. Sixty years ago it was a localized problem and few would have thought that it would have become a worldwide phenomenon.

Fifty years ago to raise the concern that the connatural sense of adoration that Catholics have towards the Blessed Sacrament of the Altar was waning would have been considered an exaggeration. But today it is sad reality that many of us can lament based on our personal experiences. This critical problem is caused by, among other things, as Raymond Cardinal Burke notes well, by an exaggerated attention to the human aspects of the liturgy that has put aside the essence of the liturgy as an encounter with God by us by means of the sacramental signs. It has neglected the nature of the liturgy as the direct action of the Glorious Christ in the Church to give us the grace of the Holy Spirit.[1]

---

[1] Raymond Leo Cardinal Burke, *Ius divinum e Sacra Liturgia*, in: Raymond Burke, Nicola Bux, Raffaele Coppola, *La danza vuota intorno al vitello d'oro* (Torino: Lindau, 2012), p. 19.

Malcolm Cardinal Ranjith points out that by making the Mass banal we have lost sight of the eminent dignity of the sacrament of the Eucharist.[2] As a consequence we have to make our outmost efforts to render back to the liturgy the sense of the sacred that is so important.

There is no doubt that one of the causes of the contemporary crisis of the Church is the collapse of the liturgy.[3] Recently Bishop Athanasius Schneider reminded us that the worst sin that humanity can commit is to refuse to adore God, to refuse to give Him the first place, the place of honor.[4] A man that does not adore God in the liturgy will not value the main gift of God, which is life. A secularized man that considers himself autonomous from God will be uncomfortable that the tabernacle would be at the center of the Church or that the cross should be at the center of the altar.

Secularization rejects the right relation of man with God. Secularization denies our dependence from God, so it refutes Him as giver of life and that man by his nature is a being that adores, giving due worship to God. We are all sensitive to the justice that is due to our neighbor, but the precedence should be given to the justice that is due to God. Catholicism has to be understood as a society of men who give to God the right worship and as a consequence they provide service to their fellow men. Service should not have priority, instead service should be the consequence of worship. In some ways we can say that service is a continuation that flows from worship.

It befalls upon all men of good will to act in accordance with nature and to desire and be proud to have children. For we Catholics, in addition to our natural inclinations, possessing the fullness of the truth about the source and the destiny of human life, this desire should be stronger. But this desire seems in the verge of fading away, both in society at large and within the Catholic community. The main cause is an anti-life attitude, or frame of mind, that has become a sinful social structure—as consequence we have a "culture of death", not life.

---

[2] "Entretien avec le Cardinal Albert Malcolm Ranjith: L'exemple du diocèse de Colombo", in: Claude Barthe, ed., *Propositions Pastorales* (Paris: Collection Hora Decima, 2012), (pp. 68–74), p. 71.

[3] "I am convinced that the crisis in the Church that we are experiencing is to a large extent due to the disintegration of the liturgy;" Joseph Cardinal Ratzinger, *Milestones: Memoirs 1927–1977* (San Francisco: Ignatius Press, 1998), pp. 148–49.

[4] Athanasius Schneider, "Guérir la sainte liturgie", in: Barthe, *Propositions Pastorales*, (pp. 86–100), p. 86.

This deeply anti-natural and pathological mind set has many causes: the militant atheism that underpins both the totalitarian and the liberal ideologies, the practical atheism that comes as a consequence of being dominated by the propaganda of a secular humanist society that leads to a shortsighted selfishness that is afraid of the cares and concerns of raising children, radical environmentalism, the fear of living that we always find in decadent societies, and as part and parcel of that fear a strong reluctance to have children that seems to have spread all over the world and which is a consequence of all the rest, and of course last but not least original sin and habitual sin.

St. John Paul II denounced how this "culture of death" had entered within the ranks of the Church, stating that:

> Too often it happens that believers, even those who take active part in the life of the Church, end up by separating their Christian faith from its ethical requirements concerning life, and thus fall into moral subjectivism and certain objectionable ways of acting. (*Evangelium Vitæ*, 95)

Reason and revelation come together to tell us that God is source of all life. Revelation also tells us, that the source of all life is present for us and for our salvation in all the tabernacles of the world, waiting to make us sharers of the most perfect form of life, which is the Divine Life. The problem that concerns us today is how we Catholics are going to be empowered to spread the Gospel of Life if we do not duly adore the source and model of all life which is present in our midst in the Blessed Sacrament of the Altar. Union with Christ in adoration necessarily leads us to evangelization, because we will give to the ones whom God places close to us what we have contemplated in adoration.[5]

God as the Source of Life

Life in its fullness resides only in God. In Him we encounter the infinite plenitude of Life. Both reason and revelation tell us that our lives on earth are totally incomplete without the presence of God. Man can neither find its meaning nor understand the reality that surrounds

---

[5] "Entretien avec Dominique Rey: L'exemple du diocèse de Fréjus-Toulon" in: Barthe, *Propositions Pastorales*, (pp. 75–85), p. 77.

except in relation to God.[6] A man separated from God will find his life empty and meaningless. He will know the world as a place where he experiences more pain than happiness. That it is dominated by dark and oppressive forces. This is why in the end a man divorced from God will lack the motivation to generate life. If there is no supernatural hope, how can a person that sees the world as place of hopeless suffering desire to bring new fellow sufferers to this world?

The Christian will also see and experience the dark and oppressive side of this world, but as he is inspired by a sense of hope because he knows that he can change the world in which he lives, and what is more important, he also knows that this world is only a brief, temporary passage that will allow him to enter afterwards into the Kingdom of Heaven if he lives his life with fidelity. He knows that his children can inherit a better world, or that they themselves can build a better society and, what it is more important, that it is possible for them to be with Him for ever and ever in the Kingdom of Heaven.

With the gift of life, man also receives the call to establish the right relation with God that comes through proper worship, which leads to the sanctification of men. In the book of Exodus we see how the people of Israel discover the type of worship that is willed by the Lord. Cult and liturgy are part of this worship. Life only becomes real life when it receives its meaning from looking towards God, because the cult exists in order to communicate this vision. To receive this vision we have to be directed towards God in adoration. This is why the liturgical orientation during the Holy Sacrifice of the Mass is of particular relevance. If the priest and the congregation are facing each other we run the risk of being enclosed in a self enclosed and self referential circle that will lose a sense of direction towards God. The liturgy can never be self-affirmation, or self-seeking.

The fullness of life is primarily communicated to us in the Eucharist, where we have the Real Presence of Christ, whilst in the other sacraments we have the grace of Christ. So if the faith in the Real Presence of Christ in the Eucharist starts to dwindle, we will be running the risk that what is left of the beliefs of Catholicism will transform themselves into a disappointing philanthropic ideology condemned to failure, like all the other ideologies that mankind has minted.

---

[6] Jean-Pierre Torrell, O.P., *Christ and Spirituality in St. Thomas Aquinas* (Washington, D.C.: Catholic University of America Press, 2011), p. 7.

The Contraceptive Risk

In the mid-sixties two things happened that show the profound relationship there is between the affirmation of human life and the celebration of a liturgy where the sense of the sacred is carefully preserved. The discussion within the Church about whether a new drug that prevented conception was in accordance or not with the constant teachings of the Magisterium or not happened at the same time that the largest liturgical reform in the history of the Church was taking place. Many of the faithful clearly saw that the acceptance of this new drug was a departure from the constant teaching of the Church. Nevertheless, they thought that if the Church was introducing profound changes in the liturgy, a rite that they had always been taught was unchangeable, it was reasonable to assume that the teachings of the Church on birth control could also change.

More than one prelate in that period took the position that Church teachings on chemical birth control were in the process of changing. Consider the foreword that Richard Cardinal Cushing wrote on 1 August 1964 to a book by Dorothy Dunbar Bromley. He states that he was preparing the people to accept a change "in the traditional presentation of the Church's position on birth control".[7] This position was strengthened when in 1966 the report of the Papal Commission on Birth Control became known as being in favor of accepting artificial birth control.[8] Finally the Church, guided by the Holy Spirit, after a long and painful process,[9] decided to maintain her traditional teachings through the Encyclical Letter of Ven. Paul VI, *Humanæ Vitæ* of 25 July 1968.

Regrettably the winds of doubt were not calmed by the manner in which Msgr. Ferdinando Lambruschini, a professor of Moral Theology

---

[7] Richard Cardinal Cushing, "Foreword" in: Dorothy Dunbar Bromley, *Catholics and Birth Control—Contemporary Views on Doctrine* (New York: The Devin-Adair Company, 1965), p. x.

[8] "Papal Commission on Birth Control—Pastoral Approaches, June 26, 1966" in: Odile M. Liebard, *Love and Sexuality* (Wilmington: McGrath, 1978), pp. 314–20.

[9] "Nel promulgare il 25 di luglio di trent'anni or sono l'Enciclica Humanæ vitæ Paolo VI era ben consapevole del l'impatto che avrebbe avuto. L'iter di formazione e quindi di redazione era stato travagliato e sofferto come nessun altro documento suo e di altri sommi Pontifici;" Gino Concetti, "Una Pietra miliare nella storia della Chiesa per la salvaguardia dell'amore coniugale" in: *L'Osservatore Romano*, 25 July 1998, p. 4.

at the Lateran University, presented the Encyclical to the press on the morning of 29 July 1968 and the way in which many authorities within the Church reacted to this document. Msgr. Lambruschini, even if he clearly stated that the Encyclical was an authentic pronouncement of the Church and that Catholics must give to it a "full and loyal assent", and that "it does not leave the question of regulation of birth in a state of vague uncertainty",[10] also pointed out that *Humanæ Vitæ* was "not irreformable" and that it did not close theological discussion on the subject of birth control.

The concern that these comments caused to the Holy See, as well as other difficult remarks coming from the secular media and from ecclesiastical environments, prompted the stern remarks that were published in *L'Osservatore Romano* a few days afterwards.[11] Cardinal Lopez Trujillo pointed out how this Encyclical suffered the attack of the dissenters and even in certain cases of those who, as teachers, had the mission of defending the Magisterium.[12]

As a consequence of the dissent within the Church on this fundamental teaching of the Magisterium, the climate of uncertainty on the teachings of the Church continued to exist at a pastoral level. This situation was reinforced by the continuation and furtherance of the liturgical reforms. This climate of liturgical uncertainty was strengthened by the end of 1969 with the introduction of the new order of Mass and all the experimentation that went with its application. Many of the unauthorized liturgical experiments that were conducted at that time, and that regrettably are still being conducted today, have brought as a consequence the lessening in the belief in the real presence of Christ in the Eucharist.[13] It is evident that wide scale changes made to the ceremonies and prayers of the Mass, or their removal, might weaken

---

[10] Ralph M. McInerny, *What Went Wrong with Vatican II—The Catholic Crisis Explained* (Manchester, N.H.: Sophia Institute Press, 1998), pp. 50-51.

[11] Federico Alessandrini, Vice-Director of *L'Osservatore Romano*, "La via più ardua" in: *L'Osservatore Romano*, 1 August 1968, p. 1.

[12] Alfonso Lopez Cardinal Trujillo, Presidente del Pontificio Consiglio per la Famiglia, "Un Documento profetico dove si incontrono la Verità che viene da Dio e la sapienza, non alterata né arrogante", in: *L'Osservatore Romano*, 25 July 1998, p. 4.

[13] Speaking of the introduction of the new missal and the norms that were adopted for its application Cardinal Ratzinger points out that, this "introduced a breach into the history of the liturgy whose consequences could only be tragic;" *Milestones*, p. 148.

the presentation of the Faith.[14] At the same time, we have to presume, that the drafters of those changes were acting with the best possible intentions.

Speaking of that historical period more than forty years ago Frederick Wilhelmsen stated that "The empty womb stripped of its child by an abortionist is analogous to the empty altar stripped of its God by the theological abortionist—the man who either denies, or, what is more frequent, ignores or plays down the Real presence of Our Lord Jesus Christ in the Sacrifice of the Mass and in the Blessed Sacrament of the Altar."[15]

Anchored in Reality

The worst fate that can befall man is to have no anchor in reality. That is the fate of the condemned souls in Hell that have lost the possibility of being united with God, who is the ground and support of all reality. It is part and parcel of man's material condition that he needs to be grounded in the objective reality of matter. Man is marked by space and time. He can only relate with ease with things when they are placed in a given place at a given time. A man who believes in the existence of God knows that He is outside of space and time in a pure spiritual realm. But if that were to be his only reference to God, that would be terribly vague and distant. That is one of the reasons for the Incarnation and why God decided to remain with us in the liturgy and in a very concrete way in the Eucharist.

In the liturgy we go from visible things to invisible realities, as we sing in the Christmas Preface (*Missale Romanum* 1962), "by the mystery of the Word made Flesh, we are drawn to the love of the things unseen through Him whom we acknowledge as God now seen by men." As the Church teaches, at the Last Supper, on the night when he was betrayed, our Savior instituted the Eucharistic sacrifice of His Body and Blood. He did this to perpetuate the sacrifice of the Cross through the centuries and as a consequence to entrust to the Church His living presence in the Holy Sacrament of the Altar. A real presence of Christ

---

[14] Cf. Anselm J. Gribbin, *Pope Benedict XVI and the Liturgy—Understanding Recent Liturgical Developments* (Leominster: Gracewing, 2011), p. 72.

[15] Frederick D. Wilhelmsen, "Empty Womb Empty Altar" in: Latin Mass Magazine, v. 2, n. 2, March-April 1993 (pp. 38–41), p. 41.

which at reception of the host fills the soul with grace and a pledge of future glory is received and in this process anchors men in God.

In the midst of the problem of our times only a man who is firmly imbedded in the reality of God, as the source and provident protector of life, will be able to be truly open to the propagation of life. His faith in the Real Presence will give him strength to live up to all the difficulties and challenges that raising a family in our adverse times will present him. This faith will convince him that he will receive over abundant graces in the same way that the Lord provided an over abundant amount of splendid wine to the poor couple of Cana who ran out of wine.

The Holy Sacrifice of the Mass as a Life-giving Sacrifice

The holy Sacrifice of the Mass is a life-giving sacrifice, because through this action of Christ we are given a new life. A failure to accept the sacrificial nature of the Mass and its connection with the supreme sacrifice of the cross distorts the essence of the Mass making our worship 'null and void.' We receive, as a consequence, a new life that recreates the old man wounded by original sin. If through the initial creating action of God we were given the gift of life, through the sacrifice of the cross we can receive a totally new life that has the potential of recreating us. I say "the potential" because it is up to us to accept or reject it. As St. Augustine used to say: "God created us without our consent but He will not save us without our consent." This offer of God is actualized in every celebration of the Mass not because the unique sacrifice of Calvary was insufficient, but because the Lord wanted to offer it to us constantly. In the Eucharist we find the same Christ who died for us on the Cross, who encountered rejection and persecution in the land that God the Father had chosen for His Incarnation. In the same way, Christianity today finds opposition and persecution in our times.

This leads us to see another fundamental link between the Holy Sacrifice of the Mass and the defense of life. The life-giving presence of Christ in the Eucharist is the consequence of the unique sacrifice that happened on Calvary and the un-bloody sacrifice of each single Mass.

As a consequence of both sacrifices Christ is present in the tabernacle. In the same way, life will be present again in the midst of our decaying societies as a consequence of our sacrifices to bring back again a culture of life. But if we celebrate liturgies that tend to obscure the sacrificial nature of the Mass, the drive to make sacrifices to defend the Faith might run the risk of dwindling, and the motivation to make the necessary efforts and sacrifices for raising and educating children might dry up.

The Mass will be perceived as a living and life giving sacrifice if it is seen in the context of a real and organic development in continuity with Tradition.[16] A development where the perception of what is substantial will always grow and become better known. On earth, the liturgy has to give us an anticipation of the eternal liturgy in which we hope to participate. We need a development that will have to avoid both the consequences of our modern technical hurried generation and of sweeping simplifications and abbreviations.[17] But it also will have to avoid an archeological fixation on the early Church, or a fixation on a given historical period like the Baroque. If on the one hand, the liturgy has to be incarnated, on the other hand it has to be otherworldly—as it eventually will become in Paradise. When we speak of the incarnation of the liturgy we have to be particularly careful when we live in deeply secularized cultures, or in cultures that retain many pagan elements.

Persecution and the Influence
of Secular Societies on the Church

Christianity is constantly being persecuted and attacked by the world. It was persecuted by the pagan world in the first centuries and it has to struggle against the post-Christian world of our times. In this opposition it has to suffer martyrdom. A result of this is that a high percentage of those who have been beatified and canonized by Pope John Paul II

---

[16] "Finally, there must be no innovations unless the good of the Church genuinely and certainly requires them; and care must be taken that any new forms adopted should in some way grow organically from forms already existing;" *Sacrosanctum Concilium*, 23.

[17] Cf. Alcuin Reid, *The Organic Development of the Liturgy*, 2nd. ed. (San Francisco: Ignatius Press, 2005), p. 296.

were martyrs.[18] Many of those martyrs suffered under different communist dictatorships—as did the thousand of martyrs of Spain. The millions of victims of communism should not obscure the fact of the growing totalitarian tendencies of the liberal secular societies where we live.

Secular humanism, which at first might look tolerant, is a monster with many faces and is in constant evolution. The current abuses we find in contemporary secular-liberal societies have always existed potentially in an ideology that enshrines relativism; remember all the crimes that were committed during the French Revolution, and all the crimes that are being perpetrated today in the name of the liberty to choose death. Many liberals are ready in the name of false human rights to destroy the true freedom of us all, as we see in recent decisions to deny freedom of conscience to those who oppose abortion.

It is of the essence of liberalism to be relativistic. As Paul VI said in his 1964 Encyclical *Ecclesiam Suam*, "Relativism, which justifies everything and treats all things as of equal value, assails the absolute character of Christian principles" (n. 49). The true liberty of mankind is rooted in the sovereign liberty of God, when man breaks his relationship with God his liberty is at risk, and that is happening in contemporary secular societies. A society that breaks its moorings with God, the Lord and giver of life, will logically turn itself into an anti-life institution. So we have to be careful that our liturgies are not influenced by the secular-humanist environment of the societies in which we happen to live.

We have to be aware of the entrance of the spirit of relativism into the Church, as Cardinal Ratzinger warned us in his homily at the Mass "Pro Eligendo Romano Pontifice" on 18 April 2005.[19] In his Audience

---

[18] Egidio Picucci, "Il Verbo non si è fatto 'carta' ma 'carne'" in: *L'Osservatore Romano, Domenica, Supplemento a L'Osservatore Romano*, 21 March 1999, p. 4.

[19] Cardinal Ratzinger stated: "How many winds of doctrine have we known in recent decades, how many ideological currents, how many ways of thinking. The small boat of the thought of many Christians has often been tossed about by these waves—flung from one extreme to another: from Marxism to liberalism, even to libertinism; from collectivism to radical individualism; from atheism to a vague religious mysticism; from agnosticism to syncretism and so forth. Every day new sects spring up, and what St. Paul says about human deception and the trickery that strives to entice people into error (cf. Eph 4:14), comes true. Today, having a clear faith based on the Creed of the Church is often labelled as fundamentalism. Whereas relativism, that is, letting oneself be 'tossed here and there, carried about by every wind of doctrine', seems the only attitude that

with the Diplomatic Corps Accredited to the Holy See of 22 March 2013 Pope Francis closely followed this important line of Benedict XVI. After denouncing the sufferings of the materially poor he added:

> But there is another form of poverty! It is the spiritual poverty of our time, which afflicts the so-called richer countries particularly seriously. It is what my much-loved predecessor, Benedict XVI, called the "tyranny of relativism", which makes everyone his own criterion and endangers the coexistence of peoples.

The Holy Father then added, with strong emphasis, "But there is no true peace without truth!"

We see how this relativistic spirit has entered into the catechesis in many countries where the truths of the Faith are not taught with clarity, due also to an anti-dogmatic mentality. To condemn this evil spirit that dominates the contemporary world requires a substantial amount of courage because it is the corner stone of the secular society in which we live.

The Church being a society which lives and acts in this world, without being of the world, runs the risk nevertheless that some of its members, even clerics, might be influenced by the world, as the history of the Church constantly shows it. This has happened many times in her history, so we should not be too surprised that it happens again today.

Jean Guitton warned us of this risk when, in 1963 during the Second Session of the Council, he published an article in *L'Osservatore Romano* on the difficult question of the updating of the Church. He underlined that some driven by the concern of pleasing the modern world could fall in the snare of changing the Catholic Faith and be conquered by the world.[20] In his first Encyclical, Paul VI saw this risk and stated in strong words:

> Men committed to the Church are greatly influenced by the climate of the world; so much that a danger bordering almost on vertiginous

---

can cope with modern times. We are building a dictatorship of relativism that does not recognize anything as definitive and whose ultimate goal consists solely of one's own ego and desires."

[20] Jean Guitton, "Approfondire" in: *L'Osservatore Romano*, 6 October 1963. Republished in: *L'Osservatore Romano*, 24 March 1999, p. 5.

confusion and bewilderment can shake the Church's very foundations and lead men to embrace most bizarre ways of thinking, as though the Church should disavow herself and take up the very latest and untried ways of life. (*Ecclesiam Suam*, 26)

Regrettably we can cite numerous instances of how many have not paid heed to this prophetic warning and have been conquered by the world, making thereby a sad caricature of the Faith that they should have proclaimed. It happened with liberation theology which has served as means of introducing Marxism in some sectors of the Catholic Church in particular in Latin America, and has lead to perceive Christianity as an instrument for refashioning the world politically. It happens also, as Michel Schooyans points out, when certain sectors of the Church are in danger of supporting theologically the totalitarian trends of liberalism.[21]

The entrance of the spirit of the world has occurred also with many who have turned the liturgy into a social gathering which seems to celebrate man more than God. This can be seen in many contemporary celebrations of the Eucharist where the priest is facing the congregation. The danger is, as Cardinal Ratzinger notes "that it can make the congregation into a closed circle which is no longer aware of the explosive Trinitarian dynamism which gives the Eucharist its greatness." He adds: "The community does not carry on a dialogue with itself, it is engaged on common journey towards the returning Lord."[22] If both the community and the priest are facing in the same direction this sense of the common journey and common destiny will be clearly expressed. If both the priest and the people face together towards God, we see how "the Church turns to her source of life, the risen and ascended Christ, whose return she desires and expects."[23] If the congregation becomes a closed circle the liturgy runs the risk of becoming centered on man, instead of being centered on God as it should.

---

[21] Michel Schooyans, *The Totalitarian Trends of Liberalism* (St. Louis: Central Bureau, CCVA, 1997), p. 219.

[22] Joseph Cardinal Ratzinger, *Feast of Faith—Approaches to a Theology of the Liturgy* (San Francisco: Ignatius Press, 1986), p. 142.

[23] U. M. Lang, *Turning Towards The Lord—Orientation in Liturgical Prayer* (San Francisco: Ignatius Press, 2004), p. 126.

Liturgy as a Foretaste of Heaven

In the Eucharist we already have a foretaste of the life which will be given to us in its fullness in the Eternal Kingdom. As the Church teaches: "In the earthly liturgy we take part in a foretaste of that heavenly liturgy which is celebrated in the holy city of Jerusalem toward which we journey as pilgrims" (*Sacrosanctum Concilium*, 8).

If we are going to desire something we need, in some way, a foretaste of that thing. This foretaste should be received in accordance with man's nature. It is impossible for human minds to attain in an immaterial way to the contemplation of heavenly things without the use of material means capable of guiding us, in a way proportionate to our nature.[24] We need material things to lead us to spiritual realities. So the liturgy has to be accompanied by proper "accidents", by appropriate external actions that will bring us to know its essence—visible and audible elements that would create a pervading sense of the sacred and of extraordinary beauty that leads to a desire of the supernatural beauty. We cannot experience substances and we can only know of substances by their accidents, externals that are perceivable by our senses which indicate the presence of a substance.

When we receive the Eucharist we perceive the accidents of bread. The externals of the liturgy which we attend might reinforce or weaken our belief in the Real Presence in the Eucharist. If we are attending a Mass that is celebrated with respect and due reverence we will be surrounded by an atmosphere that will help us to elevate our mind and heart to God, but if we attend a Mass that seems to be man centered our heart will remain on the things of this earth.

Man has a natural desire for stability, permanence, and to have a sense that he belongs in a given place which is part and parcel of the stability he desires to achieve in Heaven. Liturgy is given to us through the actions of the Holy Spirit in the Church and the faithful response of the Church. That is why the liturgy should have only the changes that are part of its organic development—development in continuity with the past actions of the Holy Spirit. For that reason the Church teaches that, "Even the supreme authority in the Church may not change the

---

[24] Pseudo-Dionysius, *Heavenly Hierarchy*, 1.

liturgy arbitrarily, but only in the obedience of faith and with religious respect for the mystery of the liturgy" (*Catechism of the Catholic Church*, 1125). We have to reject the cult of change for the sake of change that has very much entered into our society since the time of the Enlightenment. In the same way that man is the steward of the gift of life and has to take care of this gift in accordance with the plans of God, the Church is the administrator of the liturgy and should take care of divine worship in accordance with Tradition, avoiding arbitrary changes.

Perhaps the main motivation to have children is to populate heaven with souls that will enjoy the contemplation of God forever. But how are we going to be moved to do that, if we are not driven by a powerful desire of ourselves going to heaven and how can we desire to go to Heaven if previously we have not received some sort of foretaste of Heaven? If we do not receive this foretaste in the liturgy where else can we find it, in a world that is constantly being deprived of the signs of God's presence?

Traditional Worship and the Defense of Life

There is a clear relationship between traditional worship and a strong commitment to the defense and propagation of life. First and foremost, life, like tradition, is something not of our own making, but a thing which we receive, that is given to us. It is not a new object of our own creation but a reality that pre-exists our own existence. The truths of the Faith are basically a tradition, something that is given to us to be transmitted.

Only the man who has roots has a future. Part and parcel of the problems of modern man are that because he has cut his roots with his own past, he can no longer project himself to the future. Man, without an inherited and objective frame of reference, cannot even make sense of the present in which he lives. To attempt to achieve freedom by escaping from the burdens of tradition tends to result in a new enslavement to a chaotic present.[25] The person who alienates himself from his origins will live in a self-centered existence that in the end will be totally alienating and most likely will provide him a

---

[25] James Hitchcock, *Recovery of the Sacred—Reforming the Reformed Liturgy* (San Francisco: Ignatius Press, 1995), p. 78.

foretaste of hell, where every person will be curved into themselves in a total and definitive self-isolation.

The desire for a fresh start, for a new beginning is very much part and parcel of the nature of man because man has always had a sense of his wounded condition. But if we look in depth at this desire, it is not really a wish for the new, but a desire to return to the pre-existing condition that human nature had before original sin. But if this natural desire is secularized through pride and the erroneous views that the achievements of the past are irrelevant, man has nothing in his hands but a shallow present.

The healthy *Traditio*, grounded on serious theological and historical research, opens the road for developments of a dialogue that can not be interrupted under the risk of leading to the isolation of man and the reduction of the divine to insignificance.[26] God manifested Himself in many ways in the history of mankind. From the day of Pentecost onwards the Holy Spirit has guided the Church in different historical circumstances in a cumulative way. So closing our eyes to the past is closing our vision to the actions of the Holy Spirit. If reason can lead us to believe in a Provident God who takes care of His creatures, our faith and our own historical experience can strengthen this confidence a thousand fold. If God has taken care of His Church in the past through constant action in history, that must strengthen our confidence that He shall do the same in the future.

So a traditional approach to human existence is by definition pro-life because in the measure that we venerate the Faith, the wisdom and the forms of life that we have received from our ancestors, we will be eager to pass on to our children. We will see ourselves as part of a chain that passes and increases a treasure that we have inherited. On addition to that, if we look back and we see how God has protected the generations in the past, we will be confident that He will protect our descendants in the future.

Breaking with the past also creates a situation of spiritual homelessness. The religious person finds a home and shelter in the celebration of liturgical worship with his community. The rites and feasts known to the Christian and his family since childhood are intimately connected

---

[26] Biaggio Amata, "L'importanza della continuità della 'Traditio' nella Liturgia Romana" in: *L'Osservatore Romano*, 18 February 1999, p. 10.

to his faith. For him, an unchanging cult is part of his home. If the worship is constantly changed, even if the substance of the Faith is not changed, he will find himself to be in some way homeless and being without an abode will clearly not stimulate man to have children. It is obvious that the substance does not change but if the accidents change too often there is the temptation to believe that the substance has indeed changed.

We are all committed to defend life, family and the Faith, but this commitment will only bring the expected fruits if we give the reverence that is due to the source of life that is with us on earth. So we have to do everything in our power to be sure that the Holy Sacrifice of the Mass is offered with due reverence.

Implementation of the Social Doctrine of the Church and the Liturgy

There is a clear relationship between the care that we provide for the liturgy and our commitment to the implementation of the social doctrine of the Church. Man by nature is a social being, so it is logical that he should give social and public worship to God. This type of social worship should also lead him to search the common good of society inspired by what he experiences in the liturgy.

Father Paul Marx O.S.B., the founder and for many years the President of Human Life International, wrote his doctoral dissertation on the life and work of Virgil Michel O.S.B. (1888–1938), who was one of the leaders of the liturgical movement in the United States. Michel is famous in some circles for a syllogism that summarizes the focus of the papacies of the early twentieth century: "Pius X tells us that the liturgy is the indispensable source of the true Christian spirit; Pius XI says that the true Christian spirit is indispensable for social regeneration. Hence the conclusion: The liturgy is the indispensable basis of social regeneration."[27]

So it should be evident, as Benedict XVI wrote in *Sacramentum Caritatis*, that "the relationship between the Eucharistic mystery and social

---

[27] Roland Millare, The Forgotten Eucharistic Vision of Virgil Michel, http://www.truthandcharityforum.org/the-forgotten-eucharistic-vision-of-virgil-michel/

commitment must be made explicit" (n. 89). Benedict XVI also reminded us that the saints, and in particular Bl. Teresa of Calcutta, "constantly renewed their capacity of love of neighbor from their encounter with the Eucharistic Lord, and conversely this encounter acquired its realism and depth in their service to others" (*Deus Caritas Est*, 18). Our Eucharistic adoration should lead us to serve the poorest of the poor, who, as Bl. Teresa of Calcutta insisted, were the children in the womb of their mothers who were being menaced by an abortion.

As Benedict XVI taught, "A Eucharist which does not pass over into the concrete practice of love is intrinsically fragmented" (*Deus Caritas Est*, 14). Not only is it fragmented but it is incoherent. We have to build a strong Eucharistic consistency. We cannot praise the Lord in Church and forget our social commitments when we exit from the liturgy into the world:

> Worship pleasing to God can never be a purely private matter, without consequences for our relationships with others: it demands a public witness to our faith. Evidently, this is true for all the baptized, yet it is especially incumbent upon those who, by virtue of their social or political position, must make decisions regarding fundamental values, such as respect for human life, its defense from conception to natural death, the family built upon marriage between a man and a woman, the freedom to educate one's children and the promotion of the common good in all its forms. (*Sacramentum Caritatis*, 83)

The thousands of Catholics engaged in pro-life and pro-family work, are reminded through Pope Benedict's words that the Eucharist is the source of our public witness to the value of life and family.[28] It is the witness and action that we are called to give and to perform when we are sent out at the end of the Mass. So we should ask ourselves: how can we adore Christ as the King of Heaven and Earth in the liturgy if we are not committed to the instauration of His Social Kingship? We should not remain as mere witnesses. We are called to actively change the world, so that it becomes a society ruled by the teachings of the Gospel.

---

[28] Arland K. Nichols, "The Eucharist and Pro-Life Witness—What's the Connection?" http://www.truthandcharityforum.org/the-eucharist-and-pro-life-witness-whats-the-connection/

Conclusion

I would like to finish with a note of hope and, I stress, a hope that is based in reason, nature and in the supernatural hope that we have as Christians.

I believe that the negation of life, both the desire to avoid the coming about of natural life and the denial of the existence of the real presence of Our Eucharistic Lord in the altar and the refusal to pay Him due adoration are going to pass away. Man is created to worship God, so the refusal to adore God goes against nature. Therefore both our lives and the liturgy are naturally oriented towards God.

First and foremost, because as St. Thomas Aquinas stated many times, an unnatural situation cannot last forever because there is nothing more unnatural than denying life or denying the truth. Secondly, because the sin of man can never stop the saving action of God, and sooner rather than later, the saving action of God will rise again unimpeded by the errors and follies of mankind. Thirdly, because we will eventually realize that our duty is, as Cardinal Burke observes, to put into practice the first beatitude and adopt the poverty of spirit that recognizes the Lord as the creator of the world and Lord of history with humility and total trust, and offer Him due worship.[29]

In the meantime, we have to wait and fight the good battle, opening to men access to God through a liturgy that it is pervaded by a sense of adoration. I profoundly believe that in the not too distant future, the desire for truth and for life will be enkindled again in the minds and hearts of man and they will come to worship and venerate the real presence of Christ which comes to us through the Most Holy Sacrifice of the Altar and as consequence mankind will again have a strong desire to grow and multiply, sharing divine and human life.

---

[29] Burke, *Ius divinum e Sacra Liturgia*, p. 36.

20

Liturgical Law in the Mission of the Church

Raymond Leo Cardinal Burke

Prefect of the Supreme Tribunal
of the Apostolic Signatura

Introduction

Fundamental to a deeper understanding of the Sacred Liturgy, the ultimate source and highest realization of the Christian life,[1] is the study
of its juridical structure, that is, of its place in the right relationship
between God and man. Given the antinomian culture in which we
live, a culture which has also exercised a profound influence within
the Church, such a study may seem completely foreign or, at least,
esoteric. Yet, without a proper appreciation of the juridic structure of
the Sacred Liturgy, the Church's greatest treasure is subject to misunderstanding and even abuse. To speak of liturgical law in the mission
of the Church is to address perhaps the humblest aspect of the Sacred
Liturgy, but one which is, at the same time, irreplaceable in man's worship of God.

Given the cultural situation and its effect upon the life of the Church,
I propose to address the subject of the place of liturgical law in the great
mission of the Church by first examining the contemporary ecclesial
context. Then, I will address the fundamental question of the *ius divinum* and Sacred Liturgy, that is, the right relationship of man with God

---

[1] Cf. Sacrosanctum Concilium Œcumenicum Vaticanum II, Constitutio *Sacrosanctum
Concilium*, "De Sacra Liturgia", 4 Decembris 1963, *Acta Apostolicæ Sedis* 56 (1964), 102,
n. 10. ET: *Vatican Council II: The Conciliar and Post Conciliar Documents*, ed. Austin Flannery, O.P. (Collegeville: Liturgical Press, 1975), p. 6, n. 10. [Hereafter, "Flannery"].

and the divine gift of worship. Next, I will treat the place of canon law within the understanding of the *ius divinum*. Lastly, I will take up the question of the particular canonical discipline which governs the Sacred Liturgy.

For an extended treatment of the questions which I now address I recommend a recently published volume by a young Italian canonist, Daniele Nigro, who has devoted himself in particular to the study of liturgical law within the context of the *ius divinum*. The first fruit of his study, which, I anticipate, will continue and develop, is the volume entitled *I diritti di Dio: La liturgia dopo il Vaticano II*.[2] As I note in the Preface to the volume,

> Experiencing both the benefits and the deficits of the liturgical reform after the Second Vatican Ecumenical Council, the author has wished to understand the causes which have contributed to the lack of observance of liturgical law in the post-Conciliar time and therefore to the neglect of the *ius divinum*. The author, however, has not limited himself to understanding simply the causes of such lack of observance, but has devoted himself, at the same time, to discovering the most apt ways to carry out the reform desired in the Conciliar magisterium according to the demands of the *ius divinum*.[3]

The volume in question provides many helpful references to the Magisterium and to pertinent theological and canonical texts and studies.

Contemporary Ecclesial Context

Ven. Paul VI, in his homily on the Solemnity of Ss. Peter and Paul in 1972, reflected at some length upon the situation of the Church in the world during the years immediately following upon the close of the Second Vatican Ecumenical Council. Using an image with a clear

---

[2] Cf. Daniele Nigro, *I diritti di Dio. La liturgia dopo il Vaticano II* (Milano: Sugarco Edizioni, 2012).

[3] "Sperimentando i benefici e le deficienze della riforma liturgica dopo il Concilio Ecumenico Vaticano II, l'autore ha voluto capire le cause che hanno contribuito all'inosservanza del diritto liturgico nel tempo postconciliare e perciò alla trascuratezza dello *ius divinum*. L'autore, però, non si è limitato semplicemente a capire le cause di tale inosservanza, ma si è dedicato allo stesso tempo a scoprire le vie più adatte per adempiere la riforma voluta nel magistero conciliare secondo le esigenze dello *ius divinum*;" ibid., p. 21. ET by the author.

reference to the Sacred Liturgy, he spoke of his sense that "through some fissure the smoke of Satan has entered into the temple of God."[4] He spoke of a pervasive doubt, uncertainty, restlessness, dissatisfaction and dissent, and of a loss of trust in the Church, coupled with a ready placement of trust in secular prophets who speak through the press or social movements, seeking from them the formula for a true life.[5] He noted how this state of uncertainty prevailed within the Church herself, observing that after the Second Vatican Ecumenical Council it was believed that "a day of sunlight had dawned upon the Church", while, in fact, "a day of clouds, storms, darkness, wandering and uncertainty" had arrived.[6] He commented that the Church seemed to seek to dig the abysses deeper rather than to fill them.[7]

Having lived the years of the Council and those immediately following upon it in the minor and major seminary, I recall well the euphoria which accompanied the work of the Council and the reforms which the Council was said to mandate. The effects of this euphoria were perhaps most evident in the reforms introduced into the celebration of the Sacred Liturgy. The difference in the approach to the Sacred Liturgy from my first days in the seminary in the fall of 1962 to the time of the post-Conciliar reforms was, to say the least, extreme, if not violent.

I think, for instance, of what happened to the music employed in sacred worship. Upon entering the minor seminary, I was issued a personal copy of the *Liber Usualis*. During my first years in the seminary, some hours were devoted each week to perfecting the singing of Gregorian chant, especially to learning the proper chants for each Sunday and Feast. Within five years, the *Liber Usualis* was suddenly and totally abandoned, and Gregorian chant was replaced, in great part, by songs developed according to the standards of popular music and accompanied by the guitar and percussion instruments. I have recounted at some length my experience of the radical change in Sacred Music after the

---

[4] "[D]a qualche fessura sia entrato il fumo di Satana nel tempio di Dio." Paulus PP. VI, "Per il nono anniversario dell'Incoronazione di Sua Santità: «Resistite fortes in fide»", 29 giugno 1972, in: *Insegnamenti di Paolo VI*, vol. 10 (Tipografia Poliglotta Vaticana, 1973), p. 707. ET by the author.

[5] Cf. ibid., pp. 707–708.

[6] "[U]na giornata di sole per la storia della Chiesa . . . una giornata di nuvole, di tempesta, di buio, di ricerca, di incertezza;" ibid., p. 708. ET by the author.

[7] Cf. ibid., p. 708.

Council elsewhere.[8] What happened to Sacred Music happened also to the very Rite of the Mass, to the other sacred rites, and indeed to every aspect of the Sacred Liturgy.

What was the cause of such a radical, even violent, change? There was a sense that what had gone before the Council had been a gradual corruption of the purity of the Church in the first centuries of her existence. What Pope Benedict XVI has described as the battle between the hermeneutic of discontinuity and rupture and the hermeneutic of reform in continuity ensued. In other words, the liturgical reform was viewed as the repudiation of centuries of liturgical practice, in order to establish a new practice which was said to recapture the purity of the practice of the early Church. What the Conciliar teaching requested, however, was a reform within the unbroken continuity of the Tradition.

In his first Christmas address to the Roman Curia in December of 2005, which also marked the fortieth anniversary of the close of the Second Vatican Ecumenical Council, Pope Benedict XVI reflected at length upon the struggle between the two interpretations of the Council, the "hermeneutic of discontinuity and rupture" and the "hermeneutic of reform."[9] The hermeneutic of discontinuity and rupture, in the words of Pope Benedict XVI, "risks ending in a split between the pre-conciliar Church and the post-conciliar Church" and, thereby, justifies an interpretation of the Council not based upon the texts approved by the Council Fathers but upon what is called "the true spirit of the Council", which is discovered "in the impulses toward the new that are contained in the texts."[10]

---

[8] See my contribution to the Proceedings of the Third Fota International Liturgical Conference, 2010: Raymond Cardinal Burke, "The new evangelization and sacred music: the unbroken continuity of holiness, beauty and universality", in: Janet Rutherford ed., *Benedict XVI and Beauty in Sacred Music* (Dublin: Four Courts Press, 2012), (pp. 24–40), pp. 24–26.

[9] "[E]rmeneutica della discontinuità e della rottura . . . ermeneutica della riforma." Benedictus PP. XVI, Allocutio "Ad Romanam Curiam ob omina natalicia", 22 Decembris 2005, *Acta Apostolicæ Sedis* 98 (2006), p. 46. ET: Pope Benedict XVI, "Address of His Holiness Benedict XVI to the Roman Curia Offering Them His Christmas Greetings", 22 December 2005, *L'Osservatore Romano—Weekly Edition in English*, 4 January 2006, p. 5.

[10] "[R]ischia di finire in una rottura tra Chiesa preconciliare e Chiesa postconciliare . . . il vero spirito del Concilio . . . negli slanci verso il nuovo che sono sottesi ai testi;" ibid., p. 46. ET: ibid., p. 5.

The fruit of the "hermeneutic of discontinuity and rupture" is described by Pope Benedict XVI in these words:

> The nature of a Council as such is therefore basically misunderstood. In this way, it is considered as a sort of constituent that eliminates an old constitution and creates a new one. However, the Constituent Assembly needs a mandatory and then confirmation by the mandatory, in other words, the people the constitution must serve. The Fathers had no such mandate and no one had ever given them one; nor could anyone have given them one because the essential constitution of the Church comes from the Lord and was given to us so that we might attain eternal life and, starting from this perspective, be able to illuminate life in time and time itself.[11]

In the years following the Second Vatican Ecumenical Council, the hermeneutic of rupture was manifested, in a most striking way, in the betrayal of the Council's liturgical reform by means of a manipulation of the divine action of the liturgy to express the individual personality of the celebrant and of the congregation, and even to advance various human agendas, completely alien to the divine action of the Sacred Liturgy.

Already, in 1972, Pope Paul VI had the sense that some foreign, indeed diabolically hostile element, had entered into the very sanctuaries of the Church. Pope Paul VI's earlier mentioned lament pointed to a rupture in the Church caused by the failure to see the organic nature of her life, which receives from Christ, faithfully down the centuries, the gift of "worship in spirit and truth" (Jn 4:24). This rupture is embodied in the perception that everything which had happened in the Church after the time of the first disciples was somehow a corruption and that the Church must, therefore, be created *ex novo* by returning to the purity of life of the early ecclesial community. This way of thinking is profoundly naïve, for it fails to take account of the grave internal

---

[11] "Con ciò, però, si fraintende in radice la natura di un Concilio come tale. In questo modo, esso viene considerato come una specie di Costituente, che elimina una costituzione vecchia e ne crea una nuova. Ma la Costituente ha bisogno di un mandante e poi di una conferma da parte del mandante, cioè del popolo al quale la costituzione deve servire. I Padri non avevano un tale mandato e nessuno lo aveva mai dato loro; nessuno, del resto, poteva darlo, perché la costituzione essenziale della Chiesa viene dal Signore e ci è stata data affinché noi possiamo raggiungere la vita eterna e, partendo da questa prospettiva, siamo in grado di illuminare anche la vita nel tempo e il tempo stesso;" ibid., p. 46. ET: ibid., p. 5.

struggles which the Church experienced from the beginning and about which St. Luke, in the Acts of the Apostles, and Ss. Paul, John, Peter and James, in their letters, give ample testimony. In short, the rupture is caused by an abandonment of the discipline which permits us to see how the Holy Spirit has been unceasingly at work, throughout the Christian centuries, enabling man to offer true worship to God, that is, the worship which God Himself teaches us to offer in the Church.

The post-Conciliar period and accompanying euphoria manifested a general disdain for the Church's perennial discipline. There quickly developed the sense that a new age of freedom and love had been granted to the Church, in which it would be incongruous to insist upon the application of canon law and specifically of liturgical law. The matter was further complicated by the announcement of the reform of the Code of Canon Law which St. John XXIII made when he announced the convocation of the Second Vatican Ecumenical Council and of a Synod for the Diocese of Rome.[12] Clearly, the actual work of the revision of the Code of Canon Law had to wait upon the work of the Council.

In the meantime, the cultural revolution, dramatically manifested by the student riots of 1968 in Paris and profoundly characterized by a general distrust of and rebellion against all forms of authority, also had its effect upon the Church, fueling a disdain for her perennial discipline. In any case, there developed the sense that much of the Church's discipline in force up to the time of the Council was no longer relevant and that, until a new Code of Canon Law would be promulgated, a great deal of freedom could be exercised in the various aspects of the Church's life. Given the radical reform of the liturgical rites, a certain antinomian mentality easily led to a great deal of liturgical experimentation, which was completely divorced from the discipline which had formerly governed the celebration of the Sacred Liturgy.

---

[12] Cf. Ioannes PP. XXIII, Solemnis Allocutio, "In cœnobio monachorum Benedictinorum ad S. Pauli Extra Moenia, post Missarum sollemnia, quibus Beatissimus Pater in Patriarchali Basilica Ostiensi interfuerat", 25 Ianuarii 1959, *Acta Apostolicæ Sedis* 51 (1959), pp. 68–69. ET: "Pope John's Announcement of Ecumenical Council", in: Floyd Anderson ed., *Council Daybook: Vatican II, Sessions 1 and 2* (Washington, D.C.: National Catholic Welfare Conference, 1965), pp. 1–2.

Ius Divinum and the Sacred Liturgy

To speak of the *ius divinum*, the divine right, is, in the most simple terms, to speak of the right relationship between God and His creation, especially man, the only earthly creature created in the image of God Himself. It is clear that such discourse has to do, first of all, with the Sacred Liturgy, as the highest and most perfect expression of the relationship between God and man. There is no aspect of the life of the Church in which the truth about God's relationship with man should be more visible than in the Sacred Liturgy.

I speak, above all, of the relationship of the *ius divinum* to the celebration of the Holy Eucharist, in which, in the words of the Decree on the Life and Ministry of Priests of the Second Vatican Ecumenical Council, drawing upon a text of St. Thomas Aquinas, "is contained the whole spiritual good of the Church, namely Christ Himself our Pasch and the living bread which gives life to men through His flesh— that flesh which is given life and gives life through the Holy Spirit."[13] In the celebration of the Holy Eucharist, in the words of the same Decree, "men are invited and led to offer themselves, their works and all creation with Christ."[14] The Holy Eucharist, therefore, is the fundamental and preeminent manifestation of the relationship of the *ius divinum* and the Sacred Liturgy. I offer now a brief treatment of this relationship as it is articulated in the Sacred Scriptures and the Tradition.[15]

In recent years, the discussion of the relationship between the *ius divinum* and the Sacred Liturgy has been rarely engaged. It in fact can cause wonderment for some to hear divine right and the Sacred Liturgy

---

[13] "[T]otum bonum spirituale Ecclesiæ continetur, ipse scilicet Christus, Pascha nostrum panisque vivus per Carnem suam Spiritu Sancto vivificatam et vivificantem vitam præstans hominibus." Concilium Œcumenicum Vaticanum II, Decretum *Presbyterorum Ordinis*, "De Presbyterorum ministerio et vita", 7 Decembris 1965, *Acta Apostolicæ Sedis* 58 (1966), p. 997, n. 5. ET: Flannery, p. 871.

[14] "[Q]ui ita invitantur et adducuntur ad seipsos, suos labores cunctasque res creatas una cum Ipso offerendos" ibid. ET: ibid, p. 871.

[15] A more detailed treatment is found in my presentation at the Fourth Fota International Liturgical Conference in 2011; cf. Raymond Leo Cardinal Burke, "*Ius Divinum* and the Sacred Liturgy", in: Janet E. Rutherford and James O'Brien eds., *Benedict XVI and the Roman Missal* (Dublin: Four Courts Press, 2013), pp. 21–39.

named in the same context. In the time since the Second Vatican Ecumenical Council, but certainly not because of the teaching of the Council, there has been an exaggerated attention to the human aspect of the Sacred Liturgy, which has overlooked the essence of the Sacred Liturgy as the encounter of God with man by means of sacramental signs, that is, as the direct action of the glorious Christ in the Church to give to man the grace of the Holy Spirit.

The canonical discipline in what pertains to the Sacred Liturgy is securely grounded in the theological reality of the Church. In other words, it is at the service of the objective order of our life in Christ. In order to understand the deepest significance of the canonical norms which govern the Sacred Liturgy, it is first necessary to understand, at least in its essentials, the objective relationship of the *ius divinum* to the Sacred Liturgy.

Joseph Cardinal Ratzinger, in his classic work *The Spirit of the Liturgy*, reminded us of the relationship of man's worship of God to his life in general, above all to the moral rectitude of his life. He observed:

> Ultimately, it is the very life of man, man himself as living righteously, that is the true worship of God, but life only becomes real life when it receives its form from looking toward God. Cult exists in order to communicate this vision and to give life in such a way that glory is given to God.[16]

The right understanding of the Sacred Liturgy is, in fact, the key to the understanding of every dimension of life.

That right understanding respects the divine law or right (*ius divinum*), the right relationship of man with God, which is the foundation of all law. Cardinal Ratzinger concluded:

> When human affairs are so ordered that there is no recognition of God, there is a belittling of man. That is why, in the final analysis, worship and law cannot be completely separated from each other.

---

[16] "Letzlich ist das Leben des Menschen selbst, der recht lebende Mensch die wahre Anbetung Gottes, aber das Leben wird zu wirklichem Leben nur, wenn es seine Form aus dem Blick auf Gott hin empfängt. Der Kult ist dazu da, diesen Blick zu vermitteln und so Leben zu geben, das Ehre wird für Gott." Joseph Ratzinger, *Theologie der Liturgie: Die sakramentale Begründung christlicher Existenz*, Gesammelte Schriften, Band 11 (Freiburg: Herder, 2008), p. 36. ET: Joseph Cardinal Ratzinger, John Saward trans., *The Spirit of the Liturgy* (San Francisco: Ignatius Press, 2000), p. 18.

God has a right to a response from man, to man himself, and where that right of God totally disappears, the order of law among men is dissolved, because there is no cornerstone to keep the whole structure together.[17]

Reflecting on the relationship of law and sacred worship, Cardinal Ratzinger observed:

Worship, that is, the right kind of cult, of relationship with God, is essential for the right kind of human existence in the world. It is so precisely because it reaches beyond everyday life. Worship gives us a share in heaven's mode of existence, in the world of God, and allows light to fall from that divine world into ours. . . . It lays hold in advance of a more perfect life and, in so doing, gives our present life its proper measure.[18]

Cardinal Ratzinger's reflection on the *lex orandi* and the *lex vivendi* points to the fundamental importance of the study of the *ius divinum* in its relationship to the Sacred Liturgy for a right understanding of life in Christ in the Church and in the world.

When God restored the covenantal relationship of love which had been radically broken by the sin of Adam and Eve, He founded it on the Decalogue, the Ten Commandments. The first three of the Commandments, in fact, express the essence of the *ius divinum*, the right of God to be recognized as the Creator of the world and the Lord of history and, therefore, as the exclusive recipient of the worship of man.

One recalls how Satan tempted Adam and Eve to sin against the one and only commandment which the Lord had given to them, that is, "of the fruit of the tree of the knowledge of good and evil you shall not

---

[17] "Eine Ordnung der menschlichen Dinge, die Gott nicht kennt, verkleinert den Menschen. Darum sind letzlich auch Kult und Recht nicht gänzlich voneinander zu trennen: Gott hat ein Recht auf die Antwort des Menschen, auf den Menschen selbst, und wo dieses Recht Gottes gänzlich verschwindet, löst sich auch die menschliche Rechtsordnung auf, weil ihr der Eckstein fehlt, der das Ganze zusammenhält;" ibid., pp. 36–37. ET: ibid., p. 19.

[18] "Anbetung, die richtige Weise des Kultes, der Gottesbeziehung, ist konstitutiv für die rechte menschliche Existenz in der Welt; sie ist es gerade dadurch, dass sie über das Leben im Alltag hinausreicht, indem sie uns an der Existenzweise des »Himmels«, der Welt Gottes, beteiligt und damit das Licht der göttlichen Welt in die unsrige fallen lässt. . . . Er greift voraus auf ein endgültigeres Leben und gibt gerade so dem gegenwärtigen Leben sein Maß;" ibid., p. 38. ET: ibid., p. 21.

eat, for in the day that you eat of it you shall die" (Gen 2:17; cf. Gen 3:3). He told Eve: "You will not die. For God knows that when you eat of it your eyes will be opened, and you will be like God, knowing good and evil" (Gen 3:4–5). Our first parents were led into a lie by Satan, not recognizing God as the source of their being and of their every good but taking on the pretense of being equal to God. The first three commandments of the Decalogue reestablish the just relationship between God and man, based on the truth and, therefore, on divine right. The other seven commandments derive from these first commandments which establish and safeguard the divine right and, thereby, the foundation of man's relationship with God. In other words, the worship of God "in spirit and truth" (Jn 4:24) is, at the same time, the sanctification of the people.

In the Code of the Covenant, which follows the declaration of the Decalogue, the first attention is dedicated to divine worship and specifically to the altar. God, recalling the truth that He has come from heaven to speak to His children, commands: "An altar of earth you shall make for me and sacrifice on it your burnt offerings and your peace offerings, your sheep and your oxen; in every place where I cause my name to be remembered I will come to you and bless you" (Ex 20:24). After the description of the ratification of the covenant, detailed norms for divine worship are listed (cf. Gen 25:1–31, 18). Following upon the account of God's offering of the covenant and of its ratification in the book of Exodus, the book of Leviticus contains the detailed norms for the priests and Levites, in order that they might fulfill their responsibility for divine worship and, therefore, for the sanctification of the people.

This brief look at the content of the covenant between God and man underlines the fundamental principle of the covenant relationship. It is the *ius divinum*, the right of God to receive the worship of man in the manner that God desires and commands. Divine worship and the sanctification of the people, which is its fruit, are ordained by God Himself. Divine worship is not the invention of man, but the gift of God to man, by which God makes it possible for man to offer "the sacrifice of communion" with Him. Clearly, unless man recognizes and respects the *ius divinum* in what pertains to the Sacred Liturgy, he fails to recognize and respect the truth about creation and, above all, about himself. The failure to recognize and respect the *ius divinum* leads to idolatry, as the story of the Golden Calf demonstrates (cf. Ex 32). Cardinal Ratzinger, in fact, articulated the two causes of the act of idolatry: first, man's refusal to recognize God as other and his subsequent attempt to reduce God to man's dimensions; and, second, man's pretense of creating his own worship, instead of worshiping in accord with the *ius divinum*.[19]

In the Sermon on the Mount, in which Our Lord Jesus communicated the Law of the New Covenant, the first Beatitude is the poverty of spirit which recognizes the Lord as the source of being itself and of every good: "Blessed are the poor in spirit, for theirs is the kingdom of heaven" (Mt 5:3). All of the other Beatitudes depend upon this first and fundamental recognition of our relationship with God and the effective expression of the same. Through poverty of spirit, the faithful offer themselves completely to God, according to His teaching and discipline. They lose themselves in the rites of the Sacred Liturgy to discover Christ Himself at work on their behalf, for their eternal salvation.

After having announced the Beatitudes as the law of the new covenant and after having exhorted the disciples to be "the salt of the earth" and "the light of the world", so that others, seeing the holiness of the people, may give "glory to [their] Father who is in heaven" (Mt 5:16), the Lord declared His mission in what pertains to the Law:

> Think not that I have come to abolish the law and the prophets; I have come not to abolish them but to fulfil them. For truly, I say to you, till heaven and earth pass away, not an iota, not a dot, will pass from the law until all is accomplished. Whoever then relaxes one of the least of these commandments and teaches men so, shall be called least in the kingdom of heaven; but he who does them and teaches them shall be called great in the kingdom of heaven. (Mt 5:17–19)

The words of the Lord confirm the fundamental service of the Law, which is to honor and to safeguard the *ius divinum*, the divine right, and thereby to honor and safeguard the order written by God in His creation and, above all, upon every human heart.

All of the norms of the law are directed to the just relationship between God and man, upon which depends the salvation of the world,

---

[19] Cf. ibid., pp. 39–40. ET: ibid., pp. 22–23.

and thus they must be respected as the commandment of God and not the invention of man. Otherwise, the Law of God is corrupted for human purposes. After having declared the holiness of the Law, the Lord exhorted the disciples with these words: "For I tell you, unless your righteousness exceeds that of the scribes and Pharisees, you will never enter the kingdom of heaven" (Mt 5:20). Only by observing and honoring the divine right that God be known, adored, and served as He desires and commands does man find his happiness in this life and in the life to come.

When Our Lord encountered the Samaritan woman at the well of Jacob, He instructed her on the true worship of God, the adoration of God "in spirit and truth" (Jn 4:23–24). It is clear from His teaching that faith in Him as Messiah, as God the Son made man, is expressed first of all in the worship owed to God. At the Last Supper, when Our Lord instituted the Eucharistic Sacrifice, He gave directly the command: "Do this in remembrance of me. . . . Do this, as often as you drink it, in remembrance of me" (1 Cor 11:24–25). Thus, the Holy Eucharist, the worship offered to God "in spirit and truth", is not an invention of man, but a gift of God to man.

I shall now briefly review some texts of the Magisterium which indicate the irreplaceable relationship between divine right and liturgical law. The Council of Trent, in treating the question of doctrine on Holy Communion "*sub utraque specie et parvulorum* (under both species and of children)", declared that the Church from the beginning has had the authority to give dispositions regarding the administration of the Sacraments, but that she has no authority to touch in any manner the substance of the Sacraments. Here is the text from Session 19 of the Council:

> Furthermore, [the Holy Council] declares that, in the administration of the sacraments—provided their substance is preserved—there has always been in the Church that power to determine or modify what she judged more expedient for the benefit of those receiving the sacraments or for the reverence due to the sacraments themselves— according to the diversity of circumstances, times, and places.[20]

---

[20] "Præterea declarat, hanc potestatem perpetuo in Ecclesia fuisse, ut in sacramentorum dispensatione, salva illorum substantia, ea statueret vel mutaret, quæ suscipientium utilitati seu ipsorum sacramentorum venerationi, pro rerum, temporum et locorum vari-

The substance of the Sacraments cannot be touched because they are instituted by Christ and entrusted to the Church, as the worship of God the Father "in spirit and truth" (Jn 4:24).

The Second Vatican Ecumenical Council has repeated the constant teaching on the exclusive authority of the Church for the right discipline of the Sacred Liturgy, distinguishing two parts of the liturgy: "unchangeable elements divinely instituted" and "elements subject to change", which "not only may be changed but ought to be changed with the passage of time, if they have suffered from the intrusion of anything out of harmony with the inner nature of the liturgy or have become less suitable."[21] Regarding the elements susceptible to change, the Council enunciated clear rules, namely:

> 22. (1) Regulation of the Sacred Liturgy depends solely on the authority of the Church, that is, on the Apostolic See, and, as laws may determine, on the bishop.
>
> (2) In virtue of power conceded by law, the regulation of the liturgy within certain defined limits belongs also to various kinds of bishops' conferences, legitimately established, with competence in given territories.
>
> (3) Therefore no other person, not even a priest, may add, remove, or change anything in the liturgy on his own authority.[22]

The Sacred Liturgy is the worship owed to God, as He Himself has instituted it. It cannot, as the Church has always taught, be reduced to the activity of any individual, not even a priest, but must be governed,

---

etate, magis expedire iudicaret;" Heinrich Denzinger; Peter Hünermann, Robert Fastiggi and Anne Nash eds., *Enchiridion symbolorum definitionem et declarationem de rebus fidei et morum*, 43rd ed., Latin-English (San Francisco: Ignatius Press, 2012), n. 1728, p. 415.

[21] "[P]arte immutabili, utpote divinitus instituta, et partibus mutationi obnoxiis, quæ decursu temporum variare possunt vel etiam debent, si in eas forte irrepserint quæ minus bene ipsius Liturgiæ intimae naturæ respondeant, vel minus aptæ factæ sint." Sacrosanctum Concilium Œcumenicum Vaticanum II, Constitutio *Sacrosanctum Concilium*, "De Sacra Liturgia", 4 decembris 1963, *Acta Apostolicæ Sedis* 56 (1964), pp. 105–106, n. 21. ET: Flannery, p. 9.

[22] "22. §1. Sacræ Liturgiæ moderatio ab Ecclesiæ auctoritate unice pendet: quæ quidem est apud Apostolicam Sedem et, ad normam iuris, apud Episcopum. §2. Ex potestate a iure concessa, rei liturgicæ moderatio inter limites statutos pertinet quoque ad competentes varii generis territoriales Episcoporum cœtus legitime constitutos. §3. Quapropter nemo omnino alius, etiamsi sit sacerdos, quidquam proprio marte in Liturgia addat, demat, aut mutet;" ibid., p. 106, n. 22. ET: ibid., pp. 9–10.

with respect for the divine right, by the supreme authority, that is, by the Roman Pontiff and by the bishops in communion with him.

St. John Paul II underlined the divine right in what pertains to the Sacrament of Penance in his first Encyclical Letter *Redemptor Hominis*. Confronting a certain tendency to substitute communal forms of penance and conversion for individual confession, he called to mind that the act of conversion has always to be personal. Having noted the right of the individual penitent "to a more personal encounter"[23] with Christ in the Sacrament of Penance, the Holy Father quickly added that it is also a question of "a right on Christ's part with regard to every human being redeemed by him."[24]

The Holy Father continued, explaining the right and also the duty of the Church to insist on the observance of the divine right:

> His right to meet each one of us in that key moment in the soul's life constituted by the moment of conversion and forgiveness. By guarding the sacrament of Penance, the Church expressly affirms her faith in the mystery of the Redemption as a living and life-giving reality that fits in with man's inward truth, with human guilt and also with the desires of the human conscience. "Blessed are those who hunger and thirst for righteousness, for they shall be satisfied." The sacrament of Penance is the means to satisfy man with the righteousness that comes from the Redeemer himself.[25]

The solicitude of the Church for the correct celebration of the Sacrament of Penance corresponds to the divine right, to the right of Christ.

---

[23] "[A]d congressionem, uniuscuiusque hominis magis propriam, cum Christo Cruci affixo. . . ." Ioannes Paulus PP. II, Litteræ Encyclicæ *Redemptor Hominis*, "Pontificali eius ministerio ineunte", 4 martii 1979, *Acta Apostolicæ Sedis* 76 (1979), p. 314, n. 20. ET: Pope John Paul II, *Encyclicals* (Trivandrum: Carmel International Publishing House, 2005), p. 1115.

[24] "[I]us Christi est, quod is habet erga quemque hominem a se redemptum;" ibid.; ET: ibid.

[25] "Est nempe ius conveniendi unumquemque nostrum in illo decretorio tempore vitæ animæ, quod est momentum conversionis et condonationis. Ecclesia Sacramento Pænitentiæ custodiendo profitetur aperte fidem suam in Redemptionis mysterium, ut in rem veram et vivificantem, quæ etiam cum interiore veritate hominis congruit, cum humano culpæ sensu et etiam cum humanæ conscientiæ desideriis. «Beati, qui esuriunt et sitiunt iustitiam, quoniam ipsi saturabuntur». Pænitentiæ porro Sacramentum est instrumentum, quo homo illa iustitia satietur, quæ ex eodem Redemptore emanat;" ibid., pp. 314–15; ET: ibid., p. 1115.

The discipline of the Sacrament of Penance ought always to correspond to the objective relationship between God and man which is constituted by the unceasing love of God for all men, without boundary, consummated in the Passion, Death, Resurrection and Ascension of Christ.

Canon Law and the *Ius Divinum*

Pope John Paul II pursued with vigor the revision of the 1917 Code of Canon Law, first announced by Pope John XXIII. As Roman Pontiff and also as a Father of the Second Vatican Ecumenical Council, he had no question that the perennial discipline of the Church must be addressed to the present time. He understood that the Council did not intend the abandonment of the Church's discipline but rather a new appreciation of it in the context of contemporary challenges. In the Apostolic Constitution *Sacræ Disciplinæ Leges*, with which he, as Supreme Legislator in the Church, promulgated the 1983 Code of Canon Law, Pope John Paul II wrote:

> Turning our minds today to the beginning of this long journey [of the revision of the Code of Canon Law], to that January 25, 1959 ["when my predecessor of happy memory, John XXIII, announced for the first time his decision to reform the existing *corpus* of canonical legislation which had been promulgated on the feast of Pentecost in year 1917"] and to John XXIII himself who initiated the revision of the Code, I must recognize that this Code derives from one and the same intention, the renewal of Christian living. From such an intention, in fact, the entire work of the council drew its norms and its direction.[26]

---

[26] "Mentem autem hodie convertentes ad exordium illius itineris [ad Codicem Iuris Canonici recognoscendum], hoc est ad diem illam XXV Ianuarii anno MCMLIX ["qua Decessor Noster fel. rec. Ioannes XXIII primum publice nuntiavit captum abs se consilium reformandi vigens Corpus legum canonicarum, quod anno MCMXVII, in sollemnitate Pentecostes, fuerat promulgatum"], atque ad ipsum Ioannem XXIII, Codicis recognitionis initiatorem, fateri debemus hunc Codicem ad uno eodemque proposito profluxisse, rei christianæ scilicet restaurandæ; a quo quidem proposito totum Concilii opus suas normas suumque ductum præsertim accepit." Ioannes Paulus PP. II, Constitutio Apostolica *Sacræ Disciplinæ Leges*, 25 Ianuarii 1983, *Acta Apostolicæ Sedis* 75, pars II (1983), p. viii (cf. p. vii). ET: Canon Law Society of America, *Code of Canon Law: Latin-English Edition*, New English Translation (Washington, D.C.: Canon Law Society of America, 1998), p. xxviii (cf. p. xxvii).

These words point to the essential service of canon law in the life of the Church.

The saintly Pontiff described the nature of canon law, indicating its organic development from God's first covenant with His holy people. He recalled "the distant patrimony of law contained in the books of the Old and New Testament from which is derived the whole juridical-legislative tradition of the Church, as from its first source."[27] In particular, he reminded the Church how Christ Himself declared that He had not come to abolish the law but to bring it to completion, teaching us that it is, in fact, the discipline of the law which opens the way to freedom in loving God and our neighbor. He observed: "Thus the writings of the New Testament enable us to understand even better the importance of discipline and make us see better how it is more closely connected with the saving character of the evangelical message itself."[28]

Pope John Paul II then articulated the purpose of canon law, that is, the service of the Faith and of grace. He noted that, far from hindering the living of our life in Christ, canonical discipline safeguards and fosters our Christian life. He declared:

> Its purpose is rather to create such an order in the ecclesial society that, while assigning the primacy to love, grace and charisms, it at the same time renders their organic development easier in the life of both the ecclesial society and the individual persons who belong to it.[29]

As such, canon law can never be in conflict with the Church's doctrine but is, in the words of Pope John Paul II, "extremely necessary for the Church."[30]

---

[27] "[L]onginqua illa hereditas iuris, quæ in libris Veteris et Novi Testamenti continetur, ex qua tota traditio iuridica et legifera Ecclesiæ, tamquam a suo primo fonte, originem ducit." Ibid., p. x. ET: ibid., p. xxix.

[28] "Sic Novi Testamenti scripta sinunt ut nos multo magis percipiamus hoc ipsum disciplinæ momentum, utque ac melius intellegere valeamus vincula, quæ illud arctiore modo coniungunt cum indole salvifica ipsius Evangelii doctrinæ." Ibid., pp. x–xi. ET: ibid., p. xxix.

[29] "Codex eo potius spectat, ut talem gignat ordinem in ecclesiali societate, qui, præcipuas tribuens partes amori, gratiæ atque charismati, eodem tempore faciliorem reddat ordinatam eorum progressionem in vita sive ecclesialis societatis, sive etiam singulorum hominum, qui ad illam pertinent." Ibid., p. xi. ET: ibid., pp. xxix–xxx.

[30] "Ecclesiæ omnino necessarius est." Ibid., p. xii. ET: ibid., p. xxxi.

The teaching of the Church, in fact, is faithfully expressed in the daily life of the Church, as a body and in her individual members, through obedience to the discipline handed down by the canonical Tradition.[31] The Pope indicated four ways in which the Church's discipline is a necessary complement to her doctrine, declaring:

> Since the Church is organized as a social and visible structure, it must also have norms: in order that its hierarchical and organic structure be visible; in order that the exercise of the functions divinely entrusted to it, especially that of sacred power and of the administration of the sacraments, may be adequately organized; in order that the mutual relations of the faithful may be regulated according to justice based upon charity, with the rights of individuals guaranteed and well-defined; in order, finally, that common initiatives undertaken to live a Christian life ever more perfectly may be sustained, strengthened and fostered by canonical norms.[32]

Because of the essential service of canon law to the life of the Church, Pope John Paul II reminded the Church that "by their very nature canonical laws are to be observed", and, to that end, "the wording of the norms should be accurate" and "based on solid juridical, canonical and theological foundations."[33]

Liturgical Law

In the canonical tradition, the discipline of the worship owed to God has been regulated by the highest authority, that is, the Apostolic See. Can. 1247 of the Pio-Benedictine Code enunciated the perennial

---

[31] Cf. ibid., p. xi. ET: ibid., p. xxx.

[32] "Cum ad modum etiam socialis visibilisque compaginis sit constituta, ipsa normis indiget, ut eius hierarchica et organica structura adspectabilis fiat, ut exercitium munerum ipsi divinitus creditorum, sacræ præsertim potestatis et administrationis sacramentorum rite ordinetur, ut secundum iustitiam in caritate innixam mutuæ christifidelium necessitudines componantur, singulorum iuribus in tuto positis atque definitis, ut denique communia incepta, quæ ad christianam vitam perfectius usque vivendam suscipiuntur, per leges canonicas fulciantur, muniantur ac promoveantur." Ibid., pp. xii–xiii. ET: ibid., p. xxxi.

[33] "[C]anonicæ leges suapte natura observantiam exigent . . . accurate fieret normarum expressio . . . in solido iuridico, canonico ac theologico fundamento inniterentur." Ibid., p. xiii. ET: ibid., p. xxxi.

discipline of the Church: "It belongs only to the Apostolic See to order Sacred Liturgy and to approve liturgical books."[34] The Code also enunciated the responsibility of the bishops to exercise vigilance over the correct observance of the norms regarding divine worship[35] and against the introduction of abuses into ecclesiastical discipline, especially in what pertains to divine worship and the Sacred Liturgy.[36]

The present Code, promulgated by Pope John Paul II on January 25, 1983, enunciates in can. 838 the discipline formulated in the Second Vatican Ecumenical Council. The second part of the canon reads:

> It is for the Apostolic See to order the Sacred Liturgy of the universal Church, publish liturgical books and review their translations in vernacular languages, and exercise vigilance that liturgical regulations are observed faithfully everywhere.[37]

In the second paragraph of can. 392 of the 1983 Code, the responsibility of the bishop to "promote the common discipline of the whole Church and therefore to urge the observance of all ecclesiastical laws"[38] is treated. It reads:

> He is to exercise vigilance so that abuses do not creep into ecclesiastical discipline, especially regarding the ministry of the word, the celebration of the sacraments and sacramentals, the worship of God and the veneration of the saints, and the administration of goods.[39]

The 1983 Code puts together the various objects of the vigilance of the bishop over ecclesiastical discipline, and thus diminishes a bit the

---

[34] "Unius Apostolicæ Sedis est tum sacram ordinare liturgiam, tum liturgicos approbare libros." *Codex Iuris Canonici Pii X Pontificis Maximi iussu digestus Benedicti Papæ XV auctoritate promulgatus*, can. 1257. ET: Edward N. Peters ed., *The 1917 or Pio-Benedictine Code of Canon Law in English Translation* (San Francisco: Ignatius Press, 2001), p. 426.

[35] Cf. ibid., can. 1261, §1.

[36] Cf. ibid., can. 336, §2.

[37] "Apostolicæ Sedis est sacram liturgiam Ecclesiæ universæ ordinare, libros liturgicos edere eorumque versiones in linguas vernaculas recognoscere, necnon advigilare ut ordinationes liturgicæ ubique fideliter observentur." *Codex Iuris Canonici auctoritate Ioannis Pauli PP. II promulgatus*, 25 ianuarii 1983, *Acta Apostolicæ Sedis* 75, pars II (1983), p. 153, can. 838, §2. ET: *Code of Canon Law: Latin-English Edition*, p. 276.

[38] "[D]isciplinam cunctæ Ecclesiæ communem promovere et ideo observantiam omnium legum ecclesiasticarum urgere tenetur;" ibid., p. 71, can. 392, §1. ET: ibid., p. 128.

[39] "Advigilet ne abusus in ecclesiasticam disciplinam irrepant, præsertim circa ministerium verbi, celebrationem sacramentorum et sacramentalium, cultum Dei et Sanctorum, necnon bonorum administrationem;" ibid., p. 71, can. 392, §2. ET: ibid., p. 128.

particular emphasis on the vigilance over the discipline of the Sacred Liturgy which is found in can. 1261 of the Pio-Benedictine Code. The text of can. 392, §2 of the 1983 Code, however, gives clear emphasis to the primacy of the bishop's concern for everything which pertains to the Sacred Liturgy and for the life of prayer and devotion which flows from participation in the Sacred Liturgy and leads the faithful to the same participation.

Sadly, after the Second Vatican Ecumenical Council, but certainly not because of the teaching of the Council, many abuses in the celebration of the Sacred Liturgy took place. Pope Benedict XVI made explicit reference to the situation in his letter to the bishops of the world, at the time of the promulgation of the Apostolic Letter, given *motu proprio, Summorum Pontificum*. Writing about the desire of some of the faithful for the form of the Sacred Liturgy existing before the post-Conciliar reforms, he affirmed:

> Many people who clearly accepted the binding character of the Second Vatican Council, and were faithful to the Pope and the Bishops, nonetheless also desired to recover the form of the Sacred Liturgy that was dear to them. This occurred above all because in many places celebrations were not faithful to the prescriptions of the new Missal, but the latter actually was understood as authorizing or even requiring creativity, which frequently led to deformations of the liturgy which were hard to bear. I am speaking from experience, since I too lived through that period with all its hopes and its confusion. And I have seen how arbitrary deformations of the liturgy caused deep pain to individuals totally rooted in the faith of the Church.[40]

---

[40] "Molte persone, che accettavano chiaramente il carattere vincolante del Concilio Vaticano II e che erano fedeli al Papa e ai Vescovi, desideravano tuttavia anche ritrovare la forma, a loro cara, della sacra Liturgia; questo avvenne anzitutto perché in molti luoghi non si celebrava in modo fedele alle prescrizioni del nuovo Messale, ma esso veniva addirittura inteso come un'autorizzazione o perfino come un obbligo alla creatività, la quale portò spesso a deformazioni della Liturgia al limite del sopportabile. Parlo per esperienza, perché ho vissuto anch'io quel periodo con tutte le sue attese e confusioni. E ho visto quanto profondamente siano state ferite, dalle deformazioni arbitrarie della Liturgia, persone che erano totalmente radicate nella fede della Chiesa." Benedictus PP. XVI, Epistula "Ad Episcopos Catholicæ Ecclesiæ Ritus Romani", *Acta Apostolicæ Sedis* 99 (2007), p. 796, [Hereafter, Epistula]. ET: "Letter of His Holiness Benedict XVI to the Bishops", in Pope Benedict XVI, *Summorum Pontificum*, "On the use of the Roman Liturgy prior to the reform of 1970" (London: Catholic Truth Society, 2007), p. 22, [Hereafter, EpistulaEng].

There is no doubt that in many places, at the time of the post-Conciliar reform of the Sacred Liturgy, a lack of discipline was found and many abuses were introduced.

Mention of the profound concern of Pope Paul VI, expressed in the noteworthy homily of June 29, 1972, has already been made. Pope John Paul II devoted his Apostolic Letter, *Dominicæ Cenæ*, issued on Holy Thursday of 1980, to the consideration of the relationship of the priesthood to the Sacred Liturgy, above all, to the Most Blessed Sacrament. In the last part of *Dominicæ Cenæ*, he expressed concern regarding the erosion of the universal nature of the Church's worship through "a certain 'creative' freedom."[41] He declared:

> We can follow the path of this pluralism (which arises in part from the introduction itself of the various languages into the liturgy) only as long as the essential characteristics of the celebration of the Eucharist are preserved, and the norms prescribed by the recent liturgical reform are respected.[42]

Referring to the Mystery of Faith entrusted to the Church, he reminded bishops and priests of the nature of their liturgical service:

> Every priest who offers the holy Sacrifice should recall that during this Sacrifice it is not *only* he with his community that is praying but the whole Church, which is thus expressing in this sacrament her spiritual unity, among other ways by the use of the approved liturgical text. To call this position "mere insistence on uniformity" would only show ignorance of the objective requirements of authentic unity, and would be a symptom of harmful individualism.
>
> This subordination of the minister, of the celebrant, to the *Mysterium* which has been entrusted to him by the Church for the good of the whole People of God, should also find expression in the observance

---

[41] "[L]iberæ «creatici» cuidam operæ. . . ." Ioannes Paulus PP. II, Epistula *Dominicæ Cenæ*, "De Ss. Eucharistiæ Mysterio et Cultu", 24 Februarii 1980, *Acta Apostolicæ Sedis* 72 (1980), 143, n. 12. ET: Pope John Paul II, *Dominicæ Cenæ*, "On the Mystery and Worship of the Eucharist", February 24, 1980 (Boston: St. Paul, 1980), p. 30, n. 12.

[42] "Qua in pluralismi via, ut aiunt (qui ceterum iam exortus est ex variarum linguarum usu in liturgiam inducto), eatenus tantum progredi licet, quatenus necessariæ proprietates celebrationis Eucharistiæ non tollantur quatenusque obtemperetur legibus recentiore liturgica renovatione præstitutis;" ibid., p. 143, n. 12. ET: ibid., p. 30, n. 12.

of the liturgical requirements concerning the celebration of the holy Sacrifice.[43]

Although Pope John Paul II does not explicitly refer to the *ius divinum* which underlies all liturgical discipline, he in fact describes it. It is the Mystery of Faith to which St. Paul refers in his account of the institution of the Holy Eucharist, when he declares with humility and confidence: "For I received from the Lord what I also delivered to you . . ." (1 Cor 11:23).

Dominicæ Cenæ was followed by the Instruction of the Sacred Congregation for the Sacraments and Divine Worship, *Inæstimabile Donum*. While noting positive aspects of the post-Conciliar liturgical reform, the Instruction expresses:

> Concern at the varied and frequent abuses being reported from different parts of the Catholic world: the confusion of roles, especially regarding the priestly ministry and the role of the laity (indiscriminate shared recitation of the Eucharistic prayer, homilies given by lay people, lay people distributing communion while the priests refrain from doing so); an increasing loss of the sense of the sacred (abandonment of liturgical vestments, the eucharist celebrated outside church without real need, lack of reverence and respect for the Blessed Sacrament, etc.); misunderstanding of the ecclesial character of the liturgy (the use of private texts, the proliferation of unapproved Eucharistic Prayers, the manipulation of the liturgical texts for social and political ends).[44]

---

[43] "Singuli sacerdotes, qui Sanctum offerunt Sacrificium, meminerint proinde non se *solos* huius Sacrificii tempore precari cum propria communitate, verum totam simul precari Ecclesiam, quæ sic atque etiam per *usum liturgici textus approbati* aperiat hoc in Sacramento unitatem suam spiritalem. Si quis hanc rationem appellat «nimium uniformitatis studium», ostendit tantummodo se ignorare obiectivas postulationes germanæ unitatis idque signum est nocentis individualismi, quem dicunt.

"Quod autem minister sive celebrans ita subicitur ipsi «Mysterio», quod ab Ecclesia illi concreditum est in commodum totius Populi Dei, id elucere debet etiam in observatione liturgicarum normarum ad Sancti Sacrificii celebrationem attinentium;" ibid., 144, n. 12. ET: ibid., p. 31, n. 12.

[44] "[D]e sollicitudine, quacum perquam multiplices et crebros pravos usus advertimus, qui e variis partibus orbis catholici nuntiantur: confusio munerum, præsertim quod ad ministerium sacerdotale attinet et ad officium laicorum (recitatio precis eucharisticæ, quæ sine discrimine et coniuncte fit, homiliæ a laicis habitæ, laici sacram communionem distribuentes, dum sacerdotes ea dispertienda se abstinent); augescens

Quoting a text from the *Summa Theologiæ* of St. Thomas Aquinas, the Instruction declares:

> In these cases we are face to face with a real falsification of the Catho-lic liturgy: "One who offers worship to God on the Church's behalf in a way contrary to that which is laid down by the Church with God-given authority and which is customary in the Church is guilty of falsification."[45]

The Instruction then provides twenty-seven norms for the celebra-tion of the Holy Mass and of Eucharistic Worship outside Mass. It concludes by observing that the difficulties encountered in the imple-mentation of the liturgical reform mandated by the Second Vatican Ec-umenical Council "stem from the fact that neither priests nor faithful have perhaps been sufficiently aware of the theological and spiritual reasons for which the changes have been made, in accordance with the principles laid down by the Council."[46] It insists that "priests must acquire an ever deeper understanding of the authentic way of look-ing at the Church, of which the celebration of the liturgy and espe-cially of the Mass is the living expression."[47] Clearly, fundamental to the understanding of the Church and her Sacred Liturgy is the under-

---

defectus sensus illius, quo sacram percipiatur (derelictus usu vestium liturgicarum, sacræ celebrationes pro more extra ecclesias sine vera necessitate habitæ, deficiens reverentia et observantia sanctissimi Sacramenti hisque similia); neglectio indolis ecclesialis, quæ liturgiæ est propria (usus textuum privatorum, amplificata inductio precum eucharis-ticarum non approbatarum, detorta adhibitio textuum liturgicorum quatenus finibus socialibus-politicis servire iubentur)." Sacra Congregatio pro Sacramentis et Cultu Di-vino, Instructio *Inæstimabile Donum*, "De quibusdam normis circa cultum mysterii eu-charistici", 3 Aprilis 1980, *Acta Apostolicæ Sedis* 72 (1980), pp. 332–33. ET: Sacred Con-gregation for the Sacraments and Divine Worship, Instruction *Inæstimabile Donum*, "On Certain Norms Concerning Worship of the Eucharistic Mystery" (Rome: Typis Poly-glottis Vaticanis, 1980), p. 4.

[45] "Huiusmodi in casibus vera deprehenditur adulteratio liturgiæ catholicæ: «vitium falsitatis incurrit qui ex parte Ecclesiæ cultum exhibet Deo contra modum divina auc-toritate ab Ecclesia constitutum et in Ecclesia consuetum;»" ibid., p. 333. ET: ibid., p. 4. Cf. *Summa Theologiæ*, II-II, q. 93, a. 1.

[46] "[E]x eo profluit quod nonnulli sacerdotes et fideles non satis sibi exploratas et cog-nitas habuerunt ipsas rationes theologicas et spirituales, ob quas res secundum principia a Concilio statuta sunt mutatæ;" ibid., 340. ET: ibid., p. 11.

[47] "Sacerdotes oportet altius percipiant sincerum modum Ecclesiam considerandi, cuius vivum quasi documentum est celebratio liturgica, potissimum vero Missa;" ibid., 341. ET: ibid., p. 11.

standing of the *ius divinum* and of the irreplaceable service of liturgical law.

Pope John Paul II, as has been noted before, confronted the abuses regarding the celebration of the Sacrament of Penance in his first Encyclical Letter *Redemptor Hominis*. Also, in his last Encyclical Letter *Ecclesia de Eucharistia*, published on Holy Thursday of 2003, he once again confronted liturgical abuses. Commenting on the benefits of the post-Conciliar liturgical reform, he also noted the deficiencies which have followed it, with these words:

> Unfortunately, alongside these lights, *there are also shadows*. In some places the practice of Eucharistic adoration has been almost completely abandoned. In various parts of the Church abuses have occurred, leading to confusion with regard to sound faith and Catholic doctrine concerning this wonderful sacrament. At times one encounters an extremely reductive understanding of the Eucharistic mystery. Stripped of its sacrificial meaning, it is celebrated as if it were simply a fraternal banquet. Furthermore, the necessity of the ministerial priesthood, grounded in apostolic succession, is at times obscured and the sacramental nature of the Eucharist is reduced to its mere effectiveness as a form of proclamation.[48]

The pressing concern of the Supreme Pontiff is most evident.

In fact, at the end of the introductory part of the Encyclical Letter he declared:

> It is my hope that the present Encyclical Letter will effectively help to banish the dark clouds of unacceptable doctrine and practice, so that the Eucharist will continue to shine forth in all its radiant mystery.[49]

---

[48] "Dolendum tamen est quod iuxta lucida hæc *umbræ non desunt*. Etenim est ubi fere tota neglegentia cultus adorationis eucharisticæ deprehendatur. Accedunt in hoc vel illo ecclesiali ambitu abusus qui ad rectam obscurandam fidem doctrinamque catholicam super hoc mirabili Sacramento aliquid conferunt. Nonnumquam reperitur intellectus valde circumscriptus Mysterii eucharistici. Sua enim significatione et vi sacrificii destitutum, mysterium retinetur tamquam si sensum ac momentum alicuius fraterni convivii non excedat. Præterea sacerdotii ministerialis necessitas, quæ successioni apostolicæ innititur, nonnumquam absconditur atque Eucharistiæ sacramentalitas ad solam nuntiationis efficacitatem redigitur." Ioannes Paulus PP. II, Litteræ Encyclicæ *Ecclesia de Eucharistia*, "De Eucharistia eiusque necessitudine cum Ecclesia", 17 Aprilis 2003, *Acta Apostolicæ Sedis* 95 (2003), p. 439, n. 10. ET: Pope John Paul II, *Encyclicals*, pp. 9–10.

[49] "Litteras has Encyclicas Nostras conducere efficaciter posse confidimus ut doctri-

Toward the end of the Encyclical Letter, St. John Paul II wrote again about the abuses introduced with the post-Conciliar reform, in the context of the responsibility of priests for the correct celebration of the Sacred Liturgy. He made an urgent appeal "that the liturgical norms for the celebration of the Eucharist be observed with great fidelity."[50] In this context, he requested the competent Dicasteries of the Roman Curia "to prepare a more specific document, including prescriptions of a juridical nature",[51] on the liturgical norms and their profound meaning, which we may define, in a summary manner, as respect for the divine right. Thus, John Paul II concluded the discussion of the norms of the discipline of the Sacred Liturgy with these words:

> No one is permitted to undervalue the mystery entrusted to our hands: it is too great for anyone to feel free to treat it lightly and with disregard for its sacredness and its universality.[52]

As he had done in his first Encyclical Letter, so in his last, he taught the divine right, the *ius divinum* of sacred worship, in accord with the objective reality of man's relationship with God.

On March 25, 2004, the Congregation for Divine Worship and the Discipline of the Sacraments published the document requested by Pope John Paul II, the Instruction *Redemptionis Sacramentum*, "On certain matters to be observed or to be avoided regarding the Most Holy Eucharist."[53] The eighth and last chapter of the Instruction treats remedies of the delicts and abuses in the celebration of the Sacred Liturgy. After having listed the most serious delicts and the relative sanctions,[54]

---

narum umbræ dissipentur et usus reprobati submoveantur, unde omni in sui mysterii fulgore Eucharistia resplendere pergat;" ibid., p. 439, n. 10. ET: ibid., p. 10.

[50] "[U]t in eucharistica Celebratione magna quidem fidelitate liturgicæ observentur regulæ;" ibid., p. 468, n. 52. ET: ibid., p. 39.

[51] "[U]t proprium appararent documentum cum monitionibus etiam generis iuridici;" ibid., p. 468, n. 52. ET: ibid., p. 40.

[52] "Nulli quidem parvi pendere licet Mysterium nostris manibus concreditum: maius quidem illud est quam ut quisquam sibi permittat proprio id arbitratu tractare, unde nec sacra eius natura observetur nec universalis ratio;" ibid., p. 468, n. 52. ET: ibid., p. 40.

[53] Congregatio de Cultu Divino et Disciplina Sacramentorum, Instructio *Redemptionis Sacramentum*, "De quibusdam observandis et vitandis circa sanctissimam Eucharistiam", 25 Martii 2004, *Acta Apostolicæ Sedis* 96 (2004), pp. 549–601. ET: *Instruction Redemptionis Sacramentum*: "On Certain Matters to be Observed or to be Avoided Regarding the Most Holy Eucharist" (Vatican City: Libreria Editrice Vaticana, 2004).

[54] Cf. ibid., pp. 597–98, nn. 172–73. ET: ibid., pp. 65-66, nn. 172–73.

the Instruction treats other abuses, indicating that they "are not to be considered of little account, but are to be numbered among the other abuses to be carefully avoided and corrected."[55] The Instruction then indicates that all liturgical norms are to be observed and all errors corrected:

> The things set forth in this Instruction obviously do not encompass all the violations against the Church and its discipline that are defined in the canons, in the liturgical laws and in other norms of the Church for the sake of the teaching of the Magisterium or sound tradition. Where something wrong has been committed, it is to be corrected according to the norm of law.[56]

The right attention to liturgical norms does not constitute a sort of legalism or rubricism, but an act of profound respect and love for our Lord who has given us the gift of divine worship, an act of profound love which has as its irreplaceable foundation the respect for the divine right.

The legislation regarding the use of the *usus antiquior*—the older form of the Roman rite—deserves a special treatment which time has not permitted me to give. A few summary observations, however, are necessary. Of special note is Pope John Paul II's Apostolic Letter, given *motu proprio*, *Ecclesia Dei*,[57] as well as the earlier Letter *Quattuor abhinc Annos* of the Sacred Congregation for Divine Worship,[58] both of which permitted, to some degree, the celebration of the form of the Roman

---

[55] "[L]eviter non sunt æstimandæ, sed inter alios abusus sedulo vitandos et corrigendos adnumerentur." Ibid., p. 598, n. 174. ET: ibid., p. 67, n. 174

[56] "Quæ in hac Instructione exponuntur, ut patet, haud omnes contra Ecclesiam eiusque disciplinam referunt violationes, quæ in canonibus, in legibus liturgicis atque in aliis normis Ecclesiæ ob doctrinam Magisterii sanamve traditionem definiuntur. Ubi quid mali patratum est, corrigendum erit ad normam iuris." Ibid., p. 598, n. 175. ET: ibid., p. 67, n. 175.

[57] Cf. Ioannes Paulus PP. II, Litteræ Apostolicæ motu proprio datæ *Ecclesia Dei Adflicta*, 2 Iulii 1988, *Acta Apostolicæ Sedis* 80 (1988), pp. 1495–98. ET: "Apostolic Letter of John Paul II *Ecclesia Dei*" in: *L'Osservatore Romano—Weekly Edition in English*, 11 July 1988, p. 1.

[58] Cf. Sacra Congregatio pro Cultu Divino, Epistula *Quattuor abhinc annos*, "De usu Missalis Romani iuxta editionem typicam anni MCMLXII", 3 Octobris 1984, *Acta Apostolicæ Sedis* 76 (1984), pp. 1088–89. ET: "Indult for use of Roman Missal of 1962 according to judgment of diocesan bishop" in: *L'Osservatore Romano—Weekly Edition in English*, 22 October 1984, p. 9.

rite in use before the post-conciliar reforms. Pope Benedict XVI further defined and developed the discipline regarding the two forms of the one Roman rite by his Apostolic Letter, given *motu proprio*, *Summorum Pontificum*,[59] together with the accompanying Letter to the Bishops,[60] and the subsequent Instruction *Universæ Ecclesiæ* of the Pontifical Commission *Ecclesia Dei*.[61] In his just-mentioned letter to the bishops, Pope Benedict XVI made clear that the celebration of the two forms of the Roman rite "can be mutually enriching."[62] Later in the letter, employing the hermeneutic of reform in continuity, he made clear that the celebration of both forms of the Roman rite is an expression of the necessary continuity of the two forms. He wrote:

> There is no contradiction between the two editions of the Roman Missal. In the history of the liturgy there is growth and progress, but no rupture. What earlier generations held as sacred, remains sacred and great for us too, and it cannot be all of a sudden entirely forbidden or even considered harmful. It behooves all of us to preserve the riches which have developed in the Church's faith and prayer, and to given them their proper place.[63]

Through the faithful application of the juridical norms contained in *Universæ Ecclesiæ* and through their development and perfection over time, the reform desired by the Fathers of the Second Vatican Ecumenical Council will be carried out in fidelity to the Tradition. In the case of the discipline regarding the two forms of the Roman rite, one

---

[59] Cf. Benedictus PP. XVI, Litteræ Apostolicæ motu proprio datæ *Summorum Pontificum*, "De usu extraordinario antiquæ formæ Ritus Romani", 7 Iulii 2007, *Acta Apostolicæ Sedis* 99 (2007), pp. 777–81. ET: Benedict XVI, *Summorum Pontificum* (London: Catholic Truth Society, 2007), pp. 11–19.

[60] Cf. Benedictus PP. XVI, Epistula, pp. 795–99.

[61] Cf. Pontificia Commissio *Ecclesia Dei*, Instructio *Universæ Ecclesiæ*, "Ad exsequendas Litteras Apostolicas *Summorum Pontificum*", 30 Aprilis 2011, *Acta Apostolicæ Sedis*, 103 (2011), pp. 413–20. ET: http://www.vatican.va/roman_curia/pontifical_commissions/ecclsdei/documents/rc_com_ecclsdei_doc_20110430_istr-universae-ecclesiae-en.html.

[62] "[P]ossono arricchirsi a vicenda. . . ." Epistula, p. 797. ET: EpistulaEng, p. 24.

[63] "Non c'è nessuna contraddizione tra l'una e l'altra edizione del *Missale Romanum*. Nella storia della Liturgia c'è crescita e progresso, ma nessuna rottura. Ciò che per le generazioni anteriori era sacro, anche per noi resta sacro e grande, e non può essere improvvisamente del tutto proibito o, addirittura, giudicato dannoso. Ci fa bene a tutti conservare le ricchezze che sono cresciute nella fede e nella preghiera della Chiesa, e di dar loro il giusto posto." Ibid., p. 798. ET: ibid., p. 26.

sees the humble and yet irreplaceable role of liturgical law in carrying out the great mission of the Church.

Pope Benedict XVI faithfully continued the attention of Pope John Paul II to liturgical norms, especially with the publication of the Postsynodal Apostolic Exhortation *Sacramentum Caritatis*.[64] In *Sacramentum Caritatis*, he announced the publication of a compendium on the Most Holy Eucharist which was later promulgated by the Congregation for Divine Worship and the Discipline of the Sacraments.[65]

Conclusion

It is my hope that this reflection has helped to underline the humble and yet irreplaceable service of liturgical law to the Church's mission, above all, to the source and highest expression of her mission: the Sacred Liturgy. In a particular way, it is my hope that the reflection has made clear the fundamental necessity of respect for the juridical character of the Sacred Liturgy in both liturgical theology and liturgical practice. In truth, the right understanding of the Sacred Liturgy begins with the objective relationship of God with man, a relationship which demands the worship of God on the part of man as God Himself has taught in the Sacred Scriptures and in the Tradition.

Understanding the act of divine worship in its relationship to the *ius divinum*, one also understands how the norms of liturgical law are all directed to the right disposition of man in the worship of God, that is, the care to offer worship to God in the manner that God Himself asks. The disposition of divine worship is fostered by the discipline which, with the help of God's grace, purifies man of self-centered thoughts and disordered desires, and disposes him to lift up his heart to the Lord. It is in the liturgical act, above all, that man must put into practice the way of the Beatitudes, that is, the poverty of spirit which recognizes God as Creator of the world and Lord of history and which with humility and total fidelity offers to Him due worship.

---

[64] Cf. Benedictus PP. XVI, Adhortatio Apostolica postsynodalis *Sacramentum Caritatis*, "De Eucharistia vitæ missionisque Ecclesiæ fonte et culmine", 22 Februarii 2007, *Acta Apostolicæ Sedis* 99 (2007), pp. 105–80. ET: Benedict XVI, Post Synodal Exhortation on the Eucharist, *Sacramentum Caritatis* (London: Catholic Truth Society, 2007).

[65] Cf. Congregatio de Cultu Divino et Disciplina Sacramentorum, *Compendium Eucharisticum*, 25 Martii 2009, Libreria Editrice Vaticana, 2009.

21

Academic Formation and the Sacred Liturgy

PAUL GUNTER O.S.B.

Introduction

Those who thirst for God would distance themselves from the notion of academic formation in the study of liturgy being on a par with the Sacred Liturgy itself. Moreover, they would recognize that academic formation, placed alongside the Sacred Liturgy, could be nothing more than the clarion call: "Behold something greater than Solomon is here!" (Lk 11:31)[1] Nonetheless, the account of the Sign of Jonah, according to St. Luke, allows for no escape from the task in hand, as is evident in the admonition that follows it: "No one after lighting a lamp puts it in a cellar or under a basket, but on a stand, so that those who enter may see the light" (Lk 11:33).

The nineteenth- and early twentieth-century liturgiologist, Edmund Bishop, expresses the anachronism implicit in reductive and gnostic liturgical positions at the beginning of his essay "Kyrie Eleison: A Liturgical Consultation". Bishop wrote:

> "I dare say", wrote my correspondent, "some of these questions will reveal my ignorance". The word "ignorance" drew me, and for this reason: such study as I have been able to give to the subject which is called Liturgy, but which. . . . I prefer to call Christian Worship, has brought home to me with ever increasing force a sense of my real ignorance of its history. "Here is a kindred spirit" said I, "who has learnt something too."

---

[1] The English Standard Version Bible containing the Old and New Testaments with Apocrypha (Oxford University Press, 2009).

It was the word "ignorance", then, let drop by my correspondent, that made me try, for my own instruction also, to draw out a formal answer. . . . The substance of this answer, somewhat amplified, makes up the present paper. I cannot think that it will be "interesting", as the word goes now, to anybody; but here and there there may be one who may like "to know" what I too like "to know".[2]

While I suspect the second paragraph of Bishop's essay casts a prophetic optic on the challenges continually experienced in the relationship between liturgy and formation, especially where institutional ignorance of the inter-dependency of the two might emerge, the obviously disconnected historical contexts of the lamp that must shine before the world of every time and place if it is to complete its purpose, and the *anthropos*, who, finding himself on holy ground, not unlike the Magi in Matthew 2, who can only find fulfillment in adoration, illustrates the need for formation to accompany those discoveries, if their content is not to be found too rich for the unsuspecting palate.

Like modern men and women of our day, who encounter, for the first time, the treasures and treasuries hidden in the liturgy, those Magi, versed in the wisdom of the stars, had come from afar. They found what they were looking for, where *kairos* had eclipsed *chronos*, and though, as St. Matthew puts it, "they rejoiced with exceeding great joy", they did so because they had given pause for the '*kairos*-inspired' moment to draw them into the mystery. Aorist verbs in Matthew 2:11 express the process in which they were engaged. εἶδον, they saw; προσφέρω, they presented or offered, which in this context seems to stress the persons to whom and by whom the offering is made within the personal relationship that each identifies with the other; ἀναφέρω, to offer up, in the sense of leading something to a higher place, and παρίστημι, which expresses the destiny and purpose of the offering. Three stages on the way to worship, of 'vision', 'submission' and 'consecration' illustrate the process that is our concern in the relationship of academic formation to the Sacred Liturgy.

---

[2] E. Bishop, "Kyrie Eleison: A Liturgical Consultation", published in two parts in *The Downside Review* in December 1899 and March 1900. See the collection of his essays selected by Bishop's disciple Dom Hugh Connolly, *Liturgica Historica* (Oxford: Clarendon Press, 1918), (pp. 116–36), p. 116.

Sacrosanctum Concilium

The Constitution on the Sacred Liturgy of the Second Vatican Council *Sacrosanctum Concilium* is marking fifty years since its promulgation, and has become a focus of renewed inspiration in the search for the liturgical life and growth it promoted. Also, subject to no less scrutiny for the manner and extent of its implementation, the document, through its prism of fifty years, invites us to commit ourselves anew to its purpose, and to reflect on what it asked of us. Maturity comes out of reflection and those who in fifty years mark the centenary of the Second Vatican Council are likely to be in a more objective position to view its documents than we are, or, indeed, were those who received them when they were newly promulgated.

That reflection, necessary as it is for the lasting fruits of liturgical formation to blossom, has not been undertaken in the time frame since the Council and is the greatest liturgical challenge of our time. We have implemented change but we have not reflected on it, because history cannot yet have granted dispassionate reprieve to those who might be inclined to speak of the Sacred Liturgy and of its attendant liturgical formation in sentimental terms, simply because they were alive to see all, or some, of what changed and how those events unfolded. Nonetheless, the Constitution outlined clear objectives about academic formation and the Sacred Liturgy.

In the first chapter, which gives general principles for the restoration and promotion of the Sacred Liturgy, the section which deals with academic formation appears under a separate heading, "De liturgica institutione et de actuosa participatione prosequendis", but which is generally translated in English as: "The Promotion of Liturgical Instruction and Active Participation". This invites further research about different kinds of engagement in the liturgical action to identify how active the participation needs to be in order for it to be "plena et actuosa" (n. 14).[3] For the purposes of this paper, it is important to note that the document acknowledges that such participation cannot expect to be realized if it is not underpinned by adequate formation. Moreover, the

---

[3] For the Latin text see: Conc. Œcum. Vat. II, Const. de sacra Liturgia, *Sacrosanctum Concilium*, AAS 56 (1964), pp. 97–138.

document requires this formation be given so that "all the Christian faithful should be led to that fully conscious . . . participation which is demanded by the very nature of the liturgy" . . . [as] their right and duty by reason of their baptism ("Baptismatis ius habet et officium").

Article 14, covering many eventualities, establishes a list of priorities which is, of itself, revealing. Beforehand, it states unambiguously that the liturgy "is the primary and indispensable source from which the faithful are to derive the true Christian spirit". It continues: "pastors of souls must zealously strive to achieve it, by means of the necessary instruction." Then, recognizing that the importance of liturgy has not been grasped by those who to whom such a task would reasonably be entrusted, it declares that "A prime need, therefore, is that attention be directed, first of all, to the liturgical instruction of the clergy." Having explained that it is the liturgy that is primary and indispensable in the communication of the true Christian spirit to the faithful, in articles 15–18, the document requires that the instruction applicable to the different levels of those entrusted with liturgical formation should be provided. The first mentioned are professors destined to teach liturgy in seminaries, religious houses of studies and theological faculties. For such, it was required that specialized institutes be created and, in more recent years, a diversification of liturgical institutes has been established, each with its own particular strengths.

Academic Formation in the Sacred Liturgy

When *Sacrosanctum Concilium* was promulgated, such an institute had only recently been established by a decree of St. John XXIII dated June 16, 1961. The predecessor to the Pontifical Institute of Liturgy in Rome [PIL], was an Institute of Liturgical Research founded in 1950 which published the two series *Rerum Ecclesiasticarum Documenta cura Pontificii Athenæi Sancti Anselmi de Urbe*. In the preparations for the Second Vatican Council and subsequently, the Institute and its *corpus docentium* have played an important role in the teaching and renewal of the Sacred Liturgy. In 1978, the PIL was canonically erected by the Holy See as a Faculty of Sacred Liturgy and authorized to grant the academic degrees of SL.L, or Licentiate in Sacred Liturgy, the SL.D, or Doctorate in Sacred Liturgy, both of which are degrees peculiar to the PIL.

Consistent with *Sacrosanctum Concilium* 15, the goal of the Pontifical Institute of Liturgy has been to promote the scientific academic study and practice of Sacred Liturgy through teaching, research and publications. By the same token, the curriculum has been organized to give breadth of preparation for teaching, liturgical formation, liturgical leadership, and ongoing scientific academic study of liturgy and related matters.

The students are taught to develop a critical sense and a scientific method to support the scientific analysis of liturgical data studied historically and theologically. Only by working with the primary sources themselves, can they glimpse the historical, theological, spiritual, and pastoral dimensions of the Church's liturgical traditions, see the relationship between culture and liturgy, and understand the nature of the process of ritual. Then they will be able to examine liturgy in the light of Sacred Scripture and within the Tradition and apply what they find to the ecclesial and cultural circumstances of the modern world.

The curriculum at the PIL depends on the primacy of the liturgical texts that form liturgical books. The students have to acquire a familiarity with both the historical and the modern sources of the liturgy in the original languages. The concentration on the actual revised books of the Roman rite also has an historical root: many of the original faculty served in the preparations of *Sacrosanctum Concilium* and in the various groups (*cœtus*) of the post-conciliar *Consilium* for the preparation of the revised liturgical books of the Roman rite. The curriculum, therefore, is closely tied to the modern rites of the Roman Church, although the history of the development of the Roman rite and of its historical books is a solid part of the curriculum as well. For greater knowledge of the *usus antiquior*—the older form of the Roman rite,[4] major sections of the *Ritus servandus* of the Roman Missal of 1962 are read in Latin, which, not only promotes an understanding of the Missal of 1962 in itself, but which immerses students into greater depth of knowledge about the genius of the Roman rite since, following *Summorum Pontificum* of 2007, the older form of the Roman rite has again taken its place in the life of the Church. The two forms are distinctive in character

---

[4] The term "*usus antiquior*", used here in accordance with editorial policy, is taken from the "Letter of His Holiness Benedict XVI to the Bishops on the Occasion of the Publication of the Apostolic Letter 'Motu Proprio Data' *Summorum Pontificum* on the use of the Roman Liturgy Prior to the Reform of 1970", 7 July 2007, which makes use of the phrase "the *usus antiquior*."

while neither denies the legitimate place of the other within the Roman rite. Sufficient understanding of Latin and Greek is required if a student is to be capable of liturgical research and only after papers in both languages have been passed, can a student be admitted fully to the licentiate cycle. Modern languages are also important if a student is to appreciate the status quæstionis of any area of liturgical research.[5]

Another important facet of the curriculum is the comparative liturgy that derives from the school of Anton Baumstark,[6] and Bernard Botte,[7] about which, because of its importance for the integrity of academic formation in liturgical scholarship, I shall say more shortly. It is to be pointed out here that, the expression "comparative liturgy" was born of John Mason Neale,[8] more famous for his contribution to nineteenth century hymnody and less so, for his term, "liturgiology" which refers to the scientific study of liturgy. The student not only studies the Roman Latin liturgy in depth, but also the liturgies of the other Latin rites, of the seven eastern Churches and some aspects of the liturgies of the churches of the Reformation. It is important for a student to grasp the specific findings of the laws of Baumstark and to know how to apply them in objective studies of liturgical texts.

Baumstark was not merely an historian but a faithful Catholic working during the tense time of the modernist controversy. Historians faced the difficulties of that time in different ways. Some more cautiously avoided controversy by concentrating on narrow, technical topics, while others, such as Edmund Bishop, were confident that the Church would adjust to the scientific findings that historical development presented. From the middle of the nineteenth century until after the First World War, neo-scholastic theology, which drew a clear distinction between nature and grace, presented the view that reason only had the power to explore the natural world. Though it could establish the existence of God as well as the logical necessity of the Christian faith, it would never be in a position to know its mysteries. Consequently, neo-scholastic theologians constructed an epistemology of two orders of knowledge. The first of these was a theology which was certain, unlike the second of these, which was based on all other

---

[5] For more information: see http://santanselmo.org/doc_pdf/pdf/PIL_CARR.pdf
[6] Carl Anton Joseph Maria Dominikus Baumstark, 1872–1948.
[7] Dom Bernard Botte, 1883–1980, monk of Mont César.
[8] John Mason Neale, 1818–1866.

human sciences. Contrasts were marked between the Church and the world, theology and science, faith and history. While the eternal life of the Church was sealed by constancy, unity and consistency, the historical life of the world was characterized by change, plurality and contradiction. The truth of the Church, the means of eternal life, was presented as "objective, supernatural and necessary", while that of the world was held to be "natural, subjective and contingent."[9] The Jesuit, Louis Billot, professor of dogma at the Gregorian University, and who resigned from the Sacred College of Cardinals during the pontificate of Pius XI over his support for the deeply conservative movement, "Action Française", had declared: "dogmas have no history".[10]

Baumstark used neo-scholastic categories to present the place of the historian in the Church, employing comparative liturgy as a historiographical solution to a theological problem. He defined how he, a layman and an historian, could legitimately study the liturgy of the Church using natural reason. Baumstark had to establish that the study of liturgy fell into the category of natural knowledge. He argued that liturgy could be studied as both history and theology. The distinction meant his acknowledging that, since theological dimensions of liturgy referred to God, one needed to be in holy orders to study those, however quaint that sounds nowadays, stating: "It is only its subject matter which belongs to theology."[11] Nonetheless, it enabled him to pursue liturgical scholarship as an historical phenomenon. Baumstark was aware that historical data carried theological implications, the more because of the difficulties in which two liturgical scholars, Pierre Batiffol[12] and Louis Duchesne,[13] had found themselves.

Baumstark argued that the obligation of the historian is to present facts irrespective of theologians. Provocatively, he wrote: "Comparative Liturgy should always be on its guard against pre-conceived ideas and above all against theories constructed (in a way dear to theologians)

[9] F. West, *The Comparative Liturgy of Anton Baumstark*, Alcuin Club, Joint Liturgical Studies 31 (Nottingham: Grove Books, 1995), p. 10.

[10] R. Aubert, *The Church in a Secularized Society*, R. Aubert, J. Sondheimer *et al.*, *The Christian Centuries: A New History of the Catholic Church* 5 (London: Darton, Longman and Todd, 1978), p. 179.

[11] A. Baumstark, revised by B. Botte; F. L. Cross ed. and trans., *Comparative Liturgy* (London: A. R. Mowbray, 1958), p. 3.

[12] Pierre Batiffol, 1841–1929.

[13] Louis Duchesne, 1843–1922.

in the interests of a system."[14] He swiftly pointed out, however, that since theological theory is not Church dogma, this position does not, in any way, imply any contradiction of the first order of knowledge by the second: "Though facts may contradict *theories* [italics mine] of human invention, they can never contradict the *depositum fidei* handed down by Christ to the Church."[15] In fact, Baumstark was at pains to make clear that his sympathies did not rest with modernism. He wrote: "We certainly do not mean to suggest that science and dogma can be in contradiction or to propound the modernist thesis of double truth. All we insist on is that facts must be given their true value."[16] He continues, showing that he saw no contradiction for a Catholic between data and dogma:

> Now whatever be the theological considerations involved, we are not justified in conjuring the fact away. It is the theologians, not the liturgists, whose business it is to relate the historical datum to the unchangeable character of dogma. This historian, if he is a Catholic, while accepting the truth of dogma unreservedly, must no less certainly accept the fact which confronts him. In such cases he will remind himself of the saying of that great Pontiff, Leo XIII: *Veritas non erubescit nisi abscondi.*[17]

Among liturgiologists, Baumstark was among the first to reflect critically on the methodology of his work. He saw that the vocation of a liturgist is "to investigate and describe the origins and variations of the changing forms of this enduring substance of eternal value [as the] living heart of the Church".[18] This process requires the study of evidence of similarities and differences. If there were no differences, there would be nothing to explain or compare and, if there were no similarities, it would be impossible to identify the common ground from which comparisons could be launched. Baumstark wrote, indicating that comparative liturgy is not a descriptive task but an empirical science that will explain the facts and that the 'laws' of comparative liturgy will serve to explain new facts that emanate from the sources:

---

[14] Baumstark, *Comparative Liturgy*, p. 7.

[15] West, "The Comparative Liturgy of Anton Baumstark", p. 11.

[16] Baumstark, *Comparative Liturgy*, p. 7.

[17] Ibid., p. 8. "Truth has no need to blush for shame unless it be concealed."

[18] Ibid., pp. 1–2.

[Comparative liturgy] seeks to disengage from the multitude of ascertained facts certain laws which in turn will guide it in its further researches. In our modern intellectual life the idea of science . . . is bound up with the establishment of laws of some kind of evolution. . . . The laws of liturgical evolution must therefore be discovered by comparing one fact with another. Once recognized, these laws will serve as norms for the explanation of new facts which the sources will disclose.[19]

Distinguishing between the two separate sets of laws, the first category was addressed to "those capable of throwing light on the history of the great units in Liturgy"[20] seeming to refer here to liturgical rites and traditions in their entirety. Within this first category, he lists "the two laws which determine liturgical evolution . . . the Law of Organic Development" and "the second law of liturgical evolution, viz. that primitive conditions are maintained with greater tenacity in the more sacred seasons of the Liturgical Year."[21] The laws that form the second category, "illuminate the very diverse elements of which these units are compacted. These elements are of two sorts: texts and liturgical actions."[22] However, according to the exposition given by Baumstark, such is not as broad as it sounds because, what he is concerned with, is "*prose* euchological texts . . . to determine the laws which govern their evolution."[23]

Baumstark's principles embrace three distinctive areas of liturgical history. The first area provides general principles about the evolution of liturgy and liturgical rites as identified as belonging to particular liturgical families or traditions. The second area comprises two categories of 'particular laws' regarding the evolution of liturgical texts and/or the evolution of liturgical structures. The third area concerns actions and their subsequent symbolization.[24]

---

[19] Ibid., p. 15.

[20] Ibid., p. 52.

[21] Ibid., pp. 23 and 27.

[22] Ibid., p. 52.

[23] Ibid., p. 59. Italics mine.

[24] R. Taft, "Anton Baumstark's Comparative Liturgy Revisited" in: R. Taft and G. Winkler, eds., *Comparative Liturgy Fifty Years after Anton Baumstark* (1872–1948), Acts of the International Congress, Orientalia Christiana Analecta 265 (Rome: Pontificio Istituto Orientale, 2001), (pp. 191–232), p. 196.

An international congress to honour Baumstark took place in 1998 on the fiftieth anniversary of his death—the papers of which event were published by the Pontifical Oriental Institute. At this congress Robert Taft S.J. reformulated Baumstark's 'laws' and rescued them, for the benefit of liturgical scholars of our own time, from apparently inconsistent numberings that were the consequence of Baumstark's characteristic highly-technical linguistic style.[25]

The general principles referred to are, in essence, three. The first is that the evolution of liturgical rites moves from diversity to uniformity and not from uniformity to diversity. Baumstark illustrates by way of this principle that, as time progresses, diversity of local usages in a particular area of liturgical diffusion solidify into a relatively homogeneous liturgical family or rite with the effect of there being fewer diverse liturgical usages than previously was the case. Conversely, as individual rites foster internal unity, they also vary from each other where they take on specifically local characteristics that have arisen as a result of local adaptation to the specific circumstances of time and place.[26]

The second general principle is revealed when, "liturgical development proceeds from simplicity to increasing enrichment."[27] This law was originally demonstrated by Hieronymus Endberding,[28] and showed that "the growth to excessive complexity can later provoke retrograde developments of abbreviation."[29]

The third general principle is that "the liturgy is but a series of individual developments." This indicates that the history of liturgy does not consist in one progressive mono-directional growth of individual and entire rituals as homogeneous single units but of distinct developments of their individual components. Baumstark expressed this important principle "In Die Entwicklung der Liturgie nur aus Sonderentwicklung besteht" prior to 'Comparative Liturgy' and in which he did not include it. This law makes the point "that all human knowledge

---

[25] Ibid., pp. 198–210.

[26] Baumstark, *Comparative Liturgy*, pp. 15–19.

[27] Ibid., 59.

[28] Dom Hieronymus Engberding O.S.B., 1899–1969, monk of Gerleve in Germany and liturgical scholar.

[29] Cf. Baumstark, *Comparative Liturgy*, pp. 15, 19–23, 59.

remains piecework" and that our grasp of the history of a liturgical ritual only advances by means of patient examination of its component parts.[30]

In the 'particular laws', the first section that Baumstark deals with affects texts. The first of these particular laws states: "The older a text is, the less it is influenced by the Bible."[31] A literal dependence on Scripture would demonstrate that a text were more recent with the obvious exception of the texts of the sixteenth-century Protestant reformers. The second 'particular law' indicates: "The more recent a text is the more symmetrical it is."[32] A smooth style can often indicate either a more recent text or an older one that has been polished. The third 'particular' law suggests that earlier symmetry, itself a later development, can have been destroyed in a yet later period by the increasing influence of biblical language on liturgical texts,[33] "For there are many cases where symmetry which is itself clearly secondary has been destroyed in turn by the ever increasing influence of biblical language."[34] This law is particularly useful for dating documents because certain doctrinal emphases became a contention in the Church before they gained sway in the anaphora. The fourth 'particular' law decrees: "The later it is, the more liturgical prose becomes charged with doctrinal elements."[35] This law was useful in dating developing redactions of the same text, and was attested to first by Engberding, as Baumstark himself happily points out.[36] The fifth 'particular' law states that "Later liturgical prose develops in the direction of an increasingly oratorical form and becomes more and more governed by rhetoric."[37]

Regarding liturgical structures, liturgical actions and liturgical symbolisation, "in the twofold antithetical process of enrichment and pruning", which has already been mentioned, "newer elements may coexist for a time with older ones before ultimately supplanting them. When

---

[30] Taft, "Anton Baumstark's Comparative Liturgy Revisited" p. 198.
[31] Baumstark, *Comparative Liturgy*, p. 59.
[32] Ibid.
[33] Taft, "Anton Baumstark's Comparative Liturgy Revisited" p. 199.
[34] Baumstark, *Comparative Liturgy*, p. 59.
[35] Ibid., pp. 60–61.
[36] Ibid., p. 60.
[37] Ibid., pp. 61–70.

this happens, it is usually the most primitive and traditional elements that give way before the assault of the new."[38] Though Baumstark formulated this as his first general "law of organic development" in *Comparative Liturgy* (pages 23–27), "of the great units of liturgy",[39] this law has to do with the ordos of individual rituals, such as that of baptism. Baumstark showed that when the continual addition of new elements eventually overloads the structure to the point where a craving for simplicity emerges, it is always the older and more traditional elements that are suppressed, despite their previous coexistence with innovation.

The second law concerning liturgical structure, liturgical actions and liturgical symbolization enunciates "the law of the preservation of older usages in the more solemn liturgical seasons".[40] This law was first identified by Adrian Fortescue in 1912 in his work *The Mass: A Study of the Roman Liturgy*, which referred to "the constant tendency of the greatest days to keep older arrangements."[41] Baumstark asserts that in the more solemn liturgical seasons, older liturgical usages tend to resist the ordinary pruning common at other times.

The third law about liturgical structure, liturgical actions and liturgical symbolization, Baumstark called 'a new general law', explaining how merely utilitarian usages became justified by attaching symbolic meaning to them. He wrote: "Certain actions which are purely utilitarian by nature may receive a symbolic meaning either from their function in the Liturgy as such or from factors in the liturgical texts which accompany them."[42]

Over the years Baumstark's theories have never been discredited even if the intellectual framework that Baumstark sought to protect has proved exasperating for some liturgical scholars. His laws enable us to appreciate what might usefully be termed 'liturgical instinct' to underpin research. The appearance of changes in liturgical sources, whether of additions, omissions, or aberrations, constitute departures from previously established patterns. They need sifting, analyzing, cat-

---

[38] Taft, "Anton Baumstark's Comparative Liturgy Revisited" p. 200.

[39] Baumstark, *Comparative Liturgy*, p. 52.

[40] Ibid., pp. 27–30.

[41] A. Fortescue, *The Mass: A Study of the Roman Liturgy* (London: Longmans Green, 1912), p. 270.

[42] Baumstark, *Comparative Liturgy*, p. 130.

aloging or classifying, and comparing. So, the laws formulated and classified by Baumstark in *Vom geschichtlichen Werden der Liturgie*,[43] in *Liturgie comparée*, as well as in other works, crown long processes of research, analysis, synthesis and all of their conclusions. They become presumptions to the extent they provide a way of proceeding from the known to the unknown. As Dom Bernard Botte wrote following his foreword to *Comparative Liturgy*, "A method is to be judged by its results. The method here employed has proved its competence."[44]

The purpose of the processing of these laws of Baumstark is to promote and enhance understanding. As Robert Taft writes: "Understanding involves the search for meaning, and in any reality we did not invent yesterday, this meaning can be ascertained via an investigation of its origins and evolution as well as how its meaning has been explained across the trajectory of its history. . . . There is nothing so relevant as knowledge, nothing so irrelevant as ignorance."[45] We cannot expect to tailor historical findings according to personal taste, no matter how tempting, because what we are dealing with is an existing and objective reality, always intolerant of fantasy, because it depends on historical data for its expression.

The advantage of depending on historical data is that one can identify when liturgy changes. Then, there needs to be identified, what precisely has changed, and who it is that changed it. Similarly, evaluations based on historical data can assess whether the motive for change outlines a state of affairs manifestly wanting in some way, and whether envisaged changes represent improvement.

Clearly, liturgical formation is not just an historical endeavour but an interdisciplinary academic formation of mutual collaboration that must recognize that liturgy has a history in an authentic tradition as part of a broader canvas. Conscious of the demands placed on the integrity of liturgical research in the life and saving mission of the Church, an academic liturgist would be expected to demonstrate academic liturgical understanding that is consistent with the theology of the Church, by means of close textual work with the texts 'proper' to historical and

---

[43] A. Baumstark, *Vom geschichtlichen Werden der Liturgie*, Ecclesia Orans (Freiburg im Breisgau: Herder, 1923); ET: Fritz West, ed. and trans., *On the Historical Development of the Liturgy* (Collegeville: Liturgical Press, 2011).

[44] Baumstark, *Comparative Liturgy*, p. viii.

[45] Taft, "Anton Baumstark's Comparative Liturgy Revisited", p. 227.

current liturgical books, rather than from secondary sources—and it should be remembered that all liturgical books of the current Roman rite form part of the Magisterium.

The scope of possibilities for liturgical research is enormous, but Catholic liturgical scholars should, at least, have had the opportunity to engage in research in the liturgy of Sacred Scripture; in the relationship of the Bible and liturgy; in missals of the Roman rite, certainly, but also in those of other Western but non Roman rites, as well as some of the eastern anaphoras because of their place in classic Christian literature; in the Liturgy of the Hours; in Sacraments and sacramentals; in the anthropological dimensions of liturgy; in the theology of the Liturgical Year; in inculturation, or the "incarnation of the Gospel in autonomous cultures and at the same time, the introduction of these cultures into the life of the Church" (*Varietates Legitimæ*, 1994, 4); in liturgical music; in pastoral liturgy; in liturgical spirituality; in liturgical law; and, in all of the above, with many other opportunities for liturgical research, with an eye towards faithful, coherent and effective *ars celebrandi* as the application of such understanding.

Nonetheless, in noting liturgical change and development, it is necessary to note what has disappeared, how it happened to disappear and how the past, from which it disappeared, relates dynamically, with the passage of time, to the present day, rather than as a static timeframe in the past. As Taft asserts, liturgical history "does not deal with the past, but with tradition, which is a genetic vision of the present, a present conditioned by its understanding of its roots."[46] Then the liturgical researcher, by promoting understanding from historical data, can expect to carry the responsibility of implementing his understanding by the way he celebrates the liturgy, by how he preaches it, and by how accessible he makes what he has understood both at a pastoral level and in an academic context.

Some might suggest that there can be little relevance in the laws of Baumstark if those receiving liturgical instruction are not destined to undertake their own research. However, these laws provide a basis from which to filter findings for the purposes of the needs presented by different local levels, and from the basis of sound principles of litur-

---

[46] R. Taft, "The structural analysis of liturgical units. An essay in methodology" in: *Worship* 52 (1978) (pp. 314–29), pp. 316–17.

gical scholarship that will counteract sheer sentimentality, no less than short-term political and social agendas.

Liturgical Formation in Seminaries

Sacrosanctum Concilium appreciated the need for knowledge to suit the various groups it sought to educate, as well as the need for professors to specialize in different liturgical subjects. Article 16 specifically addresses the need for academic liturgical formation in seminaries and religious houses to be taken seriously. It is made clear that liturgy is to be integral to theological formation and that such formation should embrace a liturgical formation that covers its "theological, historical, spiritual, pastoral, and juridical aspects." The importance of liturgical formation is highlighted in this article as an example to all seminary professors—since, as in liturgy, so in dogma, spirituality, pastoral theology, and scripture, for all these are pillars of the seminary curriculum —in the hope that unity "may underlie all priestly training" and the interconnectedness between all of these subjects and the liturgy be adequately explained.

It should go without saying that academic formation in Sacred Liturgy within the seminary curriculum should be tailored to the needs of the seminarians and that an academic formation in Sacred Liturgy directed at those in religious life should meet the needs of the religious institute involved. Whereas, liturgical researchers might require a critical apparatus so as to understand how to edit a liturgical text in such a way as to be able to transcribe a liturgical text and identify variations, errors and corrections that different editions might have imposed on a given text, such tools do not correspond to the needs of future priests, for the most part, whose contexts will be in the diocesan structure, whether in particular ministries or in parishes.

While *Sacrosanctum Concilium* was visionary in its appeal for an academic formation in liturgy for seminarians and religious, the last fifty years have witnessed, at least in Europe, an erosion of classical culture in general. This has added challenges to the teaching of liturgy since the cultural points of reference from the past, often rooted in the Latin language, are no longer evident in the experience of many people. Moreover, knowledge of the teachings of the Church, even at a basic level, cannot be presumed among those who offer themselves for the priesthood, though some seminaries are offering a propedeutic year of Catholic catechesis to address this deficiency.

More important then, for effective teaching of liturgy to seminarians and religious, is a healthy diet that will provide immersion into such liturgical life as will nourish, not only personal spirituality, but also provide a rootedness in the liturgical life of the Church as lived within the Tradition. Regularly, I find myself saying to students whose task it will be to teach in seminaries and religious houses, that they must not forget that whatever they choose for their licence theses must be of use to the reality to which they will return. It is unlikely, then, that a student from Great Britain, for example, would further the liturgical formation of his diocese were the focus of his study to be in the liturgical implications of Christological thought in Apollinaris of Laodicea and Theodore of Mopsuestia. Students in seminaries need an intellectual appreciation of liturgical theology, an understanding of liturgical practice and a grasp of liturgical history that will encourage sound liturgical practice. Then they will be able to engage with the tradition academically, to support and promote worthy liturgical practice and have the intellectual formation to defend it. With that aim in mind, we should always be asking what, precisely, students in seminaries need to know.

The aphorism attributed to Heraclitus of Ephesus from c. 535–475 B.C. which insists on the inevitability of ever-present change in the universe, came, not from Heraclitus but from Simplicius, a neo-platonist and from 'Cratylus' by Plato. They commented: "Ever newer waters flow on those who step into the same rivers"[47] and, "All entities move and nothing remains still."[48]

We cannot deny that there has been a cultural discontinuity in the formation received in recent decades from that of the Catholic intellectual world of only fifty years ago because of the loss of linguistic dexterity in Latin which was so crucial a portal to Catholic theological thought. This sad fact was highlighted for me in May 2013 when one of the septuagenarian Benedictine professors retired from the Pontifical Athenaeum of Sant'Anselmo to his monastery in Germany. On at

---

[47] "ποταμοῖσι τοῖσιν αὐτοῖσιν ἐμβαίνουσιν, ἕτερα καὶ ἕτερα ὕδατα ἐπιρρεῖ". Quoted in "*Arius Didymus apud Eusebius, Præparatio Evangelica*" 15.20.2.

[48] Plato, *Cratylus*, 401.d.5. "τὰ ὄντα ἰέναι τε πάντα καὶ μένειν οὐδέν".

least two occasions, I have heard him speak in Latin, demonstrating a facility that has all but been lost. On Trinity Sunday in the Basilica of Sant'Anselmo, preaching for the final time, though in Italian for the benefit of the faithful, Abbot Pius Engelbert of Gerleve said:

> I am one of the last pre-conciliar students of the famous Fr. Cipriano Vagaggini, an outstanding professor of dogmatic theology in our faculty of theology. In one of his demanding lectures—always in Latin —the citations from the New Testament directly from Greek without out translation—well, in one of his lectures, he asked the question: "What is the focus of Christianity?" He responded: "The centre of the Christian Faith is not Jesus Christ. The centre is the mystery of the Most Holy Trinity."[49]

The 'same rivers' in the example given are, inevitably, contained by the mystery of the Most Holy and undivided Trinity. Unfortunately, the newer waters that flow do not permit of the skills that linked fluency in Latin with the subtlety of classical thought and the Latin genius of Catholic culture.

Given that ours is a living tradition, we can never look backwards for solutions to the future, but, from the storeroom, new and old, we can draw what is needed in liturgical formation. If authentic liturgical life is to permeate each locus of Catholic liturgical formation of clergy, religious and laity, whether in seminaries, diocesan liturgical commissions, religious houses, parishes, Catholic schools, higher institutes, Catholic universities, and other liturgical settings, the goals must be clearly stated.

Seminarians should, from the very outset of their training, be encouraged to broaden their cultural appreciation of beauty, in art, music, architecture and literature so that they encourage 'liturgical instinct' alongside the cultural sensitivity that will collaborate with theological awareness in all of the subjects taught in seminary, and provide

---

[49] "Io sono uno degli ultimi alunni preconciliari del famosissimo P. Cipriano Vagaggini, professore esimio di teologia dogmatica nella nostra Facoltà di Teologia. In una delle sue lezioni impegnative—sempre in latino, le citazione dal Nuovo Testamento direttamente dal greco senza traduzione—dunque in una delle sue lezioni poneva la domanda: Quale è il fulcro del cristianesimo, quale è il centro della fede cristiana? E rispose: Il centro della fede cristiana non è Gesù Cristo. Il centro è il mistero della Santissima Trinità." P. Engelbert, Omelia per la Solennità della Santissima Trinità, Basilica S. Anselmo, 26 maggio 2013.

acknowledged ways to express and, in turn, hand on that 'liturgical instinct' to others. A sense of the origin of liturgical practices in the wider context of liturgical history will provide intellectual equilibrium that explains the sequence of events and practices but also how they fit into explanations of theological truth and other moments of major significance in the historical and liturgical life of the Church.

With regard to liturgical resources in English, the two-volume set of *The Mass of the Roman Rite: The Origins and Development* by Joseph Jungmann are enormously valuable in explaining the origins, evolution and theology of the Mass, especially since the newer English language edition has added a chapter previously unavailable in earlier editions.[50] *The Shape of the Liturgy* by Dom Gregory Dix has withstood the test of time.[51] *The Organic Development of the Liturgy* by Alcuin Reid is an historical narration of the principles of liturgical reform and their relation to the twentieth-century liturgical movement until the cusp of the Second Vatican Council.[52] For liturgical theology, *The Theological Dimensions of the Liturgy* by Cipriano Vagaggini remains a seminal work.[53] More recently, *Theologia Prima: What is Liturgical Theology?* by David Fagerberg looks to deepen the grammar of liturgy so as to be able to describe what liturgical theology looks like. It considers human capacity for liturgy, how Leitourgia reveals how God sees the world so that "*Leitourgia* is revelation-in-motion."[54] A fascinating work by R. Gabriel Pivarnik, from the deepening perspective of trinitarian theology, in metaphysical, soteriological and ecclesiological terms, studies the concept of active participation from liturgically influential Magisterial documents of the twentieth century.[55]

There is no substitute for studying the documents of the Second

---

[50] Joseph A. Jungmann S.J., *The Mass of the Roman Rite: The Origins and Development*, 2 vols. (Notre Dame, Ind.: Christian Classics, 2012).

[51] Gregory Dix, *The Shape of the Liturgy*, first published by Dacre Press, Westminster 1945; New edition with Introduction by Simon Jones (London and New York: Continuum, 2005).

[52] Alcuin Reid, *The Organic Development of the Liturgy*, 2nd ed. (San Francisco: Ignatius Press, 2002).

[53] Cyprian Vagaggini, *Theological Dimensions of the Liturgy: A General Treatise on the Theology of the Liturgy*, (Collegeville: Liturgical Press, 1976).

[54] D. W. Fagerberg, *Theologia Prima: What is Liturgical Theology* (Chicago: Hillenbrand Books, 2004), p. 122.

[55] R. G. Pivarnik, *Toward a Trinitarian Theology of Liturgical Participation* (Collegeville: Liturgical Press, 2012).

Vatican Council in depth and, in the case of the liturgy, *Sacrosanctum Concilium* would be an important basis for the liturgical formation of any seminarian. Afterwards, in order that the context of authentic liturgical renewal should be understood in practice, without risk of ideology or liturgical polarization, it is important that seminarians know liturgical documents subsequent to *Sacrosanctum Concilium* and which serve to interpret it in the interests of genuine liturgical renewal that avoids subjectivity.

Students in seminaries need to know the liturgical books well so that, in learning what they say and what they do not say, they grasp the liturgical teaching of the Magisterium. They should be introduced to the *prænotandae* of the different rites so that they understand the mentalities of the liturgical books and of liturgical celebration. Then they will understand that liturgy is richer than "doing the red and saying the black", that it is a celebration within the Communion that is the living tradition of the Church at prayer. They will learn that since liturgical celebration is always in communion with the whole Church, they are subject to God and to truth and that, since the liturgy is not theirs to change, in the liturgy they cannot do just what they like—thus they will be opened to the wonder that is disclosed in liturgical celebration.

Pope Benedict XVI discussed the question, so redolent in our own times, in his classic *The Spirit of the Liturgy*, which liturgical professors in seminaries would do well, not only to retain as a benchmark for their own liturgical research, but to use as a key to interpreting the liturgical hermeneutic they teach their students:

> The dissolution of the subject, which coincides for us today with radical forms of subjectivism, has led to "deconstructionism"—the anarchistic theory of art. Perhaps this will help us to overcome the unbounded inflation of subjectivity and to recognize once more that a relationship with the Logos, who was at the beginning, brings salvation to the subject, that is, to the person. At the same time it puts us into a true relationship of communion that is ultimately grounded in trinitarian love.[56]

How much time seminaries can expect to allocate to liturgical formation amid many other demands is a separate question from the importance of affording liturgical formation to seminarians for the benefit

---

[56] J. Ratzinger, *The Spirit of the Liturgy* (San Francisco: Ignatius Press, 2000), p. 155.

of all the Christian faithful. *Sacrosanctum Concilium* 17 points out that a liturgical formation is indispensable for a Catholic spiritual life and for the ascetic consciousness that links liturgy to the pursuit of virtue in the quest for holiness.

Liturgical celebrants are not functionaries and always need to rediscover the 'liturgical instinct' so that they lead the Christian faithful in glorifying God in liturgy with the love with which the "good shepherd lays down his life for the sheep" (Jn 10:11). If students, at least at an initial level, are able to appreciate culture, liturgical history and liturgical theology, it will be easier for them to appreciate why liturgical laws are important and why they are not mere rubricism. Knowledge of such laws, quite apart from the benefit of protecting the faithful from liturgical abuses, their effects and their misunderstandings, will help students to understand that the liturgy encourages, no less, holiness and simplicity of life, instinctive pastoral awareness and right-ordered liturgical celebration. Rubrics and laws take their proper place in our life of worship, not to project an invincible liturgical manual, but to show us, because of whom they teach and promote, that Christ is the perfect *homo liturgicus* to the glory of the Father, because when the Church celebrates, Christ celebrates (cf. *Sacrosanctum Concilium*, 7). The Code of Canon Law of 1983 explains clearly that "the salvation of souls . . . must always be the supreme law" (canon 1752).

Authentic liturgical practice is key to communicating the integrity contained in the liturgy. *Sacrosanctum Concilium* reminds academic and pastoral liturgists alike that the riches of the liturgy are not to be kept to themselves: "Priests, both secular and religious, who are already working in the Lord's vineyard are to be helped by every suitable means to understand ever more fully what it is that they are doing when they perform sacred rites; they are to be aided to live the liturgical life and to share it with the faithful entrusted to their care" (n. 18). Clear and consistent instruction in the *ars celebrandi* of the sacred rites is of maximum importance for this purpose so that scanty preparation does not distract the priest or faithful from concentrating on their saving effects.

Students will take as their point of departure the *General Instruction of the Roman Missal* to accompany the Roman Missal in the third typical edition of 2002 and subsequently translated into English. Bishop Peter Elliott has produced two very useful volumes, now in a second edition, to present and explain what is needed for a coherent, dignified, prayerful and pastoral celebration of the Roman rite according to the liturgical books published following the Second Vatican Council.[57] While the *usus antiquior* according to the Roman Missal of 1962 requires that students gain enough knowledge of the Latin language to celebrate its liturgy worthily and well, the *Ritus servandus* found at the beginning of the missal provides the contours that steer its celebration. Nonetheless, and ordered to assist the art of the possible, there are many commentaries available that explain what is necessary in the celebration of the extraordinary form. In English, Fortescue and O'Connell's classic *The Ceremonies of the Roman Rite Described* has been updated to take account of the Roman Missal of 1962.[58]

No genuine liturgist, in any context, can afford to neglect the place of liturgical music and its integral role in the celebration of the Roman rite. Here, the crisis of liturgical understanding is at its most evident. Whether in the older rites or in the modern liturgy, tales about poor liturgical taste demonstrate institutional ignorance of liturgical norms and low cultural expectations. The Pastoral Letter to the diocese of Marquette issued in January 2013 from Bishop Alexander Sample, now Archbishop of Portland, Oregon, explains at the beginning of his letter why liturgical music is necessary:

> In any discussion of the *ars celebrandi* (the "art of celebrating") as it relates to the Holy Mass, perhaps nothing is more important or has a greater impact than the place of sacred music. The beauty, dignity and prayerfulness of the Mass depend to a large extent on the music that accompanies the liturgical action. The Holy Mass must be truly beautiful, the very best we can offer to God, reflecting his own perfect beauty and goodness.
>
> Because the place of sacred music is so important, I am issuing this pastoral letter on the nature, purpose and quality of sacred music. This is an important discussion to have, since so often the music selected for Mass is reduced to a matter of subjective "taste", i.e. what style of music appeals to this or that person or group, as if there were no

---

[57] Peter J. Elliott, *Ceremonies of the Modern Roman Rite*, revised edition (San Francisco: Ignatius Press, 2004), and *Ceremonies of the Liturgical Year* (San Francisco: Ignatius Press, 2002).

[58] Cf. Adrian Fortescue, J. B. O'Connell and Alcuin Reid, *The Ceremonies of the Roman Rite Described*, 15th ed. (London: Burns & Oates, 2009).

objective principles to be followed. There are indeed objective principles worthy of study and proper implementation.[59]

In any event, the need to protect the sacred character of liturgical music from manifestly secular influences is obvious. It should not be forgotten that the organ should be preferred to other musical instruments where possible and that Gregorian chant should not only be maintained but promoted in the interests of the sanctity of sacred music, its intrinsic beauty, and its universality. In the modern form of the Roman rite, we now have the most musical missal we have ever had. The layout indicates that it is normal to sing the Mass with as much or as little as that can entail, so realizing the principle of 'progressive solemnity.'[60] Those entrusted with musical liturgical formation should ensure that the chants of the missal are known and used as the norm, while liturgical creativity is still needed to encourage the singing of the propers, not forgetting that they form part of the texts of the Mass.

Conclusion

The New Evangelisation gives new impetus to academic formation and the Sacred Liturgy, and impetus that will long to disclose the holiness of God from an unfolding process of 'vision', 'submission' and 'consecration' in the liturgical life of the Church. Pope Francis revitalized a challenge to the Church during his homily of 16 April 2013, which happened also to be the eighty-sixth birthday of Pope Benedict: "Have we done everything the Holy Spirit was asking us to do during the Council?" he asked. The answer is "No", "We celebrate this anniversary, we put up a monument but we don't want it to upset us."

Pope Benedict XVI saw the value of the liturgy in itself as both text and celebration and knew the integrity of the liturgy had to be at the forefront of everything to be said about the hope God has for us, his Church and our salvation. Similarly, in his cordial message to the Pontifical Institute of Liturgy to mark its fiftieth anniversary in 2011, there

---

[59] Alexander K. Sample, Pastoral Letter of the Bishop of Marquette on Music in Divine Worship, *Rejoice in the Lord Always*, Diocese of Marquette, 21 January 2013.

[60] Cf. Paul VI, Apostolic Constitution, "Laudis Canticum" 1 November 1970; *The General Instruction of the Liturgy of the Hours*, n. 273.

was contained a challenge for all who are responsible for academic formation and the Sacred Liturgy throughout the Church to be faithful
to the liturgical texts, not least because they inform the *ars celebrandi*:
"Unfortunately, perhaps, we too, pastors and experts, understood the
Liturgy as an OBJECT to be reformed rather than as a SUBJECT capable of
renewing Christian life" (Address, 6 May 2011).

This urgent plea, together with that of Pope Francis for us to become docile to the voice of the Holy Spirit in the Church of our time,
are both hallmarks of the New Evangelization and of its search in the
liturgical life of the Church for the truth and beauty of God. They
are based on the knowledge that the liturgy will be the future of the
Church and that the future of the Church will be that which we live
in the liturgy.

Concluding Remarks—
The Call to a New Evangelisation

BISHOP DOMINIQUE REY

Bishop of Fréjus-Toulon, France

The new evangelisation is a challenge: spiritual, theological and pastoral; one which must get the Church back onto its feet. Indeed, at the start of this third Christian millennium we have moved to a new paradigm: that of a post-modernity which requires us to "begin again in Christ" with an evangelisation "new in its ardour, methods and expression" (John Paul II, Discourse, Nineteenth Plenary Assembly of CELAM, 9 March 1983).

The history of evangelisation throughout the centuries shows how the great missionaries were great men of prayer, and more specifically of authentic devotion. It also shows the correlation between the quality and depth of liturgical life and apostolic dynamism. Indeed, the Eucharist is the "source and summit of all Christian life" (*Lumen Gentium*, 11) and "the source and summit of the whole work of preaching the Gospel" (*Presbyterorum Ordinis*, 5). This is what Benedict XVI affirmed with emphasis in his apostolic exhortation on the Eucharist:

> The love that we celebrate in the sacrament is not something we can keep to ourselves. By its very nature it demands to be shared with all. What the world needs is God's love; it needs to encounter Christ and to believe in him. The Eucharist is thus the source and summit not only of the Church's life, but also of her mission: "an authentically eucharistic Church is a missionary Church." (*Sacramentum Caritatis*, 84)

The new evangelisation needs to anchor itself in profound Eucharistic and liturgical renewal by rediscovering the sources of liturgical

Tradition and the diversity of its expressions in the Church's heritage —especially through the mutual enrichment between the older and newer forms of the Roman rite, by its fidelity to liturgical norms and usage, and particularly through revivifying the *ars celebrandi* in order to enter into the work of redemption, of sanctification and of glorification, intended by Christ, and which continues in the Church through the celebration of the sacred mysteries.

I hope that *Sacra Liturgia 2013* has contributed to this liturgical renewal in "the spirit of the liturgy" as taught by Benedict XVI and I hope that it has been a source of inspiration and hope.

I would like to thank each person for their participation, the speakers for the quality of their presentations, the team of organizers around Dom Alcuin, the translators, all the benefactors and of course the University of *Sancta Croce* for welcoming us. A very big thank you!

Contributors

ANTONIO CARDINAL CAÑIZARES LLOVERA is a former Archbishop of Toledo, Spain, and the Prefect of the Congregation for Divine Worship and the Discipline of the Sacraments.

RAYMOND LEO CARDINAL BURKE is a former Archbishop of St. Louis, Missouri, U.S.A., and the Prefect of the Supreme Tribunal of the Apostolic Signatura, Rome.

MALCOLM CARDINAL RANJITH is a former Secretary of the Congregation for Divine Worship and the Discipline of the Sacraments and is Archbishop of Colombo, Sri Lanka.

WALTER CARDINAL BRANDMÜLLER was for many years Professor of Modern and Medieval Church History at the University of Augsburg and then President of the Pontifical Committee for Historical Sciences. In 2010 Benedict XVI named him Cardinal-Deacon of S. Giuliano dei Fiamminghi.

ARCHBISHOP ALEXANDER K. SAMPLE was appointed Bishop of Marquette, Michigan, U.S.A., in 2005. In January 2013 Benedict XVI named him Archbishop of Portland, Oregon.

BISHOP DOMINIQUE REY, a priest of the Emmanuel Community, has been the Bishop of Fréjus-Toulon, France, since his appointment by John Paul II in 2000. His reflections on the New Evangelisation *Paroisses—réveillez-vous!* were published by Éditions de l'Emmanuel in 2012.

BISHOP MARC AILLET, a priest of the Community of Saint-Martin, served as the Vicar General of the Diocese of Fréjus-Toulon before being appointed Bishop of Bayonne, Lescar and Oloron, France, by

Benedict XVI in 2008. His book *The Old Mass and the New* was published by Ignatius Press in 2010.

BISHOP PETER J. ELLIOTT, Auxiliary Bishop in Melbourne, Australia, was consecrated Titular Bishop of Manaccenser in 2007. He is Director of the John Paul II Institute for Marriage and Family, Melbourne and a member of the commission "Anglicanæ Traditiones" preparing liturgical texts for the Personal Ordinariates for former Anglicans. Amongst other works, he is the author of *Ceremonies of the Modern Roman Rite* and *Ceremonies of the Liturgical Year*, published by Ignatius Press.

MONSIGNOR KEITH NEWTON is a former Anglican Suffragan Bishop of Richborough and Provincial Episcopal Visitor in the Province of Canterbury. In 2011 he was appointed the first Ordinary of the Ordinariate of Our Lady of Walsingham, England and a Protonotary Apostolic by Benedict XVI.

DOM JEAN-CHARLES NAULT O.S.B. has been the Abbot of the Benedictine Abbey of Saint-Wandrille, France, since 2009. His doctoral work, published as *La Saveur de Dieu* (Cerf, 2006), received the praise of Joseph Cardinal Ratzinger.

ABBOT CHRISTOPHER M. J. ZIELINSKI O.S.B. OLIV. was the Abbot of Our Lady of Guadalupe in New Mexico, U.S.A., and served as Vice-President of the Pontifical Commission for the Cultural Heritage of the Church and as a Bureau Chief in the Congregation for Divine Worship and the Discipline of the Sacraments in Rome. He is the Abbot of Lendinara, Italy.

ANDREW BURNHAM is the former Anglican Bishop of Ebbsfleet and is an Assistant to the Ordinary of the Ordinariate of Our Lady of Walsingham, England, and a member of the commission "Anglicanæ Traditiones." In 2010 the Canterbury Press published his *Heaven and Earth in Little Space: The Re-enchantment of Liturgy*.

IGNACIO BARREIRO CARÁMBULA was born in Uruguay and ordained a priest in the U.S.A. He has been the Executive Director of Human Life International's Rome office since 1998 and has written extensively on liturgical and family life issues.

STEFAN HEID is a priest of the Archdiocese of Cologne, Ordinary Professor of History of Liturgy and Hagiography at the Pontifical Institute of Christian Archaeology and Associate Professor of the Faculty of Theology of the Pontifical University St. Thomas Aquinas in Rome. He is Director of the Görres-Gesellschaft Institute in Rome and editor of the journal *Römische Quartalschrift*.

UWE MICHAEL LANG is a priest of the Oratory of St. Philip Neri in London, England. He served in Rome as an official of the Congregation for Divine Worship and the Discipline of the Sacraments and a consultor of the Office of Liturgical Celebrations of the Supreme Pontiff. Amongst his publications *Turning Towards the Lord: Orientation in Liturgical Prayer* (Ignatius Press, 2004) carries a Foreword by Joseph Cardinal Ratzinger. Father Lang is editor of *Antiphon: A Journal for Liturgical Renewal*.

PAUL GUNTER O.S.B., a monk of Douai Abbey, England, is a professor at the Pontifical Liturgical Institute of St. Anselm, Rome, and a former consultor of the Office of Liturgical Celebrations of the Supreme Pontiff. He is Secretary of the Department for Christian Life and Worship of the Bishops' Conference of England and Wales.

GUIDO RODHEUDT is a priest of the Diocese of Aachen, Germany, and pastor of the parish of St. Gertrud, Herzogenrath. In 2001, he founded the Network of Catholic Priests in Frankfurt, which connects priests, deacons and seminarians who feel committed to the Church's Tradition in life, doctrine and worship. Since 2009, he has been the co-organizer and Spiritual Director of the Cologne Liturgical Conference.

NICOLA BUX is priest of the Archdiocese of Bari and a professor of Eastern liturgy and sacramental theology. He is a consultor of the Congregation for the Doctrine of the Faith and of the Congregation for Divine Worship and the Discipline of the Sacraments and a former consultor of the Office of Liturgical Celebrations of the Supreme Pontiff. His book *Benedict XVI's Reform: The Liturgy Between Innovation and Tradition* was published by Ignatius Press in 2012.

ALCUIN REID, from Melbourne, Australia, is a monk of the Monastère Saint-Benoît in the Diocese of Fréjus-Toulon, France. His publications include *Ceremonies of the Roman Rite Described*, (Burns & Oates, 2009), *Looking Again at the Question of the Liturgy with Cardinal Ratzinger* (Farnborough, 2003), and *The Organic Development of the Liturgy*, the second edition of which (Ignatius, 2005), carries a preface by Joseph Cardinal Ratzinger.

TRACEY ROWLAND is Dean of the John Paul II Institute for Marriage and Family in Melbourne, Australia, and a Permanent Fellow of the Institute in Political Philosophy and Continental Theology. She is also a Fellow of the Centre for Theology and Philosophy at the University of Nottingham, an Honorary Fellow of Campion College, Sydney, and an Adjunct Professor in the Centre for Faith, Ethics and Society of the University of Notre Dame, Sydney. Professor Rowland also serves as a member of the editorial board of the English language edition of the International Catholic Review, *Communio*.

GABRIEL M. STEINSCHULTE is the Vice-President of the *Consociatio Internationalis Musicæ Sacræ* and is the director of the Schola Cantorum Coloniensis, Cologne, Germany.

MIGUEL AYUSO is a Professor of Political Science and Constitutional Law at Comillas Pontifical University of Madrid in Spain and President of the International Union of Catholic Jurists. He is also the editor of *Verbo*, a journal of civic formation and cultural action according to natural and Christian law.

JEFFREY TUCKER is the founder of the Chant Café blog, the editor of the New Liturgical Movement website, managing editor of the journal *Sacred Music* and director of publications for the Church Music Association of America. Mr. Tucker is the author of *Sing Like a Catholic* (2009).